America in a Divided World
1945–1972

DOCUMENTARY HISTORY OF THE UNITED STATES
Richard B. Morris, *General Editor*

HISTORY OF AMERICAN DIPLOMACY
Edited by Robert H. Ferrell

Volume I: *Foundations of American Diplomacy, 1775–1872*
Volume II: *America as a World Power, 1872–1945*
Volume III: *America in a Divided World, 1945–1972*

America
in a Divided World
1945–1972

Edited by
ROBERT H. FERRELL

Cartography by
John M. Hollingsworth

UNIVERSITY OF SOUTH CAROLINA PRESS
Columbia, South Carolina

AMERICA IN A DIVIDED WORLD, 1945–1972

Copyright © 1975 by Robert H. Ferrell
All rights reserved.

First HARPER TORCHBOOK edition published 1975

This edition published by the University of South Carolina Press,
Columbia, S.C., 1975, by arrangement with Harper Torchbooks,
Harper and Row Publisher, Inc., New York, New York, from whom a
paperback edition is available (HR/1793).

Manufactured in the United States of America.

Library of Congress Cataloging in Publication Data

Ferrell, Robert H   comp.
  America in a divided world, 1945–1972.

  Continuation of America as a world power, 1872–1945.
  Bibliography: p.
  Includes index.
  1. United States—Foreign relations—1945–
—Sources. I. Title.
E744.F47 1975   327.73   75–22588
ISBN 0-87249-338-5

For Carolyn and her mother

Contents

Maps

Foreword

The following volume represents the last of a three-volume documentary history of American diplomacy from its beginning in 1775 to the present day. *Foundations of American Diplomacy* covers the period from the opening of the American Revolution through the year of the Geneva arbitration, 1872. The second volume, *America as a World Power*, treats the diplomatic record to the end of World War II. *America in a Divided World* brings us to the present, covering the period 1945 to 1972 and incorporating material through 1974.

RICHARD B. MORRIS,
General Editor

Acknowledgments

International events of recent years, since the end of the Second World War, have been fascinating, bewildering, appalling. They are important not merely for present inhabitants of the United States but also for citizens of the Republic far into the future. The decades since the victory of 1945 have been a time of great trouble. On occasion the voices of some Americans have been raised in pessimism, in the belief that international life as we have known it cannot continue much longer. The historian cannot answer the pessimists, nor even the optimists, but he can offer to all students the record of the past or, one might better say, such of the record as has come down to the present. And so this book looks to the future through the statements—treaties, executive agreements, notes, memoranda, and so forth—of the past. It seeks to discover and employ the most accurate texts, to group them according to areas of the world or (in the cases of five chapters) important topics, and to intersperse sufficient commentary in the documentary record to establish the circumstances in which individual documents originally appeared. I do wish to thank my colleague George E. Brooks, Jr., for assistance with the material on Africa; Charles B. Reafsnyder for writing the headnote on the Trust Territory of the Pacific Islands, and for otherwise helping greatly with that subject; Charles I. Bevans, assistant legal adviser of the Department of State, for kindly answering a query and, of course, providing all students with an up-to-date treaty series for instruments including executive agreements dating before the year 1950; and William M. Franklin, director of the Historical Office of the department, for reading some pages and saving me from egregious errors. John M. Hollingsworth of the department of geography of Indiana University produced the maps that are essential to the volume. Richard B. Morris, general editor of the series, scholar, friend—without his help the present three-volume series could not have been completed. I also wish to thank Harper & Row's free-lance copy editor, Russell Ann Nobles; Thomas H. Etzold, friend and colleague, who read the galleys; and Mike Robinson, Harper's production editor, who did the substantive editing—he has an unerring eye for redundancy and plain misstatement, and any good qualities the book possesses are in considerable part the result of his labors.

R.H.F.

Introduction

The first of the three principles of American foreign policy since 1945, organization of an international security community, has assumed a varying degree of importance in the country's foreign relations. Most of the people of the United States have been pleased that after the Second World War the United Nations Organization chose to establish its headquarters in an attractive skyscraper beside the East River in New York. At the same time, they have tended to regard the U.N. as an appendage of diplomacy, perhaps even an appendix, and have appeared altogether unsure of how much reliance to place upon it.

The founding of a global organization has, of course, created not merely the only large diplomatic novelty of the twentieth century, but in its origins and growth the U.N. has enjoyed a great deal of encouragement from the leading nation of the New World. When the U.N. came into being after the San Francisco Conference of 1945, it was the culmination of an ardent American interest that reached back well before the First World War, to the turn of the century, when the politics of Europe were moving toward crisis. Concern over the "international anarchy" of the time led to the Hague Peace Conferences of 1899 and 1907. A movement to codify international law was fairly well advanced by 1914 in such areas as the laws of neutrals in wartime. The somewhat inchoate theories of an international security community being talked about when the war broke out were quickly brought together after 1914, and by the time the war ended the Americans had prepared a project for the Paris Peace Conference—the League of Nations, which President Woodrow Wilson sponsored. He virtually forced it upon the conference in the French capital. Then he embroiled himself in a controversy with the Senate over its details, and the United States refrained from joining a world security organization until twenty-five years later, when it joined the U.N.

The United Nations was the direct descendant of the League of Nations, and Americans worked as enthusiastically to establish the

second world organization as they had the first. Failure of the peace
in the years after the war of 1914–18 probably came because of the
shortsightedness of European diplomacy and the distractions of the
Great Depression. But it was arguable that if the American government had joined the League and cooperated on European international questions during the 1920s a different atmosphere might
have developed between the victor and vanquished nations, and
Hitler's rise to power in Germany might not have occurred. Many
Americans felt ashamed over their nation's absence from the
League in Geneva and upon the beginning of a new world war
undertook to involve their government in whatever world organization would appear after that war. As early as 1940—which was
much too early—the Department of State began to plan for the
peace. After December, 1941, the department established an elabo-
rate structure of committees to discuss the forthcoming world
organization. A new organization was necessary because the League
had expelled the Soviet Union after its attack on Finland in 1939.
Toward the end of the war the Dumbarton Oaks meetings in
Washington showed strong international support for a new league,
and there followed the sessions of the San Francisco Conference in
April–June, 1945.

In its initial years the United Nations accomplished many
worthy projects, and yet the reality did not live up to the promise.
American sponsorship, not to mention the enormous care taken to
draft the 111 detailed articles of the charter, seemed to guarantee a
new international order. The U.S. government paid almost a third
(31.52 percent in 1972) of the U.N.'s operating costs. The agencies of the organization dispensed aid in cases of famine, earth-
quake, flood, and civil war. They compiled statistics on world economic and social problems of a reliability never achieved before.
The Security Council and General Assembly engaged in peace-
keeping in the Congo and Middle East, with military contingents
from local nations and outside neutralist powers. But within a year
or so of its founding the world organization began to run into
trouble. Supporters began to see that it was not working out the
way they had hoped. When debates droned on, it was apparent
that much important diplomacy was not being conducted at Lake
Success or in the East River building; it was being managed by
heads of state and councils of foreign ministers and occasionally by

ambassadors and special envoys; sometimes even private individuals—journalists or dedicated persons of goodwill—managed to accredit themselves. The U.N. appeared to be little more than a place for retired diplomats or inconvenient politicians. It became a showplace for visiting schoolchildren, forced onto the premises by piety or parents and teachers.

Perhaps the problem was bureaucracy. Talkativeness in the Security Council, General Assembly, and ancillary agencies inspires verbosity on paper and more functionaries to handle the paper. Years earlier the League of Nations had bogged itself down in a morass of printed proceedings and reports. In the 1930s one complaining official remarked that the cellars of Geneva were full of League paper; another said the subcommittee of a minor League committee in a single year used enough paper to allow its Polish or Swedish delegations to walk home on a path of League paper. The United Nations took over the Palais des Nations building in Geneva, along with many of the League's offices and agencies, and by 1972 had so outgrown this arrangement that it was necessary to put up a new office building in Geneva costing nearly $50 million. Annual expenditure in Geneva alone totaled a quarter of a billion, making the U.N. an industry more important to local burghers than tourism and banking. Secretary General U Thant in his last days in office complained sharply of the increase in U.N. printed matter. Perhaps nothing could be done about it.

Just how much the cold war in the late 1940s, the 1950s, and the 1960s contributed to the overshadowing of the United Nations by other diplomatic means is difficult to say. Often it proved inconvenient to take issues into the debates of a world organization. The developing contentions between the United States and the Soviet Union had their U.N. accompaniments, but from the beginning were handled mostly à deux or between the allies of each superpower, without involving the neutralist countries in the U.N. There also was a feeling that the U.N. could only talk, not act. The late Dean Acheson, who as assistant secretary of state, undersecretary, and secretary during the last four years of the Truman administration was the principal architect of American foreign policy in the early cold war era, possessed a great contempt for the U.N. In later years, when the mantle of power and responsibility was no longer about him, he openly announced it in the public press, in his memoirs, and (as if in fear that someone might miss his point of view) to the writer of his obituary for the New York Times. He told the reporter Alden Whitman, "I never thought the U.N was worth a damn. To a lot of people it was a Holy Grail, and those who set store by it had the misfortune to believe their own bunk."

The Truman administration did resort to the U.N. during the Korean War to obtain the facade of world approbation for what was virtually an American undertaking. The Soviet representative at the Security Council had absented himself because of the Nationalist Chinese representative's presence, and that gave the United States an opportunity to push through a resolution of support. Stalin eventually allowed the Russian representative to return, armed with a Big Power veto. The United States then took its case to the General Assembly and obtained the "uniting for peace" resolution of November, 1950:

> if the Security Council, because of lack of unanimity of the permanent members, fails to exercise its primary responsibility for the maintenance of international peace and security in any case where there appears to be a threat to the peace, breach of the peace, or act of aggression, the General Assembly shall consider the matter immediately with a view to making appropriate recommendations to Members for collective measures, including in the case of a breach of the peace or act of aggression the use of armed force when necessary, to maintain or restore international peace and security.

At the time this was a skillful maneuver on Acheson's part, but in solving one problem it raised others. If it continued the fiction of U.N. support in Korea, it also stretched the meaning of the charter, under which a threat to the peace was clearly and primarily the business of the Security Council. Amending the charter should have been done properly, according to the appropriate provisions, rather than by simple resolution. And the uniting-for-peace resolution created a procedure for threats to peace that could be inconvenient or downright harmful in the future. So many new nations arose in the 1950s and 1960s, especially in Africa and Asia, that Assembly membership was up to 128 by 1972, with other new nations still in the wings. Was it wise for a Great Power to place at least formal judgment of its policies in the hands of so heterogeneous a group, likely to be out of sympathy with Great Power problems? Was there also the possibility of unconscionable trading of votes within the Assembly, as in the House of Representatives of the United States, so that positions would be taken not on issues but on points of trade?*

The hope, the trust, of many Americans that the U.N. might change international relations, ending the awful alternation of wars that in the first two thirds of the twentieth century had seemed to occur closer and closer together, apparently had proved to be only a dream: it had not worked out the way planners thought. The buildings, the meetings, the people, were there. The substance of diplomacy had gone elsewhere. Indeed, it had never been present. The U.N. experience was disappointing, saddening. Another project had occupied Americans when their attention could have been elsewhere.

President Richard M. Nixon, like his predecessors, put little faith in the U.N. In 1970 he accepted the resignation of the career foreign service officer he had appointed as his U.N. ambassador, Charles W. Yost, and nominated a young Texas Republican, George H. Bush, who had just lost a Senate election. Ambassador Bush entered upon his duties with gusto and soon managed a fiasco. In 1971 he lined up opposition against mainland China's admission to the U.N., confident that once again the United States could keep the Chinese out. To his horror, and that of other administration stalwarts, the General Assembly administered him a rebuke and not long thereafter cruelly underlined it by agreeing, at the insistence of the new U.N. member, mainland China, to expel Nationalist China. In 1972 the president, protesting his dedication to the U.N., appointed Bush chairman of the Republican National Committee and gave the ambassadorship to another individual without diplomatic experience or national stature, the reporter John Scali, who had helped with some details of the president's recent trip to China.

And yet it was entirely possible that despite the president's using the U.N. ambassadorship as a reward for the political small-fry of his administration, despite American violence to the charter with

* For some citizens of the United States in later years, unhappy with their government's policies, the possibility of the country's being hoist with its own petard in the General Assembly was not unattractive. When President Richard M. Nixon in May, 1972, mined the harbors of North Vietnam and it was clear that almost no nation of the world supported this move, there was the chance that the Soviet Union might go to the Security Council with the American threat to peace, obtain an American veto, and take the issue to the Assembly under the uniting-for-peace resolution.

the uniting-for-peace resolution, despite the other effects of the cold war on the world organization, despite its unending bureaucracy and a heritage of a quarter century of moves around the periphery of international relations, the United Nations Organization during the 1970s was about to enter a new era of importance. It was possible that the dreams of the Hague Peace Conference enthusiasts at the beginning of the century, of President Woodrow Wilson, of all Americans who have sought to advance the idea of a world security community, might have some chance of coming true. The government of the United States ironically had not seen any handwriting on the wall. Ambassador Bush and the Nixon administration, whose business it was to be informed, had done their best to keep mainland China out of the U.N. China's entrance would soon be followed by the admission of West Germany and East Germany as separate U.N. members. At long last, a half century and more after the League of Nations commenced its first meetings in 1920, an international security community would obtain membership of not merely the minor powers, but all the major ones as well—the United States, the Soviet Union, Britain, France, Japan, mainland China, the two Germanys. Whether by virtue of its newly representative composition the security community could then deal with serious security matters remained to be seen. But it was possible that the U.N.'s years of ceremony might be coming to an end, an era of responsibility could begin, the battle flags might be furled. In the 1970s it behooved the government of the United States to take up a new stance in the U.N., to abandon the outworn Acheson-Nixon policy.

II

Anti-Communist ideology, the second of the post-1945 American diplomatic principles, in its origins went back futher in American history than did the idea of an international security community. It can be traced in part to the so-called new immigration beginning in the 1880s: nativist American supporters of laissez faire capitalism believed the newcomers were bringing in foreign, socialist ideas. Rapid growth of the organized labor movement at the turn of the century engendered feelings about radical beliefs. The Russian Revolution of November, 1917, and its gospel of world revolution produced American anti-Communists. Alliance with the Soviet Union during the Second World War momentarily halted their activities, but when the wartime alliance disappeared in the rancors of the cold war, anti-Communism became increasingly popular.

Several points are worth making about American anti-Communism in the years immediately after 1945. For one thing, the Truman administration did not champion anti-Communism, gathering together its adherents and pushing the issue, in order to gain easy passage of its cold war measures, such as aid to Greece and Turkey, the Marshall Plan, resistance to the Berlin blockade of 1948–49, and the North Atlantic Treaty. By the early 1970s some historians were becoming certain that President Truman was, if not the inventor, then the principal distributor of anti-Communism; the domestic political situation was so delicate, they felt, the American people were so confused, that the administration sought support through a policy of anti-Communism. They argued that Undersecretary of State Acheson in 1947 persuaded the president to raise the Communist bogey. One revisionist writer claimed that (to change the figure of speech) whenever the American people gave evidence of finding the Russians attractive, Acheson gave them immunization shots of anti-Communism. A large public pronouncement such as the Truman Doctrine, could not, of course, help but enlarge popular feelings against Communism. The critical historians were certain the administration was using the issue. The truth is that the administration did not seek whatever anti-Communism the Truman Doctrine generated. It had no intention of making the doctrine of 1947 a trumpet call for an anti-Communist crusade. The president wanted to call attention to a critical situation in Greece and Turkey. At one point in the drafting of the president's speech, the Department of State speechwriter, Joseph M. Jones, asked Acheson for tactical guidance. The undersecretary leaned back from his desk, looked over at the White House, thought a while, and said slowly, "If F.D.R. were alive I think I know what he'd do. He would make a statement of global policy but confine his request for money right now to Greece and Turkey."* And there was other evidence, public at the time, of the limited concept of the doctrine. During congressional debate over the appropriation Representative Walter H. Judd of Minnesota, a

* Joseph M. Jones, *The Fifteen Weeks (February 21–June 5, 1947)* (New York: Viking, 1955), p. 159.

former medical missionary to China, sought to get the administration to explain why it was attempting to combat Communism in Greece and, simultaneously, bring Communists and anti-Communists together in China. Acheson's response, if no model of logic, was frank enough. Circumstances in Greece and in China were entirely different, he said. It was impossible to aid China on such a modest scale as could be done for Greece and Turkey. China was forty-five times as large as Greece, its population eighty-five times as large.

It is possible that one of the contemporary inspirations of post-1945 anti-Communism was the presidential election of 1948, the loss of which infuriated the Republicans and led some of them into an excess of statement-making and accusation. They had not anticipated their fifth defeat in a presidential election. Frustration drove a few G.O.P. partisans to extremism, willingness to push any issue that would get the party back in national power. There was some truth in the remark in George F. Kennan's second volume of his *Memoirs* that after the election of 1948, "the vultures of domestic politics swarmed back on the scene, insisting that the external relations of the country were no longer important enough to be permitted to interfere with the struggle for internal political power, clamoring to be given the due of which they had so long been deprived." One might even argue that in retrospect it was unfortunate the Republicans lost in 1948, as the foreign policy of Thomas E. Dewey probably would have paralleled that of President Truman without the anti-Communist contentions that disgraced some Republican politics during Truman's last years.

And yet there were good nonpartisan, contemporary reasons for the anti-Communism that welled up in the United States in the late 1940s and early 1950s. The fear of Communism so evident among leaders of the Truman administration was no invention of partisanship or fevered imaginations. Often during the beginning of the cold war the Russians acted aggressively, and the Americans, perforce, reacted. The Soviets became difficult over the economic and political organization of Germany. They proved hostile everywhere in Western Europe, whether in the actions of their troops in Germany and Austria and elsewhere or in the acts of local Communist parties, which were anything but cooperative with other local political parties. The Russians had a chance to participate in the Marshall Plan and said no, and underlined their refusal by taking over Czechoslovakia.

Consider also the spy disclosures of the time: defection of the code clerk Igor Gouzenko from the Soviet embassy in Ottawa in 1945; the unrelated affair of Alger Hiss beginning in 1948; the confession in 1950 (through belated use of Gouzenko's documents) of the British atomic physicist Klaus Fuchs; and the arrest and execution of two American citizens, Julius and Ethel Rosenberg, for atomic espionage. These spy cases were real, not imagined, and in the instance of Fuchs involved a serious breach of security. The many Americans who went along with the exaggerations and inventions and contemptible crudities of Senator Joseph R. McCarthy, fearing a Communist conspiracy, had some considerable cause for concern.

Anti-Communism increased markedly during the Korean War, which again was no figment of someone's imagination or piece of American politics but a great Far Eastern war undoubtedly supported not merely by the North Koreans and mainland Chinese, but by the Russians as well. At the outset and at least until containment of the Chinese offensive of November–December, 1950, the war's fortunes skidded back and forth. Anti-Communism became almost a patriotic position. As long as the war continued, during the truce talks of 1951–53, the constant military confrontation with mainland Chinese troops together with Stalin's support of the North Koreans and Chinese kept anti-Communism at the front of American foreign policy.

The secretaries of state who followed Acheson beginning in 1953—first John Foster Dulles; then, briefly, Christian A. Herter; and, from 1961 until 1969, Dean Rusk—thus found it easy to bring anti-Communism to the front of their arguments. It was a natural stance after the events of the late 1940s. Of the two secretaries with long tenures who followed Acheson, Dulles was the more obvious in ideological pronouncements and the more sanctimonious in remarks, some of which do not read well today, when the difficulties with the Soviet Union have lessened. When the Central Intelligence Agency intervened in Guatemala in 1954, Dulles was sure of a Communist conspiracy:

> The master plan of international communism is to gain a solid political base in this hemisphere, a base that can be used to extend

Communist penetration to the other peoples of the other American Governments. It was not the power of the Arbenz government that concerned us but the power behind it. If world communism captures any American State, however small, a new and perilous front is established which will increase the danger to the entire free world and require even greater sacrifices from the American people.*

There was, beyond question, a misreading of affairs here at the time. The anti-Communism of Dean Rusk was far less doctrinal and descriptive, resting less on ideology than analogy. Rusk had been a professor of political science before the Second World War, but after entering the U.S. Army he briefly considered becoming a career military officer before turning to the Department of State. In the Truman administration he served in several department posts, including that of assistant secretary for Far Eastern affairs. During the Eisenhower years he was outside the government, heading the Rockefeller Foundation. Then John F. Kennedy chose him as secretary of state. It seems safe to say that his ideas of foreign policy had formed before the war. Afterward he foresaw the danger of another Munich, which could take the appearance of a compromise with the Communist fanatics. If his was a less ideological anti-Communism than Dulles's, he was just as stubborn.

Some of the critics then and later took offense because these secretaries of state of the 1950s and 1960s spoke so often and in such detail about Communism. But during much of their time there was evidence of continuing Soviet ill will. Nikita Khrushchev, who came to power in the mid-1950s, was in some ways an attractive individual, and at no time more so than when in 1956 he informed the Twentieth Party Congress of some of the sins of his predecessor, Stalin. But Khrushchev was a tough customer, whose toughness was bolstered by an unpredictable bravado and also by the increasing power of the Soviet military during his premiership. After all, it was Khrushchev who was at the center of the great crisis over Cuba in 1962. His successors were very slow to relax his enmities toward the Western world and the United States in particular. As late as September, 1971, the Soviets apparently were willing to try testing the American giant in its home base, the Western Hemisphere. They sent a submarine tender and two barges (for

* Radio and television address of June 30, 1954, in *American Foreign Policy: Current Documents, 1950–1955*, 2 vols. (Washington, D.C., 1957), I, pp. 1312–13.

reception of radioactive wastes) to Cienfuegos, Cuba, and were laying out supporting shore installations, including barracks and a soccer field (the Cubans do not play soccer; the Russians do). Only a sharp, if secret, series of American protests seems to have defeated this attempted move.*

The grand question about any policy is how long it has relevance to the course of events. In the case of anti-Communism, both the Dulles and Rusk varieties, it may have been (one says this with uncertainty, for no one yet really knows) a matter of excellent reasoning that became too set in its formulas and methods, presuming an implacable enemy in the Kremlin leadership and almost fearful of any change of policy because it might encourage the American people to let down their guard. It is an awkward judgment to say that Dulles and Rusk were too strong in their anti-Communism; one cannot be sure. The historian even now knows little about the inner political movements of the Soviet government. The successors of Stalin often fought each other in private, and while their animosities did not bring the same dire penalty to the losers that attached to failure during the Stalin era, they have generated constant efforts to rewrite the past. Each new group in the Kremlin tends to dismiss the qualities and successes of its predecessors, in a manner often confusing to outsiders. When the full truth comes out, perhaps in the twenty-first century, it may be that Stalin's successors without exception were every bit as hostile to the American government and people as was the old dictator himself. The passage of time makes judgments much easier, and the historian always has the feeling that he is using hindsight. The more complex international relations of the 1970s should not perhaps cause a kind of sweeping judgment against the anti-Communism of the 1950s and 1960s—just because the roof did not fall in, the world managed to maintain itself without nuclear wars, the sun rose in its preordained position every day, and people went about their business as usual. Only with the passage of much more time may one be sure that the anti-Communism of the years after, say, the Korean War was excessive.

At one juncture in the recent past, however, a mistake occurred. Out of anti-Communism came Vietnam. In several parts of the world there were festering local situations, civil wars, giving evi-

* Henry Brandon, *The Retreat of American Power* (Garden City, N.Y.: Doubleday, 1973), pp. 280–83.

dence of Communist support for one side and subversion of the other. An involvement could begin that, narrowly analyzed and diligently pursued, would lead to a massive military commitment. If Dulles had had his way at the time of the Vietnamese siege of the French fortress of Dien Bien Phu in 1954, the Eisenhower adminstration would have gotten involved in Vietnam ten years before another president showed less forbearance. The Korean War provided an apparently successful analogy for intervention. The physical similarities of Korea and Vietnam were striking. As the years passed and memory dimmed, intervention became ever more likely. As it happened, American support for Indochina had commenced just before the outbreak of the Korean War, but it increased greatly during the conflict, seemingly because it was another soft place along the geographical fault line between the free world and Communism. Actually involvement had come mainly because of what the blunt Acheson described at the time and later as French blackmail—a trade for French cooperation in NATO—but this fact was soon forgotten. The first American soldier was killed in Vietnam in December, 1961, and by the end of the Kennedy administration U.S. troop strength had increased to 15,500. The assassination of President Ngo Dinh Diem shortly before that of the American president then produced a swirling chaos in Saigon in 1964 that virtually invited a North Vietnamese takeover.

The Kennedy and Johnson administrations, as we now can see, rose to what should not have been an occasion. They had both become obsessed by Khrushchev's braggadocio about wars of national liberation, and Vietnam appeared to be a classic instance of this new tactic. President Lyndon B. Johnson saw behind it a dream of world conquest. His experts, military and civilian, agreed. The strength of the army in Vietnam rose to 540,000 men, not to mention supporting units in Thailand, navy vessels in Vietnamese waters, air force bases in Guam and elsewhere, and people working the long supply pipeline. Johnson deeply involved himself in the compromises of power between the sprawling executive departments in Washington, and these compromises frequently subtracted from what would have been ideal military and diplomatic solutions. Added to this blunting of policy were the miscalculations of the U.S. Army's leadership about the North Vietnamese patriot-Communists: the army's high command in Vietnam (at one point there were as many as ninety generals in and out of Saigon) moved against the North Vietnamese as if the latter were the Germans of the Second World War. And in working up an enormous administrative headquarters, with altogether insufficient hindquarters (less than 100,000 American troops in the field against the Vietcong and North Vietnamese regular army units), the generals showed an abysmal understanding of American domestic politics, no feeling at all for how the president had played dangerously fast and loose with Congress and the people to supply the troops the army said it needed for victory in an undeclared war. At the time of the lunar new year, or "Tet," offensive of the North Vietnamese in February, 1968, the only thing the leaders of the American army knew how to do was to say they were holding and winning, and then, in almost the same breath, ask for more than 200,000 additional troops, which would have run troop strength to over 700,000. Upon questioning by Johnson's new secretary of defense, Clark Clifford, they admitted they had no idea of how many more troops (in addition to the 700,000) they would need for support purposes outside of Vietnam. It was a political impossibility, a serious military miscalculation, and Johnson gave up—probably in despair, although in Texas fashion he refused to acknowledge such a state of affairs.

At this saddening juncture the incoming Nixon administration might have seized upon a great opportunity. It could have decided on complete, immediate withdrawal, cutting the national losses, and all blame could have gone to the Democrats. In retrospect it is interesting that the new Republican president did not do this. The national interest may well have dictated a dignified bug-out (the president privately used this term). Richard Nixon was not known for an excess of sympathy for political opponents in distress. But perhaps such a move was too decisive for a new man in office who according to some observers was basically timid, highly uncertain of himself. Whatever the reasoning he cautiously inched his way forward, announcing a withdrawal and making haste slowly.

The reporter Henry Brandon would write at the end of the Vietnam War in 1973 that Nixon's policy toward the Russians (Vietnam, to be sure, being only a part or it) was to move forward only along all fronts; he would move toward peace in Vietnam only as the bases of accommodation with the Soviet Union became clearer. In contrast to his predecessor, according to Brandon, the

Republican president calculated the possibilities of all pieces on the chessboard of Soviet-American relations and refused to give up even a pawn until he was sure the Soviets would produce a *quid pro quo*. This, he believed, was the only way to obtain Russian respect and make lasting diplomatic arrangements. Perhaps, therefore, the president's cautious Vietnam policy reflected this fact. If the result, the truce of January 1973, would prove lasting, then the overall strategy and the tactics in Vietnam were possibly worth it. For the war had continued at huge cost, human and physical. B-52 bombers had spewed incredible destruction over the agricultural landscape of North Vietnam. Between January, 1969, and April, 1972, air force planes dropped 3,200,000 tons of bombs (during the Second World War the *total* tonnage dropped on the British Isles was 80,000). Pilots, asked how they knew they were crossing the seventeenth parallel, laughed and said they could *see* the difference. They could not see the human cost. That, of course, was not all their doing, but the air war together with the slowness of withdrawal resulted (between January, 1969, and April, 1972) in the deaths of 20,000 more American soldiers. Another 110,000 were wounded; 340,000 Asians died; some 600,000 civilians became casualties; 4 million people became refugees. Impervious to mounting public criticism, stressing his decision to withdraw rather than the destruction with which he carried it out, counting on the average "middle American" whom he believed was on his side, the president went ahead in a manner that some critics described as, at the least, dissembling. In May, 1972, when the North Vietnamese negotiators in Paris became difficult, and faced with an offensive in Vietnam that threatened to collapse the South Vietnamese army and the Saigon regime, Nixon without batting an eyelash ordered the mining of North Vietnamese harbors and the bombing of Haiphong and Hanoi.

Nothing stopped him until the war wound down to its end. The election of November, 1972, which involved a good deal more than Vietnam, was taken by Nixon as a mandate of approval of his foreign policy. By this time the country was torn with dissension. The cities sprawled in disorder, their inner cores burned out and their suburbs filled with unaesthetic "developments" of crackerbox houses. City streets were unsafe, day or night. Pushers and dope addicts thrived; public authorities were unable to reach them with either humanity or punishment. Black Americans remained as unsatisfied as they were fifteen years before, when the black revolution began, and they were bewildered by the increasing hostility the drive for equal rights had inspired among whites. The environment deteriorated alarmingly, in country and city, with only the first signs of change evident in legislation and enforcement. Vietnam had not created these problems, but the Vietnam War had been pursued at the expense of remedying such ills. The president did not seem concerned and spoke of the greatness of America while conducting his own Vietnam War, until, in January, 1973, a negotiated settlement providing for withdrawal of American troops was reached.

III

The ideology of anti-Communism pushed the nation into Vietnam. Vietnam, in turn, appeared to demonstrate the bankruptcy of anti-Communism. The Nixon administration was nothing if not resourceful, and as one policy (on which its leader had built his political career) was losing its "credibility," it turned to another, the balance of power, which happened to be diametrically opposite.

This new policy—the third of American postwar foreign policy principles—was almost without precedent in the diplomatic history of the United States. In the past the nation's leaders had used every opportunity to stay away from the premier diplomatic practice of Europe, the balance of power. Presidents and secretaries of state calculated it, occasionally took advantage of it, but refrained from participating in it. If the country's citizens and successive national administrations could have had their way, they would have chosen to haul off from Europe and the rest of the world, as Jefferson once put it, to turn inward upon American interests, American problems, American development, presenting to the world a face much like eighteenth- and early nineteenth-century China. In time of dire necessity it was permissible to ally with a foreign nation to defeat an enemy, but the French in 1778, for example, were under few illusions as to how long American friendship might last. For the first century and more after the Revolution, the nation's diplomatic principles were preservation of independence, protection of commerce, and pursuit of manifest destiny (extension of the national territory from sea to sea). At the end of the nineteenth century and for a few years thereafter a vision of a new manifest destiny—of overseas empire—arose, but it quickly disappeared. During the First World War the country tried to make the world safe for democracy, however quaint that objective now sounds. In the Second World War it sought to preserve the national security.

Every one of the presidents except Theodore Roosevelt had refrained from taking part in balance of power politics. The only evidence of any power-balancing by an American president prior to the Nixon administration had occurred under Theodore Roosevelt in 1905 and 1906, when the Republican president arranged the Peace of Portsmouth and took part vigorously in a European conference at Algeciras. The Portsmouth Conference of 1905 was a doubtful effort to engage in balance of power politics. Roosevelt sought to halt a war in Asia before it had exhausted two great nations. One could argue that he constantly kept in mind the Asian power balance and wanted it to remain *in statu quo*. More likely his intervention was prompted by friendship and a desire to be helpful. The Algeciras Conference admittedly was something else, for according to Roosevelt's own testimony he got into the middle of a huge quarrel between France and Germany and pulled the disputants apart in the interest of a better balance of power on the Continent. He afterward catered to the egotism of Kaiser Wilhelm and bamboozled him into accepting what in reality was a German diplomatic defeat. It was a masterly performance. It was also a secret performance, most of its details remaining unknown to his countrymen until in the late 1920s his papers were opened at the Library of Congress.

Despite the lack of precedent for a policy of maintaining the balance of power, President Nixon shortly after taking office began to find it attractive. It was a curious attraction that may have derived from novelty, or from the idea of grand strategy (moving forward on all fronts), or maybe from the tuition of his adviser in political science from Harvard University, Henry A. Kissinger. Before entering the administration Kissinger had published an admiring account of the diplomacy of Prince Otto von Bismarck, who had managed to play off one European nation against another with Germany retaining a preponderance of armaments. For various reasons peace had lasted from 1871 until 1914, considerably longer than the peace, organized under a different principle, beginning in 1919. Nixon and his foreign policy adviser appeared to have calculated this fact.*

The Nixon administration ardently pursued a balance of power policy not merely in Europe but throughout the world. For the Continent it was a matter of assuring the British government that, as during the 1960s, it still occupied a special position vis-a-vis the United States. But occasionally the administration would inform the French or the West Germans that they too occupied special positions. Nor did NATO enjoy the confidence of previous years. At one point during the Arab-Israeli War of 1973, when the NATO allies were refusing to support Israel, Kissinger, by that time secretary of state, was heard to mutter that he did not care what happened to NATO. The European nations had the feeling that it was no longer one for all and all for one but that the United States was picking and choosing and each occasion contained its own logic. And the policy of balance of power was nowhere more in evidence than in diplomacy toward the Soviet Union and China. The president visited China, all the while assuring the Soviet Union that relations with Moscow remained close. There was almost constant visiting of Moscow and Peking by Kissinger, usually one after the other. That the Soviet fear of an attack by China and the Chinese fear of an attack by the Soviet Union presented an opportunity for the United States to play these hostile Communist powers off one against the other was undeniable. Nixon and Kissinger evidently believed it was wise policy to do so.

The administration would have denied absolutely—"sincerely," it would have said—that it was modeling its diplomacy after Bismarck, and yet in more ways than adoption of the policy of maintaining the balance of power were its foreign relations Bismarckian. In the 1970s the presidential progresses abroad rivaled the meetings of Europe's monarchs during the era after Sedan. The American presidency had been moving in that direction ever since the last years of Franklin D. Roosevelt, when wartime conferences and F.D.R.'s own enjoyment of travel began to produce presidential trips halfway around the world. Harry S. Truman was a traveler,

---

* It is worth remarking that Nixon's model was not the diplomacy of Prince Klemens von Metternich of Austria, who had organized post-Napoleonic Europe under the principle of legitimacy. Metternich was an ideologue, and neither Nixon nor Kissinger is an ideologue.

although he did not do anywhere near the amount of traveling that Roosevelt did; but the soil of Missouri was a part of him wherever he went, and he appeared incongruous in foreign settings. At the end of the 1950s Dwight D. Eisenhower began to undertake foreign trips, which previously he had left to Secretary Dulles (by then deceased). With Kennedy and Johnson, travel turned into a commonplace. First came the advance men and the security people. Then Air Force One and the helicopters would arrive, to be followed by parades in bubble cars. All this pageantry was light years removed from the austerities of previous presidents of the United States.

Under Nixon the presidency became ever more remote from the apparatus of government. The cabinet seldom met. Conversation between a cabinet member and the president was rare. Special White House functionaries took a cabinet member's ideas second-hand to the president.

In these circumstances the Department of State turned into a ceremonial and bookkeeping branch of government, full of busy-ness on all the minuscule problems of foreign relations and as startled, surprised, and flustered concerning the president's larger moves as (to use a description by Acheson) a little old lady trying to cross a busy street. Just a few hours before Nixon announced the mining of North Vietnamese harbors, Secretary of State William P. Rogers, who had been touring Europe, was called home aboard his big jet to be briefed by the president and White House aides; Rogers knew nothing of the new policy until told it was virtually in effect. The big issues had been removed to the White House, probably to Kissinger's office—which meant presidential preroga-tive. The office of the president's special assistant for national security affairs had increased in size dramatically from the twelve-member staff of Kissinger's predecessor, Walt W. Rostow; Kissin-ger had nearly 140 people. He also was chairman of several in-terdepartmental committees, which gave him nearly complete leverage throughout the government. During the India-Pakistani War of 1971 he chaired a subcommittee of the National Security Council with complete authority, calling upon fellow committee members—such high officials as the director of the CIA or the undersecretary of state—as if they were underlings. At last, in 1973, Secretary Rogers resigned, and Kissinger, who for more than four years had been undermining Rogers's authority, received the post.

As for congressional control of foreign relations, through the Senate Committee on Foreign Relations, the House Committee on Foreign Affairs, and the many members of both houses who not only took an interest in foreign affairs but also knew a great deal about them, it was negligible until 1972–73 when Congress at last began to exert itself. Prior to that time Congress had been as removed from diplomatic business as the Department of State. Some senators became exceedingly unhappy about the president's assumptions of authority. Bills appeared to halt the flow of power, generally considered contrary to the Constitution, from legislative to executive. Senator Clifford P. Case introduced a bill to the effect that all international agreements must go to Congress within sixty days for its information, with secret agreements to go to the Senate Committee on Foreign Relations and the House Committee on Foreign Affairs. It passed in 1972. Senator Sam J. Ervin, Jr., proposed an even stronger measure, that Congress could veto any executive agreement within sixty days of transmittal, by a majority vote of both houses, but it did not pass. Senator Jacob K. Javits in 1970 had introduced a bill to forbid use of American armed forces in combat for longer than thirty days without consent of Congress. It passed in 1973, over the president's veto, albeit watered down to sixty days.

Part of the trouble over foreign affairs between the executive and legislative branches of government during the Nixon administration concerned Congress's lack of information. How could senators object to some administration program when they did not know what it was? Or if something fell out of the executive's bag of tricks and lay on the floor visible to all onlookers, who knew what was still in the bag?

In this respect the policy of maintaining the balance of power was giving evidence of the same kind of immorality, the shading of small issues for the sake of larger concerns, that had plagued the international relations of Europe under Bismarck. After the debacle in Vietnam a subcommittee of the Senate Foreign Relations Committee in 1969 looked into American security commitments abroad and discovered not a bag of tricks but a rat's nest, the contents of which were almost unimaginable. The subcommittee, ably chaired by Senator Stuart Symington, learned that the U.S.–Philippine alliance, concluded in 1951, had undergone a change of its most crucial commitment, its casus belli, after the Philippine government balked at joining SEATO in 1954 until the United States gave something in return. Secretary Dulles had bribed the Philippines into SEATO by translating the alliance's Article IV, which said that each nation would come to the other's help "in accordance with its constitutional processes," to mean that an attack would be "instantly repelled." President Eisenhower repeated the "instantly repel" formula in 1958, and so did Johnson in 1964, in joint communiqués with Philippine leaders. This rewording of an American alliance, done by presidential fiat, was lost upon the American public until the hearings of 1969. Three years later, in 1972, the Philippine republic was changed by its president, Ferdinand E. Marcos, into a dictatorship. In view of the American experience in Vietnam there was every reason to know how many IOUs Marcos might feel free to collect.

Nor was this all. The Symington subcommittee found that the U.S. Army through an executive agreement for bases in Spain had virtually made an alliance with that country: the then-chairman of the joint chiefs of staff, General Earle G. Wheeler, admitted in an unwary moment that Spain received the best sort of guarantee against attack by allowing the stationing of American troops on its soil; an attack on the troops would be an attack on the United States. When the base agreement was up for renegotiation the Senate Committee on Foreign Relations under its able chairman, J. William Fulbright, asked the Nixon administration to communicate its terms in the form of a treaty. The administration in 1970 hastily signed another executive agreement.

In Laos both Democratic and Republican presidents had played fast and loose with the international accord on neutralization signed in 1962, and the Symington subcommittee discovered not only clear evidence of United States violations of the accord, but also a careful covering of the violations from Congress. The subcommittee chairman asked a former ambassador to Laos, William H. Sullivan, at the time deputy assistant secretary of state, how it was possible to analyze American commitments when the latter were not known. Sullivan replied with some ambiguities. It was exceedingly difficult to pin him down to anything. A Laos expert, he knew exactly what to say and what not to say. The subcommittee learned something about Laos only by interrogating less diplomatic individuals, military and civil, inquiring as to their duties in Laos.

In 1973 it became known that the Nixon administration had carried on a massive bombing of Cambodian territory for several years, under a system of false reporting that kept the attacks secret from most members of the Defense Department, from Congress, and of course from the American people. The president himself had assured his fellow Americans that there were no attacks.

The president thus conducted his own diplomacy apart from Congress, not to mention the Department of State. It was impossible for congressional committees to obtain the personal testimony, public or private, of close presidential advisers, who declined to testify, invoking executive privilege.

Meanwhile the preoccupation of the executive branch with secret, personal diplomacy took its attention from most of the other details of government, notably management of the Department of Defense. Through arduous efforts by Secretary of Defense Robert S. McNamara, the Kennedy-Johnson administrations had arranged a rough control of Pentagon spending by analyzing the cost for a given mission of programs proposed by branches of the military establishment. Systems analysis never applied to Vietnam, and in the end Vietnam consumed the Johnson presidency. During the first four years of the Nixon administration the Pentagon generals and admirals seemed much happier with Secretary of Defense Melvin R. Laird, who collected their shopping lists and passed them on to Congress. The expense of the military establishment was soaring toward $100 billion a year. Part of it was caused by inflation, and much of it was increased pay for service personnel, including a vast inflation in ranks (one general or admiral for every 1,400 men), but a great deal was for perhaps superfluous military hardware.

With the defense budget out of control, diplomacy was in great danger—one might say it was in double jeopardy, with the president's stubbornly personal conduct of foreign affairs. If in 1972 the ABM treaty and five-year freeze limited some kinds of weapons, it only gave the SALT II discussions the perplexing problem of ASW—antisubmarine warfare. Nuclear submarines were the foundation of the American and Soviet deterrents. The freeze limited the numbers of submarines and missiles but said nothing about measures of detection and destruction. At the outset of the 1970s ASW seemed an extremely difficult project. Not only could it absorb the energies of American and Russian science for years to come, but it also could cost hundreds of billions of dollars, trillions of rubles, in another race for deadlock as futile as the missile race of the 1960s. With the president and Congress so distrustful, almost at swords' point (what an ancient weapon was the sword!), it was possible for the military-industrial complex, as President Eisenhower once had dubbed the alliance of weapons producers and users, to run wild, forcing the Russians into superfluous countermeasures, the Americans into counter-countermeasures, ad infinitum. In that case foreign policy would have passed not merely beyond control of Congress or the Department of State, but out of the hands of the president who thought he was directing it.

What could be done about such a condition of affairs? For one thing, the conduct of the country's foreign policy was clearly in error, constitutionally and practically. The Constitution gave Congress oversight of foreign affairs and the president had no right to take upon the job himself. Organization was drastically, ridiculously, at fault, with the president running everything, largely in secret. By the 1970s the time had long since passed when American diplomacy could be conducted by one person with a small group of advisers. It was necessary to give the business of foreign affairs back to the Department of State, which was properly staffed.

So far as concerned the principles of American foreign relations, there was likewise room for much improvement, although change did not need to be so drastic. One of the three post-1945 principles had failed, and the failure had been so large that there was not much reason to repeat it. Another, balance of power, was nearly unprecedented in American diplomacy and had worked in Europe only under the guidance of its most distinguished nineteenth-century exponent; his successors had not proved good enough and had brought on the First World War. The remaining American principle since 1945, a world security organization, was a much more attractive policy. The United States government had done little to advance it during the quarter century since the San Francisco Conference and a good deal to hinder it. But by the time of the Nixon and Ford administrations, the at-long-last fully representative nature of the U.N. gave the security organization at least a chance to change the basis of international relations. It would be interesting to see if the harried statesmen of the power-wracked, dangerous world of the 1970s would dedicate the moment to the future or the past.

I

The United Nations

The failure of President Wilson's League of Nations haunted Americans during the Second World War, and in characteristic fashion they sought to do something about the mistake of 1919–20. Private groups planned for a world organization of peace, and the House of Representatives and Senate publicly recanted the error of a generation before. Because the League had expelled the Soviet Union after the attack on Finland in 1939, it was necessary to plan a new organization and not rearrange the old one. By the end of the war the citizens of the United States were eagerly pursuing the task, and within a year the United Nations Organization and a group of supporting institutions had come into being.

I. The Founding

A. The Fulbright and Connally Resolutions

After the Japanese attack on Pearl Harbor almost all members of Congress not merely supported the Roosevelt administration in prosecuting the war against the Axis powers in Asia and Europe, but took interest in the nature of postwar affairs. Their constituents clamored for some sort of American plan for peace. The administration was itself uncertain of a program, for President Roosevelt had entertained the idea of an international police force in which the United States would be joined by the other major powers. This idea ran counter to the Wilsonian view of collective security, according to which all of the nations, large and small, would join to protect the peace. In the momentary confusion of goals, and the need for an official statement by the government, an opportunity opened to a young member of the House of Representatives, the former dean of the law school and president of the University of Arkansas, J. William Fulbright, who moved a House concurrent resolution, which passed on September 21, 1943.

Source: *A Decade of American Foreign Policy: Basic Documents, 1941–1949* (Washington, D.C., 1950), p. 9.

Resolved by the House of Representatives (the Senate concurring), That the Congress hereby expresses itself as favoring the creation of appropriate international machinery with power adequate to establish and to maintain a just and lasting peace, among the nations of the world, and as favoring participation by the United States therein through its constitutional processes.

THE SENATE *followed with a resolution on November 5, 1943, by vote of 84 to 5, proposed by Senator Tom Connally of Texas. It is interesting that he was a veteran of the Spanish-American War. How the world, and American policy, had changed since the summer frolic of 1898!*

Resolved, That the war against all our enemies be waged until complete victory is achieved.

That the United States cooperate with its comrades-in-arms in securing a just and honorable peace.

That the United States, acting through its constitutional processes, join with free and sovereign nations in the establishment and maintenance of international authority with power to prevent aggression and to preserve the peace of the world.

That the Senate recognizes the necessity of there being established at the earliest practicable date a general international organization, based on the principle of the sovereign equality of all peace-loving states, and open to membership by all such states, large and small, for the maintenance of international peace and security.

That, pursuant to the Constitution of the United States, any treaty made to effect the purposes of this resolution, on behalf of the Government of the United States with any other nation or any association of nations, shall be made only by and with the advice and consent of the Senate of the United States, provided two-thirds of the Senators present concur.

B. THE CHARTER

THE CHARTER OF THE UNITED NATIONS ORGANIZATION *was drawn up in tentative form late in 1944 during meetings of representatives of the major allies at the Washington, D.C., mansion of Dumbarton Oaks, and the result was presented to a grand conference of all the nations enrolled in the conflict against the Axis powers. The San Francisco Conference opened on April 25, 1945, and closed on June 26 with the ceremonial signing of the charter. The Senate gave its consent on July*

SOURCE: *American Foreign Policy: 1941–1949,* p. 14.

28, 1945, by vote of 89 to 2. With its 111 articles the charter was a much more prolix document than the Covenant of the League, which contained 26 articles. It was more careful with such words as "war," which appeared only twice, in the phrase "Second World War"; it spoke of "breaches of the peace." Probably the most important articles in a limiting sense concerned the Big Power veto in the Security Council (Article 27) and regional agreements (Article 51). Designed to permit military alliances, the latter article was invoked in the North Atlantic Treaty of 1949 (p. 47).

WE THE PEOPLES OF THE UNITED NATIONS
DETERMINED

> to save succeeding generations from the scourge of war, which twice in our lifetime has brought untold sorrow to mankind, and
>
> to reaffirm faith in fundamental human rights, in the dignity and worth of the human person, in the equal rights of men and women and of nations large and small, and
>
> to establish conditions under which justice and respect for the obligations arising from treaties and other sources of international law can be maintained, and
>
> to promote social progress and better standards of life in larger freedom,

AND FOR THESE ENDS

> to practice tolerance and live together in peace with one another as good neighbors, and
>
> to unite our strength to maintain international peace and security, and
>
> to ensure, by the acceptance of principles and the institution of methods, that armed force shall not be used, save in the common interest, and
>
> to employ international machinery for the promotion of the economic and social advancement of all peoples,

HAVE RESOLVED TO COMBINE OUR EFFORTS TO
ACCOMPLISH THESE AIMS. . . .*

SOURCE: Charles I. Bevans, comp., *Treaties and Other International Agreements of the United States of America: 1776–1949* (Washington, D.C., 1968–), vol. III, pp. 1153–80.

* The style of the present volume is to use ellipses to indicate omissions with a document. However, in treaties and numbered material none are used at the end of a complete article when subsequent articles are omitted. Nor are they used at the beginning or end of an incomplete document, except when there is an omission at the beginning of the first paragraph or article cited, or at the end of the last paragraph or article cited.—ED.

Article 1

The Purposes of the United Nations are:

1. To maintain international peace and security, and to that end: to take effective collective measures for the prevention and removal of threats to the peace, and for the suppression of acts of aggression and other breaches of the peace, and to bring about by peaceful means, and in conformity with the principles of justice and international law, adjustment or settlement of international disputes or situations which might lead to a breach of the peace;
2. To develop friendly relations among nations based on respect for the principle of equal rights and self-determination of peoples, and to take other appropriate measures to strengthen universal peace;
3. To achieve international cooperation in solving international problems of an economic, social, cultural, or humanitarian character, and in promoting and encouraging respect for human rights and for fundamental freedoms for all without distinction as to race, sex, language, or religion; and
4. To be a center for harmonizing the actions of nations in the attainment of these common ends.

Article 2

The Organization and its Members, in pursuit of the Purposes stated in Article 1, shall act in accordance with the following Principles.

1. The Organization is based on the principle of the sovereign equality of all its Members.
2. All Members, in order to ensure to all of them the rights and benefits resulting from membership, shall fulfil in good faith the obligations assumed by them in accordance with the present Charter.
3. All Members shall settle their international disputes by peaceful means in such a manner that international peace and security, and justice, are not endangered.
4. All Members shall refrain in their international relations from the threat or use of force against the territorial integrity or political independence of any state, or in any other manner inconsistent with the Purposes of the United Nations.
5. All Members shall give the United Nations every assistance in any action it takes in accordance with the present Charter, and shall refrain from giving assistance to any state against which the United Nations is taking preventive or enforcement action.

6. The Organization shall ensure that states which are not Members of the United Nations act in accordance with these Principles so far as may be necessary for the maintenance of international peace and security.

7. Nothing contained in the present Charter shall authorize the United Nations to intervene in matters which are essentially within the domestic jurisdiction of any state or shall require the Members to submit such matters to settlement under the present Charter. . . .

Article 7

1. There are established as the principal organs of the United Nations: a General Assembly, a Security Council, an Economic and Social Council, a Trusteeship Council, an International Court of Justice, and a Secretariat. . . .

Article 10

The General Assembly may discuss any questions or any matters within the scope of the present Charter or relating to the powers and functions of any organs provided for in the present Charter, and, except as provided in Article 12, may make recommendations to the Members of the United Nations or to the Security Council or to both on any such questions or matters.

Article 12

1. While the Security Council is exercising in respect of any dispute or situation the functions assigned to it in the present Charter, the General Assembly shall not make any recommendation with regard to that dispute or situation unless the Security Council so requests. . . .

Article 18

1. Each member of the General Assembly shall have one vote.

2. Decisions of the General Assembly on important questions shall be made by a two-thirds majority of the members present and voting. These questions shall include: recommendations with respect to the maintenance of international peace and security, the election of the non-permanent members of the Security Council, the election of the members of the Economic and Social Council, the election of members of the Trusteeship Council in accordance

with paragraph 1(c) of Article 86, the admission of new Members to the United Nations, the suspension of the rights and privileges of membership, the expulsion of Members, questions relating to the operation of the trusteeship system, and budgetary questions.

Article 20

The General Assembly shall meet in regular annual sessions and in such special sessions as occasion may require. Special sessions shall be convoked by the Secretary-General at the request of the Security Council or of a majority of the Members of the United Nations.

Article 23

1. The Security Council shall consist of eleven Members of the United Nations. The Republic of China, France, the Union of Soviet Socialist Republics, the United Kingdom of Great Britain and Northern Ireland, and the United States of America shall be permanent members of the Security Council. The General Assembly shall elect six other Members of the United Nations to be non-permanent members of the Security Council, due regard being specially paid, in the first instance to the contribution of Members of the United Nations to the maintenance of international peace and security and to the other purposes of the Organization, and also to equitable geographical distribution. . . .

Article 27

1. Each member of the Security Council shall have one vote.
2. Decisions of the Security Council on procedural matters shall be made by an affirmative vote of seven members.
3. Decisions of the Security Council on all other matters shall be made by an affirmative vote of seven members including the concurring votes of the permanent members. . . .

Article 39

The Security Council shall determine the existence of any threat to the peace, breach of the peace, or act of aggression and shall make recommendations, or decide what measures shall be taken in accordance with Articles 41 and 42, to maintain or restore international peace and security.

Article 41

The Security Council may decide what measures not involving the use of armed force are to be employed to give effect to its decisions, and it may call upon the Members of the United Nations to apply such measures. These may include complete or partial interruption of economic relations and of rail, sea, air, postal, telegraphic, radio, and other means of communication, and the severance of diplomatic relations.

Article 42

Should the Security Council consider that measures provided for in Article 41 would be inadequate or have proved to be inadequate, it may take such action by air, sea, or land forces as may be necessary to maintain or restore international peace and security. Such action may include demonstrations, blockade, and other operations by air, sea, or land forces of Members of the United Nations.

Article 51

Nothing in the present Charter shall impair the inherent right of individual or collective self-defense if an armed attack occurs against a Member of the United Nations, until the Security Council has taken the measures necessary to maintain international peace and security. Measures taken by Members in the exercise of this right of self-defense shall be immediately reported to the Security Council and shall not in any way affect the authority and responsibility of the Security Council under the present Charter to take at any time such action as it deems necessary in order to maintain or restore international peace and security.

Article 52

1. Nothing in the present Charter precludes the existence of regional arrangements or agencies for dealing with such matters relating to the maintenance of international peace and security as are appropriate for regional action, provided that such arrange-

ments or agencies and their activities are consistent with the Purposes and Principles of the United Nations. . . .

Article 54

The Security Council shall at all times be kept fully informed of activities undertaken or in contemplation under regional arrangements or by regional agencies for the maintenance of international peace and security.

Article 55

With a view to the creation of conditions of stability and well-being which are necessary for peaceful and friendly relations among nations based on respect for the principle of equal rights and self-determination of peoples, the United Nations shall promote:

a. higher standards of living, full employment, and conditions of economic and social progress and development;

b. solutions of international economic, social, health, and related problems; and international cultural and educational cooperation; and

c. universal respect for, and observance of, human rights and fundamental freedoms for all without distinction as to race, sex, language, or religion.

Article 56

All members pledge themselves to take joint and separate action in cooperation with the Organization for the achievement of the purposes set forth in Article 55.

Article 61

1. The Economic and Social Council shall consist of eighteen Members of the United Nations elected by the General Assembly. . . .

Article 75

The United Nations shall establish under its authority an international trusteeship system for the administration and supervision of such territories as may be placed thereunder by subsequent individual agreements. These territories are hereinafter referred to as trust territories.

Article 76

The basic objectives of the trusteeship system, in accordance with the Purposes of the United Nations laid down in Article 1 of the present Charter, shall be:

a. to further international peace and security. . . .

Article 77

1. The trusteeship system shall apply to such territories in the following categories as may be placed thereunder by means of trusteeship agreements:

a. territories now held under mandate;
b. territories which may be detached from enemy states as a result of the Second World War; and
c. territories voluntarily placed under the system by states responsible for their administration. . . .

Article 82

There may be designated, in any trusteeship agreement, a strategic area or areas which may include part or all of the trust territory to which the agreement applies. . . .

Article 84

It shall be the duty of the administering authority to ensure that the trust territory shall play its part in the maintenance of international peace and security. To this end the administering authority may make use of volunteer forces, facilities, and assistance from the trust territory in carrying out the obligations towards the Security Council undertaken in this regard by the administering authority, as well as for local defense and the maintenance of law and order within the trust territory.

Article 87

The General Assembly and, under its authority, the Trusteeship Council, in carrying out their functions, may:

a. consider reports submitted by the administering authority;
b. accept petitions and examine them in consultation with the administering authority;

c. provide for periodic visits to the respective trust territories at times agreed upon with the administering authority; and

d. take these and other actions in conformity with the terms of the trusteeship agreements.

Article 88

The Trusteeship Council shall formulate a questionnaire on the political, economic, social, and educational advancement of the inhabitants of each trust territory, and the administering authority for each trust territory within the competence of the General Assembly shall make an annual report to the General Assembly upon the basis of such questionnaire.

Article 93

1. All Members of the United Nations are *ipso facto* parties to the Statute of the International Court of Justice. . . .

Article 97

The Secretariat shall comprise a Secretary-General and such staff as the Organization may require. The Secretary-General shall be appointed by the General Assembly upon the recommendation of the Security Council. He shall be the chief administrative officer of the Organization.

Article 100

1. In the performance of their duties the Secretary-General and the staff shall not seek or receive instructions from any government or from any other authority external to the Organization. They shall refrain from any action which might reflect on their position as international officials responsible only to the Organization. . . .

Article 102

1. Every treaty and every international agreement entered into by any Member of the United Nations after the present Charter comes into force shall as soon as possible be registered with the Secretariat and published by it.

2. No party to any such treaty or international agreement which has not been registered in accordance with the provisions of para-

graph 1 of this Article may invoke that treaty or agreement before any organ of the United Nations.

Article 108

Amendments to the present Charter shall come into force for all Members of the United Nations when they have been adopted by a vote of two thirds of the members of the General Assembly and ratified in accordance with their respective constitutional processes by two thirds of the Members of the United Nations, including all the permanent members of the Security Council.

2. A New Law of Nations

A. THE INTERNATIONAL COURT OF JUSTICE

AFTER THE FIRST WORLD WAR *the League of Nations in 1920, with the help of the American diplomat and jurist Elihu Root, established the Permanent Court of International Justice, usually known as the World Court. After years of controversy the Senate in 1935 refused to consent to American membership. It is an interesting commentary on the change in popular judgment about international affairs during and after the Second World War that the United States government upon joining the U.N. automatically became a member of the World Court's successor, the International Court of Justice. Participation in the U.N. court does not seem to have damaged any American vital interests and has had no notice in domestic politics. The average citizen is unaware of the U.N. court's existence. Actually it has enjoyed very few cases, and jurists have been concerned for its survival. The important parts of the court's seventy-article statute follow.*

Article 3

1. The Court shall consist of fifteen members, no two of whom may be nationals of the same state. . . .

Article 4

1. The members of the Court shall be elected by the General Assembly and by the Security Council from a list of persons

SOURCE: Bevans, *Treaties, 1776–1949,* III, pp. 1180–93.

nominated by the national groups in the Permanent Court of Arbitration. . . .

Article 10

. . . In the event of more than one national of the same state obtaining an absolute majority of the votes both of the General Assembly and of the Security Council, the eldest of these only shall be considered as elected. . . .

Article 22

1. The seat of the Court shall be established at The Hague. . . .

Article 23

1. The Court shall remain permanently in session. . . .

Article 34

1. Only states may be parties in cases before the Court. . . .

Article 36

. . . The states parties to the present Statute may at any time declare that they recognize as compulsory *ipso facto* and without special agreement, in relation to any other state accepting the same obligation, the jurisdiction of the Court. . . .

Article 38

1. The Court, whose function is to decide in accordance with international law such disputes as are submitted to it, shall apply:

a. international conventions, whether general or particular, establishing rules expressly recognized by the contesting states;
b. international custom, as evidence of a general practice accepted as law;
c. the general principles of law recognized by civilized nations;
d. subject to the provisions of Article 59, judicial decisions and the teachings of the most highly qualified publicists of the various nations, as subsidiary means for the determination of rules of law.

2. This provision shall not prejudice the power of the Court to decide a case *ex aequo et bono*, if the parties agree thereto. . . .

Article 59

The decision of the court has no binding force except between the parties and in respect of that particular case. . . .

Article 65

1. The Court may give an advisory opinion on any legal question at the request of whatever body may be authorized by or in accordance with the Charter of the United Nations to make such a request. . . .

PRESIDENT TRUMAN ON AUGUST 14, 1946, *after the consent of the Senate on August 2, declared that the United States recognized the compulsory jurisdiction of the U.N. court, with reservation of those issues essentially within the country's domestic jurisdiction. This was the same condition that the American government had begun placing in its bilateral arbitration treaties in the late 1920's and it was a loophole large enough to prevent embarrassment on any conceivable occasion.*

. . . the United States of America recognizes as compulsory *ipso facto* and without special agreement, in relation to any other state accepting the same obligation, the jurisdiction of the International Court of Justice in all legal disputes hereafter arising concerning

a. the interpretation of a treaty;
b. any question of international law;
c. the existence of any fact which, if established, would constitute a breach of an international obligation;
d. the nature or extent of the reparation to be made for the breach of an international obligation;

Provided, that this declaration shall not apply to

a. disputes the solution of which the parties shall entrust to other tribunals by virtue of agreements already in existence or which may be concluded in the future; or
b. disputes with regard to matters which are essentially within the domestic jurisdiction of the United States of America as determined by the United States of America; or
c. disputes arising under a multilateral treaty, unless (1) all parties to the treaty affected by the decision are also parties to the case before the

SOURCE: Bevans, *Treaties, 1776–1949,* IV, pp. 140–41.

Court, or (2) the United States of America specially agrees to jurisdiction.

B. The Trial of War Criminals at Nuremberg

What to do with war criminals was no novel difficulty during the Second World War, for at the end of the war of 1914–18 the Allies had sought to try the kaiser and other officials of the German government. Little had come from the effort; the Dutch government gave asylum to the kaiser, who lived quietly at Doorn until his death many years later during the Second World War, and it proved almost impossible to arrange the other trials. But the bestiality of the Hitler government together with the excesses of some of the Japanese army commanders cried out for punishment, and after a certain wavering during the war (some Allied statesmen, including Churchill, believed that a drumhead court martial was the best way to dispose of war criminals), it was decided to set up tribunals at Nuremberg and Tokyo. An agreement and charter regarding prosecution of German war criminals was signed in London on August 8, 1945.

Article 1

There shall be established after consultation with the Control Council for Germany an International Military Tribunal for the trial of war criminals whose offenses have no particular geographical location whether they be accused individually or in their capacity as members of organizations or groups or in both capacities.

Article 2

The constitution, jurisdiction and functions of the International Military Tribunal shall be those set out in the Charter annexed to this Agreement, which Charter shall form an integral part of this Agreement.

Article 3

Each of the Signatories shall take the necessary steps to make available for the investigation of the charges and trial the major war criminals detained by them who are to be tried by the International Military Tribunal. The Signatories shall also use their best

Source: Bevans, Treaties, 1776–1949, III, pp. 1238–40.

endeavors to make available for investigation of the charges against and the trial before the International Military Tribunal such of the major war criminals as are not in the territories of any of the Signatories.

Article 4

Nothing in this Agreement shall prejudice the provisions established by the Moscow Declaration concerning the return of war criminals to the countries where they committed their crimes.

It is an interesting point that Article 6, paragraph (c), of the German tribunal's accompanying charter contained a mistake in its English text, a semicolon between the words "war" and "or." The Allies on October 6, 1945, concluded a special protocol to convert the semicolon into a comma by removing the semicolon's dot. For this legality see Bevans, Treaties, 1776–1949, III, pp. 1286–87. As for the results of the Nuremberg Trials of the major war criminals, judgment was delivered on September 30–October 1, 1946, and ten men were hung on October 16. Others received prison sentences.

C. The Tokyo War Crimes Trial

General Douglas MacArthur in Tokyo *on January 19, 1946, established an International Military Tribunal for the Far East and approved its charter.*

Whereas, the United States and the Nations allied therewith in opposing the illegal wars of aggression of the Axis Nations, have from time to time made declarations of their intentions that war criminals should be brought to justice;

Whereas, the Governments of the Allied Powers at war with Japan on the 26th July 1945 at Potsdam, declared as one of the terms of surrender that stern justice shall be meted out to all war criminals including those who have visited cruelties upon our prisoners;

Whereas, by the Instrument of Surrender of Japan executed at Tokyo Bay, Japan, on the 2nd September 1945, the signatories for Japan, by command of and in behalf of the Emperor and the Japanese Government, accepted the terms set forth in such Declaration at Potsdam;

Source: Bevans, Treaties, 1776–1949, IV, pp. 20–21.

Whereas, by such Instrument of Surrender, the authority of the Emperor and the Japanese Government to rule the state of Japan is made subject to the Supreme Commander for the Allied Powers, who is authorized to take such steps as he deems proper to effectuate the terms of surrender;

Whereas, the undersigned has been designated by the Allied Powers as Supreme Commander for the Allied Powers to carry into effect the general surrender of the Japanese armed forces;

Whereas, the Governments of the United States, Great Britain and Russia at the Moscow Conference, 26th December 1945, having considered the effectuation by Japan of the Terms of Surrender, with the concurrence of China have agreed that the Supreme Commander shall issue all Orders for the implementation of the Terms of Surrender.

Now, therefore, I, Douglas MacArthur, as Supreme Commander for the Allied Powers, by virtue of the authority so conferred upon me, in order to implement the Term of Surrender which requires the meting out of stern justice to war criminals, do order and provide as follows:

Article 1

There shall be established an International Military Tribunal for the Far East for the trial of those persons charged individually, or as members of organizations or in both capacities, with offenses which include crimes against peace.

Article 2

The Constitution, jurisdiction and functions of this Tribunal are those set forth in the Charter of the International Military Tribunal for the Far East, approved by me this day.

Article 3

Nothing in this Order shall prejudice the jurisdiction of any other international, national or occupation court, commission or other tribunal established or to be established in Japan or in any territory of a United Nation with which Japan has been at war, for the trial of war criminals.

On December 23, 1948, the Allies executed seven Japanese, by hanging. Others were imprisoned for varying lengths of time.

3. Economic Cooperation

A. The IMF and the World Bank

During the Second World War the United States not only created the world's largest navy and air force and the second largest army, but also hugely subsidized the forces of its Allies. There seemed no question that the Allies would require a similarly large assistance with postwar economic problems, and even before the war was over the American government sought to organize currencies and international lending so that postwar economics would proceed in as rational a manner as possible. In the summer of 1944 at a conference at a huge vacation hotel in Bretton Woods, New Hampshire, the International Monetary Fund (IMF), which relied heavily upon the American treasury, was planned. It entered into force on December 27, 1945.

Article I

The purposes of the International Monetary Fund are:

i. To promote international monetary cooperation through a permanent institution which provides the machinery for consultation and collaboration on international monetary problems.

ii. To facilitate the expansion and balanced growth of international trade, and to contribute thereby to the promotion and maintenance of high levels of employment and real income and to the development of the productive resources of all members as primary objectives of economic policy.

iii. To promote exchange stability, to maintain orderly exchange arrangements among members, and to avoid competitive exchange depreciation.

iv. To assist in the establishment of a multilateral system of payments in respect of current transactions between members and in the elimination of foreign exchange restrictions which hamper the growth of world trade.

v. To give confidence to members by making the Fund's resources available to them under adequate safeguards, thus providing them with opportunity to correct maladjustments in their balance of payments without resorting to measures destructive of national or international prosperity.

Source: Bevans, Treaties, 1776–1949, III, pp. 1351–52, 1382–83.

vi. In accordance with the above, to shorten the duration and lessen the degree of disequilibrium in the international balances of payments of members. . . .

Article III

SECTION I. QUOTAS

Each member shall be assigned a quota. The quotas of the members represented at the United Nations Monetary and Financial Conference which accept membership before the date specified . . . shall be those set forth in Schedule A. The quotas of other members shall be determined by the Fund. . . .

SCHEDULE A: QUOTAS

	(In millions of United States dollars)
Australia	200
Belgium	225
Bolivia	10
Brazil	150
Canada	300
Chile	50
China	550
Colombia	50
Costa Rica	5
Cuba	50
Czechoslovakia	125
Denmark*	(*)
Dominican Republic	5
Ecuador	5
Egypt	45
El Salvador	2.5
Ethiopia	6
France	450
Greece	40
Guatemala	5
Haiti	5
Honduras	2.5
Iceland	1
India	400
Iran	25

* The quota of Denmark shall be determined by the Fund after the Danish Government has declared its readiness to sign this Agreement but before signature takes place.

	(In millions of United States dollars)
Iraq	8
Liberia	.5
Luxembourg	10
Mexico	90
Netherlands	275
New Zealand	50
Nicaragua	2
Norway	50
Panama	.5
Paraguay	2
Peru	25
Philippine Commonwealth	15
Poland	125
Union of South Africa	100
Union of Soviet Socialist Republics	1200
United Kingdom	1300
United States	2750
Uruguay	15
Venezuela	15
Yugoslavia	60

THE BRETTON WOODS CONFERENCE *planned an International Bank for Reconstruction and Development, usually known as the World Bank, and its articles were signed and went into effect the same day as those for the International Monetary Fund, December 27, 1945.*

Article I

The purposes of the Bank are:

i. To assist in the reconstruction and development of territories of members by facilitating the investment of capital for productive purposes, including the restoration of economies destroyed or disrupted by war, the reconversion of productive facilities to peacetime needs and the encouragement of the development of productive facilities and resources in less developed countries.

ii. To promote private foreign investment by means of guarantees or participations in loans and other investments made by private investors; and when private capital is not available on reasonable terms, to supplement private investment by providing, on suitable conditions, finance for productive purposes out of its own capital, funds raised by it and its other resources.

SOURCE: Bevans, *Treaties, 1776–1949*, III, pp. 1390–91, 1415–16.

iii. To promote the long-range balanced growth of international trade and the maintenance of equilibrium in balances of payments by encouraging international investment for the development of the productive resources of members, thereby assisting in raising productivity, the standard of living and conditions of labor in their territories.

iv. To arrange the loans made or guaranteed by it in relation to international loans through other channels so that the more useful and urgent projects, large and small alike, will be dealt with first.

v. To conduct its operations with due regard to the effect of international investment on business conditions in the territories of members and, in the immediate post-war years, to assist in bringing about a smooth transition from a wartime to a peacetime economy.

The Bank shall be guided in all its decisions by the purposes set forth above.

Article II

SECTION 1. MEMBERSHIP

a. The original members of the Bank shall be those members of the International Monetary Fund which accept membership in the Bank before the date specified.

b. Membership shall be open to other members of the Fund, at such times and in accordance with such terms as may be prescribed by the Bank.

SECTION 2. AUTHORIZED CAPITAL

a. The authorized capital stock of the Bank shall be $10,000,-000,000. . . .

b. The capital stock may be increased when the Bank deems it advisable by a three-fourths majority of the total voting power.

SECTION 3. SUBSCRIPTION OF SHARES

a. Each member shall subscribe shares of the capital stock of the Bank. The minimum number of shares to be subscribed by the original members shall be those set forth in Schedule A. . . .

SCHEDULE A: SUBSCRIPTIONS

	(millions of dollars)
Australia	200
Belgium	225
Bolivia	7

	(millions of dollars)
Brazil	105
Canada	325
Chile	35
China	600
Colombia	35
Costa Rica	2
Cuba	35
Czechoslovakia	125
*Denmark	
Dominican Republic	2
Ecuador	3.2
Egypt	40
El Salvador	1
Ethiopia	3
France	450
Greece	25
Guatemala	2
Haiti	2
Honduras	1
Iceland	400
India	400
Iran	24
Iraq	6
Liberia	.5
Luxembourg	10
Mexico	65
Netherlands	275
New Zealand	50
Nicaragua	.8
Norway	50
Panama	.2
Paraguay	.8
Peru	17.5
Philippine Commonwealth	15
Poland	125
Union of South Africa	100
Union of Soviet Socialist Republics	1200
United Kingdom	1300
United States	3175
Uruguay	10.5
Venezuela	10.5
Yugoslavia	40
Total	9100

* The quota of Denmark shall be determined by the Bank after Denmark accepts membership in accordance with these Articles of Agreement.

The Soviet Union failed to join either the International Monetary Fund or the World Bank.

B. FAO

THE CONSTITUTION OF THE UNITED NATIONS FOOD AND AGRICULTURE ORGANIZATION (FAO) was signed at Quebec on October 16, 1945. It entered into effect the same day.

Article I

1. The Organization shall collect, analyse, interpret, and disseminate information relating to nutrition, food and agriculture.

2. The Organization shall promote and, where appropriate, shall recommend national and international action with respect to

a. scientific, technological, social, and economic research relating to nutrition, food and agriculture;

b. the improvement of education and administration relating to nutrition, food and agriculture, and the spread of public knowledge of nutritional and agricultural science and practice;

c. the conservation of natural resources and the adoption of improved methods of agricultural production;

d. the improvement of the processing, marketing, and distribution of food and agricultural products;

e. the adoption of policies for the provision of adequate agricultural credit, national and international;

f. the adoption of international policies with respect to agricultural commodity arrangements.

3. It shall also be the function of the Organization

a. to furnish such technical assistance as governments may request;

b. to organize, in cooperation with the governments concerned, such missions as may be needed to assist them to fulfil the obligations arising from their acceptance of the recommendations of the United Nations Conference on Food and Agriculture; and

c. generally to take all necessary and appropriate action to implement the purposes of the Organization as set forth in the Preamble.

SOURCE: Bevans, Treaties, 1776–1949, III, pp. 1288–89.

C. GATT

THE GENERAL AGREEMENT ON TARIFFS AND TRADE (GATT) was signed at Geneva on October 20, 1947, and became provisionally effective on January 1, 1948. Subsequently amended in enormous detail, it has proved more effective than such bilateral arrangements as the United States followed beginning in 1934 with the Reciprocal Trade Agreements Act of that year. One of the interesting aspects of GATT appeared in Article I, a "general most-favored-nation" clause which extended any bilateral arrangement to all signatories.

Article I

1. With respect to customs duties and charges of any kind imposed on or in connection with importation or exportation or imposed on the international transfer of payments for imports or exports, and with respect to the method of levying such duties and charges, and with respect to all rules and formalities in connection with importation and exportation, . . . any advantage, favour, privilege or immunity granted by any contracting party to any product originating in or destined for any other country shall be accorded immediately and unconditionally to the like product originating in or destined for the territories of all other contracting parties. . . .

SOURCE: Bevans, Treaties, 1776–1949, IV, pp. 639–41.

After GATT came into force the members engaged in a series of "rounds" of tariff bargaining, of which the Kennedy Round, the sixth, beginning in November, 1964, and concluding in June, 1967, proved the most important. It provided for the gradual cutting of tariffs by as much as 50 percent over the ensuing five years. Average cuts were estimated at 35 percent. It affected almost 6,000 items and involved an estimated $40 billion of world trade in industrial products.

D. THE ILO

THE INTERNATIONAL LABOR ORGANIZATION (ILO) dated from the end of the First World War, its constitution having been signed at Versailles on June 28, 1919, the same day the statesmen signed the treaty of peace with Germany. After the Second World War it was necessary to

SOURCE: Bevans, Treaties, 1776–1949, IV, pp. 188–91.

amend the ILO constitution to bring it into relation with the new international organs. A conference in Montreal signed an instrument on October 9, 1946, which entered into force April 20, 1948. The United States deposited its acceptance with the International Labor Office on August 2, 1948.

Article 1

As from the date of the coming into force of this Instrument of Amendment, the Constitution of the International Labour Organisation, of which the text at present in force is set forth in the first column of the Annex to this Instrument, shall have effect as amended in the second column of the said Annex. . . .

Annex

THE CONSTITUTION OF THE INTERNATIONAL LABOUR ORGANISATION

Text in force on 9 October 1946	Amended Text
SECTION I	
ORGANISATION OF LABOUR	PREAMBLE
Whereas the League of Nations has for its object the establishment of universal peace, and such a peace can be established only if it is based upon social justice; And whereas. . . .	Whereas universal and lasting peace can be established only if it is based upon social justice; And whereas. . . .

4. The Human Equation

A. UNESCO

The constitution of the United Nations Educational, Scientific and Cultural Organization (UNESCO) was signed in London on November 16, 1945; the United States signed and deposited an instrument of acceptance on September 10, 1946. The constitution entered into force November 4, 1946.

Source: Bevans, Treaties, 1776–1949, III, pp. 1311–12.

The Governments of the States Parties to This Constitution on Behalf of Their Peoples

DECLARE

that since wars begin in the minds of men, it is in the minds of men that the defences of peace must be constructed;

that ignorance of each other's ways and lives has been a common cause throughout the history of mankind, of that suspicion and mistrust between the peoples of the world through which their differences have all too often broken into war;

that the great and terrible war which has now ended was a war made possible by the denial of the democratic principles of the dignity, equality and mutual respect of men, and by the propagation, in their place, through ignorance and prejudice, of the doctrine of the inequality of men and races;

that the wide diffusion of culture, and the education of humanity for justice and liberty and peace are indispensable to the dignity of man and constitute a sacred duty which all the nations must fulfill in a spirit of mutual assistance and concern;

that a peace based exclusively upon the political and economic arrangements of governments would not be a peace which could secure the unanimous, lasting and sincere support of the peoples of the world, and that the peace must therefore be founded, if it is not to fail, upon the intellectual and moral solidarity of mankind.

FOR THESE REASONS,

the States parties to this Constitution, believing in full and equal opportunities for education for all, in the unrestricted pursuit of objective truth, and in the free exchange of ideas and knowledge, are agreed and determined to develop and to increase the means of communication between their peoples and to employ these means for the purposes of mutual understanding and a truer and more perfect knowledge of each other's lives;

IN CONSEQUENCE WHEREOF

they do hereby create the United Nations Educational, Scientific and Cultural Organisation for the purpose of advancing, through the educational and scientific and cultural relations of the peoples of the world, the objectives of international peace and of the common welfare of mankind for which the United Nations Organisation was established and which its Charter proclaims.

B. WHO

THE UNITED STATES *signed the constitution of the World Health Organization (WHO) on the day it was opened for signature in New York, July 22, 1946, but it took nearly two years to obtain Senate approval of membership. That approval contained a provision that "nothing in the Constitution of the World Health Organization in any manner commits the United States to enact any specific legislative program regarding any matters referred to in said Constitution." The constitution entered into force in April, 1948, and American membership became effective on June 21.*

The States parties to this Constitution declare, in conformity with the Charter of the United Nations, that the following principles are basic to the happiness, harmonious relations and security of all peoples:

Health is a state of complete physical, mental and social well-being and not merely the absence of disease or infirmity.

The enjoyment of the highest attainable standard of health is one of the fundamental rights of every human being without distinction of race, religion, political belief, economic or social condition.

The health of all peoples is fundamental to the attainment of peace and security and is dependent upon the fullest co-operation of individuals and States.

The achievement of any State in the promotion and protection of health is of value to all.

Unequal development in different countries in the promotion of health and control of disease, especially communicable disease, is a common danger.

Healthy development of the child is of basic importance; the ability to live harmoniously in a changing total environment is essential to such development.

The extension to all peoples of the benefits of medical, psychological and related knowledge is essential to the fullest attainment of health.

SOURCE: Bevans, *Treaties, 1776–1949*, IV, pp. 119–20.

Informed opinion and active co-operation on the part of the public are of the utmost importance in the improvement of the health of the people.

Governments have a responsibility for the health of their peoples which can be fulfilled only by the provision of adequate health and social measures. . . .

Article 1

The objective of the World Health Organization . . . shall be the attainment by all peoples of the highest possible level of health.

C. THE IRO

THE INTERNATIONAL REFUGEE ORGANIZATION (IRO) was a short-term operation lasting from August 20, 1948, to December 31, 1951, but it had plenty to do, especially with the D.P. (displaced person) problems produced by the Hitler regime, which during the war had callously transported people from one end of the Continent to the other. There also were refugees from Spain, the Soviet Union, and elsewhere who were unwilling to return home. The IRO constitution was opened for signature on December 15, 1946, at Flushing Meadow, New York, the United Nations' temporary headquarters. It was signed for the United States the next day. The Senate consented to membership on July 1, 1947, reserving the immigration laws and Congress's jurisdiction in that regard.

The Governments accepting this Constitution,

Recognizing:

that genuine refugees and displaced persons constitute an urgent problem which is international in scope and character;

that as regards displaced persons, the main task to be performed is to encourage and assist in every way possible their early return to their country of origin;

that genuine refugees and displaced persons should be assisted by international action, either to return to their countries of nationality or former habitual residence, or to find new homes elsewhere, under the conditions provided for in this Constitution; or in the case of Spanish Republicans, to establish themselves temporarily in order to enable

SOURCE: Bevans, Treaties, 1776–1949, IV, pp. 284–85.

them to return to Spain when the present Falangist regime is succeeded by a democratic regime;

that re-settlement and re-establishment of refugees and displaced
persons be contemplated only in cases indicated clearly in the Constitution;

that genuine refugees and displaced persons, until such time as their
repatriation or re-settlement and re-establishment is effectively completed, should be protected in their rights and legitimate interests,
should receive care and assistance and, as far as possible, should be put
to useful employment in order to avoid the evil and anti-social consequences of continued idleness; and

that the expenses of repatriation to the extent practicable should be
charged to Germany and Japan for persons displaced by those Powers
from countries occupied by them:

Have agreed:

for the accomplishment of the foregoing purposes in the shortest
possible time, to establish and do hereby establish, a non-permanent organization to be called the International Refugee Organization, a specialized agency to be brought into relationship with
the United Nations, and accordingly

Have accepted the following articles.

II

Europe, 1945–1950

After the agonies of the Second World War people everywhere, not least in the United States, looked forward to peace and quiet. But such was not to be the condition of international relations in the half decade after V-E and V-J Days. Those first five years were wracked with crises, and indeed the decade of the 1950s opened with the Korean War; seemingly, there was no end to trouble. It may well be that American statesmen overestimated their country's peril in the years immediately after the Second World War, as some historians wrote in the late 1960s and after. Still, for people who lived through the period of the war and the first hectic years of nominal peace, the peril seemed physical and immediate, and the foreign policies of the time—the Truman Doctrine, Marshall Plan, and NATO— a series of well-executed moves.

5. Ideology and Economics

A. THE TRUMAN DOCTRINE

AMERICANS, so the distinguished diplomatic historian Dexter Perkins has written, are ardent believers in doctrines, and if anyone wishes to make a large point with the American public he should, so Perkins says, put it in the form of a doctrine. Whatever the truth of such a theory, by early 1947, when the British government announced it was going to withdraw from the task of supporting the government of Greece, and when the Russians simultaneously put pressure on the Turkish government and Ankara apparently would be unable to defend itself without economic and military assistance, President Truman decided to put the issue of Greek-Turkish aid in a forceful manner, in an address to Congress. He made the speech on March 12.

SOURCE: *Public Papers of the Presidents of the United States: Harry S. Truman, 1947* (Washington, D.C., 1963), pp. 176–80.

The gravity of the situation which confronts the world today necessitates my appearance before a joint session of the Congress.

The foreign policy and the national security of this country are involved.

One aspect of the present situation, which I present to you at this time for your consideration and decision, concerns Greece and Turkey.

The United States has received from the Greek Government an urgent appeal for financial and economic assistance. Preliminary reports from the American Economic Mission now in Greece and reports from the American Ambassador in Greece corroborate the statement of the Greek Government that assistance is imperative if Greece is to survive as a free nation.

I do not believe that the American people and the Congress wish to turn a deaf ear to the appeal of the Greek Government. . . .

The British Government, which has been helping Greece, can give no further financial or economic aid after March 31. Great Britain finds itself under the necessity of reducing or liquidating its commitments in several parts of the world, including Greece.

We have considered how the United Nations might assist in this crisis. But the situation is an urgent one requiring immediate action, and the United Nations and its related organizations are not in a position to extend help of the kind that is required. . . .

No government is perfect. One of the chief virtues of a democracy, however, is that its defects are always visible and under democratic processes can be pointed out and corrected. The government of Greece is not perfect. Nevertheless it represents 85 percent of the members of the Greek Parliament who were chosen in an election last year. Foreign observers, including 692 Americans, considered this election to be a fair expression of the views of the Greek people.

The Greek Government has been operating in an atmosphere of chaos and extremism. It has made mistakes. The extension of aid by this country does not mean that the United States condones everything that the Greek Government has done or will do. We have condemned in the past, and we condemn now, extremist measures of the right or left. We have in the past advised tolerance, and we advise tolerance now.

Greece's neighbor, Turkey, also deserves our attention.

The future of Turkey as an independent and economically sound state is clearly no less important to the freedom-loving peoples of the world than the future of Greece. The circumstances in which Turkey finds itself today are considerably different from those of Greece. Turkey has been spared the disasters that have beset Greece. And during the war, the United States and Great Britain furnished Turkey with material aid.

Nevertheless Turkey now needs our support. . . .

One of the primary objectives of the foreign policy of the United States is the creation of conditions in which we and other nations will be able to work out a way of life free from coercion. . . .

I believe that it must be the policy of the United States to support free peoples who are resisting attempted subjugation by armed minorities or by outside pressures.

I believe that we must assist free peoples to work out their own destinies in their own way.

I believe that our help should be primarily through economic and financial aid which is essential to economic stability and orderly political processes. . . .

I therefore ask the Congress to provide authority for assistance to Greece and Turkey in the amount of $400,000,000 for the period ending June 30, 1948. . . .

In addition to funds, I ask the Congress to authorize the detail of American civilian and military personnel to Greece and Turkey, at the request of those countries, to assist in the tasks of reconstruction, and for the purpose of supervising the use of such financial and material assistance as may be furnished. I recommend that authority also be provided for the instruction and training of selected Greek and Turkish personnel. . . .

This is a serious course upon which we embark.

I would not recommend it except that the alternative is much more serious.

The United States contributed $341,000,000,000 toward winning World War II. This is an investment in world freedom and world peace.

The assistance that I am recommending for Greece and Turkey amounts to little more than $\frac{1}{10}$ of 1 percent of this investment. . . .

Great responsibilities have been placed upon us by the swift movement of events.

I am confident that the Congress will face these responsibilities squarely.

In helping prepare a draft of Truman's speech, Undersecretary Acheson had advised the State Department's speechwriter, Joseph M. Jones, to make the speech apply to countries everywhere, not merely Greece and Turkey. Neither then nor later did Acheson or anyone else in authority in Washington have in mind a global policy. As Acheson told Jones, if Franklin D. Roosevelt had been living he, F.D.R., would have made the speech apply everywhere but would have confined his request for funds to Greece and Turkey. In later years the global nature —the doctrinal quality—of the Truman Doctrine seemed to some historians a mistake. The critics might have kept in mind that the nation's pristine diplomatic pronouncement, the Monroe Doctrine, theoretically encircled the Western Hemisphere but has never been invoked outside of Central America and the Caribbean.

B. The Marshall Plan

DURING THE WEEKS AFTER TRUMAN'S SPEECH *to Congress in March the economies of the European nations gave indication of deep trouble, and it became clear that piecemeal assistance, as in the cases of Greece and Turkey, was not the way to prevent the Continent's economic collapse. After turning down a proffered honorary degree at Harvard, Secretary of State George C. Marshall changed his mind. He attended the commencement in Cambridge and on the afternoon of June 5, 1947, used the occasion of the remarks permitted degree recipients to announce to the academic audience sitting under the elms of the campus an economic plan that quickly took his name.*

I need not tell you gentlemen that the world situation is very serious. That must be apparent to all intelligent people. I think one difficulty is that the problem is one of such enormous complexity that the very mass of facts presented to the public by press and radio make it exceedingly difficult for the man in the street to reach a clear appraisement of the situation. Furthermore, the people of this country are distant from the troubled areas of the earth and it is hard for them to comprehend the plight and consequent reactions of the long suffering peoples, and the effect of those reactions on their governments in connection with our efforts to promote peace in the world.

SOURCE: *A Decade of American Foreign Policy: Basic Documents, 1941–1949* (Washington, D.C., 1950), pp. 1268–70.

In considering the requirements for the rehabilitation of Europe, the physical loss of life, the visible destruction of cities, factories, mines, and railroads was correctly estimated, but it has become obvious during recent months that this visible destruction was probably less serious than the dislocation of the entire fabric of European economy. For the past 10 years conditions have been highly abnormal. The feverish preparation for war and the more feverish maintenance of the war effort engulfed all aspects of national economies. Machinery has fallen into disrepair or is entirely obsolete. Under the arbitrary and destructive Nazi rule, virtually every possible enterprise was geared into the German war machine. Long-standing commercial ties, private institutions, banks, insurance companies, and shipping companies disappeared, through loss of capital, absorption through nationalization, or by simple destruction. In many countries, confidence in the local currency has been severely shaken. The breakdown of the business structure of Europe during the war was complete. Recovery has been seriously retarded by the fact that two years after the close of hostilities a peace settlement with Germany and Austria has not been agreed upon. But even given a more prompt solution of these difficult problems, the rehabilitation of the economic structure of Europe quite evidently will require a much longer time and greater effort than had been foreseen.

There is a phase of this matter which is both interesting and serious. The farmer has always produced the foodstuffs to exchange with the city dweller for the other necessities of life. This division of labor is the basis of modern civilization. At the present time it is threatened with breakdown. The town and city industries are not producing adequate goods to exchange with the food-producing farmer. Raw materials and fuel are in short supply. Machinery is lacking or worn out. The farmer or the peasant cannot find the goods for sale which he desires to purchase. So the sale of his farm produce for money which he cannot use seems to him an unprofitable transaction. He, therefore, has withdrawn many fields from crop cultivation and is using them for grazing. He feeds more grain to stock and finds for himself and his family an ample supply of food, however short he may be on clothing and the other ordinary gadgets of civilization. Meanwhile people in the cities are short of food and fuel. So the governments are forced to use their foreign money and credits to procure these necessities abroad. This process

exhausts funds which are urgently needed for reconstruction. Thus
a very serious situation is rapidly developing which bodes no good
for the world. The modern system of the division of labor upon
which the exchange of products is based is in danger of breaking
down.

The truth of the matter is that Europe's requirements for the
next three or four years of foreign food and other essential products—principally from America—are so much greater than her
present ability to pay that she must have substantial additional
help or face economic, social, and political deterioration of a very
grave character.

The remedy lies in breaking the vicious circle and restoring the
confidence of the European people in the economic future of their
own countries and of Europe as a whole. The manufacturer and
the farmer throughout wide areas must be able and willing to exchange their products for currencies the continuing value of which
is not open to question.

Aside from the demoralizing effect on the world at large and the
possibilities of disturbances arising as a result of the desperation of
the people concerned, the consequences to the economy of the
United States should be apparent to all. It is logical that the
United States should do whatever it is able to do to assist in the
return of normal economic health in the world, without which
there can be no political stability and no assured peace. Our policy
is directed not against any country or doctrine but against hunger,
poverty, desperation, and chaos. Its purpose should be the revival
of a working economy in the world so as to permit the emergence
of political and social conditions in which free institutions can
exist. Such assistance, I am convinced, must not be on a piecemeal
basis as various crises develop. Any assistance that this Government
may render in the future should provide a cure rather than a mere
palliative. Any government that is willing to assist in the task of
recovery will find full cooperation, I am sure, on the part of the
United States Government. Any government which maneuvers to
block the recovery of other countries cannot expect help from us.
Furthermore, governments, political parties, or groups which seek
to perpetuate human misery in order to profit therefrom politically
or otherwise will encounter the opposition of the United States.

It is already evident that, before the United States Government
can proceed much further in its efforts to alleviate the situation

and help start the European world on its way to recovery, there must be some agreement among the countries of Europe as to the requirements of the situation and the part those countries themselves will take in order to give proper effect to whatever action might be undertaken by this Government. It would be neither fitting nor efficacious for this Government to undertake to draw up unilaterally a program designed to place Europe on its feet economically. This is the business of the Europeans. The initiative, I think, must come from Europe. The role of this country should consist of friendly aid in the drafting of a European program so far as it may be practical for us to do so. The program should be a joint one, agreed to by a number, if not all, European nations.

An essential part of any successful action on the part of the United States is an understanding on the part of the people of America of the character of the problem and the remedies to be applied. Political passion and prejudice should have no part. With foresight, and a willingness on the part of our people to face up to the vast responsibility which history has clearly placed upon our country, the difficulties I have outlined can and will be overcome.

C. Point Four

THE MARSHALL PLAN *was for Europe* (*although a small appropriation went to Nationalist China*). *To meet critics who said that the United States needed to send help wherever it was needed, President Truman in his inaugural address of January 20, 1949, elaborated the Point Four Program, the fourth, as it happened, of a series of suggestions in the speech.*

Fourth, we must embark on a bold new program for making the benefits of our scientific advances and industrial progress available for the improvement and growth of underdeveloped areas.

More than half the people of the world are living in conditions approaching misery. Their food is inadequate. They are victims of disease. Their economic life is primitive and stagnant. Their poverty is a handicap and a threat both to them and to more prosperous areas.

For the first time in history, humanity possesses the knowledge and skill to relieve the suffering of these people.

SOURCE: *Public Papers of the Presidents of the United States: Harry S. Truman, 1949* (Washington, D.C., 1964), pp. 112–16.

The United States is pre-eminent among nations in the development of industrial and scientific techniques. The material resources which we can afford to use for assistance of other peoples are limited. But our imponderable resources in technical knowledge are constantly growing and are inexhaustible.

I believe that we should make available to peace-loving peoples the benefits of our store of technical knowledge in order to help them realize their aspirations for a better life. And, in cooperation with other nations, we should foster capital investment in areas needing development.

Unfortunately the program was always more promise than fulfillment. It was announced without much forethought, having been proposed to one of the president's speechwriters by a subordinate official at a crucial moment. The State Department was not much in favor of it. Quite a lot of time passed before appropriations were arranged; then only $27 million was made available, and funding thereafter was never large; Congress provided $148 million in 1952 and $156 million in 1953; but in mid-1953 the Technical Cooperation Administration that managed Point Four lost its identity and specific appropriations.

6. Establishment of the Federal Republic of Germany

A. THE STUTTGART SPEECH

WITH THE RETROSPECT OF A GENERATION AND MORE *it now seems evident that in 1945 neither the Western Allies nor the Russians had thought out their postwar policies in regard to Germany and that the first months and even years of occupation were a period of improvisation. For the Russians it soon became evident that, as Stalin said at one of the Allied conferences, a free Germany would be anti-Soviet, and the U.S.S.R. was not about to allow such a solution to the German problem. For the Americans the preeminent difficulty became "getting the Germans off the American taxpayer's back." The need to raise the level of industry led to talk of giving the Germans more political rights. Secretary of State James F. Byrnes took a long step in this direction in a speech before a German-American audience in Stuttgart on September 6, 1946.*

SOURCE: Department of State *Bulletin*, September 15, 1946, pp. 496–501.

More than a year has passed since hostilities ceased. The millions of German people should not be forced to live in doubt as to their fate. It is the view of the American Government that the Allies should, without delay, make clear to the German people the essential terms of the peace settlement which they expect the German people to accept and observe. It is our view that the German people should now be permitted and helped to make the necessary preparations for setting up of a democratic German government which can accept and observe these terms.

From now on the thoughtful people of the world will judge Allied action in Germany not by Allied promises but by Allied performances. The American Government has supported and will continue to support the necessary measures to de-Nazify and de-militarize Germany, but it does not believe that large armies of foreign soldiers or alien bureaucrats, however well motivated and disciplined, are in the long run the most reliable guardians of another country's democracy.

All that the Allied governments can and should do is to lay down the rules under which German democracy can govern itself. The Allied occupation forces should be limited to the number sufficient to see that those rules are obeyed. . . .

The United States favors the early establishment of a provisional German government for Germany. Progress has been made in the American zone in developing local and state self-government in Germany, and the American Government believes similar progress is possible in all zones. . . .

The German people must realize that it was Hitler and his minions who tortured and exterminated innocent men, women, and children and sought with German arms to dominate and degrade the world. It was the massed, angered forces of humanity which had to fight their way into Germany to give the world the hope of freedom and peace.

The American people who fought for freedom have no desire to enslave the German people. The freedom Americans believe in and fought for is a freedom which must be shared with all willing to respect the freedom of others. . . .

The United States cannot relieve Germany from the hardships inflicted upon her by the war her leaders started. But the United States has no desire to increase those hardships or to deny the German people an opportunity to work their way out of those hardships so long as they respect human freedom and follow the paths of peace.

The American people want to return the government of Germany to the German people. The American people want to help the German people to win their way back to an honorable place among the free and peace-loving nations of the world.

B. THE LONDON RECOMMENDATIONS

BY THE END OF 1946 American officials saw that the Soviets did not desire the reunification of Germany and would rejoice over any economic troubles afflicting the occupation zones of the Western Allies. At foreign ministers conferences in Moscow in March–April, 1947, and in London in November–December the Russians proved intransigent on the German question. Secretary Marshall forced the breakup of the London Conference and early in 1948 assembled a second conference at London, without the Soviets, comprising the three Western nations occupying Germany, together with the three Benelux countries. The Western zones were admitted to the Marshall Plan on April 16. There remained the problem of political unity. The London Recommendations on this subject, dated June 2, were released in summary form on June 7.

Therefore the delegates have agreed to recommend to their governments that the military governors should hold a joint meeting with the Ministers-President of the western zone in Germany. At that meeting the Ministers-President will be authorized to convene a Constituent Assembly in order to prepare a constitution for the approval of the participating states.

Delegates to this Constituent Assembly will be chosen in each of the states in accordance with procedure and regulations to be determined by the legislative bodies of the individual states.

The constitution should be such as to enable the Germans to play their part in bringing to an end the present division of Germany not by the reconstitution of a centralized Reich but by means of a federal form of government which adequately protects the rights of the respective states, and which at the same time provides for adequate central authority and which guarantees the rights and freedoms of the individual.

If the constitution as prepared by the Constituent Assembly does not conflict with these general principles the military gover-

SOURCE: *American Foreign Policy: 1941–1949*, pp. 575–81.

nors will authorize its submissions for ratification by the people in the respective states.

At the meeting with the military governors the Ministers-President will also be authorized to examine the boundaries of the several States in order to determine what modifications might be proposed to the military governors for the purpose of creating a definitive system which is satisfactory to the peoples concerned. . . .

The prohibitions on the German Armed Forces and the German General Staff as contained in 4-power agreements were reaffirmed, as well as the exercise of controls by the military governors with respect to disarmament and demilitarization, level of industry and certain aspects of scientific research. To ensure the maintenance of disarmament and demilitarization in the interests of security, the three military governors should set up a military security board in the western zones of Germany to carry out the proper inspections and make the necessary recommendations to the military governors, who decide the action to be taken. . . .

The present recommendations, which in no way preclude and on the contrary should facilitate eventual 4-power agreement on the German problem, are designed to solve the urgent political and economic problems arising out of the present situation in Germany. Because of the previous failure to reach comprehensive 4-power decisions on Germany, the measures recommended mark a step forward in the policy which the powers represented at these talks are determined to follow with respect to the economic reconstruction of Western Europe, including Germany, and with respect to the establishment of a basis for the participation of a democratic Germany in the community of free peoples.

C. The Berlin Blockade

AFTER THE LONDON RECOMMENDATIONS the Western Allies instituted a currency reform in their zones and sought to introduce the new Western marks in their Berlin sectors. The Soviet government probably seized upon the currency issue as an excuse to close off land access to West Berlin. Almost certainly the Soviets were much more concerned over the London Recommendations, the already considerable political revival in the Western zones, and the forthcoming organization of a West German federal government. The blockade began on June 24, and

SOURCE: American Foreign Policy: 1941–1949, pp. 934–36.

*the airlift commenced the next day. Secretary Marshall in a note of July
6 protested vehemently to the Soviet ambassador in Washington,
Alexander S. Panyushkin.*

The rights of the United States as a joint occupying power in
Berlin derive from the total defeat and unconditional surrender of
Germany. The international agreements undertaken in connection
therewith by the Governments of the United States, United Kingdom, France and the Soviet Union defined the zones in Germany
and the sectors in Berlin which are occupied by these powers. They
established the quadripartite control of Berlin on a basis of friendly
cooperation which the Government of the United States earnestly
desires to continue to pursue.

These agreements implied the right of free access to Berlin. This
right has long been confirmed by usage. It was directly specified in
a message sent by President Truman to Premier Stalin on June 14,
1945, which agreed to the withdrawal of United States forces to
the zonal boundaries, provided satisfactory arrangements could be
entered into between the military commanders, which would give
access by rail, road and air to United States forces in Berlin.
Premier Stalin replied on June 16 suggesting a change in date but
no other alteration in the plan proposed by the President. Premier
Stalin then gave assurances that all necessary measures would be
taken in accordance with the plan. Correspondence in a similar
sense took place between Premier Stalin and Mr. Churchill. In
accordance with this understanding, the United States, whose
armies had penetrated deep into Saxony and Thuringia, parts of
the Soviet zone, withdrew its forces to its own area of occupation in
Germany and took up its position in its own sector in Berlin.
Thereupon the agreements in regard to the occupation of Germany and Berlin went into effect. The United States would not
have so withdrawn its troops from a large area now occupied by the
Soviet Union had there been any doubt whatsoever about the
observance of its agreed right of free access to its sector of Berlin.
The right of the United States to its position in Berlin thus stems
from precisely the same source as the right of the Soviet Union. It
is impossible to assert the latter and deny the former. . . .

In order that there should be no misunderstanding whatsoever
on this point, the United States Government categorically asserts
that it is in occupation of its sector in Berlin with free access
thereto as a matter of established right deriving from the defeat

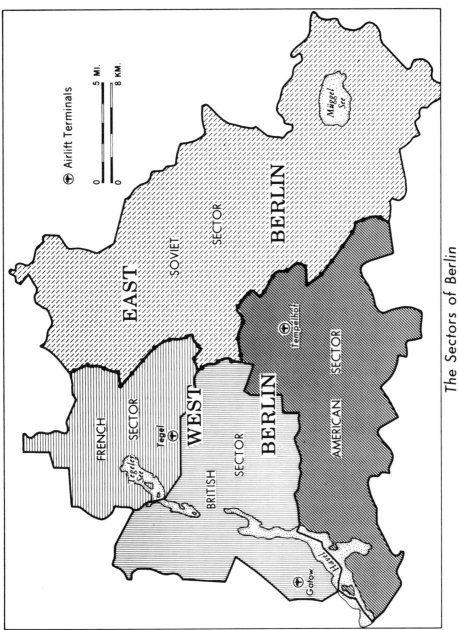

The Sectors of Berlin

and surrender of Germany and confirmed by formal agreements
among the principal Allies. It further declares that it will not be
induced by threats, pressures or other actions to abandon these
rights. It is hoped that the Soviet Government entertains no
doubts whatsoever on this point.

THE ALLIED AIRLIFT AT THE OUTSET seemed a fragile creation, and the
military governor of the American zone, General Lucius D. Clay, who
had instituted the airlift, put little faith in it. But then American
ingenuity set to work, and by the beginning of 1949 the supply of Berlin
by air was obviously succeeding. The incessant drone of Allied planes
coming and going to the three fields in West Berlin provided a great
demonstration of both the compassion and the military power of the
Western Allies. It all was too much for Premier Joseph Stalin, who
arranged an almost Byzantine diplomatic maneuver that allowed the
Soviet Union to end the blockade on Western terms. The Department
of State published an account of the negotiations in a statement of April
26, 1949, perhaps feeling that a public announcement would help
commit the Soviet dictator.

. . . the Department of State noted with particular interest that
on January 30, 1949, Premier Stalin made no mention of the currency question in Berlin in his reply to questions asked him by an
American journalist. Since the currency question had hitherto been
the announced reason for the blockade, the omission of any reference to it by Premier Stalin seemed to the Department to indicate
a development which should be explored.

With these considerations in mind, Mr. Jessup, then the U.S.
Deputy Representative on the Security Council, took occasion, in a
conversation on February 15 with Mr. Malik, the Soviet Representative on the Security Council, to comment on the omission by
Premier Stalin of any reference to the currency question. Since
this question had been the subject of much discussion in the Security Council and in the Experts Committee appointed under the
auspices of the Council, Mr. Jessup inquired whether the omission
had any particular significance.

One month later, on March 15, Mr. Malik informed Mr. Jessup
that Premier Stalin's omission of any reference to the currency
problem in regard to Berlin was "not accidental," that the Soviet
Government regarded the currency question as important but felt

SOURCE: American Foreign Policy: 1941–1949, pp. 937–38.

that it could be discussed at a meeting of the Council of Foreign Ministers if a meeting of that body could be arranged to review the whole German problem. Mr. Jessup inquired whether this meant that the Soviet Government had in mind a Foreign Ministers' meeting while the blockade of Berlin was in progress or whether it indicated that the blockade would be lifted in order to permit the meeting to take place.

The information as to the Soviet Government's attitude revealed in these informal contacts was immediately conveyed to the British and French Governments.

On March 21 Mr. Malik again asked Mr. Jessup to visit him to inform him that if a definite date could be set for the meeting of the Council of Foreign Ministers, the restrictions on trade and transportation in Berlin could be lifted reciprocally and that the lifting of the blockade could take place in advance of the meeting.

Taking advantage of the presence of the Foreign Ministers of Great Britain and France in Washington, the recent developments in regard to the Soviet attitude were discussed with them.

An agreed position was reached among the three Western Powers. In order that there should be no misunderstanding in the mind of the Soviet Government in regard to this position, a statement was read to Mr. Malik by Mr. Jessup on April 5. The purpose of this statement, which represented the agreed position of the three Western Powers, was to make clear that the points under discussion were the following:

1. Reciprocal and simultaneous lifting of the restrictions imposed by the Soviet Union since March 1, 1948, on communications, transportation, and trade between Berlin and the Western zones of Germany and the restrictions imposed by the Three Powers on communications, transportation, and trade to and from the Eastern zone of Germany.

2. The fixing of a date to be determined for a meeting of the Council of Foreign Ministers.

The Western Powers wished to be sure that these two points were not conditioned in the understanding of the Soviet Government on any of the other points which in the past had prevented agreement upon the lifting of the blockade.

The statement summarized the understanding of the three Governments of the position which the Soviet Government took concerning the proposal of lifting the blockade and the meeting of the

Council of Foreign Ministers. Its purpose was to make unmistakably clear that the position of the Soviet Government was as now stated in the release of the Tass Agency.

On April 10 Mr. Malik again asked Mr. Jessup to call upon him at that time and again stated the position of the Soviet Government. From this statement it appeared that here were still certain points requiring clarification.

As a result of this meeting, further discussions took place between the three Governments, which have resulted in a more detailed formulation of their position, which will be conveyed by Mr. Jessup to Mr. Malik.

If the present position of the Soviet Government is as stated in the Tass Agency release as published in the American press, the way appears clear for a lifting of the blockade and a meeting of the Council of Foreign Ministers. No final conclusion upon this can be reached until further exchanges of view with Mr. Malik.

The blockade came to an end on May 12, 1949, according to an agreement on the above-mentioned points initialed at the United Nations in New York on May 4 by representatives of the four occupying powers. The Paris Foreign Ministers Conference proved a face-saving affair and did nothing other than provide a screen behind which the Soviets retreated to the status quo ante the blockade. Meanwhile the Western Allies went ahead with their plans, as set out in the London Recommendations of June, 1948, for a Federal Republic of Germany. The three Western foreign ministers signed agreements in Washington on April 8, 1949, and on September 21 three high commissioners for Germany (the title of military governor having been superseded) signed a declaration at Bonn revising the occupation statute to allow establishment of the Federal Republic. The Western Allies terminated the revised occupation statute for West Germany by several agreements, signed on October 23, 1954, effective May 5, 1955 (see pp. 54-56).

7. NATO

A. THE VANDENBERG RESOLUTION

SENATOR VANDENBERG was a staunch defender—ideologically, economically, militarily—of American cooperation for the defense of Europe. He also liked to attach his name to declarations by the Senate. A

SOURCE: *American Foreign Policy: 1941-1949*, p. 197.

resolution of June 11, 1948, gave the Truman administration the green light to organize the military defense of Western Europe.

Whereas peace with justice and the defense of human rights and fundamental freedoms require international cooperation through more effective use of the United Nations: Therefore be it

Resolved, That the Senate reaffirm the policy of the United States to achieve international peace and security through the United Nations so that armed force shall not be used except in the common interest, and that the President be advised of the sense of the Senate that this Government, by constitutional process, should particularly pursue the following objectives within the United Nations Charter:

1. Voluntary agreement to remove the veto from all questions involving pacific settlements of international disputes and situations, and from the admission of new members.

2. Progressive development of regional and other collective arrangements for individual and collective self-defense in accordance with the purposes, principles, and provisions of the Charter.

3. Association of the United States, by constitutional process, with such regional and other collective arrangements as are based on continuous and effective self-help and mutual aid, and as affect its national security.

4. Contributing to the maintenance of peace by making clear its determination to exercise the right of individual or collective self-defense under article 51 should any armed attack occur affecting its national security.

B. THE NORTH ATLANTIC TREATY

In 1948 the Truman administration conducted careful talks in Washington with the representatives of the governments to be invited into the prospective North Atlantic Treaty Organization (NATO) and when the instrument was signed on April 4, 1949, signatories in addition to the United States included Great Britain, Canada, France, Italy, Portugal, Belgium, the Netherlands, Luxembourg, Denmark, Norway, and Iceland. The treaty entered into force on August 24.

SOURCE: Charles I. Bevans, comp., *Treaties and Other International Agreements of the United States of America: 1776–1949,* IV, pp. 828–831.

The Parties to this Treaty reaffirm their faith in the purposes and principles of the Charter of the United Nations and their desire to live in peace with all peoples and all governments.

They are determined to safeguard the freedom, common heritage and civilization of their peoples, founded on the principles of democracy, individual liberty and the rule of law.

They seek to promote stability and well-being in the North Atlantic area.

They are resolved to unite their efforts for collective defense and for the preservation of peace and security.

They therefore agree to this North Atlantic Treaty:

Article 1

The Parties undertake, as set forth in the Charter of the United Nations, to settle any international disputes in which they may be involved by peaceful means in such a manner that international peace and security, and justice, are not endangered, and to refrain in their international relations from the threat or use of force in any manner inconsistent with the purposes of the United Nations.

Article 2

The Parties will contribute toward the further development of peaceful and friendly international relations by strengthening their free institutions, by bringing about a better understanding of the principles upon which these institutions are founded, and by promoting conditions of stability and well-being. They will seek to eliminate conflict in their international economic policies and will encourage economic collaboration between any or all of them.

Article 3

In order more effectively to achieve the objectives of this Treaty, the Parties, separately and jointly, by means of continuous and effective self-help and mutual aid, will maintain and develop their individual and collective capacity to resist armed attack.

Article 4

The Parties will consult together whenever, in the opinion of any of them, the territorial integrity, political independence or security of any of the Parties is threatened.

Article 5

The Parties agree that an armed attack against one or more of them in Europe or North America shall be considered an attack against them all; and consequently they agree that, if such an armed attack occurs, each of them, in exercise of the right of individual or collective self-defense recognized by Article 51 of the Charter of the United Nations, will assist the Party or Parties so attacked by taking forthwith, individually and in concert with the other Parties, such action as it deems necessary, including the use of armed force, to restore and maintain the security of the North Atlantic area.

Any such armed attack and all measures taken as a result thereof shall immediately be reported to the Security Council. Such measures shall be terminated when the Security Council has taken the measures necessary to restore and maintain international peace and security.

Article 6

For the purpose of Article 5 an armed attack on one or more of the Parties is deemed to include an armed attack on the territory of any of the Parties in Europe or North America, on the Algerian departments of France, on the occupation forces of any Party in Europe, on the islands under the jurisdiction of any Party in the North Atlantic area north of the Tropic of Cancer or on the vessels or aircraft in this area of any of the Parties.

Article 7

This Treaty does not affect, and shall not be interpreted as affecting, in any way the rights and obligations under the Charter of the Parties which are members of the United Nations, or the primary responsibility of the Security Council for the maintenance of international peace and security.

Article 8

Each Party declares that none of the international engagements now in force between it and any other of the Parties or any third state is in conflict with the provisions of this Treaty, and undertakes not to enter into any international engagement in conflict with this Treaty.

Article 9

The Parties hereby establish a council, on which each of them shall be represented, to consider matters concerning the implementation of this Treaty. The council shall be so organized as to be able to meet promptly at any time. The council shall set up such subsidiary bodies as may be necessary; in particular it shall establish immediately a defense committee which shall recommend measures for the implementation of Articles 3 and 5.

Article 10

The Parties may, by unanimous agreement, invite any other European state in a position to further the principles of this Treaty and to contribute to the security of the North Atlantic area to accede to this Treaty. Any state so invited may become a party to the Treaty by depositing its instrument of accession with the Government of the United States of America. The Government of the United States of America will inform each of the Parties of the deposit of each such instrument of accession.

Article 11

This Treaty shall be ratified and its provisions carried out by the Parties in accordance with their respective constitutional processes. The instruments of ratification shall be deposited as soon as possible with the Government of the United States of America, which will notify all the other signatories of each deposit. The Treaty shall enter into force between the states which have ratified it as soon as the ratifications of the majority of the signatories, including the ratifications of Belgium, Canada, France, Luxembourg, the Netherlands, the United Kingdom and the United States, have been deposited and shall come into effect with respect to other states on the date of the deposit of their ratifications.

Article 12

After the Treaty has been in force for ten years, or at any time thereafter, the Parties shall, if any of them so requests, consult together for the purpose of reviewing the Treaty, having regard for the factors then affecting peace and security in the North Atlantic area, including the development of universal as well as regional arrangements under the Charter of the United Nations for the maintenance of international peace and security.

Article 13

After the Treaty has been in force for twenty years, any Party may cease to be a party one year after its notice of denunciation has been given to the Government of the United States of America, which will inform the Governments of the other Parties of the deposit of each notice of denunciation.

Article 14

This Treaty, of which the English and French texts are equally authentic, shall be deposited in the archives of the Government of the United States of America. Duly certified copies thereof will be transmitted by that Government to the Governments of the other signatories.

A protocol of October 17, 1951, effective the following year, admitted Greece and Turkey to NATO. The Federal Republic of Germany was included by a protocol of October 23, 1954, effective the next year.

III

Europe, 1950–1960

When the Korean War began in 1950, the attention of the American public shifted to the Far East. Europe, the Old Continent, would no longer have the interest it had held in foreign policy during the late 1940s and earlier during the coming and course of the Second World War. Leaders of the American government, nonetheless, knew that Europe, especially Western Europe, was the main prize between the contending superpowers and that no trouble elsewhere, such as Korea, should concentrate the nation's concern to a point at which Europe seemed less important, not to say unimportant. The secretary of state during the last four years of the Truman administration, Dean Acheson, was always attuned to the problems of Europe and never took his eyes off the Continent. His successor, John Foster Dulles, became a global traveler, the most traveled secretary of state in American history up to his time (he traveled 559,988 miles in 1953–59), but he too watched the Continent carefully, if not as consistently as did Acheson.

8. Bringing Germany into NATO

A. The Pleven Plan

After the beginning of the Korean War in June, 1950, the favorite explanation of some American policy makers was that the Far Eastern war was a diversion, an effort to commit the bulk of U.S. military force to a remote peninsula in Asia, whereupon the Russians would put unbearable pressure upon Western Europe. If that had happened, the Truman Doctrine, Marshall Plan, and NATO all would have come to nothing. NATO in 1950 was just beginning to be organized, and was so alarmingly weak that the American government, in view of the con-

Source: *American Foreign Policy: 1950–1955*, 2 vols. (Washington, D.C., 1957), I, pp. 1107–13.

tinuing postwar confusions of the cabinets in France, began to encourage German military growth. The Paris cabinets sought to avoid the
issue, hating the notion of a revived German army within only a few
years of the end of the war, knowing also that the methodical Germans,
untroubled with revolts in overseas possessions (for the French there
were increasing problems in Algeria and Indochina), would have more
men in the field than the French, and that this fact would give the
Germans diplomatic leverage in Europe, at the least ensuring the complete independence of the Federal Republic (which in 1949 had obtained
only partial independence). The result was the Pleven Plan of May 27,
1952, named for the French premier of the moment, René Pleven.

The President of the Federal Republic of Germany, His Majesty
the King of the Belgians, the President of the French Republic, the
President of the Italian Republic, Her Royal Highness the Grand
Duchess of Luxembourg, Her Majesty the Queen of the Netherlands. . . .
Conscious that they are thus taking a new and essential step on
the road to the formation of a united Europe. . . .

Article 1

By the present Treaty the High Contracting Parties institute
among themselves a European Defense Community, supranational
in character, consisting of common institutions, common armed
Forces and a common budget.

Article 2

1. The objectives of the Community shall be exclusively defensive.
2. Consequently, under the conditions provided for in the present Treaty, it shall ensure the security of the member States
against any aggression by participating in Western Defense within
the framework of the North Atlantic Treaty and by accomplishing
the integration of the defense forces of the member States and the
rational and economic utilization of their resources.
3. Any armed aggression directed against any one of the member
States in Europe or against the European Defense Forces shall be
considered as an attack directed against all of the member States.
The member States and the European Defense Forces shall

furnish to the State or Forces thus attacked all military and other aid and assistance in their power.

Article 8

1. The institutions of the Community shall be:
—A Council of Ministers, hereinafter called the Council.
—A Common Assembly, hereinafter called the Assembly.
—A Commissariat of the European Defense Community, hereinafter called the Commissariat.
—A Court of Justice, hereinafter called the Court. . . .

Article 9

The Armed Forces of the Community, hereinafter called "European Defense Forces" shall be composed of contingents placed at the disposal of the Community by the member States with a view to their fusion under the conditions provided for in the present Treaty. . . .

Article 15

1. The European Defense Forces shall consist of conscripted personnel and of professional personnel serving for a long term by voluntary enlistment.
2. The European Defense Forces shall be integrated. . . .

They shall wear a common uniform.
They shall be organized according to types defined in the Military Protocol. Such organization may be modified by unanimous decision of the Council. . . .

The European Defense Community (EDC) was a compromise to allow German contingents in NATO but in units no larger than the divisional level; divisions of members of EDC would be mixed at corps and army levels. The Germans would not obtain a new army; their divisions would be under Western Allied control. But the French dragged their heels over EDC. Secretary Dulles during a visit to France in December, 1953, twice announced the possibility of an agonizing reappraisal, as he put it, of American responsibilities toward Europe: the United States might pull out if EDC failed. This pressure touched the amour-propre of the French Assembly, which in August, 1954, voted down EDC.

B. Modifying the Brussels Pact

THE GERMANS soon afterward were admitted to NATO by another stratagem, which was more involved, if less soothing to French fear of a new German army. The solution was to refurbish a treaty concluded between Britain, France, and the Benelux nations in 1948—the Brussels Pact Alliance, known also as the Western Union. Its revised form, dated October 23, 1954, was christened the Western European Union (WEU).

Article I

The Federal Republic of Germany and the Italian Republic hereby accede to the Treaty as modified and completed by the present Protocol.

The High Contracting Parties to the present protocol consider the Protocol on Forces of Western European Union . . . , the Protocol on the Control of Armaments and its Annexes . . . , and the Protocol on the Agency of Western European Union for the Control of Armaments . . . to be an integral part of the present Protocol.

Article II

The sub-paragraph of the Preamble to the Treaty: "to take such steps as may be held necessary in the event of renewal by Germany of a policy of aggression" shall be modified to read: "to promote the unity and to encourage the progressive integration of Europe.". . .

Article III

The following new Article shall be inserted in the Treaty as Article IV: "In the execution of the Treaty the High Contracting Parties and any organs established by Them under the Treaty shall work in close co-operation with the North Atlantic Treaty Organization."

Recognising the undesirability of duplicating the Military Staffs of NATO, the Council and its agency will rely on the appropriate Military Authorities of NATO for information and advice on military matters.

SOURCE: *American Foreign Policy: 1950–1955*, I, pp. 972–76.

AN ACCOMPANYING PROTOCOL of the same date, on level of forces, showed close agreement with the levels of the European Defense Community.

Article 1

1. The land and air forces which each of the High Contracting Parties to the present Protocol shall place under the Supreme Allied Commander Europe in peacetime on the mainland of Europe shall not exceed in total strength and number of formations:

    a. for Belgium, France, the Federal Republic of Germany, Italy and the Netherlands, the maxima laid down for peacetime in the Special Agreement annexed to the Treaty on the Establishment of a European Defence Community signed at Paris, on 27th May, 1952; and

    b. for the United Kingdom, four divisions and the Second Tactical Air Force;

    c. for Luxembourg, one regimental combat team.

2. The number of formations mentioned in paragraph 1 may be brought up to date and adapted as necessary to make them suitable for the North Atlantic Treaty Organization, provided that the equivalent fighting capacity and total strengths are not exceeded.

3. The statement of these maxima does not commit any of the High Contracting Parties to build up or maintain forces at these levels, but maintains their right to do so if required.

SOURCE: *American Foreign Policy: 1950–1955*, I, p. 977.

IN EXCHANGE for the Federal Republic's military contingent to NATO, the Western Allies on October 23, 1954 (effective May 5, 1955) granted full sovereignty to Bonn. This involved amending a treaty signed May 26, 1952, that had anticipated the coming into effect of the Pleven Plan. The 1952 treaty follows.

Article 1

1. On the entry into force of the present Convention the United States of America, the United Kingdom of Great Britain and Northern Ireland and the French Republic (hereinafter and in the related Conventions sometimes referred to as "the Three Powers")

SOURCE: *American Foreign Policy: 1950–1955*, I, pp. 486–87.

will terminate the Occupation regime in the Federal Republic, revoke the Occupation Statute and abolish the Allied High Commission and the Offices of the Land Commissioners in the Federal Republic.

2. The Federal Republic shall have accordingly the full authority of a sovereign State over its internal and external affairs.

Article 2

In view of the international situation, which has so far prevented the reunification of Germany and the conclusion of a peace settlement, the Three Powers retain the rights and the responsibilities, heretofore exercised or held by them, relating to Berlin and to Germany as a whole, including the reunification of Germany and a peace settlement. The rights and responsibilities retained by the Three Powers relating to the stationing of armed forces in Germany and the protection of their security are dealt with in articles 4 and 5 of the present Convention.

Article 4

1. Pending the entry into force of the arrangements for the German Defence Contribution, the Three Powers retain the rights, heretofore exercised or held by them, relating to the stationing of armed forces in the Federal Republic. The mission of these forces will be the defence of the free world, of which Berlin and the Federal Republic form part. . . .

C. THE WARSAW PACT

WHEN NATO's MEMBER STATES duly ratified West Germany's entrance into the pact and the Federal Republic received full sovereignty at the hands of the Western Allies, the Russian government combined with its satellites—Albania, Bulgaria, Czechoslovakia, East Germany, Hungary, Poland, and Rumania—on May 15, 1955, to form the Warsaw Pact. The German Democratic Republic (East Germany) had been organized by the Soviet government on October 7, 1949, and the Soviet government declared it to have achieved full sovereignty on March 25, 1954.

SOURCE: American Foreign Policy: 1950–1955, I, pp. 1239–42.

Federal Republic of Germany

The Contracting Parties,

reaffirming their desire for the establishment of a system of European collective security based on the participation of all European states irrespective of their social and political systems, which would make it possible to unite their efforts in safeguarding the peace of Europe;

mindful, at the same time, of the situation created in Europe by the ratification of the Paris agreements, which envisage the formation of a new military alignment in the shape of "Western European Union," with the participation of a remilitarized Western

Germany and the integration of the latter in the North-Atlantic bloc, which increased the danger of another war and constitutes a threat to the national security of the peaceable states;

being persuaded that in these circumstances the peaceable European states must take the necessary measures to safeguard their security and in the interests of preserving peace in Europe;

guided by the objects and principles of the Charter of the United Nations Organization;

being desirous of further promoting and developing friendship, cooperation and mutual assistance in accordance with the principles of respect for the independence and sovereignty of states and of non-interference in their internal affairs,

have decided to conclude the present Treaty of Friendship, Cooperation and Mutual Assistance. . . .

Article 1

The Contracting Parties undertake, in accordance with the Charter of the United Nations Organization, to refrain in their international relations from the threat or use of force, and to settle their international disputes peacefully and in such manner as will not jeopardize international peace and security.

Article 2

The Contracting Parties declare their readiness to participate in a spirit of sincere cooperation in all international actions designed to safeguard international peace and security, and will fully devote their energies to the attainment of this end.

The Contracting Parties will furthermore strive for the adoption, in agreement with other states which may desire to cooperate in this, of effective measures for universal reduction of armaments and prohibition of atomic, hydrogen and other weapons of mass destruction.

Article 3

The Contracting Parties shall consult with one another on all important international issues affecting their common interests, guided by the desire to strengthen international peace and security.

They shall immediately consult with one another whenever, in the opinion of any one of them, a threat of armed attack on one or more of the Parties to the Treaty has arisen, in order to ensure joint defence and the maintenance of peace and security.

Article 4

In the event of armed attack in Europe on one or more of the Parties to the Treaty by any state or group of states, each of the Parties to the Treaty, in the exercise of its right to individual or collective self-defence in accordance with Article 51 of the Charter of the United Nations Organization, shall immediately, either individually or in agreement with other Parties to the Treaty, come to the assistance of the state or states attacked with all such means as it deems necessary, including armed force. The Parties to the Treaty shall immediately consult concerning the necessary measures to be taken by them jointly in order to restore and maintain international peace and security.

Measures taken on the basis of this Article shall be reported to the Security Council in conformity with the provisions of the Charter of the United Nations Organization. These measures shall be discontinued immediately the Security Council adopts the necessary measures to restore and maintain international peace and security.

Article 5

The Contracting Parties have agreed to establish a Joint Command of the armed forces that by agreement among the Parties shall be assigned to the Command, which shall function on the basis of jointly established principles. They shall likewise adopt other agreed measures necessary to strengthen their defensive power, in order to protect the peaceful labours of their peoples, guarantee the inviolability of their frontiers and territories, and provide defence against possible aggression.

Article 6

For the purpose of the consultations among the Parties envisaged in the present Treaty, and also for the purpose of examining questions which may arise in the operation of the Treaty, a Political Consultative Committee shall be set up, in which each of the Parties to the Treaty shall be represented by a member of its Government or by another specifically appointed representative.

The Committee may set up such auxiliary bodies as may prove necessary.

Article 7

The Contracting Parties undertake not to participate in any coalitions or alliances and not to conclude any agreements whose objects conflict with the objects of the present Treaty.

The Contracting Parties declare that their commitments under existing international treaties do not conflict with the provisions of the present Treaty.

Article 8

The Contracting Parties declare that they will act in a spirit of friendship and cooperation with a view to further developing and fostering economic and cultural intercourse with one another, each adhering to the principle of respect for the independence and sovereignty of the others and non-interference in their internal affairs.

Article 9

The present Treaty is open to the accession of other states, irrespective of their social and political systems, which express their readiness by participation in the present Treaty to assist in uniting the efforts of the peaceable states in safeguarding the peace and security of the peoples. Such accession shall enter into force with the agreement of the Parties to the Treaty after the declaration of accession has been deposited with the Government of the Polish People's Republic

Article 10

The present Treaty is subject to ratification, and the instruments of ratification shall be deposited with the Government of the People's Republic.

The Treaty shall enter into force on the day the last instrument of ratification has been deposited. The Government of the Polish People's Republic shall notify the other Parties to the Treaty as each instrument of ratification is deposited.

Article 11

The present Treaty shall remain in force for twenty years. For such Contracting Parties as do not at least one year before the expiration of this period present to the Government of the Polish People's Republic a statement of denunciation of the Treaty, it shall remain in force for the next ten years.

Should a system of collective security be established in Europe, and a General European Treaty of Collective Security concluded for this purpose, for which the Contracting Parties will unswervingly strive, the present Treaty shall cease to be operative from the day the General European Treaty enters into force.

9. The Geneva Summit Conference

IN THE SUMMER OF 1955, on July 18–23, the president of the United States, Dwight D. Eisenhower; the prime minister of Great Britain, Anthony Eden; the premier of France, Guy Mollet; and the premier of the Soviet Union, Nikolai Bulganin, met for a few days in Geneva. This was the first Big Four meeting since Potsdam at the end of the Second World War. Photographers took pictures of the gala occasion, showing the four leading statesmen sitting on chairs on the grassy grounds of the old League of Nations building, by that time used by the United Nations. The faces in the pictures looked benign, and people everywhere rejoiced that the rancors of the so-called cold war had come to an end: the crisis-ridden era in Europe from 1945 to 1950 was over; the Korean War was over; Stalin had died in 1953, and his successors showed no desire to carry on the animosities that had marked the old dictator's last crotchety years. The concrete results of the Geneva Summit were less than the spiritual results—the meetings of the Big Four did not produce much in the way of actual changes in international relations—but there did seem to be a new atmosphere of hope and pleasantness. After his return to Washington, President Eisenhower reported to the American people by radio and television on July 25, 1955.

Secretary Dulles and I, with our associates, went to the Big Four Conference at Geneva resolved to represent as accurately as we could the aspirations of the American people for peace and the

SOURCE: *American Foreign Policy: 1950–1955*, I, pp. 111–14.

principles upon which this country believes that peace should be based. . . .

Probably no question caused us as much trouble as that of German reunification and European security. At first we thought that these could be dealt with separately, but the American delegation concluded that they had to be dealt with as one subject. We held that Germany should be reunited under a government freely chosen by themselves, and under conditions that would provide security both for nations of the East and for nations of the West— in fact in a framework that provided European security.

In the matter of disarmament, the American Government believes that an effective disarmament system can be reached only if at its base there is an effective reciprocal inspection and overall supervision system, one in which we can have confidence and each side can know that the other side is carrying out his commitments. Now, because of this belief, we joined with the French and the British in making several proposals. Some were global, some were local, some were sort of budgetary in character. But all were in furtherance of this one single objective, that is, to make inspection the basis of disarmament proposals.

One proposal suggested aerial photography, as between the Soviets and ourselves, by unarmed peaceful planes, and to make this inspection just as thorough as this kind of reconnaissance can do. The principal purpose, of course, is to convince everyone of Western sincerity in seeking peace. But another idea was this: If we could go ahead and establish this kind of an inspection as initiation of an inspection system, we could possibly develop it into a broader one and eventually build on it an effective and durable disarmament system.

In the matter of increasing contacts, many items were discussed. We talked about a freer flow of news across the Curtains of all kinds. We talked about the circulation of books, and particularly we talked about peaceful trade. But the subject that took most of our attention in this regard was the possibility of increased visits by the citizens of one country into the territory of another, doing this in such a way as to give each the fullest possible opportunity to learn about the people of the other nation. In this particular subject there was the greatest possible degree of agreement. As a matter of fact, it was agreement often repeated and enthusiastically supported by the words of the members of each side.

As a matter of fact, each side assured the other earnestly and often that it intended to pursue a new spirit of conciliation and cooperation in its contacts with the other. Now, of course, we are profoundly hopeful that these assurances will be faithfully carried out. . . .

Now, for myself, I do not belittle the obstacles lying ahead on the road to a secure and just peace. By no means do I underestimate the long and exhausting work that will be necessary before real results are achieved. I do not blink the fact that all of us must continue to sacrifice for what we believe to be best for the safety of ourselves and for the preservation of the things in which we believe.

But I do know that the people of the world want peace. Moreover, every other individual who was at Geneva likewise felt this longing of mankind. So there is great pressure to advance constructively, not merely to reenact the dreary performances—the negative performances—of the past.

We, all of us, individually and as a people now have possibly the most difficult assignment of our Nation's history. Likewise, we have the most shining opportunity ever possessed by Americans. May these truths inspire, never dismay us.

I believe that only with prayerful patience, intelligence, courage, and tolerance, never forgetting vigilance and prudence, can we keep alive the spark ignited at Geneva. But if we are successful in this, then we will make constantly brighter the lamp that will one day guide us to our goal—a just and lasting peace.

Among his colleagues in the American government, the president in his dramatic proposal of "open skies" evoked both hearty approval and dismay. Some individuals foresaw the last of the country's secrets passing to the Russians via aerial photography. Others envisioned a wonderful chance to photograph the Soviet Union. In the end the Soviets refused to agree to the president's proposition. The American government the next year undertook a program of aerial reconnaissance, about which there will be more later (see pp. 75–82). In the 1960s the entire issue became academic because of reconnaissance by satellites, and it is interesting that because both the U.S. and the U.S.S.R. benefitted from satellite photography, they signed a treaty in 1967 providing for noninterference with the satellites (see pp. 309–10).

10. The Ebullient Diplomacy of Nikita Khrushchev

A. The Speech to the Twentieth Party Congress

COMMUNIST PARTY MEETINGS have been as much addicted to speech-making as the quadrennial assemblages of American political parties, and it is safe to add that speeches at Soviet conventions, like those at American, usually do not last beyond the evening of their making. The speech to the Twentieth Party Congress in Moscow on February 25, 1956, by Nikita Khrushchev, at the time first secretary of the Soviet Communist party, was a notable exception to this rule. First, it told a good deal about the long, anguished era of the late dictator, Stalin, which before had been the subject of hearsay and surmise. In the address before a huge audience, which was punctuated by stormy applause and gasps of incredulity and horror, Khrushchev announced that some Soviet policies under Stalin had been wrong and should have been challenged either from within the Soviet Union by the ruling hierarchy or by Communist parties outside the U.S.S.R. He thereby opened Communism to more criticism than it ever had received before. Khrushchev gave the speech to an audience composed only of delegates from the U.S.S.R. but its text seems to have circulated among high party members elsewhere. The State Department obtained a copy and released it to newspaper reporters on June 4, 1956. The text was later published in book form.

COMRADES! In the report of the Central Committee of the Party of the XXth Congress, in a number of speeches by delegates to the Congress, as also formerly during the plenary CC/CPSU sessions, quite a lot has been said about the cult of the individual and about its harmful consequences.

After Stalin's death the Central Committee of the Party began to implement a policy of explaining concisely and consistently that it is impermissible and foreign to the spirit of Marxism-Leninism to elevate one person, to transform him into a superman possessing supernatural characteristics akin to those of a god. Such a man supposedly knows everything, sees everything, thinks for everyone, can do anything, is infallible in his behavior.

SOURCE: Columbia University, Russian Institute, *The Anti-Stalin Campaign and International Communism* (New York: Columbia University Press, 1956), pp. 1–89.

Such a belief about a man, and specifically about Stalin, was cultivated among us for many years. . . .

In addition to the great accomplishments of V. I. Lenin for the victory of the working class and of the working peasants, for the victory of our Party and for the application of the ideas of scientific Communism to life, his acute mind expressed itself also in this, that he detected in Stalin in time those negative characteristics which resulted later in grave consequences. Fearing for the future fate of the Party and of the Soviet nation, V. I. Lenin made a completely correct characterization of Stalin, pointing out that it was necessary to consider the question of transferring Stalin from the position of the Secretary General because of the fact that Stalin is excessively rude, that he does not have a proper attitude toward his comrades, that he is capricious and abuses his power. . . .

COMRADES! . . . Since Stalin could behave in this manner during Lenin's life, could thus behave toward Nadezhda Konstantinovna Krupskaya [Lenin's wife], whom the Party knows well and highly as a loyal friend of Lenin and as an active fighter for the cause of the Party since its creation—we can easily imagine how Stalin treated other people. These negative characteristics of his developed steadily and during the last years acquired an absolutely insufferable character. . . .

Worth noting is the fact that even during the progress of the furious ideological fight against the Trotskyites, the Zinovievites, the Bukharinites and others, extreme repressive measures were not used against them. The fight was on ideological grounds. But some years later when socialism in our country was fundamentally constructed, when the exploiting classes were generally liquidated, when the Soviet social structure had radically changed, when the social basis for political movements and groups hostile to the Party had violently contracted, when the ideological opponents of the Party were long since defeated politically—then the repression directed against them began.

It was precisely during this period (1935-1937-1938) that the practice of mass repression through the government apparatus was born, first against the enemies of Leninism—Trotskyites, Zinovievites, Bukharinites, long since politically defeated by the Party, and subsequently also against many honest Communists, against those Party cadres who had borne the heavy load of the Civil War and the first and most difficult years of industrialization and collectivization, who actively fought against the Trotskyites and the rightists for the Leninist Party line.

Stalin originated the concept "enemy of the people." This term automatically rendered it unnecessary that the ideological errors of a man or men engaged in a controversy be proven; this term made possible the usage of the most cruel repression, violating all norms of revolutionary legality, against anyone who in any way disagreed with Stalin, against those who were only suspected of hostile intent, against those who had bad reputations. This concept, "enemy of the people," actually eliminated the possibility of any kind of ideological fight or the making of one's views known on this or that issue, even those of a practical character. In the main, and in actuality, the only proof of guilt used, against all norms of current legal science, was the "confession" of the accused himself; and, as subsequent probing proved, "confessions" were acquired through physical pressures against the accused. . . .

It was determined that of the 139 members and candidates of the Party's Central Committee who were elected at the XVIIth Congress, 98 persons, i.e., 70 percent, were arrested and shot (mostly in 1937–1938). (*Indignation in the hall.*) . . .

The same fate met not only the Central Committee members but also the majority of the delegates to the XVIIth Party Congress. Of 1,966 delegates with either voting or advisory rights, 1,108 persons were arrested on charges of anti-revolutionary crimes, i.e., decidedly more than a majority. This very fact shows how absurd, wild and contrary to common sense were the charges of counter-revolutionary crimes made out, as we now see, against a majority of participants at the XVIIth Party Congress. (*Indignation in the hall.*). . .

A large part of these cases are being reviewed now and a great part of them are being voided because they were baseless and falsified. Suffice it to say that from 1954 to the present time the Military Collegium of the Supreme Court has rehabilitated 7,679 persons, many of whom were rehabilitated posthumously. . . .

. . . Stalin was a very distrustful man, sickly suspicious; we knew this from our work with him. He could look at a man and say: "Why are your eyes so shifty today," or "Why are you turning so much today and avoiding to look me directly in the eyes?" The sickly suspicion created in him a general distrust even toward eminent Party workers whom he had known for years. Everywhere and in everything he saw "enemies," "two-facers" and "spies."

Possessing unlimited power he indulged in great willfulness and choked a person morally and physically. A situation was created where one could not express one's own will. . . .

When the Fascist armies had actually invaded Soviet territory and military operations began, Moscow issued the order that the German fire was not to be returned. Why? It was because Stalin, despite evident facts, thought that the war had not yet started, that this was only a provocative action on the part of several undisciplined sections of the German army, and that our reaction might serve as a reason for the Germans to begin the war. . . .

As you see, everything was ignored: warnings of certain army commanders, declarations of deserters from the enemy army, and even the open hostility of the enemy. Is this an example of the alertness of the Chief of the Party and of the state at this particularly significant historical moment?

And what were the results of this carefree attitude, this disregard of clear facts? The result was that already in the first hours and days the enemy had destroyed in our border regions a large part of our air force, artillery and other military equipment; he annihilated large numbers of our military cadres and disorganized our military leadership; consequently we could not prevent the enemy from marching deep into the country.

Very grievous consequences, especially in reference to the beginning of the war, followed Stalin's annihilation of many military commanders and political workers during 1937–1941 because of his suspiciousness and through slanderous accusations. During these years repressions were instituted against certain parts of military cadres beginning literally at the company and battalion commander level and extending to the higher military centers; during this time the cadre of leaders who had gained military experience in Spain and in the Far East was almost completely liquidated.

The policy of large-scale repression against the military cadres led also to undermined military discipline, because for several years officers of all ranks and even soldiers in the Party and Komsomol cells were taught to "unmask" their superiors as hidden enemies. (*Movement in the hall.*) It is natural that this caused a negative influence on the state of military discipline in the first war period. . . .

It would be incorrect to forget that after the first severe disaster and defeats at the front, Stalin thought that this was the end. In one of his speeches in those days he said: "All that which Lenin created we have lost forever."

After this Stalin for a long time actually did not direct the military operations and ceased to do anything whatever. He returned to active leadership only when some members of the Political Bureau visited him and told him that it was necessary to take certain steps immediately in order to improve the situation at the front.

Therefore, the threatening danger which hung over our Fatherland in the first period of the war was largely due to the faulty methods of directing the nation and the Party by Stalin himself. . . .

We must state that after the war the situation became even more complicated. Stalin became even more capricious, irritable and brutal; in particular his suspicion grew. His persecution mania reached unbelievable dimensions. Many workers were becoming enemies before his very eyes. After the war Stalin separated himself from the collective even more. Everything was decided by him alone without any consideration for anyone or anything. . . .

The willfulness of Stalin showed itself not only in decisions concerning the internal life of the country but also in the international relations of the Soviet Union. . . .

I recall the first days when the conflict between the Soviet Union and Yugoslavia began artificially to be blown up. Once, when I came from Kiev to Moscow, I was invited to visit Stalin who, pointing to the copy of a letter lately sent to Tito, asked me, "Have you read this?" Not waiting for my reply he answered, "I will shake my little finger—and there will be no more Tito. He will fall." . . .

You see to what Stalin's mania for greatness led. He had completely lost consciousness of reality; he demonstrated his suspicion and haughtiness not only in relation to individuals in the USSR, but in relation to whole parties and nations. . . .

In organizing the various dirty and shameful cases, a very base role was played by the rabid enemy of our Party, an agent of a foreign intelligence service—Beria, who had stolen into Stalin's confidence. In what way could this provocateur gain such a position in the Party and in the state, so as to become the First Deputy

Chairman of the Council of Ministers of the Soviet Union and a member of the Central Committee Political Bureau? It has now been established that this villain had climbed up the government ladder over an untold number of corpses. . . .

Beria was unmasked by the Party's Central Committee shortly after Stalin's death. As a result of the particularly detailed legal proceedings it was established that Beria had committed monstrous crimes and Beria was shot. . . .

COMRADES! The cult of the individual acquired such monstrous size chiefly because Stalin himself, using all conceivable methods, supported the glorification of his own person. This is supported by numerous facts. One of the most characteristic examples of Stalin's self-glorification and of his lack of even elementary modesty is the edition of his *Short Biography*, which was published in 1948.

This book is an expression of the most dissolute flattery, an example of making a man into a godhead, of transforming him into an infallible sage, "the greatest leader," "sublime strategist of all times and nations." Finally no other words could be found with which to lift Stalin up to the heavens. . . .

Some comrades may ask us: Where were the members of the Political Bureau of the Central Committee? Why did they not assert themselves against the cult of the individual in time? And why is this being done only now?

First of all we have to consider the fact that the members of the Political Bureau viewed these matters in a different way at different times. Initially, many of them backed Stalin actively because Stalin was one of the strongest Marxists and his logic, his strength and his will greatly influenced the cadres and Party work. . . .

In the situation which then prevailed I have talked often with Nikolai Alexandrovich Bulganin; once when we two were traveling in a car, he said, "It has happened sometimes that a man goes to Stalin on his invitation as a friend. And when he sits with Stalin, he does not know where he will be sent next, home or to jail."

It is clear that such conditions put every member of the Political Bureau in a very difficult situation. And when we also consider the fact that in the last years the Central Committee plenary sessions were not convened and that the sessions of the Political Bureau occurred only occasionally, from time to time, then we will understand how difficult it was for any member of the Political Bureau to take a stand against one or another injust or improper procedure, against serious errors and shortcomings in the practices of leadership. . . .

One of the oldest members of our Party, Kliment Yefremovich Voroshilov, found himself in an almost impossible situation. For several years he was actually deprived of the right of participation in Political Bureau sessions. Stalin forbade him to attend the Political Bureau sessions and to receive documents. When the Political Bureau was in session and Comrade Voroshilov heard about it, he telephoned each time and asked whether he would be allowed to attend. Sometimes Stalin permitted it, but always showed his dissatisfaction. Because of his extreme suspicion, Stalin toyed also with the absurd and ridiculous suspicion that Voroshilov was an English agent. (*Laughter in the hall.*) It's true—an English agent. A special tapping device was installed in his home to listen to what was said there. (*Indignation in the hall.*) . . .

Let us consider the first Central Committee Plenum after the XIXth Party Congress when Stalin, in his talk at the Plenum, characterized Vyacheslav Mikhailovich Molotov and Anastas Ivanovich Mikoyan and suggested that these old workers of our Party were guilty of some baseless charges. It is not excluded that had Stalin remained at the helm for another several months, Comrades Molotov and Mikoyan would probably have not delivered any speeches at this Congress.

Stalin evidently had plans to finish off the old members of the Political Bureau. . . .

We should in all seriousness consider the question of the cult of the individual. We cannot let this matter get out of the Party, especially not to the press. It is for this reason that we are considering it here at a closed Congress session. We should know the limits; we should not give ammunition to the enemy; we should not wash our dirty linen before their eyes. I think that the delegates to the Congress will understand and assess properly all these proposals. (*Tumultuous applause.*)

The speech sent tremors of hope through the satellite regimes and led directly to great revolts in Poland and Hungary. In Poland a national Communist, Wladyslaw Gomulka, took control in October, 1956, and held out for autonomy despite the appearance in Warsaw of a distinguished Moscow delegation led by Khrushchev. Gomulka threatened an armed uprising against any Soviet-inspired military coup, and Khru-

shchev backed down. In Hungary affairs got out of hand under the national Communist Imre Nagy. When the Roman Catholic primate, Cardinal Joseph Mindszenty, entered Budapest in triumph, to the ringing of all the city's church bells broadcast for the world to hear, it was too much for the Russians. After feigning a withdrawal from Budapest, the Red Army on November 4 reappeared and reconquered the capital from its people. During these developments the Suez crisis (see pp. 173–80) was preoccupying and embarrassing the American government. It could have done little anyway about the fate of Hungarian democracy other than appeal to the United Nations, which it did.

B. KHRUSHCHEV'S VISIT TO THE UNITED STATES

A PART OF KHRUSHCHEV'S FLAMBOYANT DIPLOMACY consisted of visiting countries all over the world, and from the beginning of his power in the Soviet Union he wanted to come to America. The wish came true in September, 1959, and his tour turned into a cross-country progress, in the course of which he stopped off in Iowa to visit the farm of the corn expert Roswell Garst. In California he wanted to visit Disneyland, but problems of security made the visit impossible, to his vast disappointment. President Eisenhower at a news conference on September 28, 1959, discussed the visit.

First of all, I want to thank the American people. I think their restraint and their conduct [during the Khrushchev visit] on the whole was a credit to them. And if there is a better understanding on the part of Mr. Khrushchev of our people, of their aspirations, of their general attitudes about international questions, and particularly about their desire for peace, then that has been done by the American people.

I invited Mr. Khrushchev, as you know, to come here so that we might have a chance to discuss some of the obvious reasons for tensions in the world, and particularly between our two countries, because of the outstanding unsettled matters. I did not ask him here for substantive negotiations, because those are impossible without the presence of our associates. But I thought that, through this visit of his and through these conversations, possibly, I think as I have said to you before, some of the ice might be melted.

Now, if any of this has been done, again it's due to the American people; and I make special acknowledgements to the Mayors,

SOURCE: *American Foreign Policy: Current Documents, 1959* (Washington, D.C., 1963), pp. 931–34.

Governors, the local officials who carried so much of the responsibility for making these visits possible and for directing so many of the activities necessarily involved.

With respect to one other point, I think this: I think the American people have proved that they have an enlightened outlook toward these international problems; that they have got the strength in their own beliefs and convictions to listen to the other man politely, attentively, although reserving to themselves a right to oppose bitterly any imposition upon themselves of some of the practices, the beliefs and convictions that are proposed and supported by another ideology; that they came through this with a very much better understanding and proving that they themselves are very sophisticated and, if not sophisticated, let us say enlightened and understanding in these matters. . . .

I assure you there is no sinister or no ulterior motive behind it [the postponement of the President's trip to the Soviet Union]. This has been a rather trying period, the last year, and we have both set up for ourselves rather large and full schedules. He [Khrushchev] is going to China, for example, the day after he gets back to Moscow. I have Mr. Segni here on Wednesday; I have the Ministers from the old Baghdad Pact here within a week; I have the President of Mexico I'm very anxious to have some long talks with; I have a number of heads of state coming along. It just looked like too much to put these things all together and get some of the other things that we want to do. So, I was personally the first one that said, "Well, maybe in the spring." . . .

He [Khrushchev] is a dynamic and arresting personality. He is a man that uses every possible debating method available to him. He is capable of great flights, you might say, of mannerism and almost disposition, from one of almost negative, difficult attitude to the most easy, affable, genial type of discussion. I think that the American people sensed, as they [the members of Mr. Khrushchev's group] went around, that they were seeing some man who is an extraordinary personality, there is no question about it.

Now, I thoroughly believe that he is sure that the basic tenets of the socialistic, or communistic, doctrine are correct. He has made great dents into the original concept of this doctrine. For example, he very definitely stated that he had made much better use of the incentive system in the Soviet economy than we. He knows all about our taxes and all the rest of it, but he talks in terms that if you do a better job you get a better house. He talked about some of the things they are providing for their people who really perform. So, in a number of ways, he shows how the application of the doctrine has been changed very greatly in modern usage in the Soviet region.

. . . I think that there are a number of people close to him [Khrushchev] that are quite aware of some of the problems that come about unless we do melt some ice [in the cold war]. For example, he himself deplored the need for spending so much money on defenses. We tried, between ourselves, to talk for a little bit about our comparative costs, therefore how we could calculate just exactly how much of our wealth is going into these things that are, after all, negative and sterile and purely defensive. Well, this was an interesting exercise, but, of course, we got nowhere except his continued insistence they're just too expensive; we must find better ways.

IV

Europe, 1960–1972

The era of Khrushchev, from 1958, when he succeeded Bulganin as premier, until his departure from power in 1964, continued—for the most part—the détente in Soviet-American relations that had set in with the death of Stalin in 1953. This is not to say that everything was sweetness and light between the two superpowers, as Khrushchev's behavior during the U–2 affair of 1960 showed, not to mention his threats about Berlin and his support of Premier Fidel Castro in Cuba (see pp. 229–36). Nonetheless, in retrospect it is becoming clear that Khrushchev, despite his bombast, was willing to ease relations with the United States. He and his successors did not show Stalin's presistent ill will for America and Americans. By the beginning of the 1970s something approaching goodwill had begun to appear in relations between the U.S. and the U.S.S.R.— inspired, the Kremlinologists said, by the Russians' intense fear of mainland China.

11. The U.S.–U.S.S.R. Confrontation of May, 1960

A. The U–2 Incident

Francis Gary Powers, *an employee of the Central Intelligence Agency, flew his Utility-2 (or U–2) plane—a jet with enormous wingspan that was almost like a glider and could soar at very high altitudes—out of Pakistan on May 1, 1960, and across the Soviet Union, photographing as he went, on a route toward Norway. As he was passing over Sverdlovsk, a Soviet Pittsburgh, a rocket downed his plane. Powers bailed out and was picked up and turned over to the authorities, together with most of his plane, which had glided down to earth and crashed. As the United States had been sending planes across the Soviet Union on "milk run"*

Source: *American Foreign Policy: Current Documents, 1960* (Washington, D.C., 1964), pp. 423–25.

spying expeditions since 1956, the government perhaps presumed that both Powers and his plane had been blown up (the planes contained destruct devices). In that belief it issued a cover story that Powers had been on a mission for the National Aeronautics and Space Agency. Khrushchev gave out just enough information to inspire the State Department to stick to the cover story, whereupon the Soviet leader triumphantly produced both the pilot and unmistakable pieces of the plane. President Eisenhower on May 11 read a statement to a press conference about the U–2 incident.

I have made some notes from which I want to talk to you about this U–2 incident.

A full statement about this matter has been made by the State Department, and there have been several statesmanlike remarks by leaders of both parties.

For my part, I supplement what the Secretary of State has had to say with the following four main points. After that, I shall have nothing further to say—for the simple reason I can think of nothing to add that might be useful at this time.

First point is this: the need for intelligence-gathering activities.

No one wants another Pearl Harbor. This means that we must have knowledge of military forces and preparations around the world, especially those capable of massive surprise attack.

Secrecy in the Soviet Union makes this essential. In most of the world no large-scale attack could be prepared in secret. But in the Soviet Union there is a fetish of secrecy and concealment. This is a major cause of international tension and uneasiness today. Our deterrent must never be placed in jeopardy. The safety of the whole free world demands this.

As the Secretary of State pointed out in his recent statement, ever since the beginning of my administration I have issued directives to gather, in every feasible way, the information required to protect the United States and the free world against surprise attack and to enable them to make effective preparations for defense.

My second point: the nature of intelligence-gathering activities.

These have a special and secret character. They are, so to speak, "below the surface" activities.

They are secret because they must circumvent measures designed by other countries to protect secrecy of military preparations.

They are divorced from the regular, visible agencies of government, which stay clear of operational involvement in specific detailed activities.

These elements operate under broad directives to see and gather intelligence short of the use of force, with operations supervised by responsible officials within this area of secret activities.

We do not use our Army, Navy, or Air Force for this purpose, first, to avoid any possibility of the use of force in connection with these activities and, second, because our military forces, for obvious reasons, cannot be given latitude under broad directives but must be kept under strict control in every detail.

These activities have their own rules and methods of concealment, which seek to mislead and obscure—just as in the Soviet allegations there are many discrepancies. For example, there is some reason to believe that the plane in question was not shot down at high altitude. The normal agencies of our Government are unaware of these specific activities or of the special efforts to conceal them.

Third point: How should we view all of this activity?

It is a distasteful but vital necessity.

We prefer and work for a different kind of world—and a different way of obtaining the information essential to confidence and effective deterrence. Open societies, in the day of present weapons, are the only answer.

This was the reason for my open-skies proposal in 1955, which I was ready instantly to put into effect, to permit aerial observation over the United States and the Soviet Union which would assure that no surprise attack was being prepared against anyone. I shall bring up the open-skies proposal again at Paris, since it is a means of ending concealment and suspicion.

My final point is that we must not be distracted from the real issues of the day by what is an incident or a symptom of the world situation today.

This incident has been given great propaganda exploitation. The emphasis given to a flight of an unarmed, nonmilitary plane can only reflect a fetish of secrecy.

The real issues are the ones we will be working on at the summit—disarmament, search for solutions affecting Germany and Berlin, and the whole range of East-West relations, including the reduction of secrecy and suspicion.

Frankly, I am hopeful that we may make progress on these great issues. This is what we mean when we speak of "working for peace."

And, as I remind you, I will have nothing further to say about this matter.

B. THE PARIS SUMMIT CONFERENCE

BECAUSE OF THE U–2 AFFAIR *the American government found itself in a weak position to face the Russians at the summit conference scheduled to open in Paris on May 16. But as President Eisenhower had said in his explanation of the U–2 flight, he was planning to attend the summit nonetheless. The American embassy in Moscow, in a note of May 12, 1960, gave assurances on this point.*

The Embassy of the United States of America refers to the Soviet Government's note of May 10 concerning the shooting down of an American unarmed civilian aircraft on May 1, and under instruction from its Government, has the honor to state the following.

The United States Government, in the statement issued by the Department of State on May 9, has fully stated its position with respect to this incident.

In its note the Soviet Government has stated that the collection of intelligence about the Soviet Union by American aircraft is a "calculated policy" of the United States. The United States Government does not deny that it has pursued such a policy for purely defensive purposes. What it emphatically does deny is that this policy has any aggressive intent, or that the unarmed U–2 flight of May 1 was undertaken in an effort to prejudice the success of the forthcoming meeting of the Heads of Government in Paris or to "return the state of American-Soviet relations to the worst times of the cold war." Indeed, it is the Soviet Government's treatment of this case which, if anything, may raise questions about its intentions in respect to these matters.

For its part, the United States Government will participate in the Paris meeting on May 16 prepared to cooperate to the fullest extent in seeking agreements designed to reduce tensions, including effective safeguards against surprise attack which would make unnecessary issues of this kind.

SOURCE: *Current Documents, 1960,* p. 425.

EISENHOWER AND KHRUSHCHEV *journeyed to Paris. After some confusion the Soviet premier then refused to take part in the summit conference because of the U–2 affair. He may have had little to propose at the summit and felt relief that the Americans had given him an excuse for nonattendance. Perhaps he desired to prolong American mortification. He surely was not as angry as he appeared: the Soviets had known of the flights for some time; Khrushchev had been aware of them when he visited the United States and had said nothing, for until Powers's flight the Russians had been unable to intercept the American planes. But Khrushchev broke up the summit, and the president returned home. Eisenhower explained the American view of the ill-starred meeting in a radio and television address of May 25.*

MY FELLOW AMERICANS: Tonight I want to talk with you about the remarkable events last week in Paris, and their meaning to our future. . . .

. . . before leaving Washington I had directed that these U–2 flights be stopped. Clearly their usefulness was impaired. Moreover, continuing this particular activity in these new circumstances could not but complicate the relations of certain of our allies with the Soviets. And of course, new techniques, other than aircraft, are constantly being developed.

Now I wanted no public announcement of this decision until I could personally disclose it at the summit meeting in conjunction with certain proposals I had prepared for the conference.

At my first Paris meeting with Mr. Khrushchev, and before his tirade was made public, I informed him of this discontinuance and the character of the constructive proposals I planned to make. These contemplated the establishment of a system of aerial surveillance operated by the United Nations.

The day before the first scheduled meeting, Mr. Khrushchev had advised President de Gaulle and Prime Minister Macmillan that he would make certain demands upon the United States as a precondition for beginning a summit conference.

Although the United States was the only power against which he expressed his displeasure, he did not communicate this information to me. I was, of course, informed by our allies.

At the four-power meeting on Monday morning, he demanded of the United States four things: first, condemnation of U–2 flights as a method of espionage; second, assurance that they would not be

SOURCE: *Current Documents, 1960,* pp. 434–41.

continued; third, a public apology on behalf of the United States; and, fourth, punishment of all those who had any responsibility respecting this particular mission.

I replied by advising the Soviet leader that I had, during the previous week, stopped these flights and that they would not be resumed. I offered also to discuss the matter with him in personal meetings, while the regular business of the summit might proceed. Obviously, I would not respond to his extreme demands. He knew, of course, by holding to those demands the Soviet Union was scuttling the summit conference.

In torpedoing the conference, Mr. Khrushchev claimed that he acted as the result of his own high moral indignation over alleged American acts of aggression. As I said earlier, he had known of these flights for a long time. It is apparent that the Soviets had decided even before the Soviet delegation left Moscow that my trip to the Soviet Union should be canceled and that nothing constructive from their viewpoint would come out of the summit conference.

In evaluating the results, however, I think we must not write the record all in red ink. There are several things to be written in the black. Perhaps the Soviet action has turned the clock back in some measure, but it should be noted that Mr. Khrushchev did not go beyond invective—a time-worn Soviet device to achieve an immediate objective, in this case, the wrecking of the conference.

On our side, at Paris, we demonstrated once again America's willingness, and that of her allies, always to go the extra mile in behalf of peace. Once again Soviet intransigence reminded us all of the unpredictability of despotic rule and the need for those who work for freedom to stand together in determination and in strength.

The conduct of our allies was magnificent. My colleagues and friends—President de Gaulle and Prime Minister Macmillan—stood sturdily with the American delegation in spite of persistent Soviet attempts to split the Western group. The NATO meeting after the Paris conference showed unprecedented unity and support for the alliance and for the position taken at the summit meeting. I salute our allies for us all. . . .

Here in our country anyone can buy maps and aerial photographs showing our cities, our dams, our plants, our highways—indeed, our whole industrial and economic complex. We know that

Soviet attachés regularly collect this information. Last fall Chairman Khrushchev's train passed no more than a few hundred feet from an operational ICBM, in plain view from his window. Our thousands of books and scientific journals, our magazines, newspapers and official publications, our radio and television, all openly describe to all the world every aspect of our society.

This is as it should be. We are proud of our freedom.

'Soviet distrust, however, does still remain. To allay these misgivings I offered 5 years ago to open our skies to Soviet reconnaissance aircraft on a reciprocal basis. The Soviets refused. That offer is still open. At an appropriate time America will submit such a program to the United Nations, together with the recommendation that the United Nations itself conduct this reconnaissance. Should the United Nations accept this proposal, I am prepared to propose that America supply part of the aircraft and equipment required.

[At this point, an aerial photograph was shown on the television screen.]

This is a photograph of the North Island Naval Station in San Diego, California. It was taken from an altitude of more than 70 thousand feet. You may not perhaps be able to see them on your television screens, but the white lines in the parking strips around the field are clearly discernible from 13 miles up. Those lines are just 6 inches wide.

Obviously most of the details necessary for a military evaluation of the airfield and its aircraft are clearly distinguishable.

I show you this photograph as an example of what could be accomplished through United Nations aerial surveillance. . . .

Fellow Americans, long ago I pledged to you that I would journey anywhere in the world to promote the cause of peace. I remain pledged to pursue a peace of dignity, of friendship, of honor, of justice.

Operating from the firm base of our spiritual and physical strength, and seeking wisdom from the Almighty, we and our allies together will continue to work for the survival of mankind in freedom—and for the goal of mutual respect, mutual understanding, and openness among all nations.

Thank you, and good night.

The Presidium of the Supreme Soviet of the U.S.S.R. pardoned Powers in February, 1962, and he was exchanged for Colonel Rudolf

Abel, a Soviet spy captured in New York City in 1957 and sentenced to prison by an American court.

12. Berlin Again

A. 1958–1959

IN THE YEARS AFTER THE SECOND WORLD WAR the position of Berlin, deep within East Germany, was a major concern of the Department of State, for whenever American foreign policy might seem to the Soviets overbearing or unsatisfactory, it would be a fairly easy matter for them to, as President Kennedy put it in 1962, close out Berlin. Armed force would be necessary, but not much of it, and short of starting a Third World War the United States would be unable to retaliate. Or so Berlin's situation appeared in the late 1950s. Doubtless sensing his advantage, Premier Khrushchev used the Berlin issue for one démarche after another. His initial maneuver began when the Soviet government, in a note of November 27, 1958, proposed to transfer East Berlin from Soviet to East German jurisdiction and establish a "free city" of West Berlin.

. . . the Government of the USSR hereby notifies the United States Government that the Soviet Union regards as null and void the "Protocol of the Agreement between the Governments of the Union of Soviet Socialist Republics, the United States of America, and the United Kingdom on the zones of occupation in Germany and on the administration of Greater Berlin," of September 12, 1944, and the related supplementary agreements, including the agreement on the control machinery in Germany, concluded between the governments of the USSR, the USA, Great Britain, and France on May 1, 1945, i.e., the agreements that were intended to be in effect during the first years after the capitulation of Germany. . . .

Pursuant to the foregoing and proceeding from the principle of respect for the sovereignty of the German Democratic Republic, the Soviet Government will enter into negotiations with the Government of the GDR at an appropriate time with a view to

SOURCE: *American Foreign Policy: Current Documents, 1958* (Washington, D.C., 1962), pp. 591–96.

transferring to the German Democratic Republic the functions temporarily performed by the Soviet authorities by virtue of the above-mentioned Allied agreements and under the agreement between the USSR and the GDR of September 20, 1955. The best way to solve the Berlin problem would undoubtedly be to adopt a decision based on the enforcement of the Potsdam Agreement on Germany. But this is possible only in the event that the three Western Powers return to a policy in German affairs that would be pursued jointly with the USSR and in conformity with the spirit and principles of the Potsdam Agreement. In the present circumstances this would mean the withdrawal of the Federal Republic of Germany from NATO with the simultaneous withdrawal of the German Democratic Republic from the Warsaw Treaty [organization], and an agreement whereby, in accordance with the principles of the Potsdam Agreement, neither of the two German states would have any armed forces except those needed to maintain law and order at home and guard the frontiers. . . .

One cannot of course fail to take into account the fact that the political and economic development of West Berlin during the period of its occupation by the three Western powers has progressed in a different direction from the development of East Berlin and the GDR, as a result of which the way of life in the two parts of Berlin are at the present time entirely different. The Soviet Government considers that when the foreign occupation is ended the population of West Berlin must be granted the right to have whatever way of life it wishes for itself. If the inhabitants of West Berlin desire to preserve the present way of life, based on private capitalistic ownership, that is up to them. The USSR, for its part, would respect any choice of the West Berliners in this matter.

In view of all these considerations, the Soviet Government on its part would consider it possible to solve the West Berlin question at the present time by the conversion of West Berlin into an independent political unit—a free city, without any state, including both existing German states, interfering in its life. Specifically, it might be possible to agree that the territory of the free city be demilitarized and that no armed forces be contained therein. The free city, West Berlin, could have its own government and run its own economic, administrative, and other affairs. . . .

The Soviet Government seeks to have the necessary change in Berlin's situation take place in a cold atmosphere, without haste and unnecessary friction, with maximum possible consideration for the interests of the parties concerned.

. . . the Soviet Government proposes to make no changes in the present procedure for military traffic of the USA, Great Britain, and France from West Berlin to the FRG for half a year.

THE STATE DEPARTMENT *the same day, November 27, affirmed the responsibilities of the Western Allies in relation to Berlin.*

The Soviets seem to be proposing that, while they keep their grip on East Berlin, the three Western allies abandon their rights in West Berlin and retire in favor of what is called a "free city." Their "free city" proposal is limited to West Berlin. The Soviet Government indicates that, unless the three Western allies accept this Soviet proposal within 6 months, the Soviet Union will consider itself free of its obligations to them in relation to Berlin.

It is clear that a number of fundamental considerations are raised which will have to be kept in mind while we study the Soviet note.

One of these is that the United States, along with Britain and France, is solemnly committed to the security of the Western sectors of Berlin. Two and a quarter million West Berliners in reliance thereon have convincingly and courageously demonstrated the good fruits of freedom.

Another consideration is that the United States will not acquiesce in a unilateral repudiation by the Soviet Union of its obligations and responsibilities formally agreed upon with Britain, France, and the United States in relation to Berlin. Neither will it enter into any agreement with the Soviet Union which, whatever the form, would have the end result of abandoning the people of West Berlin to hostile domination.

SOURCE: *Current Documents, 1958,* pp. 596–97.

B. 1961–1962

KHRUSHCHEV'S SIX-MONTH ULTIMATUM *came and went, by chance expiring in May, 1959, at the time of the death of Secretary of State Dulles (who, afflicted with cancer, had resigned some weeks before, his office passing*

SOURCE: *American Foreign Policy: Current Documents, 1961* (Washington, D.C., 1965), pp. 586–87.

to Christian A. Herter). Perhaps the Russian premier, who respected Dulles, felt that the obsequies of the time constituted an inopportune moment to press his Berlin policy, especially as he was about to take a trip to the United States. Not much more happened concerning Berlin until the 1961 meeting in Vienna between President John F. Kennedy and Khrushchev, which, according to most contemporary and later accounts, came off rather badly for the former, perhaps leading the Soviet premier to believe that he was dealing with an ineffective young man. Back in Moscow, Khrushchev, on June 21, 1961, at ceremonies marking the twentieth anniversary of the beginning of the Great Patriotic War, announced that the Soviet Union "will sign a peace treaty with the German Democratic Republic at the end of this year."

The Soviet people do not want war, and for this very reason we are striving to eliminate the causes of its outbreak. For the sake of this, we and the other peace-loving states will sign a peace treaty with the German Democratic Republic at the end of this year.

The Soviet Union is not proposing war or an alliance of some countries against others for the purpose of amassing strength for war. We have only one aspiration—a lasting peace. It is to strengthen peace that it is necessary to conclude a peace treaty and thereby eliminate the vestiges of the second world war. We openly state this and want everyone to understand us correctly. The Soviet Union wants to sign a peace treaty with Germany together with our former allies.

In urging the conclusion of a peace treaty we by no means threaten West Berlin, as the advocates of the preservation of international tension are screaming. We would sincerely like to reach agreement on this question, as well, with those countries with whom we fought against Hitlerite Germany and with whom we have common obligations with respect to Germany.

We propose giving West Berlin the status of a free city. We do not at all intend to change West Berlin's social and political system. This is the internal affair of its population. Neither the Soviet Union nor the German Democratic Republic intends to restrict West Berlin's ties with all countries of the world. But, in accordance with international law, the sovereign rights of the German Democratic Republic, through whose territory the communications linking West Berlin with the outside world pass, must be respected.

In regard to West Berlin, the Governments of the U.S.A., Britain and France are defending the past. . . .

We are told that the peace treaty that we intend to conclude with the G.D.R. will be a separate treaty. I have already pointed out in my radio and television address that when the U.S.A. signed a peace treaty with Japan, it did not take us into account, although we were its allies in the war against Japan. It thereby showed that it felt it had the right to sign a treaty without us, although our rights, as one of the victorious countries, were indisputable.

Now we, in turn, want in the German question to enjoy the same rights enjoyed by the U.S.A. and its friends in the Japanese question. We are following their example, no more.

As for those who are trying to threaten us with war if we sign a peace treaty with the G.D.R., they will bear full responsibility for their actions.

THE SOVIET POINT ABOUT JAPAN *inspired a reply by Secretary of State Dean Rusk during a press conference of June 22.*

There are several important differences between the Japanese Peace Treaty and this proposal to sign a treaty with the so-called East German Republic. In the case of Japan, there was a representative, elected government representing a unified nation with which to sign a peace treaty. There were 49 nations, I believe, which did in fact sign that peace treaty. The Soviet Union was consulted by the then Ambassador, John Foster Dulles, in the early stages and had an opportunity to consult freely prior to the meeting of the Japanese Peace Conference in San Francisco. They did not avail themselves of the full opportunity that was there for them for consultation.

At the conference itself, the Russians attended, and the conference agreed to proceed to sign a treaty. That treaty did not purport to, nor did it, affect any tangible rights of the Soviet Union in Japan.

The situation in Berlin involves quite a different situation, with the United States and France and the United Kingdom exercising very specific rights and obligations in West Berlin. There was nothing like that in the Japanese situation at all. Nor did we have a representative government in Germany to decide for all of Germany, and certainly not a respresentative government in the so-

SOURCE: *Current Documents, 1961,* p. 587.

called East German Republic. I think the situations are quite different.

ON JULY 25, 1961, President Kennedy in a television address announced a crisis over Berlin and asked for additional military forces.

Seven weeks ago tonight I returned from Europe to report on my meeting with Premier Khrushchev and the others. His grim warnings about the future of the world, his aide memoire on Berlin, his subsequent speeches and threats which he and his agents have launched, and the increase in the Soviet military budget that he has announced have all prompted a series of decisions by the administration and a series of consultations with the members of the NATO organization. In Berlin, as you recall, he intends to bring to an end, through a stroke of the pen, first, our legal rights to be in West Berlin and, secondly, our ability to make good on our commitment to the 2 million free people of that city. That we cannot permit. . . .

Accordingly I am now taking the following steps:

1. I am tomorrow requesting of the Congress for the current fiscal year an additional $3,247,000,000 of appropriations for the Armed Forces.

2. To fill out our present Army divisions and to make more men available for prompt deployment, I am requesting an increase in the Army's total authorized strength from 875,000 to approximately 1 million men.

3. I am requesting an increase of 29,000 and 63,000 men, respectively, in the active-duty strength of the Navy and the Air Force.

4. To fulfill these manpower needs, I am ordering that our draft calls be doubled and tripled in the coming months; I am asking the Congress for authority to order to active duty certain ready reserve units and individual reservists and to extend tours of duty; and, under that authority, I am planning to order to active duty a number of air transport squadrons and Air National Guard tactical air squadrons to give us the airlift capacity and protection that we need. Other reserve forces will be called up when needed.

5. Many ships and planes once headed for retirement are to be retained or reactivated, increasing our air power tactically and our sealift, airlift, and antisubmarine warfare capability. In addition, our

SOURCE: *Current Documents, 1961*, pp. 604–12.

strategic air power will be increased by delaying the deactivation of B-47 bombers.

6. Finally, some $1.8 billion—about half of the total sum—is needed for the procurement of nonnuclear weapons, ammunition, and equipment. . . .

I would like to close with a personal word. When I ran for the Presidency of the United States, I knew that this country faced serious challenges, but I could not realize—nor could any man realize who does not bear the burdens of this office—how heavy and constant would be those burdens.

Three times in my lifetime our country and Europe have been involved in major wars. In each case serious misjudgments were made on both sides of the intentions of others, which brought about great devastation. Now, in the thermonuclear age, any misjudgment on either side about the intentions of the other could rain more devastation in several hours than has been wrought in all the wars of human history.

Therefore I, as President and Commander in Chief, and all of us as Americans are moving through serious days. I shall bear this responsibility under our Constitution for the next 3½ years, but I am sure that we all, regardless of our occupations, will do our very best for our country and for our cause. For all of us want to see our children grow up in a country at peace and in a world where freedom endures.

With Russian instruction or assent, the authorities of the German Democratic Republic erected the Berlin Wall in August, 1961, partly because of the lack of response to Khrushchev's Berlin proposals by the Western Allies. The inhumanity of the wall was obvious, for it forced the separation of relatives and friends and created a highly artificial division in the life of one of Europe's greatest cities. In subsequent years stories of sensational escapes over or under the wall filled Western newspapers (including saddening but equally sensational accounts of failures). It gradually became evident that an economic purpose had inspired the raising of the wall: hundreds of thousands of East Germany's able-bodied young people had fled to the West, responding to the economic opportunities in West Berlin and West Germany; the East Germans had been losing too much of their minuscule population (the G.D.R. contained approximately 16 million people, compared to the 53 million of the Federal Republic). The wall had been necessary to prevent the East German state from bleeding to death.

C. The Accords of 1971–1972

By the beginning of the 1970s the economy of East Germany had undergone a large improvement, and it became possible to consider removing the wall between East and West Berlin. The Western Allies had refused to negotiate with the German Democratic Republic, but their position weakened when West Germany's Chancellor Willy Brandt engaged in conversations with his East German opposite. The days of the Hallstein Doctrine (named for a West German foreign minister, Walter Hallstein, it said that the Federal Republic would break diplomatic relations with any nation recognizing the G.D.R.) long since had passed. In this easier environment the Western Allies and the Soviet Union signed an accord in Berlin on September 3, 1971.

Part I. General Provisions

1. The four Governments will strive to promote the elimination of tension and the prevention of complications in the relevant area.

2. The four Governments, taking into account their obligations under the Charter of the United Nations, agree that there shall be no use or threat of force in the area and that disputes shall be settled solely by peaceful means.

3. The four Governments will mutually respect their individual and joint rights and responsibilities, which remain unchanged.

4. The four Governments agree that, irrespective of the differences in legal views, the situation which has developed in the area, and as it is defined in this Agreement as well as in the other agreements referred to in this Agreement, shall not be changed unilaterally.

Part II. Provisions Relating to the Western Sectors of Berlin

A. The Government of the Union of Soviet Socialist Republics declares that transit traffic by road, rail and waterways through the territory of the German Democratic Republic of civilian persons and goods between the Western Sectors of Berlin and the Federal Republic of Germany will be unimpeded; that such traffic will be

Source: Department of State *Bulletin*, September 27, 1971, pp. 318–19.

facilitated so as to take place in the most simple and expeditious manner; and that it will receive preferential treatment.

Detailed arrangements concerning this civilian traffic, as set forth in Annex I, will be agreed by the competent German authorities.

B. The Governments of the French Republic, the United Kingdom and the United States of America declare that the ties between the Western Sectors of Berlin and the Federal Republic of Germany will be maintained and developed, taking into account that these Sectors continue not to be a constituent part of the Federal Republic of Germany and not to be governed by it.

Detailed arrangements concerning the relationship between the Western Sectors of Berlin and the Federal Republic of Germany are set forth in Annex II.

C. The Government of the Union of Soviet Socialist Republics declares that communications between the Western Sectors of Berlin and areas bordering on these Sectors and those areas of the German Democratic Republic which do not border on these Sectors will be improved. Permanent residents of the Western Sectors of Berlin will be able to travel to and visit such areas for compassionate, family, religious, cultural or commercial reasons, or as tourists, under conditions comparable to those applying to other persons entering these areas.

The problems of the small enclaves, including Steinstuecken, and of other small areas may be solved by exchange of territory.

Detailed arrangements concerning travel, communications and the exchange of territory, as set forth in Annex III, will be agreed by the competent German authorities.

D. Representation abroad of the interests of the Western Sectors of Berlin and consular activities of the Union of Soviet Socialist Republics in the Western Sectors of Berlin can be exercised as set forth in Annex IV.

Part III.   Final Provisions

This Quadripartite Agreement will enter into force on the date specified in a Final Quadripartite Protocol to be concluded when the measures envisaged in Part II of this Quadripartite Agreement and in its Annexes have been agreed.

Its conditions having been duly arranged, the agreement took effect on October 17, 1972, at midnight. The West German and East German governments, incidentally, had concluded a treaty containing the agreement, but did not consider the treaty as constituting recognition; at least the West German government took this anomalous point of view (according to international law, a treaty implies ordinary relations between the signatories). On November 9 representatives of the two Germanys initialed a treaty to normalize relations, and signed it on December 21. According to its first article, "The Federal Republic of Germany and the German Democratic Republic will develop normal good-neighborly relations with one another on the basis of equality."

13. De Gaulle and NATO

THE CHARISMATIC FRENCH FIGURE of the Second World War, Charles de Gaulle, had enjoyed a short rule over France at the end of the war, and then, like Churchill in Britain, he was retired by his countrymen. Neither Churchill nor de Gaulle had any inclination to remain in retirement, and both men returned to office, Churchill in 1951, de Gaulle in 1958. In his second period in power the French leader stressed France's independence; it seemed necessary to him that he should assert his nation's freedom while remaining loosely within the bonds of the North Atlantic Pact. He therefore forced NATO troops out of France, which meant movement of supplies to the NATO troops in Germany through Antwerp and German ports, the loss of bases laboriously constructed and reinforced, and removal of planes to other and sometimes more vulnerable airfields. The general stated his case in a letter of March 7, 1966, to President Lyndon B. Johnson.

DEAR MR. PRESIDENT: In 3 years, our Atlantic alliance will complete its first term. I wish to tell you that France appreciates the extent to which the solidarity of defense thus established among 15 free Western nations helps insure their security, and, especially, what an essential role the United States of America plays in this respect. Therefore, France now expects to remain, when the time comes, a party to the treaty signed at Washington on April 4, 1949. This means that, unless events in the course of the next 3 years should change the fundamental elements of the relations between

SOURCE: *American Foreign Policy: Current Documents, 1966* (Washington, D.C., 1969), pp. 317–18.

East and West, she would be, in 1969 and later, determined, just as today, to fight beside her allies if one of them should suffer unprovoked aggression.

However, France considers that the changes that have occurred, or are in the process of occurring, since 1949, in Europe, Asia, and elsewhere, as well as the evolution of her own situation and her own forces, no longer justify, insofar as she is concerned, the arrangements of a military nature made after the conclusion of the alliance, either jointly in the form of multilateral agreements, or by special agreements between the French Government and the American Government.

That is why France intends to recover, in her territory, the full exercise of her sovereignty, now impaired by the permanent presence of Allied military elements or by the habitual use being made of its airspace, to terminate her participation in the "integrated" commands, and no longer to place forces at the disposal of NATO. It goes without saying that, in order to implement these decisions, she is prepared to make arrangements with the Allied Governments, and in particular with the Government of the United States, regarding the practical measures that concern them. Furthermore, she is prepared to reach agreement with them regarding the military facilities to be accorded on a mutual basis in the event of a conflict in which she would join battle at their side, and regarding the conditions governing the cooperation between her forces and theirs in the event of joint action, especially in Germany.

And, so, Mr. President, my government will get in touch with yours regarding all these points. However, in order to act in the spirit of friendly candor that should inspire the relations between our two countries, and, allow me to add, between you and me, I have sought, first of all, to let you know personally, for what reasons, to what end, and within what limits France believes that she must, for her part, change the form of our Alliance without altering its substance.

V

China

Unhappy relations with China—with Nationalist China before 1949, the China of Mao Tse-tung thereafter—constituted one of the main themes in American foreign policy after the Second World War. In actual fact, support of Nationalist China virtually ceased after the Marshall mission of 1946. The head of that mission came home to become secretary of state, and he and President Harry S. Truman decided that they could do nothing more to assist Generalissimo Chiang Kai-shek until the dust settled. A new regime established itself in Peking in 1949, and a short era followed when, had events in the Korean War gone differently, it might have been possible to establish relations with the Communist regime. Chinese intervention in the Korean War made early recognition impossible. It hardened opinion in the United States, and twenty years passed before feelings between Peking and Washington began to soften, and then only after a spectacular visit to Peking by, of all personages, a Republican president of the United States. Even after the visit the course of China policy remained unclear.

14. The Nationalist Collapse

A. The Marshall Mission

At the outset of the Second World War the United States government had extended aid to Nationalist China, and, indeed, one of the causes of the Japanese attack on Pearl Harbor was this support against the encroachments of the Japanese. In subsequent years, to the end of the Pacific war, American policy veered from enthusiastic sup-

Source: *Foreign Relations of the United States: 1945*, VII (Washington, D.C., 1969), pp. 722–24.

port toward considerable doubt. The latter sentiment increased markedly once it became evident that conquest of the Chinese coast from the Japanese invaders would not be a necessary preliminary to attacking the Japanese home islands. At the end of the war the Japanese collapsed because of aerial bombardment including the atomic bombs, because of the invasion of Manchuria by Soviet troops, and because of the imminence of a mighty American invasion mounted from Okinawa and the other American bases that by that time ringed the Japanese homeland. Chiang Kai-shek thus found himself the beneficiary of a primarily American victory with lesser assistance from the Soviet Union and America's other allies. The Chinese themselves had done virtually nothing against the Japanese. Indeed, toward the end of the great conflict some of the American diplomatic staff in China, especially the observers in Yenan, the Communist stronghold, believed that the Nationalists could not long maintain themselves in postwar China and that the time was quickly coming when the United States should turn to the Chinese Communists as the future regime. In the autumn of 1945 the last wartime ambassador to Nationalist China, Patrick J. Hurley, an Oklahoma oilman and onetime secretary of war (in the Hoover administration), came home to the United States to report to the Department of State, with every apparent intention of returning to his post. While talking to members of Congress he suddenly lost his temper and blurted out his intense dissatisfaction with his role in China. Hurley followed up these commentaries with a rambling communication to President Truman dated November 26, 1945.

MY DEAR MR. PRESIDENT: I hereby resign as Ambassador to China.

In tendering my resignation I wish you to know that I am in agreement with the foreign policy outlined by you in your recent Navy Day address.

I am grateful to both you and the Secretary of State for the support you have given me and for your kind offer in requesting me to return to China as Ambassador.

In one capacity or another I have been on the perimeter of America's influence since the beginning of the war. During the war I have served in Java, Australia, New Zealand, and generally in the southwest Pacific, in Egypt, Palestine, The Lebanon, Syria, Trans-Jordan, Iraq, Saudi Arabia, Iran, Russia, Afghanistan, India, Ceylon, Burma and China. Of all the assignments China was the most intricate and the most difficult. It is a source of gratification to me that in all my missions I had the support of President Roosevelt, Secretary Hull, Secretary Stettinius, yourself, Mr. President, and Secretary Byrnes.

In the higher echelon of our policy-making officials American objectives were nearly always clearly defined. The astonishing feature of our foreign policy is the wide discrepancy between our announced policies and our conduct of international relations. For instance, we began the war with the principles of the Atlantic Charter and democracy as our goal. Our associates in the war at that time gave eloquent lip service to the principles of democracy. We finished the war in the Far East furnishing lend-lease supplies and using all our reputation to undermine democracy and bolster imperialism and Communism. Inasmuch as I am in agreement with you and the Secretary of State on our foreign policy I think I owe it to you as well as to the country to point out the reasons for the failure of the American foreign policy in reaching the objectives for which we said we were fighting the war. I will confine my remarks in this letter to Asia, although I wish to assure you that I will be at your service in discussing frankly other phases of our international relations.

I was assigned to China at a time when statesmen were openly predicting the collapse of the National Government of the Republic of China and the disintegration of the Chinese Army. I was directed by President Roosevelt to prevent the collapse of the Government and to keep the Chinese Army in the war. From both a strategical and diplomatic viewpoint the foregoing constituted our chief objective. The next in importance was the directive to harmonize the relations between the Chinese and American military establishments and between the American Embassy in Chungking and the Chinese Government. It will readily appear that the former objective could not be accomplished without the accomplishment of the secondary objective as a condition precedent. Both of these objectives were accomplished. While these objectives had the support of the President and the Secretary of State it is no secret that the American policy in China did not have the support of all the career men in the State Department. The professional foreign service men sided with the Chinese Communist armed party and the imperialist bloc of nations whose policy it was to keep China divided against herself. Our professional diplomats continuously advised the Communists that my efforts in preventing the collapse of the National Government did not represent the policy of the United States. These same professionals openly advised the Communist armed party to decline unification of the Chinese Communist Army with the National Army unless the Chinese Communists were given control.

Despite these handicaps we did make progress toward unification of the armed forces of China. We did prevent civil war between the rival factions, at least until after I had left China. We did bring the leaders of the rival parties together for peaceful discussions. Throughout this period the chief opposition to the accomplishment of our mission came from the American career diplomats in the Embassy at Chungking and in the Chinese and Far Eastern Divisions of the State Department.

I requested the relief of the career men who were opposing the American policy in the Chinese Theater of war. These professional diplomats were returned to Washington and placed in the Chinese and Far Eastern Divisions of the State Department as my supervisors. Some of these same career men whom I relieved have been assigned as advisors to the Supreme Commander in Asia. In such positions most of them have continued to side with the Communist armed party and at times with the imperialist bloc against American policy. This, Mr. President, is an outline of one of the reasons why American foreign policy announced by the highest authority is rendered ineffective by another section of diplomatic officials.

PAT HURLEY'S SUDDEN DENUNCIATION OF CHINA POLICY nonplussed the Truman administration, and after a cabinet discussion the president decided to appoint General George C. Marshall in Hurley's stead, a move that would take the heat off Hurley's resignation. Marshall had just retired from the army. Although unenthusiastic about the assignment, he agreed immediately to go to China and was appointed on November 27, 1945. There followed some very frank discussions of China policy within the administration. Marshall himself drew up a memorandum of the discussion of December 11 with President Truman, Secretary of State Byrnes, and Admiral William D. Leahy.

The President stated that he wished to have a clear and complete understanding among us as to just what was the basis on which I was to operate in China in representing him. Mr. Byrnes outlined the policy of this Government as he understood it and advocated it. In effect he stated this, that first of all we, that is the Army and Navy, were being authorized to proceed at once with the

SOURCE: *Foreign Relations: 1945*, VII, pp. 767–69.

arrangement of shipping for the transfer of the armies of the Generalissimo to Manchuria and for their logistical support; also for the evacuation of Japanese from China; and finally, though this was to be maintained in a status of secrecy, for the present, for the transfer of the Generalissimo's troops into North China for the purpose, on our part, of releasing the Japanese forces in that area and facilitating their evacuation and deportation to Japan.

Mr. Byrnes stated that the reason for holding secret for the present the preparations for the movement of the Generalissimo's troops into North China was to enable General Marshall to utilize that uncertainty for the purpose of bringing influence to bear both on the Generalissimo and the Communist leaders towards concluding a successful negotiation for the termination of hostilities and the development of a broad unified Chinese government.

The President stated his concurrence with the proposition outlined by Mr. Byrnes and informed General Marshall that he would back him in his, General Marshall's, efforts whatever they might be to bring about the desired result.

General Marshall stated that his understanding then was that he would do his best to influence the Generalissimo to make reasonable concessions in his negotiations with the democratic and communist leaders, holding in abeyance the information that this Government was actually preparing shipping to assist the Generalissimo in moving his troops into North China for the purpose of releasing the Japanese in that region and, incidentally, taking over control of the railroads. That, on the other hand, he, General Marshall, was to utilize the same uncertainty as to the attitude of our Government toward the establishment of the Generalissimo's troops in North China in the effort to bring the Communist leaders to the point of making reasonable concessions in order to bring about desirable political unification. That in the event that the Communist leaders refused to make what, in General Marshall's opinion, were reasonable concessions, he was authorized to back the Generalissimo by assisting in the movement of troops into the region for the U.S. purpose of removing the Japanese.

Finally, General Marshall stated, that if the Generalissimo, in his (General Marshall's) opinion, failed to make reasonable concessions, and this resulted in the breakdown of the efforts to secure a political unification, and the U.S. abandoned continued support of the Generalissimo, there would follow the tragic consequences of a divided China and of a probable Russian reassumption of power in Manchuria, the combined effect of this resulting in the defeat or loss of the major purpose of our war in the Pacific. Under these circumstances, General Marshall inquired whether or not it was intended for him, in that unfortunate eventuality, to go ahead and assist the Generalissimo in the movement of troops into North China. This would mean that this Government would have to swallow its pride and much of its policy in doing so.

The President and Mr. Byrnes concurred in this view of the matter; that is, that we would have to back the Generalissimo to the extent of assisting him to move troops into North China in order that the evacuation of the Japanese might be completed.

There was some discussion and Mr. Byrnes re-stated the policy of this Government adding specifically that it was not the purpose of the U.S. to send additional troops, divisions—he mentioned, to China, that he was opposed to that and that it would be contrary to the expressions of policy he had made public up to this time. The President agreed with this point of view of the Secretary of State.

The President approved the paper from the State Department containing the draft for a release to the press regarding our policy in China. . . .

The Secretary stated that he was having a draft of a letter prepared for the President to General Marshall formally stating these various policies. The draft was not then available.

THE NEW AMBASSADOR made notes of a meeting with the president and Undersecretary of State Acheson on December 14, 1945.

The President handed me a final draft of his letter of instructions together with the enclosures and asked me if these were satisfactory to me. I replied in the affirmative. The President stated that if I desired a directive from him in any other form for me to prepare it and he would sign it, that he wished to back me in every way possible.

I stated that my understanding of one phase of my directive was not in writing but I thought I had a clear understanding of his desires in the matter, which was that in the event that I was unable

SOURCE: *Foreign Relations: 1945*, VII, p. 769.

to secure the necessary action by the Generalissimo, which I thought reasonable and desirable, it would still be necessary for the U.S. Government, through me, to continue to back the National Government of the Republic of China—through the Generalissimo within the terms of the announced policy of the U.S. Government.

The President stated that the foregoing was a correct summation of his direction regarding that possible development of the situation.

The Under Secretary of State, Mr. Acheson, confirmed this as his understanding of my directions.

The President repeated his assurances that the U.S. Government, that he would back me in my decisions, that he had confidence in my judgment.

THE PRESIDENT'S SPECIAL ENVOY went out to China in December, 1945, and remained until January, 1947, when he returned to Washington to replace Byrnes as secretary of state. At the outset of the Marshall mission there seemed evidence that the two quarreling sides in China, Nationalists and Communists, could come together, and that the forceful personality of Marshall would bring them together. The general arranged a cease-fire on January 10, 1946, and managed to extend it to cover all Manchuria, the area where the antagonists were in sharpest conflict. When he went home for a short time in March the truce fell apart. Between June 7 and 30 he arranged another cease-fire, but it too fell apart. The latter months of 1946 marked a time when both sides in China thought they could win without American mediation, and the mediator found himself reduced to the position of an observer while each side blamed the other and civil war extended throughout Manchuria and elsewhere. When Marshall returned home he made a personal statement on January 7, 1947, a frank report to the American people that showed that his mission and the policy of the government of the United States had failed.

In the first place, the greatest obstacle to peace has been the complete, almost overwhelming suspicion with which the Chinese Communist Party and the Kuomintang regard each other.

On the one hand, the leaders of the Government are strongly opposed to a communistic form of government. On the other, the

SOURCE: *United States Relations with China, with Special Reference to the Period 1944–1949* (Washington, D.C., 1949), pp. 686–89.

Communists frankly state that they are Marxists and intend to work toward establishing a communistic form of government in China, though first advancing through the medium of a democratic form of government of the American or British type. . . .

I think the most important factors involved in the recent breakdown of negotiations are these: On the side of the National Government, which is in effect the Kuomintang, there is a dominant group of reactionaries who have been opposed, in my opinion, to almost every effort I have made to influence the formation of a genuine coalition government. This has usually been under the cover of political or party action, but since the Party was the Government, this action, though subtle or indirect, has been devastating in its effect. They were quite frank in publicly stating their belief that cooperation by the Chinese Communist Party in the government was inconceivable and that only a policy of force could definitely settle the issue. This group includes military as well as political leaders.

On the side of the Chinese Communist Party there are, I believe, liberals as well as radicals, though this view is vigorously opposed by many who believe that the Chinese Communist Party discipline is too rigidly enforced to admit of such differences of viewpoint. Nevertheless, it has appeared to me that there is a definite liberal group among the Communists, especially of young men who have turned to the Communists in disgust at the corruption evident in the local governments—men who would put the interest of the Chinese people above ruthless measures to establish a Communist ideology in the immediate future. The dyed-in-the-wool Communists do not hesitate at the most drastic measures to gain their end as, for instance, the destruction of communications in order to wreck the economy of China and produce a situation that would facilitate the overthrow or collapse of the Government, without any regard to the immediate suffering of the people involved. They completely distrust the leaders of the Kuomintang and appear convinced that every Government proposal is designed to crush the Chinese Communist Party. I must say that the quite evidently inspired mob actions of last February and March, some within a few blocks of where I was then engaged in completing negotiations, gave the Communists good excuse for such suspicions.

However, a very harmful and immensely provocative phase of

the Chinese Communist Party procedure has been in the character of its propaganda. I wish to state to the American people that in the deliberate misrepresentation and abuse of the action, policies and purposes of our Government this propaganda has been without regard for the truth, without any regard whatsoever for the facts, and has given plain evidence of a determined purpose to mislead the Chinese people and the world and to arouse a bitter hatred of Americans. It has been difficult to remain silent in the midst of such public abuse and wholesale disregard of facts, but a denial would merely lead to the necessity of daily denials; an intolerable course of action for an American official. In the interest of fairness, I must state that the Nationalist Government publicity agency has made numerous misrepresentations, though not of the vicious nature of the Communist propaganda. Incidentally, the Communist statements regarding the Anping incident which resulted in the death of three Marines and the wounding of twelve others were almost pure fabrication, deliberately representing a carefully arranged ambuscade of a Marine convoy with supplies for the maintenance of Executive Headquarters and some UNRRA supplies, as a defence against a Marine assault. The investigation of this incident was a tortuous procedure of delays and maneuvers to disguise the true and privately admitted facts of the case.

Sincere efforts to achieve settlement have been frustrated time and again by extremist elements of both sides. The agreements reached by the Political Consultative Conference a year ago were a liberal and forward-looking charter which then offered China a basis for peace and reconstruction. However, irreconcilable groups within the Kuomintang, interested in the preservation of their own feudal control of China, evidently had no real intention of implementing them. Though I speak as a soldier, I must here also deplore the dominating influence of the military. Their dominance accentuates the weakness of civil government in China. At the same time, in pondering the situation in China, one must have clearly in mind not the workings of small Communist groups or committees to which we are accustomed in America, but rather of millions of people and an army of more than a million men.

I have never been in a position to be certain of the development of attitudes in the innermost Chinese Communist circles. Most certainly, the course which the Chinese Communist Party has pursued in recent months indicated an unwillingness to make a fair compromise. It has been impossible even to get them to sit down at a conference table with Government representatives to discuss given issues. Now the Communists have broken off negotiations by their last offer which demanded the dissolution of the National Assembly and a return to the military positions of January 13th which the Government could not be expected to accept.

Between this dominant reactionary group in the Government and the irreconcilable Communists who, I must state, did not so appear last February, lies the problem of how peace and well-being are to be brought to the long-suffering and presently inarticulate mass of the people of China. The reactionaries in the Government have evidently counted on substantial American support regardless of their actions. The Communists by their unwillingness to compromise in the national interest are evidently counting on an economic collapse to bring about the fall of the Government, accelerated by extensive guerrilla action against the long lines of rail communications—regardless of the cost in suffering to the Chinese people. . . .

I have spoken very frankly because in no other way can I hope to bring the people of the United States to even a partial understanding of this complex problem. I have expressed all these views privately in the course of negotiations; they are well known, I think, to most of the individuals concerned. I express them now publicly, as it is my duty, to present my estimate of the situation and its possibilities to the American people who have a deep interest in the development of conditions in the Far East promising an enduring peace in the Pacific.

B. "Nothing Can Be Done. . . ."

AFTER MARSHALL RETURNED, *China policy lapsed. There seemed little to do other than wait to see what the Chinese people wished to do about their future. The administration found its attention turning to the press of events in Europe. In 1947–49, the era when the Nationalist regime collapsed and the Communists took over, it was almost impossible to pursue a strong Chinese policy because of the need to give attention to the economic and military future of Europe. The only really effective intervention by the United States would have had to be military, and neither the Truman administration nor its Republican opposition was willing to send troops in force to China. To have preserved China for*

SOURCE: *U.S. Relations with China,* pp. 758–63.

the Nationalists might have required thirty or forty divisions, and no one in the United States at that time was willing to endure a partial mobilization for such a purpose. Meanwhile the Truman administration found itself forced to give the appearance of action or at least interest in the affairs of China, and Marshall in 1947, in accord with a well-known practice of American government, sent an investigatory mission to China headed by Lieutenant General Albert C. Wedemeyer. The general had held command positions in China during the Second World War and immediately after, and seemed a suitable person to estimate the state of affairs. Wedemeyer took his mission very seriously and at its end, on August 22, 1947, gave a lecture to a group of the highest officials of the Chinese government including Generalissimo Chiang. Ambassador John Leighton Stuart transmitted a summary of these remarks to Secretary Marshall on August 25.

Taxation

Approximately 80 percent of the people of China are hard working peasants, their crops are visible and officials can easily appraise the amounts the peasants are able to give toward government. Corrupt officials in many instances take more than the peasants are able to give and this results finally in the peasants leaving the land and forming bandit groups.

In contrast to the taxation of peasants, Chinese businessmen and rich Chinese resort to devious and dishonest methods to avoid payment of proper taxes to their government. It is commonly known that Chinese business firms maintain two sets of books, one showing the true picture of business transactions and the other showing a distorted picture so that they do not pay as much tax as they should.

Military

For the first year after the war, in my opinion it was possible to stamp out or at least to minimize the effect of Chinese Communists. This capability was predicated upon the assumption that the Central Government disposed its military forces in such a manner as to insure control of all industrial areas, food producing areas, important cities and lines of communication. It was also assumed that the Central Government appointed highly efficient and scrupulously honest officials as provincial governors, district magistrates, mayors, and throughout the political and economic structure. If these assumptions had been accomplished, political and economic stability would have resulted, and the people would not have been receptive, in fact, would have strongly opposed the infiltration or penetration of communistic ideas. It would not have been possible for the Chinese Communists to expand so rapidly and acquire almost undisputed control of such vast areas. I believe that the Chinese Communist movement cannot be defeated by the employment of force. Today China is being invaded by an idea instead of strong military forces from the outside. The only way in my opinion to combat this idea successfully is to do so with another idea that will have stronger appeal and win the support of the people. This means that politically and economically the Central Government will have to remove corruption and incompetence from its ranks in order to provide justice and equality and to protect the personal liberties of the Chinese people, particularly of the peasants. To recapitulate, the Central Government cannot defeat the Chinese Communists by the employment of force, but can only win the loyal, enthusiastic and realistic support of the masses of the people by improving the political and economic situation immediately. The effectiveness and timeliness of these improvements will determine in my opinion whether or not the Central Government will stand or fall before the Communist onslaught. . . .

Final Remarks

The Government should not be worried about criticism. I think constructive criticism should be encouraged. It makes the people feel that they are participating in government; that they are members of the team. I have mentioned earlier the terrible economic conditions that exist in England. Criticism of the government is expressed freely in meetings on the streets, and in the press, and on the radio. This is in my opinion a healthy condition. The Government should point out that it is made up of human beings who are of course fallible and can make mistakes. The Government should emphasize, however, that once the mistakes are pointed out, effective steps will be taken to remedy them. The Government should publish information freely concerning expenditures, taxation. Let all the people know how much income tax each individual, particularly wealthy people and big business firms are paying. Announce publicly when any official or any individual has been guilty of some crime or offense and also indicate the punishment meted out. By the same token, announce publicly the accomplishment or good work of individual Government activities. All of these matters would contribute to confidence on the part of the people in the Government. They want to know what is going on and they have a right to know. Open and public official announcements on the part of the Government will also serve to stop malicious conjectures and adverse propaganda of opponents of the Government.

I realize that many of the ideas that I have expressed are quite contrary to Chinese tradition. However, I have carefully studied the philosophy of Confucius and I am sure that all of these ideas are in consonance with the fine principles of conduct that he prescribed. I have confidence in the good sound judgment and in the decency of the bulk of the Chinese peoples. I hope sincerely that you will accept my remarks in the same spirit in which they were given, namely, in the interest of China. Anything that I can do to help China become a strong, happy and prosperous nation, I would gladly do. Anything I could do to protect the sovereignty of China and to insure her a place of respect in the eyes of the world in the family of nations, I would gladly do.

THE TOPICS INCLUDED in this frank address, in addition to those mentioned above, were conscription, the relationship between military and civilians, government organization, corruption, national assets and resources, punishment and secret police, and restoration and revitalization of the Chinese economy. After giving his final remarks, Wedemeyer dealt with the following additional points: (1) general frustration on the part of Chinese officialdom, (2) the Generalissimo's dabbling in all strata of government, (3) the lack of authority among the Generalissimo's cabinet officers, (4) the necessity for a closer relationship with the Generalissimo, who should encourage criticism. Apparently, the address met with restrained enthusiasm from the Nationalist officials in attendance. Ambassador Stuart's memoirs (Fifty Years in China [New York: Random House, 1954]) criticize Wedemeyer for indiscretion, although there is some evidence that Stuart, a long-time missionary to China, put Wedemeyer up to the speech. Wedemeyer on August 24 made a public statement to the American people about his mission that included generally some of the comments he had offered Nationalist officials three days earlier. In his long report to the Department of State he recommended a trusteeship for Manchuria that would include the Soviet Union. Making public Wedemeyer's report, Secretary Marshall sup-

SOURCE: U.S. Relations with China, pp. iii–xvii.

pressed this recommendation. As the Secretary explained a few years later, it was completely unrealistic. At the time of the Nationalist collapse in the summer of 1949, Marshall's successor, Acheson, arranged for the department to gather together a huge compilation of its records on China policy, the so-called China White Paper (U.S. Relations with China, cited above), which was thereupon released. In his letter of transmittal to President Truman, dated July 30, 1949, Secretary Acheson set out the nation's point of view with the same honesty and clarity as his predecessor.

THE PRESIDENT: In accordance with your wish, I have had compiled a record of our relations with China, special emphasis being placed on the last five years. This record is being published and will therefore be available to the Congress and to the people of the United States. . . .

This is a frank record of an extremely complicated and most unhappy period in the life of a great country to which the United States has long been attached by ties of closest friendship. No available item has been omitted because it contains statements critical of our policy or might be the basis of future criticism. The inherent strength of our system is the responsiveness of the Government to an informed and critical public opinion. It is precisely this informed and critical public opinion which totalitarian governments, whether Rightist or Communist, cannot endure and do not tolerate. . . .

When peace came [in 1945] the United States was confronted with three possible alternatives in China: (1) it could have pulled out lock, stock and barrel; (2) it could have intervened militarily on a major scale to assist the Nationalists to destroy the Communists; (3) it could, while assisting the Nationalists to assert their authority over as much of China as possible, endeavor to avoid a civil war by working for a compromise between the two sides.

The first alternative would, and I believe American public opinion at the time so felt, have represented an abandonment of our international responsibilities and of our traditional policy of friendship for China before we had made a determined effort to be of assistance. The second alternative policy, while it may look attractive theoretically and in retrospect, was wholly impracticable. The Nationalists had been unable to destroy the Communists during the 10 years before the war. Now after the war the Nationalists were . . . weakened, demoralized, and unpopular. . . . We therefore came to the third alternative policy whereunder we faced the facts of the situation and attempted to assist in working out a *modus vivendi* which would avert civil war but nevertheless preserve and even increase the influence of the National Government. . . .

The reasons for the failures of the Chinese National Government . . . do not stem from any inadequacy of American aid. Our military observers on the spot have reported that the Nationalist armies did not lose a single battle during the crucial year of 1948 through lack of arms or ammunition. The fact was that the decay which our observers had detected in Chungking early in the war had fatally sapped the powers of resistance of the Kuomintang. Its leaders had proved incapable of meeting the crisis confronting them, its troops had lost the will to fight, and its Government had lost popular support. The Communists, on the other hand, through a ruthless discipline and fanatical zeal, attempted to sell themselves as guardians and liberators of the people. The Nationalist armies did not have to be defeated; they disintegrated. History has proved again and again that a regime without faith in itself and an army without morale cannot survive the test of battle. . . .

It must be admitted frankly that the American policy of assisting the Chinese people in resisting domination by any foreign power or powers is now confronted with the gravest difficulties. The heart of China is in Communist hands. The Communist leaders have foresworn their Chinese heritage and have publicly announced their subservience to a foreign power, Russia, which during the last 50 years, under czars and Communists alike, has been most assiduous in its efforts to extend its control in the Far East. In the recent past, attempts at foreign domination have appeared quite clearly to the Chinese people as external aggression and as such have been bitterly and in the long run successfully resisted. Our aid and encouragement have helped them to resist. In this case, however, the foreign domination has been masked behind the façade of a vast crusading movement which apparently has seemed to many Chinese to be wholly indigenous and national. Under these circumstances, our aid has been unavailing.

The unfortunate but inescapable fact is that the ominous result of the civil war in China was beyond the control of the government of the United States. Nothing that this country did or could have done within the reasonable limits of its capabilities could have changed that result; nothing that was left undone by this country has contributed to it. It was the product of internal Chinese forces, forces which this country tried to influence but could not. A decision was arrived at within China, if only a decision by default.

President Truman in mid-1949 told the chairman of the Atomic Energy Commission, David E. Lilienthal, that the "grafters and crooks" and their lot in China had no interest in the millions and millions of Chinese who did not have enough to eat. Two and a half billion dollars of U.S. government money had gone into China in recent years and, "I'll bet you that a billion dollars of it is in New York banks today." The President also said that "nothing can be done about China until things kind of settle down."

15. The Korean War and the China Problem

A. Leashing and Unleashing the Nationalist Chinese

When the Nationalist positions collapsed on the mainland, the *regime moved to Formosa, now known as Taiwan, and established itself in the provincial capital of Taipei. The Formosa Strait was not wide, the Nationalists gave little evidence of being able to protect themselves from invasion, and the United States government virtually wrote off the regime as indefensible, bound sooner or later to fall. With the outbreak of the Korean War on June 25, 1950, all this changed. Two days later the Truman administration announced a new policy.*

The attack upon Korea makes it plain beyond all doubt that communism has passed beyond the use of subversion to conquer independent nations and will now use armed invasion and war. It has defied the orders of the Security Council of the United Nations issued to preserve international peace and security. In these circumstances, the occupation of Formosa by Communist forces would be a direct threat to the security of the Pacific area and to United States forces performing their lawful and necessary functions in that area.

Source: *American Foreign Policy: Current Documents, 1950–1955,* 2 vols. (Washington, D.C., 1957), II, p. 2468.

Accordingly, I have ordered the Seventh Fleet to prevent any attack on Formosa. As a corollary of this action, I am calling upon the Chinese Government on Formosa to cease all air and sea operations against the mainland. The Seventh Fleet will see that this is done. The determination of the future status of Formosa must await the restoration of security in the Pacific, a peace settlement with Japan, or consideration by the United Nations.

IT WAS SAID at the time that the order of June 27 was a "leashing" of Chiang, as it prevented him from achieving his often-announced goal of invading the mainland and restoring himself to power there. After the mainland Chinese intervention in the Korean War and as that war slowly moved along toward an armistice in the summer of 1953, a good deal of criticism arose over Truman's order, the thought being that the American government had denied itself an able ally who at the very least could make some trouble for the mainland government in Peking. In 1953 President Eisenhower, then newly elected, announced, in a message to Congress on February 2, a change of policy, the unleashing of Chiang.

In June 1950, following the aggressive attack on the Republic of Korea, the United States Seventh Fleet was instructed both to prevent attack upon Formosa and also to insure that Formosa should not be used as a base of operations against the Chinese Communist mainland.

This has meant, in effect, that the United States Navy was required to serve as a defensive arm of Communist China. Regardless of the situation of 1950, since the date of that order the Chinese Communists have invaded Korea to attack the United Nations forces there. They have consistently rejected the proposals of the United Nations Command for an armistice. They recently joined with Soviet Russia in rejecting the armistice proposal sponsored in the United Nations by the Government of India. This proposal had been accepted by the United States and 53 other nations.

Consequently there is no longer any logic or sense in a condition that required the United States Navy to assume defensive responsibilities on behalf of the Chinese Communists. This permitted those Communists, with greater impunity, to kill our soldiers and those of our United Nations allies in Korea.

SOURCE: *American Foreign Policy: 1950–1955*, II, p. 2476.

I am, therefore, issuing instructions that the Seventh Fleet no longer be employed to shield Communist China. Permit me to make this crystal clear: This order implies no aggressive intent on our part. But we certainly have no obligation to protect a nation fighting us in Korea.

B. The U.S.–Nationalist Chinese Alliance

Nearly two years after President Eisenhower's withdrawal of the Seventh Fleet from the Formosa Strait and after Generalissimo Chiang's troops had shown either inability or unwillingness to attack the mainland, moving not one inch from their positions on Taiwan, the Eisenhower administration returned to the Truman policy, "releashing" Chiang's regime, albeit with a treaty of alliance of December 2, 1954.

The Parties to this Treaty,

Reaffirming their faith in the purposes and principles of the Charter of the United Nations and their desire to live in peace with all peoples and all Governments, and desiring to strengthen the fabric of peace in the West Pacific Area,

Recalling with mutual pride the relationship which brought their two peoples together in a common bond of sympathy and mutual ideals to fight side by side against imperialist aggression during the last war,

Desiring to declare publicly and formally their sense of unity and their common determination to defend themselves against external armed attack, so that no potential aggressor could be under the illusion that either of them stands alone in the West Pacific Area, and

Desiring further to strengthen their present efforts for collective defense for the preservation of peace and security pending the development of a more comprehensive system of regional security in the West Pacific Area,

Have agreed as follows:

Article I

The Parties undertake, as set forth in the Charter of the United Nations, to settle any international dispute in which they may be involved by peaceful means in such a manner that international

Source: *United States Treaties and Other International Agreements: 1955*, pt. 1 (Washington, D.C., 1956), pp. 433–38.

peace, security and justice are not endangered and to refrain in their international relations from the threat or use of force in any manner inconsistent with the purposes of the United Nations.

Article II

In order more effectively to achieve the objective of this Treaty, the Parties separately and jointly by self-help and mutual aid will maintain and develop their individual and collective capacity to resist armed attack and communist subversive activities directed from without against their territorial integrity and political stability.

Article III

The Parties undertake to strengthen their free institutions and to cooperate with each other in the development of economic progress and social well-being and to further their individual and collective efforts toward these ends.

Article IV

The Parties, through their Foreign Ministers or their deputies, will consult together from time to time regarding the implementation of this Treaty.

Article V

Each Party recognizes that an armed attack in the West Pacific Area directed against the territories of either of the Parties would be dangerous to its own peace and safety and declares that it would act to meet the common danger in accordance with its constitutional processes.

Any such armed attack and all measures taken as a result thereof shall be immediately reported to the Security Council of the United Nations. Such measures shall be terminated when the Security Council has taken the measures necessary to restore and maintain international peace and security.

Article VI

For the purposes of Articles II and V, the terms "territorial" and "territories" shall mean in respect of the Republic of China,

Taiwan and the Pescadores; and in respect of the United States of America, the island territories in the West Pacific under its jurisdiction. The provisions of Articles II and V will be applicable to such other territories as may be determined by mutual agreement.

Article VII

The Government of the Republic of China grants, and the Government of the United States of America accepts, the right to dispose such United States land, air and sea forces in and about Taiwan and the Pescadores as may be required for their defense, as determined by mutual agreement.

Article VIII

This Treaty does not affect and shall not be interpreted as affecting in any way the rights and obligations of the Parties under the Charter of the United Nations or the responsibility of the United Nations for the maintenance of international peace and security.

As PART OF THE ALLIANCE *Secretary of State Dulles initiated an exchange of notes with the Nationalist Chinese foreign minister, George K. C. Yeh, on December 10, 1954.*

EXCELLENCY: I have the honor to refer to recent conversations between representatives of our two Governments and to confirm the understandings reached as a result of those conversations, as follows:

The Republic of China effectively controls both the territory described in Article VI of the Treaty of Mutual Defense between the Republic of China, and the United States of America signed on December 2, 1954, at Washington and other territory. It possesses with respect to all territory now and hereafter under its control the inherent right of self-defense. In view of the obligations of the two Parties under the said Treaty and of the fact that the use of force from either of these areas by either of the Parties affects the other, it is agreed that such use of force will be a matter of joint agreement, subject to action of an emergency character which is clearly an exercise of the inherent right of self-defense. Military elements which are a product of joint effort and contribu-

SOURCE: *American Foreign Policy: 1950–1955,* I, pp. 947–48.

tion by the two Parties will not be removed from the territories described in Article VI to a degree which would substantially diminish the defensibility of such territories without mutual agreement.

In a response of the same date Foreign Minister Yeh agreed to this "releashing" of Chiang Kai-shek's regime on Taiwan.

C. The Quemoy Resolution

In the autumn of 1954 *and again in* 1958, *trouble occurred in connection with Nationalist-occupied islands—the Tachen, Quemoy, and Matsu island groups—between Taiwan and the mainland. These island groups are much closer to the mainland than to Taiwan; the two Quemoys lie about 5 miles off the mainland and about 105 miles west of Taiwan. The Quemoys and Matsus command the approaches to important harbors, Foochow and Amoy, in the Fukien province of mainland China. On September 3,* 1954, *the mainland Chinese began shelling some of the Tachen Islands with coastal batteries. The Nationalists replied with their own artillery and with announcements of a fight to the finish. With the fall of the island of Yikiangshan in January,* 1955, *the situation looked dangerous, and President Eisenhower obtained from Congress an extraordinary resolution dated January 29.*

Whereas the primary purpose of the United States, in its relations with all other nations, is to develop and sustain a just and enduring peace for all; and

Whereas certain territories in the West Pacific under the jurisdiction of the Republic of China are now under armed attack, and threats and declarations have been and are being made by the Chinese Communists that such armed attack is in aid of and in preparation for armed attack on Formosa and the Pescadores,

Whereas such armed attack if continued would gravely endanger the peace and security of the West Pacific Area and particularly of Formosa and the Pescadores; and

Whereas the secure possession by friendly governments of the Western Pacific Island chain, of which Formosa is a part, is essential to the vital interests of the United States and all friendly nations in or bordering upon the Pacific Ocean; and

Whereas the President of the United States on January 6, 1955, submitted to the Senate for its advice and consent to ratification a Mutual Defense Treaty between the United States of America and

Source: *American Foreign Policy: 1950–1955,* II, pp. 2486–87.

Chinese Offshore Islands

the Republic of China, which recognizes that an armed attack in the West Pacific Area directed against territories, therein described, in the region of Formosa and the Pescadores, would be dangerous to the peace and safety of the parties to the treaty: Therefore be it

Resolved by the Senate and House of Representatives of the United States of America in Congress assembled, That the President of the United States be and he hereby is authorized to employ the Armed Forces of the United States as he deems necessary for the specific purpose of securing and protecting Formosa and the Pescadores against armed attack, this authority to include the securing and protection of such related positions and territories of that area now in friendly hands and the taking of such other measures as he judges to be required or appropriate in assuring the defense of Formosa and the Pescadores.

This resolution shall expire when the President shall determine that the peace and security of the area is reasonably assured by international conditions created by action of the United Nations or otherwise, and shall so report to the Congress.

The fall of Yikiangshan made evacuation of the Tachen group necessary, but the Nationalists retained the other two island groups, bombardment of which resumed for a while in 1958.

16. Nixon's Visit to China

THE MOST SPECTACULAR EVENT *during President Nixon's first administration was his trip to China. Upon arrival in the People's Republic, he and his entourage engaged in a series of talks with Chinese officials, and on February 27, 1972, the president and Premier Chou En-lai issued a joint communiqué. The Nixon-Chou statement could not, of course, detail the physical impact of the trip—the receptions in Peking and other places; the trips to the Forbidden City, the Great Wall, the Ming tombs. Nor could it quite describe what the president himself found difficult to put into words upon his return: "In a technical sense we were at peace . . . before this trip, but a gulf of almost 12,000 miles and 22 years of noncommunication and hostility separated the United States of America from the 750 million who live in the People's Republic of China, and that is one-fourth of all the people in the world."*

President Richard Nixon of the United States of America visited the People's Republic of China at the invitation of Premier Chou En-lai of the People's Republic of China from February 21 to February 28, 1972. Accompanying the President were Mrs. Nixon, U.S. Secretary of State William Rogers, Assistant to the President Dr. Henry Kissinger, and other American officials.

President Nixon met with Chairman Mao Tse-tung of the Communist Party of China on February 21. The two leaders had a serious and frank exchange of views on Sino-U.S. relations and world affairs.

SOURCE: Department of State *Bulletin*, March 20, 1972, pp. 435–38.

During the visit, extensive, earnest and frank discussions were held between President Nixon and Premier Chou En-lai on the normalization of relations between the United States of America and the People's Republic of China, as well as on other matters of interest to both sides. In addition, Secretary of State William Rogers and Foreign Minister Chi Peng-fei held talks in the same spirit.

President Nixon and his party visited Peking and viewed cultural, industrial and agricultural sites, and they also toured Hangchow and Shanghai where, continuing discussions with Chinese leaders, they viewed similar places of interest.

The leaders of the People's Republic of China and the United States of America found it beneficial to have this opportunity, after so many years without contact, to present candidly to one another their views on a variety of issues. They reviewed the international situation in which important changes and great upheavals are taking place and expounded their respective positions and attitudes.

The U.S. side stated: Peace in Asia and peace in the world requires efforts both to reduce immediate tensions and to eliminate the basic causes of conflict. The United States will work for a just and secure peace: just, because it fulfills the aspirations of peoples and nations for freedom and progress; secure, because it removes the danger of foreign aggression. The United States supports individual freedom and social progress for all the peoples of the world, free of outside pressure or intervention. The United States believes that the effort to reduce tensions is served by improving communication between countries that have different ideologies so as to lessen the risks of confrontation through accident, miscalculation or misunderstanding. Countries should treat each other with mutual respect and be willing to compete peacefully, letting performance be the ultimate judge. No country should claim infallibility and each country should be prepared to re-examine its own attitudes for the common good. The United States stressed that the peoples of Indochina should be allowed to determine their destiny without outside intervention; its constant primary objective has been a negotiated solution; the eight-point proposal put forward by the Republic of Vietnam and the United States on January 27, 1972, represents a basis for the attainment of that objective; in the absence of a negotiated settlement the United

States envisages the ultimate withdrawal of all U.S. forces from the region consistent with the aim of self-determination for each country of Indochina. The United States will maintain its close ties with and support for the Republic of Korea; the United States will support efforts of the Republic of Korea to seek a relaxation of tension and increased communication in the Korean peninsula. The United States places the highest value on its friendly relations with Japan; it will continue to develop the existing close bonds. Consistent with the United Nations Security Council Resolution of December 21, 1971, the United States favors the continuation of the ceasefire between India and Pakistan and the withdrawal of all military forces to within their own territories and to their own sides of the ceasefire line in Jammu and Kashmir; the United States supports the right of the peoples of South Asia to shape their own future in peace, free of military threat, and without having the area become the subject of great power rivalry.

The Chinese side stated: Wherever there is oppression, there is resistance. Countries want independence, nations want liberation and the people want revolution—this has become the irresistible trend of history. All nations, big or small, should be equal; big nations should not bully the small and strong nations should not bully the weak. China will never be a superpower and it opposes hegemony and power politics of any kind. The Chinese side stated that it firmly supports the struggles of all the oppressed people and nations for freedom and liberation and that the people of all countries have the right to choose their social systems according to their own wishes and the right to safeguard the independence, sovereignty and territorial integrity of their own countries and oppose foreign aggression, interference, control and subversion. All foreign troops should be withdrawn to their own countries.

The Chinese side expressed its firm support to the peoples of Vietnam, Laos and Cambodia in their efforts for the attainment of their goal and its firm support to the seven-point proposal of the Provisional Revolutionary Government of the Republic of South Vietnam and the elaboration of February this year on the two key problems in the proposal, and to the Joint Declaration of the Summit Conference of the Indochinese Peoples. It firmly supports the eight-point program for the peaceful unification of Korea put forward by the Government of the Democratic People's Republic of Korea on April 12, 1971, and the stand for the abolition of the

"U.N. Commission for the Unification and Rehabilitation of Korea." It firmly opposes the revival and outward expansion of Japanese militarism and firmly supports the Japanese people's desire to build an independent, democratic, peaceful and neutral Japan. It firmly maintains that India and Pakistan should, in accordance with the United Nations resolutions on the India-Pakistan question, immediately withdraw all their forces to their respective territories and to their own sides of the ceasefire line in Jammu and Kashmir and firmly supports the Pakistan Government and people in their struggle to preserve their independence and sovereignty and the people of Jammu and Kashmir in their struggle for the right of self-determination.

There are essential differences between China and the United States in their social systems and foreign policies. However, the two sides agreed that countries, regardless of their social systems, should conduct their relations on the principles of respect for the sovereignty and territorial integrity of all states, non-aggression against other states, non-interference in the internal affairs of other states, equality and mutual benefit, and peaceful coexistence. International disputes should be settled on this basis, without resorting to the use or threat of force. The United States and the People's Republic of China are prepared to apply these principles to their mutual relations.

With these principles of international relations in mind the two sides stated that:

> —progress toward the normalization of relations between China and the United States is in the interests of all countries;
> —both wish to reduce the danger of international military conflict;
> —neither should seek hegemony in the Asia-Pacific region and each is opposed to efforts by any other country or group of countries to establish such hegemony; and
> —neither is prepared to negotiate on behalf of any third party or to enter into agreements or understandings with the other directed at other states.

Both sides are of the view that it would be against the interests of the peoples of the world for any major country to collude with another against other countries, or for major countries to divide up the world into spheres of interest.

The two sides reviewed the long-standing serious disputes between China and the United States. The Chinese side reaffirmed its position: The Taiwan question is the crucial question obstructing the normalization of relations between China and the United States; the Government of the People's Republic of China is the sole legal government of China; Taiwan is a province of China which has long been returned to the motherland; the liberation of Taiwan is China's internal affair in which no other country has the right to interfere; and all U.S. forces and military installations must be withdrawn from Taiwan. The Chinese Government firmly opposes any activities which aim at the creation of "one China, one Taiwan," "one China, two governments," "two Chinas," and "independent Taiwan" or advocate that "the status of Taiwan remains to be determined."

The U.S. side declared: The United States acknowledges that all Chinese on either side of the Taiwan Strait maintain there is but one China and that Taiwan is a part of China. The United States Government does not challenge that position. It reaffirms its interest in a peaceful settlement of the Taiwan question by the Chinese themselves. With this prospect in mind, it affirms the ultimate objective of the withdrawal of all U.S. forces and military installations from Taiwan. In the meantime, it will progressively reduce its forces and military installations on Taiwan as the tension in the area diminishes.

The two sides agreed that it is desirable to broaden the understanding between the two peoples. To this end, they discussed specific areas in such fields as science, technology, culture, sports and journalism, in which people-to-people contacts and exchanges would be mutually beneficial. Each side undertakes to facilitate the further development of such contacts and exchanges.

Both sides view bilateral trade as another area from which mutual benefit can be derived, and agreed that economic relations based on equality and mutual benefit are in the interest of the peoples of the two countries. They agree to facilitate the progressive development of trade between their two countries.

The two sides agreed that they will stay in contact through various channels, including the sending of a senior U.S. representative to Peking from time to time for concrete consultations to further the normalization of relations between the two countries and continue to exchange views on issues of common interest.

The two sides expressed the hope that the gains achieved during this visit would open up new prospects for the relations between the two countries. They believe that the normalization of relations between the two countries is not only in the interest of the Chinese and American peoples but also contributes to the relaxation of tension in Asia and the world.

President Nixon, Mrs. Nixon and the American party expressed their appreciation for the gracious hospitality shown them by the Government and people of the People's Republic of China.

VI

The Korean War

The Korean War of 1950–53, a war undeclared by Congress but supported by the president and Congress and by the United Nations, marked the first of a series of at least two informal military actions by the government of the United States. For American military and foreign policy these wars raised problems of considerable magnitude. A limited action produces questions about how war can be limited and whether one fights to preserve the *status quo ante* or improve his position. Fighting in the Far East, in areas that never before had involved the American national interest, also raised questions of diplomatic gravity. If either of the two Far Eastern wars had been of short duration and small cost the questions might have become academic, if one may use that word; but such was not to be. The Korean War probably is easier to analyze than the Vietnam War because the conflict in Korea was, by the 1970s, a generation into the past and its lessons should for that reason be more apparent.

17. Police Action

A. ATTACK AND RESPONSE

THE KOREAN WAR started suddenly, unexpectedly; the American government was hardly prepared for the news that arrived in Washington at 8:00 P.M. Saturday, June 24 (the attack began on Sunday, June 25, Korean time). The Truman administration immediately requested a meeting of the U.N. Security Council, which assembled on Sunday without its Russian member, who had been boycotting Council meetings because of the presence of the Nationalist Chinese representative. The Council passed the following resolution.

SOURCE: *American Foreign Policy: Current Documents, 1950–1955,* 2 vols. (Washington, D.C., 1957), II, pp. 2538–39.

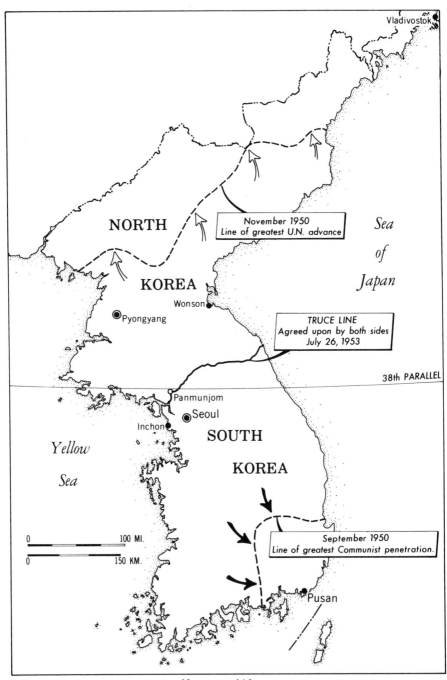

Korean War

THE SECURITY COUNCIL

Recalling the finding of the General Assembly in its resolution of 21 October 1949 that the Government of the Republic of Korea is a lawfully established government having effective control and jurisdiction over that part of Korea where the United Nations Temporary Commission on Korea was able to observe and consult and in which the great majority of the people of Korea reside; and that this Government is based on elections which were a valid expression of the free will of the electorate of that part of Korea and which were observed by the Temporary Commission; and that this is the only such government in Korea;

Mindful of the concern expressed by the General Assembly in its resolutions of 12 December 1948 and 21 October 1949 of the consequences which might follow unless Member States refrained from acts derogatory to the results sought to be achieved by the United Nations in bringing about the complete independence and unity of Korea; and the concern expressed that the situation described by the United Nations Commission on Korea in its report menaces the safety and well being of the Republic of Korea and of the people of Korea and might lead to open military conflict there;

Noting with grave concern the armed attack on the Republic of Korea by forces from North Korea,

Determines that this action constitutes a breach of the peace,

I. *Calls for* the immediate cessation of hostilities; and

Calls upon the authorities in North Korea to withdraw forthwith their armed forces to the 38th parallel;

II. *Requests* the United Nations Commission on Korea

a. To communicate its fully considered recommendations on the situation with the least possible delay.
b. To observe the withdrawal of North Korean forces to the 38th parallel, and
c. To keep the Security Council informed on the execution of this resolution;

III. *Calls upon* all Members to render every assistance to the United Nations in the execution of this resolution and to refrain from giving assistance to the North Korean authorities.

PRESIDENT TRUMAN'S STATEMENT *followed on June 27.*

In Korea, the Government forces, which were armed to prevent border raids and to preserve internal security, were attacked by

SOURCE: *American Foreign Policy: 1950–1955,* II, pp. 2539–40.

invading forces from North Korea. The Security Council of the United Nations called upon the invading troops to cease hostilities and to withdraw to the 38th Parallel. This they have not done but, on the contrary, have pressed the attack. The Security Council called upon all members of the United Nations to render every assistance to the United Nations in the execution of this resolution. In these circumstances, I have ordered United States air and sea forces to give the Korean Government troops cover and support.

The attack upon Korea makes it plain beyond all doubt that communism has passed beyond the use of subversion to conquer independent nations and will now use armed invasion and war. It has defied the orders of the Security Council of the United Nations issued to preserve international peace and security. In these circumstances, the occupation of Formosa by Communist forces would be a direct threat to the security of the Pacific area and to United States forces performing their lawful and necessary functions in that area.

Accordingly, I have ordered the Seventh Fleet to prevent any attack on Formosa. As a corollary of this action, I am calling upon the Chinese Government on Formosa to cease all air and sea operations against the mainland. The Seventh Fleet will see that this is done. The determination of the future status of Formosa must await the restoration of security in the Pacific, a peace settlement with Japan, or consideration by the United Nations.

I have also directed that United States forces in the Philippines be strengthened and that military assistance to the Philippine Government be accelerated.

I have similarly directed acceleration in the furnishing of military assistance to the forces of France and the Associated States in Indochina and the dispatch of a military mission to provide close working relations with those forces.

I know that all members of the United Nations will consider carefully the consequences of this latest aggression in Korea in defiance of the Charter of the United Nations. A return to the rule of force in international affairs would have far-reaching effects. The United States will continue to uphold the rule of law.

I have instructed Ambassador Austin, as the representative of the United States to the Security Council, to report these steps to the Council.

A SECOND SECURITY COUNCIL RESOLUTION *passed on June 27.*

The Security Council

Having determined that the armed attack upon the Republic of Korea by forces from North Korea constitutes a breach of the peace;

Having called for an immediate cessation of hostilities; and

Having called upon the authorities of North Korea to withdraw forthwith their armed forces to the 38th parallel; and

Having noted from the report of the United Nations Commission for Korea that the authorities in North Korea have neither ceased hostilities nor withdrawn their armed forces to the 38th parallel, and that urgent military measures are required to restore international peace and security; and

Having noted the appeal from the Republic of Korea to the United Nations for immediate and effective steps to secure peace and security,

Recommends that the Members of the United Nations furnish such assistance to the Republic of Korea as may be necessary to repel the armed attack and to restore international peace and security in the area.

SOURCE: *American Foreign Policy: 1950–1955*, II, pp. 2540–41.

HAVING AUTHORIZED NAVAL AND AIR SUPPORT *on June 27, Truman gave consent for ground troops on June 30, and a press release announced this fact.*

At a meeting with Congressional leaders at the White House this morning, the President, together with the Secretary of Defense, the Secretary of State, and the Joint Chiefs of Staff, reviewed the latest developments of the situation in Korea.

The Congressional leaders were given a full review of the intensified military activities.

In keeping with the United Nations Security Council's request for support to the Republic of Korea in repelling the North Korean invaders and restoring peace in Korea, the President announced that he had authorized the United States Air Force to conduct missions on specific military targets in Northern Korea, wherever militarily necessary, and had ordered a naval blockade of the entire Korean coast.

SOURCE: *American Foreign Policy: 1950–1955*, II, p. 2541.

General MacArthur has been authorized to use certain supporting ground units.

B. The Invasion of North Korea

The initial North Korean attack seemed almost irresistible and
pushed the United Nations forces—almost entirely those of the United
States—down toward the tip of the peninsula, the area surrounding the
port of Pusan. Some question arose as to whether the troops could hold
Pusan, but the port was held and was reinforced. General Douglas
MacArthur in his headquarters in Tokyo arranged a risky undertaking, a
landing at the port of Inchon high up on Korea's west coast, which was
made successfully in September. The result was the outflanking of the
North Korean forces, which were trapped in a pincer, and the North
Korean army collapsed. Apparently secure in this victory MacArthur and
the Truman administration and the members of the U.N. all believed
they were about to succeed in the first attempt to conquer a Communist
satellite. The U.N. on October 7, 1950, confidently established a commission for the unification and rehabilitation of Korea (UNCURK).
Two days later MacArthur, who had been designated U.N. commander,
issued a second call that he described as "for the last time" for all North
Korean forces to surrender. Shortly thereafter President Truman met
with MacArthur on Wake Island and received assurances that the
Chinese would not intervene and that victory was imminent. The president on October 15, announced that policy and strategy had been coor-
dinated. The United States government then took an important action
when, after the Soviet delegate to the Security Council had returned
and obviously was willing to block any further Council move with a
veto, it supported a declaration by the General Assembly concerning
policy toward Korea. The U.N. Charter specified that policy, especially
matters pertaining to international peace and security, was to be handled
by the Security Council. To take a matter of policy to the Assembly was
to set a precedent that might well, and indeed did, prove sometimes
against the interest of the American government (there was no Big
Power veto in the Assembly). The needs of the moment prevailed over
the theoretical dangers of the future, and the Assembly on November 3,
1950, passed the "uniting for peace" resolution.

The General Assembly . . .

1. Resolves that if the Security Council, because of lack of
unanimity of the permanent members, fails to exercise its primary
responsibility for the maintenance of international peace and security in any case where there appears to be a threat to the peace,

Source: American Foreign Policy: 1950–1955, I, pp. 187–92.

breach of the peace, or act of aggression, the General Assembly shall consider the matter immediately with a view to making appropriate recommendations to Members for collective measures, including in the case of a breach of the peace or act of aggression the use of armed force when necessary, to maintain or restore international peace and security. If not in session at the time, the General Assembly may meet in emergency special session within twenty-four hours of the request therefor. Such emergency special session shall be called if requested by the Security Council on the vote of any seven members, or by a majority of the Members of the United Nations.

The invasion of North Korea by U.N. forces turned into a near-debacle when on Sunday, November 26, 1950, the Chinese, having mobilized directly in front of the U.N. lines just over the border from Manchuria, made a massive assault. MacArthur found himself in deepest embarrassment, for he had predicted that the war might be finished by Christmas and had assured Truman at Wake Island that the Chinese would not intervene. He was the more embarrassed, if that were possible, because in the movement beyond the 38th parallel he had split his forces and placed X Corps in command of an officer who reported directly to Tokyo rather than to the commander of the U.S. Eighth Army, whose troops were moving northward on the west side of the peninsula. It proved necessary to evacuate X Corps by sea, with the loss of almost all its equipment. The Eighth Army moved backward to the perimeter of Pusan. Slowly the front stabilized again. After a change of commanders (General Walton Walker had been killed in a jeep accident, and General Matthew B. Ridgway took over), there began a slow, grinding operation that killed tens of thousands of Chinese and took the Eighth Army northward above Seoul to a position roughly along the 38th parallel. In the meantime MacArthur chafed at the restrictions placed upon his movements by the Truman administration, which absolutely forbade any thought of resort to atomic weapons, and became ever more outspoken. Finally, he sent a letter to a leading Republican congressman, Representative Joseph W. Martin, Jr., who read the letter to the assembled House. The letter contained the phrase "There is no substitute for victory." Since the general had sent this missive after explicitly being told that he should not communicate with anyone outside military channels, President Truman with the support of all the joint chiefs of staff and of Secretary of Defense Marshall relieved MacArthur and replaced him with Ridgway.

18. Uneasy Settlement

A. The Armistice

THE WAR continued until the armistice of July 27, 1953. The military situation had stabilized by the spring of 1951, when U.N. forces retook Seoul for the second time and pushed north until in some places they had crossed a short way above the 38th parallel. For more than two years the North Korean regime conducted truce talks, mostly in a place named Panmunjom. The talks did not get too far, although at least there was only minor fighting while the two sides were conferring. The Korean War became a major issue in the 1952 U.S. presidential campaign, and General Eisenhower as the Republican candidate announced during a speech in Detroit that if chosen for the presidency he would "go to Korea." After making a reconnaissance and after becoming president, he permitted Secretary of State Dulles to communicate indirectly to the Chinese Communists, whom Eisenhower and Dulles both suspected of encouraging the North Koreans to intransigence at the truce talks, that if the Korean War did not come swiftly to an end it might prove necessary to extend the conflict and perhaps employ atomic weapons, presumably against China. The negotiations quickly moved to a conclusion, and the armistice of July, 1953, has continued to the present day.

The undersigned, the Commander-in-Chief, United Nations Command, on the one hand, and the Supreme Commander of the Korean People's Army and the Commander of the Chinese People's Volunteers, on the other hand, in the interest of stopping the Korean conflict, with its great toll of suffering and bloodshed on both sides, and with the objective of establishing an armistice which will insure a complete cessation of hostilities and of all acts of armed force in Korea until a final peaceful settlement is achieved, do individually, collectively, and mutually agree to accept and to be bound and governed by the conditions and terms of armistice set forth in the following Articles and Paragraphs, which said conditions and terms are intended to be purely military in character and to pertain solely to the belligerents in Korea.

SOURCE: *American Foreign Policy: 1950–1955*, I, pp. 724–43.

Article I. Military Demarcation Line and Demilitarized Zone

1. A Military Demarcation Line shall be fixed and both sides shall withdraw two (2) kilometers from this line so as to establish a Demilitarized Zone between the opposing forces. A Demilitarized Zone shall be established as a buffer zone to prevent the occurrence of incidents which might lead to a resumption of hostilities. . . .

6. Neither side shall execute any hostile act within, from, or against the Demilitarized Zone.

7. No person, military or civilian, shall be permitted to cross the Military Demarcation Line unless specifically authorized to do so by the Military Armistice Commission.

8. No person, military or civilian, in the Demilitarized Zone shall be permitted to enter the territory under the military control of either side unless specifically authorized to do so by the Commander into whose territory entry is sought.

9. No person, military or civilian, shall be permitted to enter the Demilitarized Zone except persons concerned with the conduct of civil administration and relief and persons specifically authorized to enter by the Military Armistice Commission. . . .

Article II. Concrete Arrangements for Cease-fire and Armistice

A. General

12. The Commanders of the opposing sides shall order and enforce a complete cessation of all hostilities in Korea by all armed forces under their control, including all units and personnel of the ground, naval, and air forces, effective twelve (12) hours after this Armistice Agreement is signed. . . .

Article III. Arrangements Relating to Prisoners of War

51. The release and repatriation of all prisoners of war held in the custody of each side at the time this Armistice Agreement becomes effective shall be effected in conformity with the following provisions agreed upon by both sides prior to the signing of this Armistice Agreement.

a. Within sixty (60) days after this Armistice Agreement becomes effective, each side shall, without offering any hindrance, directly repatriate and hand over in groups all those prisoners of war in its custody who insist on repatriation to the side to which they belonged at the time of capture. Repatriation shall be accomplished in accordance with the related provisions of this Article. In order to expedite the repatriation process of such personnel, each side shall, prior to the signing of the Armistice Agreement, exchange the total numbers, by nationalities, of personnel to be directly repatriated. Each group of prisoners of war delivered to the other side shall be accompanied by rosters, prepared by nationality, to include name, rank (if any) and internment or military serial number.

b. Each side shall release all those remaining prisoners of war, who are not directly repatriated, from its military control and from its custody and hand them over to the Neutral Nations Repatriation Commission for disposition in accordance with the provisions in the Annex hereto: "Terms of Reference for Neutral Nations Repatriation Commission." . . .

B. The U.S.–Korean Alliance

IT WAS DIFFICULT for American forces to leave Korea until a final peace settlement was reached or at least until South Korean forces were trained to take over positions along the armistice line. The logical outcome of this situation was an alliance signed on October 1, 1953.

The Parties to this Treaty,

Reaffirming their desire to live in peace with all peoples and all governments, and desiring to strengthen the fabric of peace in the Pacific area,

Desiring to declare publicly and formally their common determination to defend themselves against external armed attacks so that no potential aggressor could be under the illusion that either of them stands alone in the Pacific area,

Desiring further to strengthen their efforts for collective defense for the preservation of peace and security pending the development of a more comprehensive and effective system of regional security in the Pacific area,

Have agreed as follows:

SOURCE: *United States Treaties and Other International Agreements: 1954*, pt. 3 (Washington, D.C., 1956), pp. 2368–76.

Article I

The Parties undertake to settle any international disputes in which they may be involved by peaceful means in such a manner that international peace and security and justice are not endangered and to refrain in their international relations from the threat or use of force in any manner inconsistent with the Purposes of the United Nations, or obligations assumed by any Party toward the United Nations.

Article II

The Parties will consult together whenever, in the opinion of either of them, the political independence or security of either of the Parties is threatened by external armed attack. Separately and jointly, by self help and mutual aid, the Parties will maintain and develop appropriate means to deter armed attack and will take suitable measures in consultation and agreement to implement this Treaty and to further its purposes.

Article III

Each Party recognizes that an armed attack in the Pacific area on either of the Parties in territories now under their respective administrative control, or hereafter recognized by one of the Parties as lawfully brought under the administrative control of the other, would be dangerous to its own peace and safety and declares that it would act to meet the common danger in accordance with its constitutional processes.

Article IV

The Republic of Korea grants, and the United States of America accepts, the right to dispose United States land, air and sea forces in and about the territory of the Republic of Korea as determined by mutual agreement.

In ADVISING RATIFICATION on January 26, 1954, the Senate placed the following understanding upon the treaty, to which the Korean government agreed.

SOURCE: *U.S. Treaties, 1954, pt. 3, pp. 2375–76.*

It is the understanding of the United States that neither party is obligated, under Article III of the above Treaty, to come to the aid of the other except in case of an external armed attack against such party; nor shall anything in the present Treaty be construed as requiring the United States to give assistance to Korea except in the event of an armed attack against territory which has been recognized by the United States as lawfully brought under the administrative control of the Republic of Korea.

The treaty entered into force on November 17, 1954.

VII

The Western Pacific

Because of the Open Door notes at the turn of the twentieth century and the gradual involvement of the United States in the contentions with Japan that led to Pearl Harbor, most Americans have had the impression that the policy of their government has been marked by serious participation in Far Eastern affairs for many, many years. Actually, however, this has not been so. Intense involvement with the affairs of the Western Pacific has been essentially a phenomenon of the years after 1945. In the future, when Americans come to understand what has happened, the manner in which their country's power has flowed into this area surely will seem one of the major changes in American foreign relations.

19. Japan

A. The Postsurrender Policy

AT THE END OF THE PACIFIC WAR IN 1945, *United States troops occupied Tokyo—an incredible situation, had one thought about it in, say, 1941, before the nation was shoved into war. But by 1945 the enormous growth of American military power had made American physical presence in Japan seem natural. With considerable assurance the government drew up its initial policy concerning postwar Japan. The Department of State, the War Department, and the Navy Department prepared a policy statement that the president approved on September 6, 1945.*

SOURCE: *A Decade of American Foreign Policy: Basic Documents, 1941–1949* (Washington, D.C., 1950), pp. 627–33.

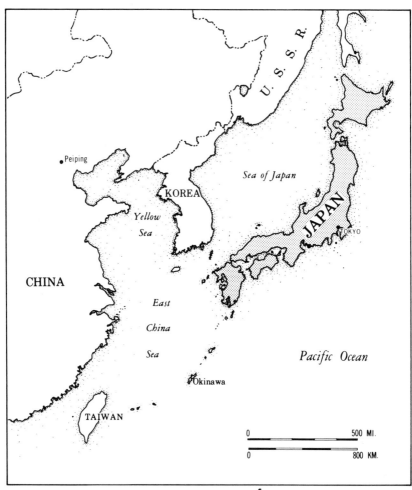

Peiping

KOREA

Sea of Japan

Yellow
Sea

CHINA

JAPAN

TOKYO

East

China

Sea

Pacific Ocean

Okinawa

TAIWAN

U. S. S. R.

| 0 | 500 MI. |
| 0 | 800 KM. |

Strategic Position of Japan

Part II. Allied Authority

1. MILITARY OCCUPATION

There will be a military occupation of the Japanese home islands to carry into effect the surrender terms and further the achievement of the ultimate objectives stated above. The occupation shall have the character of an operation in behalf of the principal allied powers acting in the interests of the United Nations at war with Japan. For that reason, participation of the forces of other nations that have taken a leading part in the war against Japan will be welcomed and expected. The occupation forces will be under the command of a Supreme Commander designated by the United States.

Although every effort will be made, by consultation and by constitution of appropriate advisory bodies, to establish policies for the conduct of the occupation and the control of Japan which will satisfy the principal Allied powers, in the event of any differences of opinion among them, the policies of the United States will govern.

2. RELATIONSHIP TO JAPANESE GOVERNMENT

The authority of the Emperor and the Japanese Government will be subject to the Supreme Commander, who will possess all powers necessary to effectuate the surrender terms and to carry out the policies established for the conduct of the occupation and the control of Japan. . . .

3. PUBLICITY AS TO POLICIES

The Japanese people, and the world at large, shall be kept fully informed of the objectives and policies of the occupation, and of progress made in their fulfilment.

Part III. Political

1. DISARMAMENT AND DEMILITARIZATION

Disarmament and demilitarization are the primary tasks of the military occupation and shall be carried out promptly and with determination. Every effort shall be made to bring home to the Japanese people the part played by the military and naval leaders, and those who collaborated with them, in bringing about the existing and future distress of the people.

Japan is not to have an army, navy, air force, secret police organization, or any civil aviation. . . .

2. WAR CRIMINALS

Persons charged by the Supreme Commander or appropriate United Nations Agencies with being war criminals, including those charged with having visited cruelties upon United Nations prisoners or other nationals, shall be arrested, tried and, if convicted, punished. Those wanted by another of the United Nations for offenses against its nationals, shall, if not wanted for trial or as witnesses or otherwise by the Supreme Commander, be turned over to the custody of such other nation.

· 3. ENCOURAGEMENT OF DESIRE FOR INDIVIDUAL LIBERTIES AND DEMOCRATIC PROCESSES

Freedom of religious worship shall be proclaimed promptly on occupation. At the same time it should be made plain to the Japanese that ultra-nationalistic and militaristic organizations and movements will not be permitted to hide behind the cloak of religion.

The Japanese people shall be afforded opportunity and encouraged to become familiar with the history, institutions, culture, and the accomplishments of the United States and the other democracies. Association of personnel of the occupation forces with the Japanese population should be controlled, only to the extent necessary, to further the policies and objectives of the occupation.

Democratic political parties, with rights of assembly and public discussion, shall be encouraged, subject to the necessity for maintaining the security of the occupying forces.

Laws, decrees and regulations which establish discriminations on grounds of race, nationality, creed or political opinion shall be abrogated. . . .

Part IV.   Economic

1. ECONOMIC DEMILITARIZATION

The existing economic basis of Japanese military strength must be destroyed and not be permitted to revive. . . .

2. PROMOTION OF DEMOCRATIC FORCES

Encouragement shall be given and favor shown to the development of organizations in labor, industry, and agriculture, organized on a democratic basis. Policies shall be favored which permit a wide distribution of income and of the ownership of the means of production and trade.

Those forms of economic activity, organization and leadership shall be favored that are deemed likely to strengthen the peaceful disposition of the Japanese people, and to make it difficult to command or direct economic activity in support of military ends.

To this end it shall be the policy of the Supreme Commander:

a. To prohibit the retention in or selection for places of importance in the economic field of individuals who do not direct future Japanese economic effort solely toward peaceful ends; and

b. To favor a program for the dissolution of the large industrial and banking combinations which have exercised control of a great part of Japan's trade and industry.

4. REPARATIONS AND RESTITUTION

Reparations

Reparations for Japanese aggression shall be made:

a. Through the transfer—as may be determined by the appropriate Allied authorities—of Japanese property located outside of the territories to be retained by Japan.

b. Through the transfer of such goods or existing capital equipment and facilities as are not necessary for a peaceful Japanese economy or the supplying of the occupying forces. Exports other than those directed to be shipped on reparation account or as restitution may be made only to those recipients who agree to provide necessary imports in exchange or agree to pay for such exports in foreign exchange. No form of reparation shall be exacted which will interfere with or prejudice the program for Japan's demilitarization. . . .

Restitution

Full and prompt restitution will be required of all identifiable looted property.

5. FISCAL, MONETARY, AND BANKING POLICIES

The Japanese authorities will remain responsible for the management and direction of the domestic fiscal, monetary, and credit policies subject to the approval and review of the Supreme Commander.

6. INTERNATIONAL TRADE AND FINANCIAL RELATIONS

Japan shall be permitted eventually to resume normal trade relations with the rest of the world. . . .

B. THE PEACE TREATY

SHORTLY AFTER THE COLD WAR *began between the United States and the Soviet Union the State Department took up the business of a Japanese peace treaty. The initial policies of the occupation seemed to have been accomplished, and a continued occupation was proving inconvenient with the situation in Europe becoming so uncertain. The*

Truman administration early in 1949 carefully gave the task of drawing up a treaty to John Foster Dulles, a well-known Republican, who they hoped could keep the issue bipartisan. Republican political leaders were raising questions over China policy, and it seemed desirable to keep Japanese affairs away from partisanship. General MacArthur's personal politics were considered Republican, and until 1949 his presence in Tokyo had tended to deter Republican critics; to assign Dulles to the negotiations of the peace treaty was apparently a wise move. Dulles took up his task with enthusiasm. He found an enormous draft of a peace treaty in the files of the State Department, an instrument that might prove at least as involved as the Versailles treaty with Germany following the First World War (the Treaty of Versailles contained over 400 articles and was as large as a book). He decided to keep the Japanese treaty simple and also undertook to arrange its details in advance with all of the interested nations, which he did in a series of diplomatic visits and consultations. When finally the Japanese Peace Conference met at San Francisco in 1951, the treaty's success was assured. Soviet representatives were in attendance but refused to sign the treaty when it was opened for signature on September 8, eventually making their own arrangements with the Japanese government. The treaty entered into force on April 28, 1952.

Article I

a. The state of war between Japan and each of the Allied Powers is terminated as from the date on which the present Treaty comes into force between Japan and the Allied Power concerned as provided for in Article 23.

b. The Allied Powers recognize the full sovereignty of the Japanese people over Japan and its territorial waters.

Article 2

a. Japan, recognizing the independence of Korea, renounces all right, title and claim to Korea, including the islands of Quelpart, Port Hamilton and Dagelet.

b. Japan renounces all right, title and claim to Formosa and the Pescadores.

c. Japan renounces all right, title and claim to the Kurile Islands, and to that portion of Sakhalin and the islands adjacent to it over which Japan acquired sovereignty as a consequence of the Treaty of Portsmouth of September 5, 1905.

Source: *United States Treaties and Other International Agreements: 1952*, pt. 3 (Washington, D.C., 1955), pp. 3169–3191.

d. Japan renounces all right, title and claim in connection with the League of Nations Mandate System, and accepts the action of the United Nations Security Council of April 2, 1947, extending the trusteeship system to the Pacific Islands formerly under mandate to Japan.

e. Japan renounces all claim to any right or title to or interest in connection with any part of the Antarctic area, whether deriving from the activities of Japanese nationals or otherwise.

f. Japan renounces all right, title and claim to the Spratly Islands and to the Paracel Islands.

Article 3

Japan will concur in any proposal of the United States to the United Nations to place under its trusteeship system, with the United States as the sole administering authority, Nansei Shoto south of 29° north latitude (including the Ryukyu Islands and the Daito Islands), Nanpo Shoto south of Sofu Gan (including the Bonin Islands, Rosario Island and the Volcano Islands) and Parece Vela and Marcus Island. Pending the making of such a proposal and affirmative action thereon, the United States will have the right to exercise all and any powers of administration, legislation and jurisdiction over the territory and inhabitants of these islands, including their territorial waters.

Article 5

. . . c. The Allied Powers for their part recognize that Japan as a sovereign nation possesses the inherent right of individual or collective self-defense referred to in Article 51 of the Charter of the United Nations and that Japan may voluntarily enter into collective security arrangements.

Article 6

a. All occupation forces of the Allied Powers shall be withdrawn from Japan as soon as possible after the coming into force of the present Treaty, and in any case not later than 90 days thereafter. Nothing in this provision shall, however, prevent the stationing or retention of foreign armed forces in Japanese territory under or in consequence of any bilateral or multilateral agreements which have been or may be made between one or more of the Allied Powers, on the one hand, and Japan on the other.

b. The provisions of Article 9 of the Potsdam Proclamation of July 26, 1945, dealing with the return of Japanese military forces to their homes, to the extent not already completed, will be carried out. . . .

Article 9

Japan will enter promptly into negotiations with the Allied Powers so desiring for the conclusion of bilateral and multilateral agreements providing for the regulation or limitation of fishing and the conservation and development of fisheries on the high seas.

Article 10

Japan renounces all special rights and interests in China, including all benefits and privileges resulting from the provisions of the final Protocol signed at Peking on September 7, 1901, and all annexes, notes and documents supplementary thereto, and agrees to the abrogation in respect to Japan of the said protocol, annexes, notes and documents.

Article 11

Japan accepts the judgments of the International Military Tribunal for the Far East and of other Allied War Crimes Courts both within and outside Japan, and will carry out the sentences imposed thereby upon Japanese nationals imprisoned in Japan. The power to grant clemency, to reduce sentences and to parole with respect to such prisoners may not be exercised except on the decision of the Government or Governments which imposed the sentence in each instance, and on the recommendation of Japan. In the case of persons sentenced by the International Military Tribunal for the Far East, such power may not be exercised except on the decision of a majority of the Governments represented on the Tribunal, and on the recommendation of Japan.

Article 14

a. It is recognized that Japan should pay reparations to the Allied Powers for the damage and suffering caused by it during the war.

Nevertheless it is also recognized that the resources of Japan are not presently sufficient, if it is to maintain a viable economy, to make complete reparation for all such damage and suffering and at the same time meet its other obligations. . . .

Article 23

a. The present Treaty shall be ratified by the States which sign it, including Japan, and will come into force for all the States which have then ratified it, when instruments of ratification have been deposited by Japan and by a majority, including the United States of America as the principal occupying Power, of the following States, namely Australia, Canada, Ceylon, France, Indonesia, the Kingdom of the Netherlands, New Zealand, Pakistan, the Republic of the Philippines, the United Kingdom of Great Britain and Northern Ireland, and the United States of America. The present Treaty shall come into force for each State which subsequently ratifies it, on the date of the deposit of its instrument of ratification.

b. If the Treaty has not come into force within nine months after the date of the deposit of Japan's ratification, any State which has ratified it may bring the Treaty into force between itself and Japan by a notification to that effect given to the Governments of Japan and the United States of America not later than three years after the date of deposit of Japan's ratification.

Article 26

Japan will be prepared to conclude with any State which signed or adhered to the United Nations Declaration of January 1, 1942, and which is at war with Japan, or with any State which previously formed a part of the territory of a State named in Article 23, which is not a signatory of the present Treaty, a bilateral Treaty of Peace on the same or substantially the same terms as are provided for in the present Treaty, but this obligation on the part of Japan will expire three years after the first coming into force of the present Treaty. Should Japan make a peace settlement or war claims settlement with any State granting that State greater advantages than those provided by the present Treaty, those same advantages shall be extended to the parties to the present Treaty.

YEARS LATER the Nixon administration arranged a treaty on June 17, 1971, giving Okinawa back to Japan. The treaty was signed in a novel fashion, in Tokyo and Washington, by Foreign Minister Kiichi Aichi and Secretary of State William P. Rogers, the televised signings in the two faraway capitals being broadcast by satellite under arrangement with the International Telecommunications Satellite Organization, IN-TELSAT (agreements for which were concluded in May, 1971, replacing interim arrangements negotiated in 1964). It entered into force in 1972.

Article I

1. With respect to the Ryukyu Islands and the Daito Islands, as defined in paragraph 2 below, the United States of America relinquishes in favor of Japan all rights and interests under Article 3 of the Treaty of Peace with Japan signed at the city of San Francisco on September 8, 1951, effective as of the date of entry into force of this Agreement. Japan, as of such date, assumes full responsibility and authority for the exercise of all and any powers of administration, legislation and jurisdiction over the territory and inhabitants of the said islands.

2. For the purpose of this Agreement, the term "the Ryukyu Islands and the Daito Islands" means all the territories and their territorial waters with respect to which the right to exercise all and any powers of administration, legislation and jurisdiction was accorded to the United States of America under Article 3 of the Treaty of Peace with Japan other than those with respect to which such right has already been returned to Japan in accordance with the Agreement concerning the Amami Islands and the Agreement concerning Nanpo Shoto and other islands signed between Japan and the United States of America respectively on December 24, 1953, and April 5, 1968.

Article II

It is confirmed that treaties, conventions and other agreements concluded between Japan and the United States of America, including, but without limitation, the Treaty of Mutual Cooperation and Security between Japan and the United States of America signed at Washington on January 19, 1960, and its related arrangements and the Treaty of Friendship, Commerce and Navigation

SOURCE: Department of State *Bulletin*, July 12, 1971, pp. 35–40.

between Japan and the United States of America signed at Tokyo on April 2, 1953, become applicable to the Ryukyu Islands and the Daito Islands as of the date of entry into force of this Agreement.

Article III

1. Japan will grant the United States of America on the date of entry into force of this Agreement the use of facilities and areas in the Ryukyu Islands and the Daito Islands in accordance with the Treaty of Mutual Cooperation and Security between Japan and the United States of America signed at Washington on January 19, 1960, and its related arrangements. . . .

Article IV

1. Japan waives all claims of Japan and its nationals against the United States of America and its nationals and against the local authorities of the Ryukyu Islands and the Daito Islands, arising from the presence, operations or actions of forces or authorities of the United States of America in these islands, or from the presence, operations or actions of forces or authorities of the United States of America having had any effect upon these islands, prior to the date of entry into force of this Agreement. . . .

Article VI

1. The properties of the Ryukyu Electric Power Corporation, the Ryukyu Domestic Water Corporation and the Ryukyu Development Loan Corporation shall be transferred to the Government of Japan on the date of entry into force of this Agreement, and the rights and obligations of the said Corporations shall be assumed by the Government of Japan on that date in conformity with the laws and regulations of Japan. . . .

Article VII

Considering, inter alia, that United States assets are being transferred to the Government of Japan under Article VI of this Agreement, that the Government of the United States of America is carrying out the return of the Ryukyu Islands and the Daito Islands to Japan in a manner consistent with the policy of the Government of Japan . . . and that the Government of the United States of America will bear extra costs, particularly in the area of employment after reversion, the Government of Japan will pay to the Government of the United States of America in United States dollars a total amount of three hundred and twenty million United States dollars (U.S. $320,000,000) over a period of five years from the date of entry into force of this Agreement. Of the said amount, the Government of Japan will pay one hundred million United States dollars (U.S. $100,000,000) within one week after the date of entry into force of this Agreement and the remainder in four equal annual installments in June of each calendar year subsequent to the year in which this Agreement enters into force.

Article VIII

The Government of Japan consents to the continued operation by the Government of the United States of America of the Voice of America relay station in Okinawa Island for a period of five years from the date of entry into force of this Agreement in accordance with the arrangements to be concluded between the two Governments. The two Governments shall enter into consultation two years after the date of entry into force of this Agreement on future operation of the Voice of America in Okinawa Island.

20. Securing the Western Pacific

IT WAS ONE THING to make a peace treaty with Japan, hold a peace conference, and sign an instrument, but another to convince the nations of the Western Pacific that the pledges of that treaty made them safe from a revival of Japanese imperialism. During his flying trips to the capitals of states interested in the peace treaty Dulles discovered that only special security arrangements—bilateral alliances with the United States—would ensure the success of the peace conference. Such alliances would have been inconceivable in the years before the Second World War, but after conclusion of the North Atlantic Treaty in 1949 they became fairly easy to have approved by the Senate.

A. THE U.S.–PHILIPPINE ALLIANCE

ACCORDING TO THE INTERPRETATION of some historians, it was the proximity of the Philippine Islands to the Japanese Islands that involved the United States in Far Eastern political problems after the turn of the

SOURCE: *U.S. Treaties, 1952, pt. 3, pp. 3947–51.*

twentieth century. Whatever the truth of this theory, it was certainly true that the Filipinos in 1945 were extremely sensitive to future dangers from Japan. It was a precondition for signing the Japanese peace treaty by the government of the Philippines that the United States sign bilateral alliance, which was dated August 30, 1951, a few days before the San Francisco peace conference.

The Parties to this Treaty,

Reaffirming their faith in the purposes and principles of the Charter of the United Nations and their desire to live in peace with all peoples and all Governments, and desiring to strengthen the fabric of peace in the Pacific Area,

Recalling with mutual pride the historic relationship which brought their two peoples together in a common bond of sympathy and mutual ideals to fight side-by-side against imperialist aggression during the last war,

Desiring to declare publicly and formally their sense of unity and their common determination to defend themselves against external armed attack, so that no potential aggressor could be under the illusion that either of them stands alone in the Pacific Area,

Desiring further to strengthen their present efforts for collective defense for the preservation of peace and security pending the development of a more comprehensive system of regional security in the Pacific Area,

Agreeing that nothing in this present instrument shall be considered or interpreted as in any way or sense altering or diminishing any existing agreements or understandings between the United States of America and the Republic of the Philippines,

Have agreed as follows:

Article I

The Parties undertake, as set forth in the Charter of the United Nations, to settle any international disputes in which they may be involved by peaceful means in such a manner that international peace and security and justice are not endangered and to refrain in their international relations from the threat or use of force in any manner inconsistent with the purposes of the United Nations.

Article II

In order more effectively to achieve the objective of this Treaty, the Parties separately and jointly by self-help and mutual aid will maintain and develop their individual and collective capacity to resist armed attack.

Article III

The Parties, through their Foreign Ministers or their deputies, will consult together from time to time regarding the implementation of this Treaty and whenever in the opinion of either of them the territorial integrity, political independence or security of either of the Parties is threatened by external armed attack in the Pacific.

Article IV

Each Party recognizes that an armed attack in the Pacific Area on either of the Parties would be dangerous to its own peace and safety and declares that it would act to meet the common dangers in accordance with its constitutional processes.

Any such armed attack and all measures taken as a result thereof shall be immediately reported to the Security Council of the United Nations. Such measures shall be terminated when the Security Council has taken the measures necessary to restore and maintain international peace and security.

Article V

For the purpose of Article IV, an armed attack on either of the Parties is deemed to include an armed attack on the metropolitan territory of either of the Parties, or on the island territories under its jurisdiction in the Pacific or on its armed forces, public vessels or aircraft in the Pacific.

Article VI

This Treaty does not affect and shall not be interpreted as affecting in any way the rights and obligations of the Parties under the Charter of the United Nations or the responsibility of the United Nations for the maintenance of international peace and security.

The State Department in 1969 informed a subcommittee of the Senate Foreign Relations Committee of an interesting—constitutionally as well as diplomatically—change in the vital Article IV of the Philippine alliance. In its original form, the text given above, this article had related that the United States would help the Philippines only "in accordance with its constitutional processes." The SEATO treaty in 1954 (see pp. 152–56) contained the same formula. But in 1954, in order to help persuade the Philippines to sign the SEATO treaty, Secretary Dulles agreed to a new formula for the 1951 alliance, a pledge that an attack on the Philippines would be "instantly repelled." In joint communiqués with Philippine leaders, President Eisenhower in 1958, then President Johnson in 1964, publicly used the "instantly repel" language, but few individuals in the United States noticed the change until this executive arrangement was publicized during the hearings of 1969. See 91st Cong., Hearings before the Subcommittee on US Security Agreements and Commitments Abroad of the Committee on Foreign Relations, 11 pts. (Washington, D.C., 1969–1970), pt. 1, pp. 5–41.

B. ANZUS

By the time of American entrance into the Second World War it had become evident that Australia and New Zealand, although members of the British Commonwealth, could expect little protection against Japanese imperialism from the British government in faraway London and that any serious security arrangements in the Western Pacific had to involve American forces. During the progress of the Pacific war the contribution of the British government was nominal, the major forces against the Japanese being American. In the postwar years the clearly American nature of security in the Western Pacific was unquestioned by the governments of Australia and New Zealand. The Japanese peace conference provided an occasion for a firm American commitment, the "Anzus" treaty of alliance between Australia, New Zealand, and the United States, signed in San Francisco on September 1, 1951, three days before the peace conference opened.

The Parties to This Treaty,

Reaffirming their faith in the purposes and principles of the Charter of the United Nations and their desire to live in peace with all peoples and all Governments, and desiring to strengthen the fabric of peace in the Pacific Area,

Noting that the United States already has arrangements pursuant to which its armed forces are stationed in the Philippines, and has armed forces and administrative responsibilities in the Ryukyus, and upon the coming into force of the Japanese Peace Treaty may also station armed forces in and about Japan to assist in the preservation of peace and security in the Japan Area,

Recognizing that Australia and New Zealand as members of the

SOURCE: *U.S. Treaties*, 1952, pt. 3, pp. 3420–25.

British Commonwealth of Nations have military obligations outside as well as within the Pacific Area,

Desiring to declare publicly and formally their sense of unity, so that no potential aggressor could be under the illusion that any of them stand alone in the Pacific Area, and

Desiring further to coordinate their efforts for collective defense for the preservation of peace and security pending the development of a more comprehensive system of regional security in the Pacific Area,

Therefore declare and agree as follows:

Article I

The Parties undertake, as set forth in the Charter of the United Nations, to settle any international disputes in which they may be involved by peaceful means in such a manner that international peace and security and justice are not endangered and to refrain in their international relations from the threat or use of force in any manner inconsistent with the purposes of the United Nations.

Article II

In order more effectively to achieve the objective of this Treaty the Parties separately and jointly by means of continuous and effective self-help and mutual aid will maintain and develop their individual and collective capacity to resist armed attack.

Article III

The Parties will consult together whenever in the opinion of any of them the territorial integrity, political independence or security of any of the Parties is threatened in the Pacific.

Article IV

Each Party recognizes that an armed attack in the Pacific Area on any of the Parties would be dangerous to its own peace and safety and declares that it would act to meet the common danger in accordance with its constitutional processes.

Any such armed attack and all measures taken as a result thereof shall be immediately reported to the Security Council of the United Nations. Such measures shall be terminated when the

Security Council has taken the measures necessary to restore and maintain international peace and security.

Article V

For the purpose of Article IV, an armed attack on any of the Parties is deemed to include an armed attack on the metropolitan territory of any of the Parties, or on the island territories under its jurisdiction in the Pacific or on its armed forces, public vessels or aircraft in the Pacific.

Article VI

This Treaty does not affect and shall not be interpreted as affecting in any way the rights and obligations of the Parties under the Charter of the United Nations or the responsibility of the United Nations for the maintenance of international peace and security.

Article VII

The Parties hereby establish a Council, consisting of their Foreign Ministers or their Deputies, to consider matters concerning the implementation of this Treaty. The Council should be so organized as to be able to meet at any time.

Article VIII

Pending the development of a more comprehensive system of regional security in the Pacific Area and the development by the United Nations of more effective means to maintain international peace and security, the Council, established by Article VII, is authorized to maintain a consultative relationship with States, Regional Organizations, Associations of States or other authorities in the Pacific Area in a position to further the purposes of this Treaty and to contribute to the security of that Area.

C. The U.S.–Japanese Alliance

DULLES ALSO ARRANGED an alliance with Japan, signed September 8, 1951, the same day as the peace treaty. For this instrument see United States Treaties and Other International Agreements: 1952, pt. 3, pp.

SOURCE: United States Treaties and Other International Agreements: 1960, pt. 2 (Washington, D.C., 1961), pp. 1633–35.

3329–33. On January 19, 1960, the two nations signed a new treaty reflecting the increased stature of Japan; the governments now dealt with each other on a basis of virtual equality.

The United States of America and Japan,

Desiring to strengthen the bonds of peace and friendship traditionally existing between them, and to uphold the principles of democracy, individual liberty, and the rule of law,

Desiring further to encourage closer economic cooperation between them and to promote conditions of economic stability and well-being in their countries,

Reaffirming their faith in the purposes and principles of the Charter of the United Nations, and their desire to live in peace with all peoples and all governments,

Recognizing that they have the inherent right of individual or collective self-defense as affirmed in the Charter of the United Nations,

Considering that they have a common concern in the maintenance of international peace and security in the Far East,

Having resolved to conclude a treaty of mutual cooperation and security,

Therefore agree as follows:

Article I

The Parties undertake, as set forth in the Charter of the United Nations, to settle any international disputes in which they may be involved by peaceful means in such a manner that international peace and security and justice are not endangered and to refrain in their international relations from the threat or use of force against the territorial integrity or political independence of any state, or in any other manner inconsistent with the purposes of the United Nations.

The Parties will endeavor in concert with other peace-loving countries to strengthen the United Nations so that its mission of maintaining international peace and security may be discharged more effectively.

Article II

The Parties will contribute toward the further development of peaceful and friendly international relations by strengthening their free institutions, by bringing about a better understanding of the principles upon which these institutions are founded, and by promoting conditions of stability and well-being. They will seek to eliminate conflict in their international economic policies and will encourage economic collaboration between them.

Article III

The Parties, individually and in cooperation with each other, by means of continuous and effective self-help and mutual aid will maintain and develop, subject to their constitutional provisions, their capacities to resist armed attack.

Article IV

The Parties will consult together from time to time regarding the implementation of this Treaty, and, at the request of either Party, whenever the security of Japan or international peace and security in the Far East is threatened.

Article V

Each Party recognizes that an armed attack against either Party in the territories under the administration of Japan would be dangerous to its own peace and safety and declares that it would act to meet the common danger in accordance with its constitutional provisions and processes.

Any such armed attack and all measures taken as a result thereof shall be immediately reported to the Security Council of the United Nations in accordance with the provisions of Article 51 of the Charter. Such measures shall be terminated when the Security Council has taken the measures necessary to restore and maintain international peace and security.

Article VI

For the purpose of contributing to the security of Japan and the maintenance of international peace and security in the Far East, the United States of America is granted the use by its land, air and naval forces of facilities and areas in Japan. . . .

21. SEATO

As SPECIAL AMBASSADOR during the last years of the Truman administration, Dulles arranged the alliances with the Philippines, Australia and New Zealand, and Japan, all of which were connected with the Japanese peace treaty. It may well be that this experience with a series of treaties covering a region of the world convinced him that a multilateral engagement complementing the Rio Pact for the Western Hemisphere (see pp. 212–17) and the North Atlantic Treaty would be in the interest of the United States government. He also realized that the alliances negotiated for the Japanese peace conference said nothing about Southeast Asia, which was close to Japan and impinged upon Japanese problems. The Korean War emphasized the importance of the littoral of Asia. Most important to Dulles's calculations was the Geneva Conference of 1954, which, nominally called to discuss Korean problems, turned to consideration of the war between France and the Vietminh, under the leadership of Ho Chi Minh. (For U.S. participation in the conference see pp. 243–47.) After the Geneva Conference it seemed desirable to organize a security treaty for Southeast Asia, which Secretary of State Dulles accomplished within a few weeks, signing the Southeast Asia Collective Defense Treaty and attached protocol at Manila on September 8, 1954, the third anniversary of the signing of the Japanese peace treaty. Also signing were representatives of Britain, France, Australia, New Zealand, the Philippines, Pakistan, and Thailand.

Dulles would have preferred to have the Manila treaty known by the acronym MANPAC, for Manila Pact, but the analogy with the North Atlantic Treaty proved irresistible, even to inclusion of the final "O" that was euphonically necessary.

The Parties to this Treaty,

Recognizing the sovereign equality of all the Parties,

Reiterating their faith in the purposes and principles set forth in the Charter of the United Nations and their desire to live in peace with all peoples and all governments,

Reaffirming that, in accordance with the Charter of the United Nations, they uphold the principle of equal rights and self-determina-

SOURCE: *United States Treaties and Other International Agreements: 1955*, pt. 1 (Washington, D.C., 1956), pp. 81–87.

tion of peoples, and declaring that they will earnestly strive by every peaceful means to promote self-government and to secure the independence of all countries whose peoples desire it and are able to undertake its responsibilities,

Desiring to strengthen the fabric of peace and freedom and to uphold the principles of democracy, individual liberty and the rule of law, and to promote the economic well-being and development of all peoples in the treaty area,

Intending to declare publicly and formally their sense of unity, so that any potential aggressor will appreciate that the Parties stand together in the area, and

Desiring further to coordinate their efforts for collective defense for the preservation of peace and security,

Therefore agree as follows:

Article I

The Parties undertake, as set forth in the Charter of the United Nations, to settle any international disputes in which they may be involved by peaceful means in such a manner that international peace and security and justice are not endangered, and to refrain in their international relations from the threat or use of force in any manner inconsistent with the purposes of the United Nations.

Article II

In order more effectively to achieve the objectives of this Treaty, the Parties, separately and jointly, by means of continuous and effective self-help and mutual aid will maintain and develop their individual and collective capacity to resist armed attack and to prevent and counter subversive activities directed from without against their territorial integrity and political stability.

Article III

The Parties undertake to strengthen their free institutions and to cooperate with one another in the further development of economic measures, including technical assistance, designed both to promote economic progress and social well-being and to further the individual and collective efforts of governments toward these ends.

Article IV

1. Each Party recognizes that aggression by means of armed attack in the treaty area against any of the Parties or against any State or territory which the Parties by unanimous agreement may hereafter designate, would endanger its own peace and safety, and agrees that it will in that event act to meet the common danger in accordance with its constitutional processes. Measures taken under this paragraph shall be immediately reported to the Security Council of the United Nations.

2. If, in the opinion of any of the Parties, the inviolability or the integrity of the territory or the sovereignty or political independence of any Party in the treaty area or of any other State or territory to which the provisions of paragraph 1 of this Article from time to time apply is threatened in any way other than by armed attack or is affected or threatened by any fact or situation which might endanger the peace of the area, the Parties shall consult immediately in order to agree on the measures which should be taken for the common defense.

3. It is understood that no action on the territory of any State designated by unanimous agreement under paragraph 1 of this Article or on any territory so designated shall be taken except at the invitation or with the consent of the government concerned.

Article V

The Parties hereby establish a Council, on which each of them shall be represented, to consider matters concerning the implementation of this Treaty. The Council shall provide for consultation with regard to military and any other planning as the situation obtaining in the treaty area may from time to time require. The Council shall be so organized as to be able to meet at any time.

Article VI

This Treaty does not affect and shall not be interpreted as affecting in any way the rights and obligations of any of the Parties under the Charter of the United Nations or the responsibility of the United Nations for the maintenance of international peace and security. Each Party declares that none of the international engagements now in force between it and any other of the Parties or any third party is in conflict with the provisions of this Treaty, and undertakes not to enter into any international engagement in conflict with this Treaty.

Article VII

Any other State in a position to further the objectives of this Treaty and to contribute to the security of the area may, by unanimous agreement of the Parties, be invited to accede to this Treaty. . . .

Article VIII

As used in this Treaty, the "treaty area" is the general area of Southeast Asia, including also the entire territories of the Asian Parties, and the general area of the Southwest Pacific not including the Pacific area north of 21 degrees 30 minutes north latitude. . . .

THE SENATE advised ratification of the treaty with the understanding that Article IV, paragraph 1, applied "only to communist aggression" and that otherwise the parties would consult under provisions of the same article. Much more important was the accompanying protocol which was signed the same day as the treaty, and which included Laos, Cambodia, and South Vietnam under Article IV.

The Parties to the Southeast Asia Collective Defense Treaty unanimously designate for the purposes of Article IV of the Treaty the States of Cambodia and Laos and the free territory under the jurisdiction of the State of Vietnam.

The Parties further agree that the above mentioned states and territory shall be eligible in respect of the economic measures contemplated by Article III.

This Protocol shall enter into force simultaneously with the coming into force of the Treaty.

In the 1960s SEATO came under attack and gradually passed into a state of disarray approaching disintegration. Because of dislike for American policy in Vietnam the French at an early point became inactive. The pact never enrolled many Asian countries—only Pakistan, the Philippines, and Thailand. Zulfikar Ali Bhutto, then foreign minister of Pakistan, pursued a friendly policy toward mainland China, and when

SOURCE: *U.S. Treaties, 1955*, pt. 1, p. 87.

the United States and Britain aided India in the 1962 Chinese-Indian War, he ended most of his country's participation in SEATO. After he became president of Pakistan, perhaps unhappy over the Nixon administration's ineffective policy during the India-Pakistan War of 1971 (see pp. 156–62), he announced in July, 1972, that his country was dropping out altogether. Pakistan formally withdrew on November 8, 1972, having recognized North Vietnam the preceding day. Meanwhile the foreign minister of the Philippines, Carlos Romulo, borrowing a word from Richard M. Nixon (who prior to his presidency had described the pact as "a somewhat anachronistic relic"), remarked that SEATO was an anachronism that "needs a massive transformation." That left only one ardent local supporter, Thailand. Critics noted the proximity of Thailand to Vietnam and the Nixon administration's heavy use of Thai territory in the air war against the Hanoi regime. The New York Times in an editorial on July 24, 1972, remarked that SEATO's principal purpose was to provide "a fig leaf of collective security respectability to a predominantly unilateral undertaking."

22. The India-Pakistan War

DURING THE SECOND WORLD WAR the Roosevelt administration had differed sharply with the British government over London's treatment of India, and it was only in the interest of Allied unity that F.D.R. desisted from urging Churchill to give the Indians more freedom. The United States looked with approval in 1947 upon the retirement of the British and the division of the subcontinent between two independent native governments, India, with its capital in Delhi, and Pakistan, with its capital in Karachi (now Islamabad). Few Americans worried about the geographical separation of Moslem-dominated Pakistan into East Pakistan and West Pakistan and the tactics of the West Pakistanis in turning East Pakistan into a virtual province. After Pakistan's inclusion in SEATO and CENTO (see pp. 186–88), it was touchy to offer suggestions. Uprisings occurred in East Pakistan and in March, 1971, the West Pakistan regime instituted a crackdown, using American military equipment against the relatively unarmed dissidents. Officers of the Pakistan army allowed troops to butcher tens of thousands of East Pakistanis; ten million refugees poured into India. All this led to an invasion of East Pakistan by Indian government troops early in December and proclamation of a breakaway state, Bangladesh. In the course of the two-week India-Pakistan War the Nixon administration sought not to criticize the Pakistan government nor to pursue a policy of neutrality, but to "tilt" in favor of the Pakistanis. Documents illustra-

SOURCE: New York Times, January 6, 1972.

tive of this course came into the hands of the syndicated columnist Jack Anderson, who used them in his column and then released them to the press. The New York Times on January 6, 1972, published memoranda, in one case apparently a verbatim transcript, of three meetings of an informal committee of the National Security Council (the Washington Special Action Group, or WSAG) on December 3, 4, and 6, 1971. The December 3d session in the situation room of the White House was attended by, among other individuals, the presidential assistant for national security affairs, Henry A. Kissinger; the deputy administrator for the Agency for International Development, Maurice J. Williams; the under secretary of state, John N. Irwin; and Assistant Secretary of State Joseph J. Sisco.

KISSINGER: I am getting hell every half-hour from the President that we are not being tough enough on India. He has just called me again. He does not believe we are carrying out his wishes. He wants to tilt in favor of Pakistan. He feels everything we do comes out otherwise. . . .

KISSINGER: The President wants no more irrevocable letters of credit issued under the $99-million credit. He wants the $72-million P.L. 480 credit also held.

WILLIAMS: Word will soon get around when we do this. Does the President understand that?

KISSINGER: That is his order, but I will check with the President again. If asked, we can say we are reviewing our whole economic program and that the granting of fresh aid is being suspended in view of conditions on the subcontinent. The next issue is the U.N.

IRWIN: The Secretary is calling in the Pak Ambassador this afternoon, and the Secretary leans toward making a U.S. move in the U.N. soon.

KISSINGER: The President is in favor of this as soon as we have some confirmation of the large-scale new action. If the U.N. can't operate in this kind of situation effectively, its utility has come to an end and it is useless to think of U.N. guarantees in the Middle East.

SISCO: We will have a recommendation for you this afternoon, after the meeting with the Ambassador. In order to give the Ambassador time to wire home, we could tentatively plan to convene the Security Council tomorrow.

KISSINGER: We have to take action. The President is blaming me, but you people are in the clear.

SISCO: That's ideal!

India, Pakistan, and Bangladesh

KISSINGER: The earlier draft for Bush [George Bush, ambassador to the UN] is too even-handed.

SISCO: To recapitulate, after we have seen the Pak Ambassador, the Secretary will report to you. We will update the draft speech for Bush.

KISSINGER: We can say we favor political accommodation but the real job of the Security Council is to prevent military action.

SISCO: We have never had a reply either from Kosygin or Mrs. Gandhi [the Russian premier, Aleksei N. Kosygin, and the prime minister of India, Indira Gandhi].

WILLIAMS: Are we to take economic steps with Pakistan also?

KISSINGER: Wait until I talk with the President. He hasn't addressed this problem in connection with Pakistan yet.

SISCO: If we act on the Indian side, we can say we are keeping the Pakistan situation "under review."

KISSINGER: It's hard to tilt toward Pakistan if we have to match every Indian step with a Pakistan step. If you wait until Monday, I can get a Presidential decision.

AMONG THOSE PRESENT at the session of WSAG on December 4 were Assistant Secretary of State Samuel De Palma, Deputy Assistant Secretary Christopher Van Hollen, and Director Richard Helms of the CIA. The memorandum of this meeting was of a summary nature, in numbered paragraphs.

14. Dr. Kissinger then asked what was happening in the U.N., to which Mr. De Palma responded that the U.K., Belgium, Japan and possibly France were joining for a call for a Security Council meeting. The Japanese had detected some slight tilt in our letter requesting the meeting. The Japanese preferred a blander formulation. We have not, however, reacted to the Japanese.

15. Dr. Kissinger asked to see the letter and requested that it be promulgated in announcing our move in the U.N., to which Mr. De Palma responded affirmatively.

16. Dr. Kissinger stated that while he had no strong view on the letter, our position must be clearly stated in the announcement.

17. Dr. Kissinger stated he did not care how third parties might react, so long as Ambassador Bush understands what he should say.

18. Dr. Kissinger said that whoever was putting out background information relative to the current situation is provoking Presidential wrath. The President is under the "illusion" that he is giving instructions, not that he is merely being kept apprised of affairs as they progress. Dr. Kissinger asked that this be kept in mind.

20. Mr. De Palma asked whether we wanted to get others lined up with our resolution before we introduce it. This, however, would take time. Dr. Kissinger suggested rather than follow this course, we had better submit the resolution as quickly as possible, alone if necessary. According to Dr. Kissinger the only move left for us at the present time is to make clear our position relative to

our greater strategy. Everyone knows how all this will come out and everyone knows that India will ultimately occupy East Pakistan. We must, therefore, make clear our position, table our resolution. We want a resolution which will be introduced with a speech by Ambassador Bush. If others desire to come along with us, fine; but in any event we will table the resolution with a speech by Ambassador Bush.

21. Dr. Kissinger continued that it was important that we register our position. The exercise in the U.N. is likely to be an exercise in futility, inasmuch as the Soviets can be expected to veto. The U.N., itself, will in all probability do little to terminate the war. . . .

22. Dr. Kissinger asked how long the Indians could delay action in the Council. Mr. De Palma said they could make long speeches or question our purpose. Mr. Van Hollen said that they would draw out as long as possible which would allow them to concentrate on the situation in East Pakistan. Mr. De Palma said that they could shilly-shally for three or four days which, Mr. Helms stated, would be long enough for them to occupy East Pakistan. Mr. De Palma stated that we could always try to force a vote. Dr. Kissinger reiterated that there was no chance in getting anything useful in the U.N.

THE SESSION of December 6 had a large cast, among which were Undersecretary of Defense David Packard, Deputy Administrator Maurice J. Williams of AID, and Under Secretary of State U. Alexis Johnson.

4. Mr. Helms opened the meeting by briefing the current situation. He stated that the Indians had recognized Bangladesh and the Paks had broken diplomatic ties with India. Major fighting continued in the East but India is engaged in a holding action in the West. Mr. Helms felt that the Indians will attempt to force a decision in the East within the next 10 days. . . .

6. Dr. Kissinger asked what is to be done with Bangladesh. Mr. Helms stated that for all practical purposes it is now an independent country, recognized by India. . . .

8. Dr. Kissinger stated that the next state of play will involve determining our attitude toward the state of Bangladesh.

21. Dr. Kissinger then asked about U.N. initiatives. Mr. Sisco said that we are now reviewing the situation with Ambassador Bush. Two Security Council resolutions have been vetoed by the

Soviets. However, there is a groundswell building in New York for an emergency session by the General Assembly to be convened under the provisions of the "threat to peace" ["uniting for peace"] mechanism. The crisis could be moved into the Assembly through a simple majority vote.

22. Dr. Kissinger and Mr. Sisco agreed that any resolution introduced into the General Assembly must retain two key elements: Cease fire and withdrawal of military forces. Dr. Kissinger agreed that our U.N. delegation has handled the situation extremely well to date. Mr. Sisco said that although it is very likely that the crisis will be introduced in the General Assembly, we must remember that there are 136 countries represented therein and we can expect all sorts of pressure to be generated. . . .

26. Dr. Kissinger also directed that henceforth we show a certain coolness to the Indians; the Indian Ambassador is not to be treated at too high a level.

29. Dr. Kissinger then asked whether we have the right to authorize Jordan or Saudi Arabia to transfer military equipment to Pakistan. Mr. Van Hollen stated the United States cannot permit a third country to transfer arms which we have provided them when we, ourselves, do not authorize sale direct to the ultimate recipient, such as Pakistan. As of last January we made a legislative decision not to sell to Pakistan. Mr. Sisco said that the Jordanians would be weakening their own position by such a transfer and would probably be grateful if we could get them off the hook. Mr. Sisco went on to say that as the Paks increasingly feel the heat we will be getting emergency requests from them.

30. Dr. Kissinger said that the President may want to honor those requests. The matter has not been brought to Presidential attention but it is quite obvious that the President is not inclined to let the Paks be defeated. Mr. Packard then said that we should look at what could be done. Mr. Sisco agreed but said it should be done very quietly. Dr. Kissinger indicated he would like a paper by tomorrow (7 Dec.).

35. Dr. Kissinger inquired about a possible famine in East Pakistan. Mr. Williams said that we will not have a massive problem at this time, but by next spring this will quite likely be the case. Dr. Kissinger asked whether we will be appealed to bail out Bangladesh. Mr. Williams said that the problem would not be terribly great if we could continue to funnel 140 tons of food a month

through Chittagong, but at this time nothing is moving. He further suggested that Bangladesh will need all kinds of help in the future, to which Ambassador Johnson added that Bangladesh will be an "international basket case." Dr. Kissinger said, however, it will not necessarily be our basket case.

23. The Trust Territory of the Pacific Islands

CONQUEST OF JAPAN'S PACIFIC ISLANDS *during the Second World War proved so costly that at the end of the war the American military forces and the public at large were unwilling to give them up. An arrangement needed to be made, for the United States government probably would not annex them and yet did not want to get rid of them. The obvious analogue to this situation had occurred when Japan and Great Britain during the First World War had divided Germany's Pacific islands and the League of Nations afterward placed them under mandate. A resolution of the U.N. Security Council on April 2, 1947, created the Trust Territory of the Pacific Islands.*

> WHEREAS Article 75 of the Charter of the United Nations provides for the establishment of an international trusteeship system for the administration and supervision of such territories as may be placed thereunder by subsequent agreements; and
>
> WHEREAS under Article 77 of the said Charter the trusteeship system may be applied to territories now held under mandate; and
>
> WHEREAS on 17 December 1920 the Council of the League of Nations confirmed a mandate for the former German islands north of the equator to Japan, to be administered in accordance with Article 22 of the Covenant of the League of Nations; and
>
> WHEREAS Japan, as a result of the Second World War, has ceased to exercise any authority in these islands;

Now, THEREFORE, the Security Council of the United Nations, having satisfied itself that the relevant articles of the Charter have been complied with, hereby resolves to approve the following terms of trusteeship for the Pacific Islands formerly under mandate to Japan.

Article 1

The Territory of the Pacific Islands, consisting of the islands formerly held by Japan under mandate in accordance with Article

SOURCE: *American Foreign Policy: 1941–1949*, pp. 1031–35.

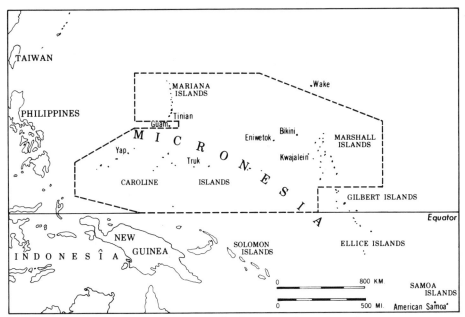

Trust Territory of the Pacific Islands

Guam, which belongs to the Mariana island group, has been American territory since the Spanish-American War of 1898; its population is approximately 50,000. The remaining Marianas contain about 13,000 people. The native peoples of the Marshalls and Carolines number nearly 90,000; they are of a different ethnic background from the Marianas people, although all are included within the broad Micronesian racial grouping.

22 of the Covenant of the League of Nations, is hereby designated as a strategic area and placed under the trusteeship system established in the Charter of the United Nations. The territory of the Pacific Islands is hereinafter referred to as the trust territory.

Article 2

The United States of America is designated as the administering authority of the trust territory.

Article 3

The administering authority shall have full powers of administration, legislation, and jurisdiction over the territory subject to the provisions of this agreement, and may apply to the trust territory, subject to any modifications which the administering authority may consider desirable, such of the laws of the United States as it may deem appropriate to local conditions and requirements.

Article 5

In discharging its obligations under Article 76 (a) and Article 84, of the Charter, the administering authority shall ensure that the trust territory shall play its part, in accordance with the Charter of the United Nations, in the maintenance of international peace and security. To this end the administering authority shall be entitled:

1. to establish naval, military and air bases and to erect fortifications in the trust territory;
2. to station and employ armed forces in the territory; and
3. to make use of volunteer forces, facilities and assistance from the trust territory in carrying out the obligations towards the Security Council undertaken in this regard by the administering authority, as well as for the local defense and the maintenance of law and order within the trust territory.

Article 8

. . . 3. Nothing in this Article shall be so construed as to accord traffic rights to aircraft flying into and out of the trust territory. Such rights shall be subject to agreement between the administering authority and the state whose nationality such aircraft possesses. . . .

Article 13

The provisions of Articles 87 and 88 of the Charter shall be applicable to the trust territory, provided that the administering authority may determine the extent of their applicability to any areas which may from time to time be specified by it as closed for security reasons.

Article 15

The terms of the present agreement shall not be altered, amended or terminated without the consent of the administering authority.

Representatives of the United States and the Congress of Micronesia (Trust Territory of the Pacific Islands) met in May, 1970, to negotiate an end to the UN trusteeship agreement. The United States, seeking to protect its strategic interests, proposed a detailed plan of commonwealth status similar in many ways to the status of Puerto Rico. The Congress of Micronesia in July, 1970, rejected the proposal. Only representatives from the Marianas Islands spoke in favor of the United States offer. At a negotiating session held on Maui, Hawaii, in October 1971, the United States retreated from its earlier position and engaged the Micronesian side in a general discussion of principles and issues. Agreement on some principles was reached. These agreements were broadened and more sharply defined in April, 1972, at Koror, Palau, into a preliminary "Compact of Free Association" that left the United States in charge of foreign affairs and defense matters, guaranteed the use of certain lands for military purposes, and granted internal self-government to Micronesians. Left unresolved were differences over the financial support to be provided by the United States, specific matters of authority on foreign affairs, and the time during which the compact would be binding on both parties. The United States delegation announced its willingness to negotiate separately with the Marianas representatives who desired a closer form of association than that favored by the rest of Micronesia. Of course any agreement on termination of the trusteeship had to gain approval of the United States Congress, the United Nations, and the Micronesian people through a plebiscite.

VIII

The Middle East

Before the Second World War the United States government sometimes had shown interest in the affairs of the Middle East, but it had been a desultory and almost haphazard interest, occasioned by problems of American citizens in the area, by the spill-over of European concerns, and generally by the interest of Americans in Palestine as the cradle of Christianity. With the war of 1941–45 American troops went into the area to reinforce British power, and Middle Eastern—chiefly Saudi Arabian—oil became almost an obsession of the U.S. Navy because of fear for the exhaustion of American and Western Hemisphere sources. Then with the end of the war another new concern (the first had been strategic; the second was oil) appeared, the need of world Jewry for a place to which oppressed Jews could go and live in peace, and the desire of a large group of Jews that their ethnic group might have what one of the British foreign secretaries during the First World War, Lord Balfour, had described as a national home. The government of the United States after the end of the Second World War found itself with so many problems all over the world that the hypersensitivity of the Middle East's Arab peoples to the creation of a State of Israel did not register itself very strongly with the makers of policy, especially President Truman. Thus Middle Eastern policy became a tangle of strategic, economic, and sentimental interests that probably will not be unwound in the latter half of the twentieth century.

24. The State of Israel

A. Partition

No SINGLE EVENT of the years after 1945 made such an impression upon the domestic and foreign policies of the Arab governments of the Middle East, and upon the Middle Eastern policy of the United States, as did creation of the State of Israel in 1948. Contrary to popular belief, the American government did not do a great deal to create Israel; the state was created largely by Adolf Hitler, whose terrible oppression of Europe's Jews brought an urgency to Zionism that it never had possessed in its roughly half century of existence prior to the 1930s. The Palestine issue arose in American politics toward the end of the Second World War. As President Truman remarked to a group of American diplomatic representatives who were seeking to insure at least American neutrality toward the possible creation of a Jewish state in Palestine, it was difficult for the United States government to remain neutral because the Arab vote in America was virtually nonexistent. Despite this presidential opinion offered in 1946 and despite some statements of friendship in regard to the Jewish desire for a national home, Truman did little more; he hoped the problem could be worked out in the United Nations. The General Assembly passed a resolution on November 29, 1947, after a U.N. Special Commission for Palestine (UNSCOP) had made a detailed study of the problem.

1. The Mandate for Palestine shall terminate as soon as possible but in any case not later than 1 August 1948.

2. The armed forces of the Mandatory Power shall be progressively withdrawn from Palestine, the withdrawal to be completed as soon as possible but in any case not later than 1 August 1948.

The Mandatory Power shall advise the Commission, as far in advance as possible, of its intention to terminate the Mandate and to evacuate each area.

The Mandatory Power shall use its best endeavours to ensure that an area situated in the territory of the Jewish State, including a seaport and hinterland adequate to provide facilities for a substantial immigration, shall be evacuated at the earliest possible date and in any event not later than 1 February 1948.

SOURCE: *A Decade of American Foreign Policy: Basic Documents, 1941–1949* (Washington, D.C., 1950), pp. 820–39.

3. Independent Arab and Jewish States and the Special International Regime for the City of Jerusalem . . . shall come into existence in Palestine two months after the evacuation of the armed forces of the Mandatory Power has been completed but in any case not later than 1 October 1948. The boundaries of the Arab State, the Jewish State, and the City of Jerusalem shall be as described. . . .

4. The period between the adoption by the General Assembly of its recommendation on the question of Palestine and the establishment of the independence of the Arab and Jewish States shall be a transitional period.

B. RECOGNITION

JEWS IN THE UNITED STATES *together with representatives of the Jewish Agency, the Palestine organization that was the forerunner of the State of Israel, put enormous pressure upon delegations to the General Assembly to support the resolution of November 29. The pressure became so obvious, so crude, that it offended Truman, who thereafter did virtually nothing to assist the creation of the Jewish state in Palestine until shortly before the state's proclamation on May 14, 1948. Actually he needed to do little other than avoid military intervention in support of the U.N. resolution. The U.N. could not enforce its own resolution. The United States could not enforce it. Intervention by United States armed forces appeared completely impractical because, as became evident during cabinet discussion of the problem, over 100,000 troops would have been necessary, and they could not have been furnished without a partial mobilization. Such a mobilization would have been politically difficult to achieve. Besides, too many issues were arising in Europe, where early in 1948 the United States government was putting the Marshall Plan into effect and the Russian government was preparing the Berlin blockade. By early May, therefore, it seemed best for the American government to recognize an independent Israeli state. The representative of the Jewish Agency in Washington, Eliahu Epstein (later Elath), asked for recognition in a letter dated May 15, 1948, but whose content showed it was communicated beforehand.*

MY DEAR MR. PRESIDENT: I have the honor to notify you that the state of Israel has been proclaimed as an independent republic within frontiers approved by the General Assembly of the United Nations in its Resolution of November 29, 1947, and that a provisional government has been charged to assume the rights and duties of government for preserving law and order within the

SOURCE: *American Foreign Policy: 1941–1949*, pp. 843–44.

boundaries of Israel, for defending the state against external aggression, and for discharging the obligations of Israel to the other nations of the world in accordance with international law. The Act of Independence will become effective at one minute after six o'clock on the evening of 14 May 1948, Washington time.

With full knowledge of the deep bond of sympathy which has existed and has been strengthened over the past thirty years between the Government of the United States and the Jewish people of Palestine, I have been authorized by the provisional government of the new state to tender this message and to express the hope that your government will recognize and will welcome Israel into the community of nations.

THE UNITED STATES recognized Israel at 6:11 P.M., May 14, 1948, Washington, D.C., time, which was 12:11 P.M., May 15, Palestine time. Fighting broke out in Palestine, with the Arabs halfheartedly cooperating to prevent establishment of the new state. The war continued into 1949 when the Arab states and Israel concluded an armistice that lasted for a few years. The State of Israel did not, of course, conform in all particulars to the U.N. resolution of November 29, 1947. There was no economic union with the Arab portions of former Palestine. The city of Jerusalem was not placed under international jurisdiction; it was divided between Jews and Arabs, until in 1967 the Jews took all of it (see pp. 189–90). Nor were the borders of Israel in accord with the resolution, for the Israelis desired the area around the Sea of Galilee (Lake Tiberias). Meanwhile, after U.S. recognition, the Truman administration began to support the Israeli state in a liberal way, as shown by the private letter sent by Truman to President Chaim Weizmann on November 29, 1948.

DEAR MR. PRESIDENT:

Today—the first anniversary of the Partition Resolution—is a most appropriate time for me to answer your last letter, dated November 5th.

As I read your letter, I was struck by the common experience you and I have recently shared. We had both been abandoned by the so-called realistic experts to our supposedly forlorn lost cause. Yet we both kept pressing for what we were sure was right—and we were both proven to be right. My feeling of elation on the morning of

SOURCE: Harry S. Truman, *Memoirs: Years of Trial and Hope* (Garden City, N.Y.: Doubleday, 1956), pp. 168–69.

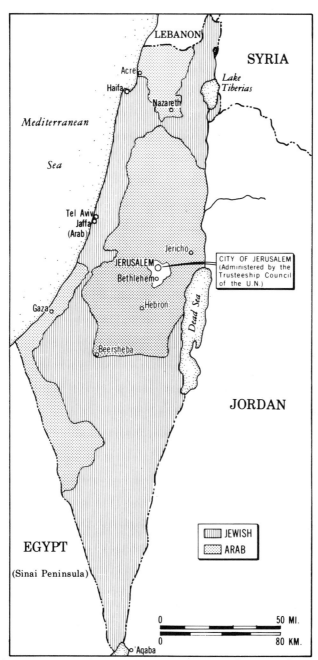

Palestine – The Partition Boundary of 1947

November 3rd must have approximated your own feelings one year ago today, and on May 14th and on several occasions since then.

However, it does not take long for bitter and resourceful opponents to regroup their forces after they have been shattered. You in Israel have already been confronted with that situation; and I expect to be all too soon. So I understand very well your concern to prevent the undermining of your well-earned victories.

I remember well our conversations about the Negeb, to which you referred in your letter. I agree fully with your estimate of the importance of the area to Israel, and I deplore any attempt to take it away from Israel. I had thought that my position would have been clear to all the world, particularly in the light of the specific wording of the Democratic Party platform. But there were those who did not take this seriously, regarding it as "just another campaign promise" to be forgotten after the election. I believe they have recently realized their error. I have interpreted my re-election as a mandate from the American people to carry out the Democratic platform—including, of course, the plank on Israel. I intend to do so.

Since your letter was written, we have announced in the General Assembly our firm intention to oppose any territorial changes in the November 29th Resolution which are not acceptable to the State of Israel. I am confident that the General Assembly will support us in this basic position.

We have already expressed our willingness to help develop the new State through financial and economic measures. As you know, the Export-Import Bank is actively considering a substantial long-term loan to Israel on a project basis. I understand that your Government is now in process of preparing the details of such projects for submission to the Bank. Personally, I would like to go even further, by expanding such financial and economic assistance on a large scale to the entire Middle East, contingent upon effective mutual cooperation.

Thank you so much for your warm congratulations and good wishes on my re-election. I was pleased to learn that the first Israeli elections have been scheduled for January 25th. That enables us to set a definite target date for extending de jure recognition.

In closing, I want to tell you how happy and impressed I have been at the remarkable progress made by the new State of Israel.

What you have received at the hands of the world has been far less than was your due. But you have more than made the most of what you have received, and I admire you for it. I trust that the present uncertainty, with its terribly burdensome consequences, will soon be eliminated. We will do all we can to help by encouraging direct negotiations between the parties looking toward a prompt peace settlement.

Very sincerely yours,
Harry S. Truman

25. The Suez Crisis

IN THE MIDDLE and later years of the 1950s, crisis followed crisis, largely because of the political insecurity of the area after Israeli independence. It is true that if Israel had not existed it might have had to be invented: the Arabs needed a scapegoat for their own inadequacies. It is true also that American support of Israel, if not before 1948, then beginning with the extraordinary recognition of the new state only eleven minutes after it came into existence, involved the U.S. government in the Arabs' hostilities and hatreds in a most inconvenient way considering the problems of American foreign policy elsewhere since 1945.

A. THE TRIPARTITE DECLARATION

THE UNITED STATES, Great Britain, and France on May 25, 1950, a year after the Arab-Israeli armistice and in spite of the simmering animosities of the Arab nations that had been defeated by the Israelis, sought to put the lid on war in the Middle East by ensuring that neither side would get enough weapons to tempt it to hostilities.

1. The three Governments recognize that the Arab states and Israel all need to maintain a certain level of armed forces for the purposes of assuring their internal security and their legitimate self-defense and to permit them to play their part in the defense of the area as a whole. All applications for arms or war material for these countries will be considered in the light of these principles. In this connection the three Governments wish to recall and reaffirm the terms of the statements

SOURCE: *American Foreign Policy: 1950–1955*, 2 vols. (Washington, D.C., 1957), II, p. 2237.

made by their representatives on the Security Council on August 4, 1949, in which they declared their opposition to the development of an arms race between the Arab states and Israel.

2. The three Governments declare that assurances have been received from all the states in question, to which they permit arms to be supplied from their countries, that the purchasing state does not intend to undertake any act of aggression against any other state. Similar assurances will be requested from any other state in the area to which they permit arms to be supplied in the future.

3. The three Governments take this opportunity of declaring their deep interest in and their desire to promote the establishment and maintenance of peace and stability in the area and their unalterable opposition to the use of force or threat of force between any of the states in that area. The three Governments, should they find that any of these states was preparing to violate frontiers or armistice lines, would, consistently with their obligations as members of the United Nations, immediately take action, both within and outside the United Nations, to prevent such violation.

B. THE WAR OF 1956

THE SOVIET UNION *did not sign the Tripartite Declaration, and in 1955 trouble commenced when Egypt mortgaged its cotton crop for years thereafter in exchange for arms made available by Czechoslovakia. The Russians had failed to make headway in Europe in 1945–50; the Korean War armistice brought an end to a military action in Asia; and within the U.S.S.R. the succession to Stalin had been determined (Khrushchev was rising to power, although he had not yet taken over as premier). The Soviets must have calculated that it was time to intervene in the Middle East, where the anger of the Arabs over Israel was so great that the new Egyptian government of Gamal Abdel Nasser would purchase arms from any quarter to avoid the equalities of the Tripartite Declaration. The Nasser government had itself arisen on the ruins of the Arab-Israeli War: the war had so discredited the corrupt regime of King Farouk that Nasser toppled it in 1952 and after a short time established himself as president of Egypt. The American and British governments had tried to prevent trouble from the new Egyptian regime by tying it into a long-cherished Egyptian project for a higher dam at Aswan that would open vast areas to cultivation, create hydroelectric power, and regulate the flow of the Nile's waters throughout Egypt, preventing the sudden flooding that occurred annually. The idea in Washington and London was that the Egyptian contribution to the Aswan dam project*

SOURCE: *American Foreign Policy: Current Documents, 1956* (Washington, D.C., 1959), pp. 603–04.

would be so large that no funds would be left over for military opera-
tions against Israel. Instead, Nasser went to the Russians, via the
Czechs. He then tried to blackmail Secretary Dulles into going ahead
with the dam project anyway; he announced that the Russians were
showing interest in the project and that he was ready to sign with the
Americans and British. This was too much for Dulles, who withdrew
the United States from the Aswan dam project in an announcement of
July 19, 1956.

At the request of the Government of Egypt, the United States
joined in December 1955 with the United Kingdom and with the
World Bank in an offer to assist Egypt in the construction of a
high dam on the Nile at Aswan. This project is one of great magnitude. It would require an estimated 12 to 16 years to complete at a
total cost estimated at some $1,300,000,000, of which over $900,-
000,000 represents local currency requirements. It involves not
merely the rights and interests of Egypt but of other states whose
waters are contributory, including Sudan, Ethiopia, and Uganda.

The December offer contemplated an extension by the United
States and United Kingdom of grant aid to help finance certain
early phases of the work, the effects of which would be confined
solely to Egypt, with the understanding that accomplishment of
the project as a whole would require a satisfactory resolution of the
question of Nile water rights. Another important consideration
bearing upon the feasibility of the undertaking and thus the
practicability of American aid was Egyptian readiness and ability to
concentrate its economic resources upon this vast construction
program.

Developments within the succeeding 7 months have not been
favorable to the success of the project, and the U.S. Government
has concluded that it is not feasible in present circumstances to
participate in the project. Agreement by the riparian states has not
been achieved, and the ability of Egypt to devote adequate resources to assure the project's success has become more uncertain
than at the time the offer was made.

This decision in no way reflects or involves any alteration in the
friendly relations of the Government and people of the United
States toward the Government and people of Egypt.

The United States remains deeply interested in the welfare of
the Egyptian people and in the development of the Nile. It is
prepared to consider at an appropriate time and at the request of

the riparian states what steps might be taken toward a more effective utilization of the water resources of the Nile for the benefit of the peoples of the region. Furthermore, the United States remains ready to assist Egypt in its effort to improve the economic condition of its people and is prepared, through its appropriate agencies, to discuss these matters within the context of funds appropriated by the Congress.

IT WAS NOT IMMEDIATELY CLEAR *that Dulles had made a mistake (sometimes a great nation, contrary to the belief of such individuals as Theodore Roosevelt, must submit to blackmail), and a series of confusing events occurred. In an inflammatory speech at Alexandria a few days later, a speech full of invective, exaggeration, and plain misstatement, Nasser nationalized the Suez Canal. He announced a takeover of the rights exercised by the Universal Company of the Suez Maritime Canal and promised to indemnify the company's stockholders. Secretary Dulles flew to London and gave evidence of supporting the anti-Nasser position of the British and French governments, although almost at once international lawyers began to observe a certain weakness in the position of the American government because of its possession of the Panama Canal. These observations led Dulles to a press conference statement of August 28, 1956.*

There has been a good deal of speculation as to possible similarities between the Suez Canal and the Panama Canal. Actually, the situation is totally dissimilar in two vital respects. First, the juridical, the legal aspect of the problem. The Suez Canal by the treaty of 1888 is internationalized. The Panama Canal is a waterway in a zone where, by treaty, the United States has all the rights which it would possess if it were the sovereign "to the entire exclusion of the exercise by the Republic of Panama of any such sovereign rights, power or authority." And there is no international treaty giving other countries any rights at all in the Panama Canal except for a treaty with the United Kingdom which provides that it has the right to have the same tolls for its vessels as for ours.

Now the second aspect of the matter, which is totally different, is the practical situation. In the case of the Suez Canal a large number of countries, whose very livelihood almost depends upon the free and efficient and impartial operation of the canal, are in fact gravely disturbed because they fear that there will not be that

SOURCE: *Current Documents, 1956,* pp. 619–20.

kind of operation and that their lifeline—and to them it is almost literally a lifeline—that their lifeline may be cut. As far as I am aware, no country anywhere in the world fears that its economy is jeopardized by possible misuse, abuse, of our rights in the Panama Canal.

To REPORTERS ON SEPTEMBER 11, 1956, President Eisenhower gave the impression of supporting the British and French without going all the way.

As you know, this country will not go to war ever while I am occupying my present post unless the Congress is called into session, and Congress declares such a war; and the only exception to that would be in the case of unexpected and unwarranted attack on this nation, where self-defense itself would dictate some quick response while you call Congress into action.

So, as far as going into any kind of military action under present conditions, of course, we are not.

Now, if after all peaceful means are exhausted, . . . there is some kind of aggression on the part of Egypt against a peaceful use of the Canal, you might say that we would recognize that Britain and France had no other recourse than to continue to use it even if they had to be more forceful than merely sailing through it.

. . . There are so many things that can occur that I believe it is best to say we are consulting . . . with other nations on every possible line of action that could occur.

SOURCE: *Current Documents, 1956*, p. 624.

SECRETARY DULLES *busied himself consulting the British and French and arranged a Suez Canal Users Association (S.C.U.A.) that would collect tolls from vessels using the canal and in a somewhat complicated and confusing manner pass on some of the tolls to the Egyptians so that the latter could maintain the canal. The question arose whether American ships, either registered under the American flag or under the flags of convenience of Panama or Liberia, would observe the rules of S.C.U.A., and the secretary answered it in a press conference of September 26, 1956.*

It is planned, as I indicated in a letter which I left with the Foreign Minister of the United Kingdom in London just before I

SOURCE: *Current Documents, 1956*, p. 635.

left last week, it is indicated that we will take steps to amend the present Treasury license so as to preclude any direct payments to Egypt, and to permit such payments to Egypt only as they might occur through payments to the Users Association. Of course, you know the Users Association under its charter is authorized to make certain payments over to the Government of Egypt, because we do not expect Egypt to help maintain the canal entirely out of its own funds. And there could in that way be payments to Egypt through the Users Association which would act, you might say, as an agent for the vessels. But outside of that, we would not expect that there would be any payments to Egypt by United States flag vessels. We do not have in mind extending that to vessels which are not of United States registry. That involves possible questions of conflict of laws and until we know more clearly what the views might be of the countries of registry, we do not expect, certainly initially, to impose a restriction upon those vessels. We would hope that they might find it desirable voluntarily to conform to the same practice as U.S. flag vessels. But the extension of our authority to vessels which are owned by corporations of other nations and incorporated under the laws of other nations and which fly under the flag of other nations is a step which we do not contemplate taking at the present time.

IT BECAME APPARENT that Dulles was trying to smooth over the whole affair; he was stalling for time, hoping that the British and French governments would get over their anger at nationalization of the Suez Canal. In this effort he grossly miscalculated, for since the end of the Second World War nations everywhere had been pushing the British, and Egyptian support of an Arab rebellion in Algeria had enormously discomfited the French. Prime Minister Anthony Eden believed that Nasser was another Hitler and decided to put him down. He arranged a low intrigue with the French and Israeli governments by which the Israelis would attack the Egyptians and the British and French would issue an ultimatum to the two contestants, Israel and Egypt, to withdraw to positions ten miles from the Suez Canal. That would leave Israel in possession of all of Sinai and the Anglo-French holding the canal. It was a Byzantine maneuver that failed not because of the brilliant military action of Israel during October 29–November 2, but because of the slow military tactics of the British and French, who could not get their troops into the canal zone fast enough, thus giving the Egyptians an opportunity to block the canal by sinking ships in it. Lon-

SOURCE: Current Documents, 1956, pp. 657–58.

don and Paris also miscalculated the humor of their American ally, whom they had thoughtfully failed to inform prior to the Israeli attack and their October 30 ultimatum to Egypt. President Eisenhower and Secretary Dulles were incensed and took the issue to the United Nations Security Council, where on the day of the ultimatum the French and British vetoed a U.S. resolution. Under the Korean precedent—the uniting-for-peace resolution—Washington called the first emergency special session of the General Assembly, and a resolution passed on November 2 with the enthusiastic support of the Soviet Union, and with abstentions and support by some members of the British Commonwealth.

The General Assembly,

Noting the disregard on many occasions by parties to the Israel-Arab armistice agreements of 1949 of the terms of such agreements, and that the armed forces of Israel have penetrated deeply into Egyptian territory in violation of the General Armistice Agreement between Egypt and Israel of 24 February 1949,

Noting that armed forces of France and the United Kingdom of Great Britain and Northern Ireland are conducting military operations against Egyptian territory,

Noting that traffic through the Suez Canal is now interrupted to the serious prejudice of many nations,

Expressing its grave concern over these developments,

1. Urges as a matter of priority that all parties now involved in hostilities in the area agree to an immediate cease-fire and, as part thereof, halt the movement of military forces and arms into the area;

2. Urges the parties to the armistice agreements promptly to withdraw all forces behind the armistice lines, to desist from raids across the armistice lines into neighbouring territory, and to observe scrupulously the provisions of the armistice agreements;

3. Recommends that all Member States refrain from introducing military goods in the area of hostilities and in general refrain from any acts which would delay or prevent the implementation of the present resolution;

4. Urges that, upon the cease-fire being effective, steps be taken to reopen the Suez Canal and restore secure freedom of navigation;

5. Requests the Secretary-General to observe and report promptly on the compliance with the present resolution to the Security Council and to the General Assembly, for such further action as they may deem appropriate in accordance with the Charter;

6. Decides to remain in emergency session pending compliance with the present resolution.

The British, French, and Israelis gave in and complied with the U.N. resolution. Shortly thereafter a special U.N. force took over Anglo-French positions and the Israelis retreated to their home base.

26. Lebanon

A. THE EISENHOWER DOCTRINE

ISRAELI INDEPENDENCE led to a revolution in Egypt, which in turn brought the Czech arms deal and then the debacle at Suez, in which the United States, supported by the Soviet Union, opposed two members of the North Atlantic Treaty Organization. The American government, having miscalculated both with the Egyptians and with the British and French, albeit momentarily earning the appreciation of the Arab peoples because of its strong stand against aggression in the Middle East, proceeded to complicate its position by a third miscalculation. The Eisenhower administration believed that a little money, judiciously applied, would soothe Arab passions and arranged for $200 million to go to the Arab governments under a special congressional resolution approved by the president on March 9, 1957. This was known as the Eisenhower Doctrine.

Resolved by the Senate and House of Representatives of the United States of America in Congress assembled,

That the President be and hereby is authorized to cooperate with and assist any nation or group of nations in the general area of the Middle East desiring such assistance in the development of economic strength dedicated to the maintenance of national independence.

SEC. 2. The President is authorized to undertake, in the general area of the Middle East, military assistance programs with any nation or group of nations of that area desiring such assistance. Furthermore, the United States regards as vital to the national interest and world peace the preservation of the independence and integrity of the nations of the Middle East. To this end, if the President determines the necessity thereof, the United States is prepared to use armed forces to assist any such nation or group of

SOURCE: *American Foreign Policy: Current Documents, 1957* (Washington, D.C., 1961), pp. 829–31.

such nations requesting assistance against armed aggression from any country controlled by international communism: *Provided,* That such employment shall be consonant with the treaty obligations of the United States and with the Constitution of the United States.

SEC. 3. The President is hereby authorized to use during the balance of fiscal year 1957 for economic and military assistance under this joint resolution not to exceed $200,000,000. . . .

SEC. 6. This joint resolution shall expire when the President shall determine that the peace and security of the nations in the general area of the Middle East are reasonably assured by international conditions created by action of the United Nations or otherwise except that it may be terminated earlier by a concurrent resolution of the two Houses of Congress.

B. THE INTERVENTION OF 1958

THE EISENHOWER DOCTRINE *involved a special mission to the Middle East under former congressman James P. Richards to dispense the appropriation. The Arab states wanted the money but hesitated to ask for it under the circumstances. An exception was the government of Lebanon, which was in difficulty because its president, Camille Chamoun, a Maronite Christian, desired a second term in office. Bolstered by American money, he overturned the delicate political balance in Lebanon between town and countryside, Christians and Arabs, and the country slipped into civil war. On July 14, 1958, a murderous revolt in Baghdad overthrew the Hashemite monarchy and appeared to be under the direction of Nasser. The cousin of the murdered King Faisal of Iraq, King Hussein of Jordan, came under intense Nasserite pressure. President Eisenhower gave a radio and television address on July 15 invoking the Eisenhower Doctrine.*

Yesterday was a day of grave developments in the Middle East. In Iraq a highly organized military blow struck down the duly constituted Government and attempted to put in its place a committee of Army officers. The attack was conducted with great brutality. Many of the leading personalities were beaten to death or hanged and their bodies dragged through the streets. At about the same time there was discovered a highly organized plot to overthrow the lawful Government of Jordan.

SOURCE: *American Foreign Policy: Current Documents, 1958* (Washington, D.C., 1962), pp. 969–72.

Warned and alarmed by these developments, President Chamoun of Lebanon sent me an urgent plea that the United States station some military units in Lebanon to evidence our concern for the independence of Lebanon, that little country which itself has for about 2 months been subjected to civil strife. This has been actively fomented by Soviet and Cairo broadcasts and abetted and aided by substantial amounts of arms, money, and personnel infiltrated into Lebanon across the Syrian border.

President Chamoun stated that without an immediate show of United States support the Government of Lebanon would be unable to survive against the forces which had been set loose in the area. The plea of President Chamoun was supported by the unanimous action of the Lebanese Cabinet.

After giving this plea earnest thought and after taking advice from leaders of both the executive and congressional branches of the Government, I decided to comply with the plea of the Government of Lebanon. A few hours ago a battalion of the United States Marines landed and took up stations in and about the city of Beirut.

The mission of these forces is to protect American lives—there are about 2,500 Americans in Lebanon—and by their presence to assist the Government of Lebanon to preserve its territorial integrity and political independence.

The United States does not, of course, intend to replace the United Nations, which has a primary responsibility to maintain international peace and security. We reacted as we did within a matter of hours because the situation was such that only prompt action would suffice. We have, however, with equal promptness moved in the United Nations. This morning there was held at our request an emergency meeting of the United Nations Security Council. At this meeting we reported the action which we had taken. We stated the reasons therefor. We expressed the hope that the United Nations would itself take measures which would be adequate to preserve the independence of Lebanon and permit of the early withdrawal of the United States forces.

I should like now to take a few minutes to explain the situation in Lebanon.

Lebanon is a small country, a little less than the size of Connecticut, with a population of about 1½ million. It has always had close and friendly relations with the United States. Many of you no doubt have heard of the American University at Beirut, which has a distinguished record. Lebanon has been a prosperous, peaceful country, thriving on trade largely with the West. A little over a year ago there were general elections, held in an atmosphere of total calm, which resulted in the establishment, by an overwhelming popular vote, of the present Parliament for a period of 4 years. The term of the President, however, is of a different duration and would normally expire next September. The President, Mr. Chamoun, has made clear that he does not seek reelection.

When the attacks on the Government of Lebanon began to occur, it took the matter to the United Nations Security Council, pointing out that Lebanon was the victim of indirect aggression from without. As a result, the Security Council sent observers to Lebanon in the hope of thereby insuring that hostile intervention would cease. Secretary-General Hammarskjold undertook a mission to the area to reinforce the work of the observers. We believe that his efforts and those of the United Nations observers were helpful. They could not eliminate arms or ammunition or remove persons already sent into Lebanon. But we believe they did reduce such aid from across the border.

It seemed, last week, that the situation was moving toward a peaceful solution which would preserve the integrity of Lebanon and end indirect aggression from without. Those hopes were, however, dashed by the events of yesterday in Iraq and Jordan. These events demonstrate a scope of aggressive purpose which tiny Lebanon could not combat without further evidence of support. That is why Lebanon's request for troops from the United States was made. That is why we have responded to that request.

Some will ask, does the stationing of some United States troops in Lebanon involve any interference in the internal affairs of Lebanon? The clear answer is "no."

First of all, we have acted at the urgent plea of the Government of Lebanon, a Government which has been freely elected by the people only a little over a year ago. It is entitled, as are we, to join in measures of collective security for self-defense. Such action, the United Nations Charter recognizes, is an "inherent right."

In the second place what we now see in the Middle East is the same pattern of conquest with which we became familiar during the period of 1945 to 1950. This involves taking over a nation by means of indirect aggression; that is, under the cover of a fomented civil strife the purpose is to put into domestic control those whose real loyalty is to the aggressor. It was by such means that the Communists attempted to take over Greece in 1947. That effort was thwarted by the Truman Doctrine. It was by such means that the Communists took over Czechoslovakia in 1948. It was by such means that the Communists took over the mainland of China in 1949. It was by such means that the Communists attempted to take over Korea and Indochina, beginning in 1950.

You will remember at the time of the Korean war that the Soviet Government claimed that this was merely a civil war, because the only attack was by north Koreans upon south Koreans. But all the world knew that the north Koreans were armed, equipped, and directed from without for the purpose of aggression.

This means of conquest was denounced by the United Nations General Assembly when it adopted in November 1950 its resolution entitled "Peace Through Deeds." It thereby called upon every nation to refrain from "fomenting civil strife in the interest of a foreign power" and denounced such action as "the gravest of all crimes against peace and security throughout the world."

We had hoped that these threats to the peace and to the independence and integrity of small nations had come to an end. Unhappily, now they reappear. Lebanon was selected to become a victim.

Last year the Congress of the United States joined with the President to declare that "the United States regards as vital to the national interest and world peace the preservation of the independence and integrity of the nations of the Middle East." I believe that the presence of the United States forces now being sent to Lebanon will have a stabilizing effect which will preserve the independence and integrity of Lebanon. It will also afford an increased measure of security to the thousands of Americans who reside in Lebanon.

We know that stability and well-being cannot be achieved purely by military measures. The economy of Lebanon has been gravely strained by civil strife. Foreign trade and tourist traffic have almost come to a standstill. The United States stands ready, under its mutual security program, to cooperate with the Government of Lebanon to find ways to restore its shattered economy. Thus we shall help to bring back to Lebanon a peace which is not merely the absence of fighting but the well-being of the people.

I am well aware of the fact that landing of United States troops in Lebanon could have some serious consequences. That is why this step was taken only after the most serious consideration and broad consultation. I have, however, come to the sober and clear conclusion that the action taken was essential to the welfare of the United States. It was required to support the principles of justice and international law upon which peace and a stable international order depend. That, and that alone, is the purpose of the United States.

We are not actuated by any hope of material gain or by any emotional hostility against any person or any government. Our dedication is to the principles of the United Nations Charter and to the preservation of the independence of every state. That is the basic pledge of the United Nations Charter. Yet indirect aggression and violence are being promoted in the Near East in clear violation of the provisions of the United Nations Charter.

There can be no peace in the world unless there is fuller dedication to the basic principles of the United Nations Charter. If ever the United States fails to support these principles, the result would be to open the floodgates to direct and indirect aggression throughout the world.

In the 1930s the members of the League of Nations became indifferent to direct and indirect aggression in Europe, Asia, and Africa. The result was to strengthen and stimulate aggressive forces that made World War II inevitable. The United States is determined that that history shall not now be repeated.

We are hopeful that the action which we are taking will both preserve the independence of Lebanon and check international violations which, if they succeeded, would endanger world peace. We hope that this result will quickly be attained and that our forces can be promptly withdrawn.

We must, however, be prepared to meet the situation, whatever be the consequences. We can do so, confident that we strive for a world in which nations, be they great or be they small, can preserve their independence. We are striving for an ideal which is close to the heart of every American and for which in the past many Americans have laid down their lives. To serve these ideals is also to serve the cause of peace, security, and well-being, not only for us but for all men everywhere.

ALMOST A DIVISION OF AMERICAN TROOPS, 14,000 men, landed in Lebanon, and the commander of the Lebanese army, General Fuad Chehab, succeeded Chamoun as president. British troops, violating Israeli air space, flew from Cyprus to Jordan and stiffened Hussein. The revolution in Baghdad detached Iraq from the Baghdad Pact. In the subsequent military regime the Nasserite faction failed to gain the upper hand, however, and the Iraqis settled down to a policy separate from Egypt that has confused observers ever since.

27. CENTO

THE EISENHOWER DOCTRINE encouraged the United States to assume an obligation under the Baghdad Pact, an organization arranged in 1955 as an alliance between Iraq and Turkey but which soon included Great Britain, Iran, and Pakistan in what appeared to be an anti-Communist front. Actually, the pact represented the rump of a project by the British to organize the Arab nations of the Middle East, which failed because of the confusions of Middle Eastern politics due to the emergence of Israel, together with the declining importance in the area of Great Britain. President Eisenhower's press secretary announced at a news conference at Tucker's Town, Bermuda, where the president was meeting the British prime minister, that the United States was willing, if invited, to join the Military Committee of the Baghdad Pact. It was invited, but arrangements were not completed until July 28, 1958, after the revolution in Iraq had brought the withdrawal of that country from the Baghdad Pact and the United States had involved itself in a short-term military operation in Lebanon.

1. The members of the Baghdad Pact attending the Ministerial meeting in London have reexamined their position in the light of recent events and conclude that the need which called the Pact into being is greater than ever. These members declare their determination to maintain their collective security and to resist aggression, direct or indirect.

2. Under the Pact collective security arrangements have been instituted. Joint military planning has been advanced and area economic projects have been promoted. Relationships are being established with other free world nations associated for collective security.

SOURCE: Current Documents, 1958, pp. 894–95.

3. The question of whether substantive alterations should be made in the Pact and its organization or whether the Pact will be continued in its present form is under consideration by the Government concerned. However, the nations represented at the meeting in London reaffirmed their determination to strengthen further their united defence posture in the area.

4. Article I of the Pact of Mutual Co-operation signed at Baghdad on February 24, 1955 provides that the parties will co-operate for their security and defence and that such measures as they agree to take to give effect to this co-operation may form the subject of special agreements. Similarly, the United States, in the interest of world peace, and pursuant to existing Congressional authorisation, agrees to co-operate with the nations making this Declaration for their security and defence, and will promptly enter into agreements designed to give effect to this co-operation.

AT ANKARA ON MARCH 5, 1959, *the United States signed separate but mutatis mutandis identical executive agreements with Iran, Turkey, and Pakistan. The Pakistan agreement follows.*

Article I

The Government of Pakistan is determined to resist aggression. In case of aggression against Pakistan, the Government of the United States of America, in accordance with the Constitution of the United States of America, will take such appropriate action, including the use of armed forces, as may be mutually agreed upon and as is envisaged in the Joint Resolution to Promote Peace and Stability in the Middle East, in order to assist the Government of Pakistan at its request.

Article II

The Government of the United States of America, in accordance with the Mutual Security Act of 1954, as amended, and related laws of the United States of America, and with applicable agreements heretofore or hereafter entered into between the Government of the United States of America and the Government of

SOURCE: *United States Treaties and Other International Agreements: 1959,* pt. 1 (Washington, D.C., 1960), pp. 317–19.

Pakistan, reaffirms that it will continue to furnish the Government of Pakistan such military and economic assistance as may be mutually agreed upon between the Government of the United States of America and the Government of Pakistan, in order to assist the Government of Pakistan in the preservation of its national independence and integrity and in the effective promotion of its economic development.

Article III

The Government of Pakistan undertakes to utilize such military and economic assistance as may be provided by the Government of the United States of America in a manner consonant with the aims and purposes set forth by the Governments associated in the Declaration signed at London on July 28, 1958, and for the purpose of effectively promoting the economic development of Pakistan and of preserving its national independence and integrity.

Article IV

The Government of the United States of America and the Government of Pakistan will cooperate with the other Governments associated in the Declaration signed at London on July 28, 1958, in order to prepare and participate in such defensive arrangements as may be mutually agreed to be desirable, subject to the other applicable provisions of this agreement.

Article V

The provisions of the present agreement do not affect the cooperation between the two Governments as envisaged in other international agreements or arrangements.

Article VI

This agreement shall enter into force upon the date of its signature and shall continue in force until one year after the receipt by either Government of written notice of the intention of the other Government to terminate the agreement.

The Baghdad Pact's name was changed to Central Treaty Organization (CENTO) in 1959.

28. The Israeli-Egyptian War of 1967

INCREASING BORDER PRESSURE and the braggadocio of the Egyptians persuaded the Israeli government early in June, 1967, that the Egyptian army needed another lesson à la 1956. The result, the Six Day War of June 5–11, was a sudden invasion of the Egyptian-held Gaza strip along the Mediterranean, the Sinai peninsula, Arab-held Jerusalem, and the Egyptian side of the Gulf of Aqaba, where an Egyptian force had prevented use of the Israeli port of Elath. An annoyed, even outraged, U.N. Security Council demanded a cease-fire on June 7.

The Security Council,

Noting that, in spite of its appeal to the Governments concerned to take forthwith as a first step all measures for an immediate cease-fire and for a cessation of all military activities in the Near East . . . military activities in the area are continuing,

Concerned that the continuation of military activities may create an even more menacing situation in the area,

1. Demands that the Governments concerned should as a first step cease fire and discontinue all military activities at 2000 hours GMT on 7 June 1967;

2. Requests the Secretary-General to keep the Council promptly and currently informed on the situation.

SOURCE: American Foreign Policy: Current Documents, 1967 (Washington, D.C., 1969), p. 516.

THE ISRAELIS obliged with a cease-fire after they had accomplished all their military objectives, including occupation of the Sinai up to the Suez Canal. Egyptian troops had been abjectly defeated, and the Israelis captured many millions of dollars worth of Russian equipment. The Israelis refused to move their troops back within their prewar boundaries until the Egyptians promised free transit of the Suez Canal, and the situation came to a stalemate. The U.N. Security Council on November 22, 1967, drew up a statement of principles for a peace settlement and proposed a mediation; the latter failed, and the former remained the U.N. program for solution of the Arab-Israeli confrontation.

SOURCE: Current Documents, 1967, pp. 616–617.

The Security Council,

Expressing its continuing concern with the grave situation in the Middle East,

Emphasizing the inadmissibility of the acquisition of territory by war and the need to work for a just and lasting peace in which every State in the area can live in security,

Emphasizing further that all Member States in their acceptance of the Charter of the United Nations have undertaken a commitment to act in accordance with Article 2 of the Charter,

1. *Affirms* that the fulfilment of Charter principles requires the establishment of a just and lasting peace in the Middle East which should include the application of both the following principles:

i. Withdrawal of Israeli armed forces from territories occupied in the recent conflict;

ii. Termination of all claims or states of belligerency and respect for and acknowledgement of the sovereignty, territorial integrity and political independence of every State in the area and their right to live in peace within secure and recognized boundaries free from threats or acts of force;

2. *Affirms further* the necessity

a. For guaranteeing freedom of navigation through international waterways in the area;

b. For achieving a just settlement of the refugee problem;

c. For guaranteeing the territorial inviolability and political independence of every State in the area, through measures including the establishment of demilitarized zones;

3. *Requests* the Secretary-General to designate a Special Representative to proceed to the Middle East to establish and maintain contacts with the States concerned in order to promote agreement and assist effort to achieve a peaceful and accepted settlement in accordance with the provisions and principles in this resolution;

4. *Requests* the Secretary-General to report to the Security Council on the progress of the efforts of the Special Representative as soon as possible.

From 1967 onward, relations between the Arabs and Israelis moved uncertainly between war and peace. In 1967 the canal was again closed to traffic; it began to silt up, with several ships of assorted nationalities trapped inside, perhaps permanently. Aerial warfare and shelling con-

tinued in the vicinity of the canal until in 1970 the two sides managed a modest truce, arranged by Secretary of State Rogers. The Israelis remained in possession of their captured territories and considered the occupation of all of Jerusalem a fait accompli. They moved their capital from Tel Aviv to Jerusalem. As the years passed the Egyptians gave some evidence of mellowing. They finished the Soviet-financed higher dam at Aswan. Nasser died in 1970. In 1972 his successor, President Anwar el-Sadat, expelled the thousands of Soviet military advisers who had been training Egyptian troops after the debacle of 1967, helping Egypt defend the Suez Canal area against the Israelis, and using Egyptian territory somewhat mysteriously as a base for planes shadowing the U.S. Sixth Fleet. The Egyptians angrily denied any intention of negotiating with the Israelis. Then to the complete surprise of the American government a fourth Arab-Israeli war broke out on October 6, 1973, the day of Yom Kippur. Egyptian troops attacked Israeli positions on the east bank of the canal, and the Syrians simultaneously attacked the Golan heights on the Israeli-Syrian border. The Iraqis and Jordanians entered the war. After gains by the Egyptians, with heavy losses of Israeli tanks and planes because of Egyptian use of Russian-made missiles, the Israelis began to counterattack, and crossed over to the west bank of the canal and seized the city of Suez. A U.N. cease-fire was arranged on October 22. The Israelis broke it to complete the encirclement of an Egyptian corps, cutting off its water supply, thus putting intense pressure on Cairo. President Sadat proposed a joint intervention by the U.S. and U.S.S.R. to enforce the cease-fire. There followed, on the night of October 24, 1973, what President Nixon afterward said was "the most difficult crisis we have had since the Cuban confrontation of 1962." A message from Chairman Brezhnev said the Soviet Union was willing to accept the Sadat proposal, and if necessary might intervene without the United States. Seven Soviet divisions were known to have been alerted. American military forces thereupon went on "Defense Condition 3," the middle on a scale of five alert stages. The Soviets were advised not to intervene unilaterally. The crisis ended when the U.N. organized a peace-keeping force and the Israelis allowed the supply of the Egyptian corps. The Soviet Union meanwhile had undertaken to replace the Arabs' losses of equipment, and the United States did likewise for the Israelis. There was a proposal to Congress for a massive grant of funds and talk of an alliance with Israel. In retaliation the Arabs cut off oil exports and Americans faced an energy crisis. Secretary of State Kissinger remarked publicly that the United States, too, might have to retaliate.

IX

Africa

Prior to the Second World War the interest of the people and government of the United States in the continent of Africa was connected with the inhuman exportation of thousands upon thousands of Africans to the North American subcontinent which had begun over three centuries earlier in 1619. The American government had made the slave trade illegal in 1808 and effectively ended it during the Civil War with the assistance of the British navy. In the years thereafter the so-called Dark Continent engaged popular attention mainly as a field for missionary endeavor, as the ancestral home of a tenth of the American people, and incidentally of course, as a place of exploration—Henry M. Stanley was an American newspaperman. The government took special interest in the trials and tribulations of Liberia, founded by private philanthropy in the 1820s. The only other independent state in Africa until after the war of 1939–45 was Ethiopia, a feudal country that briefly moved across the stage of world history in the mid-1930s when it was conquered by Fascist Italy. Commerce between the United States and Africa was slight, investment almost nonexistent, until the Second World War brought the mineral resources of the continent, notably the copper and uranium of the Congo, to American attention. The postwar era marked a movement of capital into the booming economy of South Africa. Politically, Africa lingered in a kind of limbo, tied to the colonial powers. The United States was preoccupied with the developing cold war with Russia. As late as October, 1957, according to the *Foreign Service List*, the foreign service had only 248 officers in its 33 African posts, whereas it had 256 officers in the single nation of West Germany alone. The officers in African posts concerned themselves largely with American citizens resident in or visiting the localities and with the colonial rulers. Chester Bowles, well-qualified as an observer of American foreign relations, passed through Africa in 1955 and visited four American consulates. Only one had ever had an African to dinner. But then came the announcements of independence: the Sudan (1956), Ghana (1957), Guinea (1958), and a total of eighteen countries in 1960. The Congo—present-day Zäire —became independent that year. By the end of the 1960s more than forty African states had sent delegations to the United Nations. A desire for freedom was agitating the politics of the remaining parts of Africa. In the course of all this change, and the efforts to effect more change, the diplomatic position of the United States gradually became discernible. The nation from 1776 had been dedicated to freedom. It had fought the Civil War in part for the purpose of ensuring freedom. In the late 1950s and throughout the 1960s its black minority was making a mighty effort to advance its own rights—political, social, cultural. When freedom was rising throughout most of Africa, America's blacks and their many supporters among the whites began to find themselves "turned on" by African problems. In South Africa a repressive government was attempting to keep the whites and blacks separate, and restrict the economic and other opportunities of the blacks. In Southern Rhodesia a white-dominated government refused suffrage to the vast black majority. Most Americans strongly objected to these repressions, and were willing to use all suitable diplomatic means to help right them.

29. The Congo

THE UNITED NATIONS' first major experience with an international police action (the stationing of truce observers between Egypt and Israel in 1956 was a small-scale operation) came shortly after the Congo received its independence from Belgium. Following riots in Léopoldville on January 4-6, 1959, the Belgian king on May 19, 1960, promulgated a fundamental law granting independence to the Congo, and the two nations, old and new, signed a treaty on June 29. The United States recognized the Congo that same day. Shortly thereafter the Force Publique rebelled and widespread disorder broke out. After a request from the Congolese government, the Security Council on July 14 authorized military and technical assistance.

SOURCE: American Foreign Policy: Current Documents, 1960 (Washington, D.C., 1964), p. 528.

Africa

1. *Calls upon* the Government of Belgium to withdraw their troops from the territory of the Republic of the Congo;

2. *Decides* to authorize the Secretary-General to take the necessary steps, in consultation with the Government of the Republic of the Congo, to provide the Government with such military assistance, as may be necessary, until, through the efforts of the Congolese Government with the technical assistance of the United Nations, the national

SOURCE: *Current Documents, 1960*, p. 529.

security forces may be able, in the opinion of the Government, to meet fully their tasks;

3. Requests the Secretary-General to report to the Security Council as appropriate.

THE U.N. CONGO RESOLUTION *asked for the immediate departure of Belgian troops in the belief that their continued presence in the Congo was exacerbating the confused political situation there. This section of the resolution was embarrassing to the United States, for Belgium was a NATO ally. The Belgians obviously had not prepared the Congo for independence, but it did not help much for the U.N. to become so obviously critical. A statement of July 14, 1960, by the American representative at the U.N., Henry Cabot Lodge, Jr., sought to explain the American vote on the Security Council resolution.*

The United States voted for the Tunisian resolution in spite of its doubts about the wisdom of the first operative paragraph, and we did so because of the vital urgency which we attach to prompt United Nations action to meet the tragic and highly dangerous situation in the Congo.

In voting for this resolution the United States expressly interprets the first paragraph calling upon the Government of Belgium to withdraw its troops as being contingent upon the successful carrying out by the United Nations of the second paragraph, that is, in providing the Government of the Republic of the Congo with the military assistance necessary until national security forces are able to fulfill their task.

The situation we face in the Congo is unique. At the outset of its independence, as power was being passed from the Government of Belgium to the Government of the Republic of the Congo, public law and order collapsed. In these circumstances the United Nations must not contribute to the perpetuation of public disorder by insisting upon the withdrawal of military units capable of assisting in the protection of life and property without establishment of alternate methods to accomplish the task.

The resolution can only be read as a whole in this sense, and it is with this understanding that the United States has supported it.

The United States has confidence that the Government of Belgium will cooperate wholeheartedly with the United Nations along these lines, in accordance with the long tradition which it has of loyal membership in support of the Organization. May I say to the representative of Belgium that he has in fact just this evening made a statement expressing his Government's willingness to withdraw its troops upon introduction of United Nations forces, a statement of Belgium's full cooperation with the United Nations for which the Belgian Government should be congratulated and which reflects credit on the Belgian representative here.

U.N. FORCES, *eventually numbering almost 18,000 troops, entered the Congo, brought in by U.S. Air Force planes. The troops were contributed by the smaller countries, mostly African. Meanwhile relations between Belgium and the Congo had snapped on July 14, the same day the Security Council voted to intervene. In other respects, however, the Congolese government's politics were not easy to follow, especially its internal politics. There was a dispute involving Premier Patrice Lumumba, who had been expelled from the post of premier by President Joseph Kasavubu but refused to acknowledge that Kasavubu had the authority to remove him. The Soviet Union became unhappy over what it considered an American military presence in the Congo (the U.S. government had sent in supporting personnel for the airlift), and threw its support to Lumumba. All the while a secessionist movement employing European mercenaries was in control of the copper-rich province of Katanga, under the presidency of Moïse Tshombé, and there was some question as to whether the taxes Tshombé collected from the great Belgian ore firm, the Union Minière du Haut Katanga, were paid under duress or from a feeling that a secessionist government might be more pliable than the regime seeking to control all of the Congo from Léopoldville. In a statement on December 17, 1960, the government of the United States sought to make its position clear through its representative to the U.N., James J. Wadsworth.*

From the outset of the emergency in the Congo the United States, along with the great majority of the United Nations members, has wholeheartedly supported this Organization as the only possible instrument to restore peace and independence to the suffering people of the Congo. We have channeled all our aid, military transport, technical, administrative, and financial, through the United Nations and have repeatedly urged others to follow our example. Today we believe that more than ever. Only the United Nations has at its disposal both the great resources and the great and impartial principles which the emergency demands.

I would remind the Assembly once again that the United States could have taken another course. At the very beginning, just after the Belgian intervention, the Congolese Government asked the United States for direct military assistance. We refused, Mr. Presi-

SOURCE: *Current Documents, 1960,* pp. 619–25.

dent, and insisted that all military aid be channeled through the United Nations. We provided a massive airlift, in which 15,000 troops from every quarter of the globe were brought to the Congo. We did not pick and choose and say, "We will not carry your troops because we disagree with your policy." We carried all the troops which the United Nations asked us to carry.

As to the Soviet Union, it has already become quite clear that the Soviet Union has other aims as regards the Congo. Its preferred candidates for power are those who are least likely to achieve a solution to the Congo's problems without violence and bloodshed. It wishes to foment hatred between races and between tribes. It wishes to disarm the only Congolese military force. It wishes to cut the Congo off from technical aid through the United Nations. It wants a civil war in the Congo in order to promote its own evil designs. In short, every aspect of Soviet policy is designed either to weaken and divide or to gain power in the Congo for those who will do the will of Moscow. It is a straight policy of "rule or ruin." It is a policy fraught with danger for international peace and security.

That is not our attitude toward the people of the Republic of the Congo. They have suffered much, and they still face a difficult future. To overcome the difficulties three things are needed:

First, that the Congo should not become an unwilling victim in the struggle of an ambitious nation or group of nations eager to build new empires.

Second, that the Congolese people and their leaders should make the most strenuous and disciplined efforts on their own behalf to win their birthright as an independent nation and in this task should cooperate willingly with the United Nations.

And, finally, that we, the members of the United Nations, should support the Organization in foul weather as well as fair. Only great problems and great difficulties can truly measure our fidelity to the charter. Let us meet our difficulties in such a way that freedom and peace in Africa may be advanced and that we shall have no reason to fear the judgment of history.

IN EARLY 1961 *the Congo situation seemed as far from solution as it had during the preceding summer, with disorder rampant in large parts of*

SOURCE: *American Foreign Policy: Current Documents, 1961* (Washington, D.C., 1965), pp. 774–75.

the country. In the U.N. sessions over the issue the Soviet Union sought to censure Secretary General Dag Hammarskjold and vetoed attempts by the Security Council to carry on the intervention. An emergency special session of the General Assembly proved necessary. President Kennedy read the following statement in a news conference on February 15.

Ambassador Stevenson in the Security Council today has expressed fully and clearly the attitude of the United States Government toward the attempts to undermine the effectiveness of the United Nations Organization. The United States can take care of itself, but the United Nations system exists so that every nation can have the assurance of security. Any attempt to destroy this system is a blow aimed directly at the independence and security of every nation, large and small.

I am also, however, seriously concerned at what appears to be a threat of unilateral intervention in the internal affairs of the Republic of Congo. I find it difficult to believe that any government is really planning to take so dangerous and irresponsible a step. Nevertheless, I feel it important that there should be no misunderstanding of the position of the United States in such an eventuality. The United States has supported and will continue to support the United Nations' presence in the Congo. The United States considers that the only legal authority entitled to speak for the Congo as a whole is a government established under the Chief of State, President Kasavubu, who has been seated in the General Assembly of the United Nations by a majority vote of its members. The broadening of the government under President Kasavubu is a quite legitimate subject of discussion, and such discussions have been going on in Léopoldville and in New York, but the purported recognition of Congolese factions as so-called governments in other parts of that divided country can only confuse and make more difficult the task of securing Congolese independence and unity.

The United Nations offers the best, if not only, possibility for the restoration of conditions of stability and order in the Congo.

The press reports this afternoon that Prime Minister Nehru has stated, "If the United Nations goes out of the Congo, it will be a disaster." I strongly agree with this view. Only by the presence of the United Nations in the Congo can peace be kept in Africa.

I would conceive it to be the duty of the United States and, indeed, all members of the United Nations to defend the charter of the United Nations by opposing any attempt by any government to intervene unilaterally in the Congo.

FORMER PREMIER LUMUMBA *was murdered in Katanga in February 1961, and secessionist sentiment was increasing in Katanga and elsewhere, with danger that the new African state would dissolve into several, perhaps even several dozen, tribal entities. Gradually the U.N. force created order, but not before Secretary General Hammarskjold was killed in a plane accident on September 18, 1961, together with his entire party of assistants. Tshombé arranged a cease-fire with the central government and after some hesitation recognized the authority of that government on December 21, 1961. Two days before, Undersecretary of State George W. Ball in an address in Los Angeles discussed the American position on Tshombé's attempted secession.*

Prime Minister Adoula's ability to concentrate the energies of his Government on the prime tasks of the Congo has been undermined by the danger of two major defections—the defection of Moïse Tshombé who has claimed to set up an "independent" government in Elisabethville in the Katanga in the Southern Congo, and the defection of Antoine Gizenga who is pursuing his own ambitions in Stanleyville in the Orientale Province of the Eastern Congo.

In these circumstances, the Congo's main political issue—perhaps the only really "modern" issue—is Congolese unity. If Prime Minister Adoula should prove unable to deal effectively with the Katanga secession of Mr. Tshombé, militant extremists such as the Communist-chosen instrument, Mr. Gizenga, would bid to take over the Central Government—in the name of Congolese unity. In the resulting civil war, our main objectives of all the Western countries in Central Africa would be drowned in blood.

The Congo is not characterized by homogeneity.

The road to nationhood will at best be rough indeed.

As many of you are aware, the Congo is composed of a large number of tribes—some large, some small. They speak over one hundred tribal languages, and four varieties of lingua-franca. Out of this diverse material, there was created in the last fifty years a single country, administered as six major provinces.

Both the nation and the provinces were given their unity essentially by a common colonial administration and a structure of

SOURCE: *Current Documents, 1961,* pp. 865–69.

political institutions which created the habit of common government. It was on this structure—the only one the Congo has ever known except for tribal institutions—that the federal constitution was based. This federal constitution, adopted and placed into force at the time of independence, is the fundamental law of the Congo.

In view of the absence of any experience with federalism it was not surprising that under the stress and strain of political turmoil a number of the larger tribes in the Congo and the political leaders who drew their strength from those tribes, should begin to develop ambitions towards separate national existence, albeit a separate national existence for which there was in fact no historical basis. This was the case with Mr. Tshombé with his Lunda and Bayeke supporters in the south Katanga; of Mr. Kalonji with his Baluba supporters in the south of Kasai, of the Mongo tribe in the northeast; and even of some of President Kasavubu's Bakongo supporters in the area around Léopoldville.

What distinguishes Mr. Tshombé's particular brand of secession from the others is that the slice of territory which his supporters inhabit—less than one-twelfth of the area of the Congo, with about ½0th of its population—happens to contain a disproportionate part of the mineral wealth that is the Congo's greatest natural resource. It is the revenues Mr. Tshombé has been able to obtain by taxing the production under his control, the soldiers of fortune and writers of propaganda he has been able to mobilize with these revenues, and the encouragement he has received from outside financial interests, that have given the peculiar flavor to the Katangese attempt at secession.

The question may, of course, be asked: Why shouldn't the Katanga be independent? For that matter, why shouldn't every other tribe in Central Africa that wishes to declare its independence have a right to do so? There are, I think, two answers to this question—one political and the other legal.

To pose the question as I have posed it answers the political question without need for much elaboration. The Government structure which the Belgians left behind in the Congo is the only political structure the Congo has ever known. Under it, the Congo has evolved from a primitive area to a potentially prosperous power in Africa, with a relatively high standard of basic education and a level of economic development that many other African areas could envy. To break up this entity into a number of conflicting and competing tribal satrapies could only confirm and render permanent the chaos we have already seen in the Congo. And that—as I hope I have made clear—would open the way inevitably for the Soviets and their friends to fish where they can catch the most—in troubled waters.

To those who approach the problem from the viewpoint of protecting particular interests, something may perhaps be said for carving enclaves out of the Congo—though I am convinced that even this calculation is mistaken. But if one looks at the problem from the viewpoint of saving all of Central Africa from chaos and Communist infiltration, then clearly the acceptance of armed secession by a tribal area, no matter how rich and well-supported, can lead only to disaster.

At no time has any responsible leader in the Congo itself advocated that the Congo be split into sovereign states. The absurdity of such a notion is clear if the Congo were split into separate states with populations equivalent to the population of the Katanga Province, we would wind up with over twenty governments; indeed, Katanga itself would split in two if the concept of tribal separatism were given full play. There simply is no legal case, no political case, no economic case, and no moral case for Balkanizing the heart of Africa.

But there may be a case for injecting an element of decentralization in a country the size of the Congo. The Congo is a very large country; its institutions for governing are still in the "less developed" category; its leadership cadres are still dangerously thin; many of its people still lack a sense of nationhood. In these circumstances most of the political leaders of the Congo appear to believe that there should be enough local autonomy on local matters to discourage secession.

Yet if the Congo is to be a nation, it can hardly permit provincial leaders to break off pieces of the country—especially when such provincial leaders are heavily influenced from the outside. What I am saying applies not only to the Katanga, but equally to the northern provinces and to the efforts of Antoine Gizenga, the agent of Communist designs, to set up shop as leader of a leftward-leaning separatism in Stanleyville.

It is clearly in the direction of constitutional changes brought about on the basis of agreement among the regional leaders that the solution must be sought. But this has so far proved impossible because the Katanga authorities, confident they were secure behind their mercenary-led private army, have shown little interest in real negotiations, and have blocked talks by insisting, in effect, on a prior recognition of independent status.

The continuation of this situation, which has lasted for over a year, has posed an increasingly serious threat of civil war. Pressures have grown progressively greater on the Central Government to break the deadlock and put an end to secession by military means. The moderate leadership in the present government has made statesmanlike efforts to resist these pressures and rely on the UN. But it has been perfectly clear that an explosion into civil war became every day more likely if no political solution were found. Gizenga and his Communist advisers have based their hopes on this explosion.

The United Nations forces were stationed in Elisabethville—in the Katanga—over a year ago for the same purposes as in the rest of the Congo—to assist in the maintenance of law and order and the prevention of civil war. As the threat of civil war has steadily grown, the importance of the United Nations mission—to interpose itself between the rival forces in the Katanga—has grown in equal measure. But during the same period these forces have been subjected to a continuing and growing campaign of harassment by the Katanga authorities and their military appendages—African and European—designed apparently to make the position of the United Nations in the Katanga untenable. These efforts have been spearheaded by mercenaries, adventurers, soldiers of fortune who have flocked to the well-heeled standard of the "independent" Katanga.

Even the cease fire that followed the outbreak of fighting in the Katanga last September served only to exacerbate the situation: While the United Nations stuck strictly to the terms of the cease fire, the Katanga authorities engaged in a steady build-up of men, munitions and equipment (including airplanes) obtained through the devious channels of the international arms trade in spite of the sincere efforts of Western European governments to stop the traffic.

The result was, of course, the series of incidents that began about two weeks ago. The Katanga forces and authorities arrested and beat up the top leaders of the United Nations in Elisabethville, kidnapped a number of their troops including one officer, kept up a steady propaganda barrage against the UN, and finally tried to cut off the United Nations forces from their base of supplies and communications. The United Nations leadership on the spot showed commendable patience. But it was finally necessary for the UN command in Elisabethville to recognize that these repeated breaches of the cease fire agreement could no longer be tolerated, and to take the necessary limited action to restore the ability of the United Nations to carry out its mandate in the Katanga.

No one can be happy about the bloodshed on either side that accompanied these military operations. Peacekeeping is not necessarily wholly peaceful. But in this case it was necessary to prevent a civil war that would have made the past few days in Elisabethville look like a picnic.

The UN action in Elisabethville has now largely achieved its limited objective—to maintain freedom of movement for the peacekeeping forces, without the daily, bloody harassment by local Katanga troops, whipped into excited and irresponsible action by rumor, radio and beer. The UN forces have stuck loyally to the limited aims set for them by Acting Secretary General U Thant in New York. Now that talks are hopefully about to start between Prime Minister Adoula and Mr. Tshombé, the fighting has stopped. We hope it is over for keeps.

The most urgent unfinished business now is to get on with negotiations between Prime Minister Adoula and Mr. Tshombé for the peaceful reintegration of the Katanga into the Congo. Just before he left on his Latin American trip, President Kennedy took a major initiative to bring these efforts to fruition. As a result Ambassador Gullion, our Ambassador in Léopoldville, has embarked on a series of arrangements to facilitate Mr. Tshombé's meeting with the Prime Minister.

We are watching developments hourly. In a situation as fluid as this, it is rash to be optimistic, but I am convinced that we are on the right path.

In the final analysis, the interests of the Katanga and those of the moderate leadership in Léopoldville are parallel. The sooner they can pull in the same direction, the better for both of them—and for us as well.

I said before that a solution to the Katanga problem should contribute decisively to the ability of the Léopoldville Government to cope with the diversionary activities of Antoine Gizenga. Although technically Vice Premier in the Government, he has never worked at his job. His basis of real support in the country is narrow. His policy is founded upon the hope that the Adoula Government and the United Nations will be unable to deal with the Katanga problem and that the country must then turn to him for a solution. But if the Katanga problem can be disposed of, I am convinced that Mr. Gizenga—who has already slipped badly—will cease to be of much use to the Communist bloc. He can then be dealt with effectively by the genuine nationalists in the Congo Government.

30. Trials of Freedom

A. SOUTH AFRICA

THE RACIAL POLICIES of the Union of South Africa—the practices known in Afrikaans as apartheid—troubled the American government from the outset of the postwar era and became serious in the 1950s, when they ran directly counter to the development of most of the rest of the African continent toward freedom. The United Nations, both the Security Council and the General Assembly, took increasing interest in apartheid, and a typical resolution (they began to appear almost annually) was that taken by the General Assembly on December 6, 1955.

The General Assembly,

Recalling its previous resolutions on the question of race conflict in South Africa resulting from the policies of apartheid of the Government of the Union of South Africa, . . .

1. Commends the United Nations Commission on the Racial Situation in the Union of South Africa for its constructive work;
2. Notes with regret that the Government of the Union of South Africa again refused to co-operate with the Commission;
3. Recommends the Government of the Union of South Africa to take note of the Commission's report;
4. Expresses its concern at the fact that the Government of the Union of South Africa continues to give effect to the policies of

SOURCE: American Foreign Policy: 1950–1955, 2 vols. (Washington, D.C., 1957), I, pp. 2308–09.

apartheid, notwithstanding the request made to it by the General Assembly to reconsider its position in the light of the high principles contained in the Charter and taking into account the pledge of all Member States to promote respect for human rights and fundamental freedoms without distinction as to race;

5. *Reminds* the Government of the Union of South Africa of the faith it had reaffirmed, in signing the Charter, in fundamental human rights and in the dignity and worth of the human person;

6. *Calls on* the Government of the Union of South Africa to observe the obligations contained in Article 56 of the Charter.

YEAR AFTER YEAR *the U.N. passed its resolutions, and year after year the Union of South Africa defied its critics. It withdrew from the British Commonwealth and became a republic on May 31, 1961. As the years passed and the republic flourished economically, attracting much American capital, a movement began to obtain United States government prohibition of investment in South Africa and then failing that, stockholders' actions to sell South African plants and withdraw from other affiliations. The Nixon administration refused to go along with this public feeling, which by the early 1970s had become intense. Assistant Secretary of State for African Affairs David D. Newsom sought to explain the administration's position in a speech in Chicago on June 28, 1972.*

Finally, there is the question of U.S. investments in South Africa. There are those who see the failure of the U.S. Government to seek to restrict such investments as an indication of sympathy for the policies of South Africa. There are those who assume that the presence of these investments automatically means that we will intervene in the event of trouble in that area. Neither assumption is correct. Here, again, the record needs to be set straight:

—First, U.S. investment in South Africa represents only 16 percent of total foreign investment in that country. It represents only a fourth of total U.S. investment in Africa, a ratio that is decreasing all the time. It is not likely that U.S. withdrawal of this investment, assuming this were feasible, would force change in South Africa. There is no valid basis for speculating that the United States would take extraordinary measures to protect this investment in the event of civil or other disturbance when, among other factors, more substantial investment in the rest of the continent would need to be weighed in the balance.

—Second, much of this investment is linked with South African

SOURCE: Department of State *Bulletin*, July 24, 1972, pp. 119–25.

business interests; withdrawal would not be easy even if the United States had authority to force withdrawal by American companies. New U.S. investment in South Africa comes to a large extent from current profits of U.S. firms operating there.

—Third, the United States does not encourage investment in South Africa nor extend guarantees covering such investment. It is the economic situation in that country that attracts investment.

—Fourth, while there is debate in the United States and in South Africa on this point, our surroundings indicate that the black and colored populations of South Africa do not want to see U.S. investment withdrawn. The majority see U.S. investment as a constructive force; they wish to see it remain and make an impact on that society.

The United States Government, therefore, neither encourages nor discourages investment in South Africa. It does encourage U.S. firms that are there to lead the way in upgrading the status of non-white workers and in contributions to social and educational improvement. It is a misleading oversimplification to suggest that the presence of that investment either draws us into the conflict of races in that area or commits us to a policy favorable to apartheid.

B. Southern Rhodesia

WHILE SOUTH AFRICA defied the U.N. Charter's guarantees of human rights and political freedom, civil war wracked the Congo and a revolutionary movement appeared in Angola. At the same time the prosperous British enclave in southern Africa known as Southern Rhodesia—named after the nineteenth-century British colonizer—stirred in confusion and uncertainty. The white settlers determined not to yield much, if any, political power to the colony's vast majority of blacks. The same contention was heard in Southern Rhodesia as elsewhere, namely, that the white colonists were themselves natives and could not properly be dispossessed of their property, in particular, their land. The settlers had a good deal less reason to feel this way than the South African whites, for Southern Rhodesia had been settled largely in the past half century. Still, it was a lovely country, productive farmland and rich mineral resources. The British government sought to control the situation and appeared to have a better chance of success than in South Africa because there were far fewer whites in Rhodesia. By the time the Southern Rhodesia problem got into the United Nations, there had been the intervention in the Congo, and the British seem to have hoped that the

SOURCE: *American Foreign Policy: Current Documents, 1962* (Washington, D.C., 1966), pp. 980–81.

U.N. might be able to handle the matter. At the outset the United States government made its position clear, as in the remarks by the U.S. representative, Jonathan B. Bingham, to a committee of the General Assembly on October 26, 1962.

The United States continues to be ever more deeply concerned, not only with the situation in Southern Rhodesia, but equally with the effect that situation as it unfolds may have on wider issues involving the future of parts, if not the whole of the continent of Africa. The recent civil disturbances in Southern Rhodesia, the adoption by the Government of Southern Rhodesia of extraordinary measures, including the banning of the Zimbabwe African People's Union as a legitimate political party, and the placing of many of its leaders under varying degrees of restraint if not imprisonment, have accentuated my Government's anxiety. We are faced today with the consideration of a situation which is, to say the least, potentially explosive. . . .

In view of this tragic prospect, it seems to my delegation that the time has arrived when some third party, some outside agency, is needed to help the various groups in Southern Rhodesia allay the deepening fears and mistrusts and reverse the trend toward one of growing mutual confidence. The cycle which is now vicious could then be made benign. Communication is an essential element of confidence and, as each side learned to know and understand the other better, all would come increasingly to recognize that it is their common interests that are truly compelling and that the welfare of all depend on the willingness of all to recognize their mutual interdependence.

To us it would seem that the Government of the United Kingdom is a natural agency to play the role of third-party conciliator, and we would hope that it would undertake to do so.

THE BRITISH GOVERNMENT did its best to persuade the "settler minority government of Southern Rhodesia" (as a U.N. special committee referred to the regime there in 1964) but was unable to get a lever under that government, which was dominated by its stalwart white supremacist prime minister, Ian Smith. On November 11, 1965, the Smith regime made a unilateral declaration of independence. Next day the U.N. Security Council condemned the move and called upon all U.N.

SOURCE: American Foreign Policy: Current Documents, 1965 (Washington, D.C., 1968), pp. 686–88.

members not to recognize "this illegal racist minority regime in Southern Rhodesia and to refrain from rendering any assistance to this illegal regime." The U.S. representative to the U.N., Arthur Goldberg, that day announced the measures his government would take.

As a first step, the United States yesterday recalled its consul general from Salisbury. We have also informed the British Government that the Minister for Southern Rhodesian Affairs in the United Kingdom Embassy in Washington, and his four staff members, no longer have any diplomatic status in the United States.

We are immediately instituting a comprehensive embargo on the shipment of all arms and military equipment to Southern Rhodesia.

We will withhold the establishment of any quota for the importation of sugar from Southern Rhodesia in 1966.

The United States Government will suspend action on all applications for United States Government loans and credit guarantees to Southern Rhodesia and will make clear to any potential American investors in Southern Rhodesia the risks which we perceive in any further investment of American capital.

Finally, we will discourage all American private travel to Southern Rhodesia.

The U.N. Security Council on December 16, 1966, passed a resolution imposing selective mandatory economic sanctions against Southern Rhodesia, and the United States cooperated. But then an act of Congress in 1971 recognized the fact that Rhodesian sanctions had forced Americans to pay higher prices to the Soviet Union for strategic materials, and it exempted such materials from Rhodesian sanctions and allowed their importation unless there was a similar embargo on such materials from Communist countries. The United States found itself condemned by resolutions in the U.N. and in the Organization of African Unity. The State Department was deeply embarrassed. Congress had undercut the negotiations then in progress between the British government and the Smith regime, which, after having given some indication of arriving at a modus vivendi, failed.

X

Good Neighbor in Latin America

If anyone could have inquired of American officials in the 1930s whether the government of the United States ever again would pursue a policy of intervention in the affairs of Latin America, he would have been met with a resounding "No!" But as affairs turned out, there were several interventions in the years after 1945—Guatemala in 1954, Cuba in 1961, the Dominican Republic in 1965. The proportions of these interventions were different from those of the Theodore Roosevelt–Taft–Wilson era for several reasons: they were very temporary affairs; the Cuban intervention did not succeed; in two of the three countries they were conducted by non-U.S. nationals; and all were against Communism, or at least that was the contention of the United States government. Nor were these interventions the most important part of American policy toward Latin America after the Second World War, for one single situation—the Cuban missile crisis of 1962—was by far the most dangerous threat to international peace to arise anywhere in the world in the years after the war. In a sense, of course, the missile crisis does not belong in the present chapter, for it held only a geographical meaning for Cuba and Latin America: it was a great world crisis that happened to occur in Cuba.

31. Organizing the Hemisphere

A. THE RIO PACT

THE FIRST of the post-1945 regional agreements of the United States (the others were the North Atlantic Treaty of 1949, the Southeast Asia Treaty of 1954, and adherence to the Central Treaty in 1957) was the Inter-American Treaty of Reciprocal Assistance, known as the Rio Pact, a regional agreement under Article 51 of the U.N. Charter, which was signed September 2, 1947.

Article 1

The High Contracting Parties formally condemn war and undertake in their international relations not to resort to the threat or the use of force in any manner inconsistent with the provisions of the Charter of the United Nations or of this Treaty.

Article 2

As a consequence of the principle set forth in the preceding Article, the High Contracting Parties undertake to submit every controversy which may arise between them to methods of peaceful settlement and to endeavor to settle any such controversy among themselves by means of the procedures in force in the Inter-American System before referring it to the General Assembly or the Security Council of the United Nations.

Article 3

1. The High Contracting Parties agree that an armed attack by any State against an American State shall be considered as an attack against all the American States and, consequently, each one of the said Contracting Parties undertakes to assist in meeting the attack in the exercise of the inherent right of individual or collec-

SOURCE: Charles I. Bevans, comp., *Treaties and Other International Agreements of the United States of America: 1776–1949* (Washington, D.C., 1968–), IV, pp. 559–66.

tive self-defense recognized by Article 51 of the Charter of the United Nations.

2. On the request of the State or States directly attacked and until the decision of the Organ of Consultation of the Inter-American System, each one of the Contracting Parties may determine the immediate measures which it may individually take in fulfillment of the obligation contained in the preceding paragraph and in accordance with the principle of continental solidarity. The Organ of Consultation shall meet without delay for the purpose of examining those measures and agreeing upon the measures of a collective character that should be taken.

3. The provisions of this Article shall be applied in case of any armed attack which takes place within the region described in Article 4 or within the territory of an American State. When the attack takes place outside of the said areas, the provisions of Article 6 shall be applied.

4. Measures of self-defense provided for under this Article may be taken until the Security Council of the United Nations has taken the measures necessary to maintain international peace and security.

Article 4

The region to which this Treaty refers is bounded as follows: beginning at the North Pole; thence due south to a point 74 degrees north latitude, 10 degrees west longitude; thence by a rhumb line to a point 47 degrees 30 minutes north latitude, 50 degrees west longitude; thence by a rhumb line to a point 35 degrees north latitude, 60 degrees west longitude; thence due south to a point in 20 degrees north latitude; thence by a rhumb line to a point 5 degrees north latitude, 24 degrees west longitude; thence due south to the South Pole; thence due north to a point 30 degrees south latitude, 90 degrees west longitude; thence by a rhumb line to a point on the Equator at 97 degrees west longitude; thence by a rhumb line to a point 15 degrees north latitude, 120 degrees west longitude; thence by a rhumb line to a point 50 degrees north latitude, 170 degrees east longitude; thence due north to a point in 54 degrees north latitude; thence by a rhumb line to a point 65 degrees 30 minutes north latitude, 168 degrees 58 minutes 5 seconds west longitude; thence due north to the North Pole.

Article 5

The High Contracting Parties shall immediately send to the Security Council of the United Nations, in conformity with Articles 51 and 54 of the Charter of the United Nations, complete information concerning the activities undertaken or in contemplation in the exercise of the right of self-defense or for the purpose of maintaining inter-American peace and security.

Article 6

If the inviolability or the integrity of the territory or the sovereignty or political independence of any American State should be affected by an aggression which is not an armed attack or by an extra-continental or intra-continental conflict, or by any other fact or situation that might endanger the peace of America, the Organ of Consultation shall meet immediately in order to agree on the measures which must be taken in case of aggression to assist the victim of the aggression or, in any case, the measures which should be taken for the common defense and for the maintenance of the peace and security of the Continent.

Article 7

In the case of a conflict between two or more American States, without prejudice to the right of self-defense in conformity with Article 51 of the Charter of the United Nations, the High Contracting Parties, meeting in consultation shall call upon the contending States to suspend hostilities and restore matters to the *status quo ante bellum,* and shall take in addition all other necessary measures to reestablish or maintain inter-American peace and security and for the solution of the conflict by peaceful means. The rejection of the pacifying action will be considered in the determination of the aggressor and in the application of the measures which the consultative meeting may agree upon.

Article 8

For the purposes of this Treaty, the measures on which the Organ of Consultation may agree will comprise one or more of the following: recall of chiefs of diplomatic missions; breaking of

The region defined by Article 4 of the Inter-American Treaty of Reciprocal Assistance, signed at Río de Janeiro on September 2, 1947.

Boundaries of the Río Pact

diplomatic relations; breaking of consular relations; partial or complete interruption of economic relations or of rail, sea, air, postal, telegraphic, telephonic, and radiotelephonic or radio-telegraphic communications; and use of armed force.

Article 9

In addition to other acts which the Organ of Consultation may characterize as aggression, the following shall be considered as such:

a. Unprovoked armed attack by a State against the territory, the people, or the land, sea or air forces of another State;

b. Invasion, by the armed forces of a State, of the territory of an American State, through the trespassing of boundaries demarcated in accordance with a treaty, judicial decision, or arbitral award, or, in the absence of frontiers thus demarcated, invasion affecting a region which is under the effective jurisdiction of another State.

Article 10

None of the provisions of this Treaty shall be construed as impairing the rights and obligations of the High Contracting Parties under the Charter of the United Nations.

Article 11

The consultations to which this Treaty refers shall be carried out by means of the Meetings of Ministers of Foreign Affairs of the American Republics which have ratified the Treaty, or in the manner or by the organ which in the future may be agreed upon.

Article 12

The Governing Board of the Pan American Union may act provisionally as an organ of consultation until the meeting of the Organ of Consultation referred to in the preceding Article takes place.

Article 13

The consultations shall be initiated at the request addressed to the Governing Board of the Pan American Union by any of the Signatory States which has ratified the Treaty.

Article 14

In the voting referred to in this Treaty only the representatives of the Signatory States which have ratified the Treaty may take part.

Article 15

The Governing Board of the Pan American Union shall act in all matters concerning this Treaty as an organ of liaison among the

Signatory States which have ratified this Treaty and between these States and the United Nations.

Article 16

The decisions of the Governing Board of the Pan American Union referred to in Articles 13 and 15 above shall be taken by an absolute majority of the Members entitled to vote.

Article 17

The Organ of Consultation shall take its decisions by a vote of two-thirds of the Signatory States which have ratified the Treaty.

Article 18

In the case of a situation or dispute between American States, the parties directly interested shall be excluded from the voting referred to in two preceding Articles.

Article 19

To constitute a quorum in all the meetings referred to in the previous Articles, it shall be necessary that the number of States represented shall be at least equal to the number of votes necessary for the taking of the decision.

B. THE ORGANIZATION OF AMERICAN STATES

THE NINTH REGULAR PAN-AMERICAN CONFERENCE held at Bogotá in 1948 drew up a constitution for a new organization of the hemisphere, the Organization of American States (O.A.S.), with organs and membership arranged in such a manner as to make possible the inclusion of Canada. The treaty of April 30, 1948, went into effect in 1951.

Article 1

The American States establish by this Charter the international organization that they have developed to achieve an order of peace and justice, to promote their solidarity, to strengthen their collaboration, and to defend their sovereignty, their territorial integ-

SOURCE: United States Treaties and Other International Agreements: 1951, pt. 2 (Washington, D.C., 1951), pp. 2416–37.

rity and their independence. Within the United Nations, the Organization of American States is a regional agency.

Article 4

The Organization of American States, in order to put into practice the principles on which it is founded and to fulfill its regional obligations under the Charter of the United Nations, proclaims the following essential purposes:

   a. To strengthen the peace and security of the continent;
   b. To prevent possible causes of difficulties and to ensure the pacific settlement of disputes that may arise among the Member States;
   c. To provide for common action on the part of those States in the event of aggression;
   d. To seek the solution of political, juridical and economic problems that may arise among them; and
   e. To promote, by cooperative action, their economic, social and cultural development.

Article 20

Decisions which require the application of the measures specified in Article 8 shall be binding upon all the Signatory States which have ratified this Treaty, with the sole exception that no State shall be required to use armed force without its consent.

Article 32

The Organization of American States accomplishes its purposes by means of:

   a. The Inter-American Conference;
   b. The Meeting of Consultation of Ministers of Foreign Affairs;
   c. The Council;
   d. The Pan American Union;
   e. The Specialized Conferences; and
   f. The Specialized Organizations.

Article 78

The Pan American Union is the central and permanent organ of the Organization of American States and the General Secretariat of the Organization. It shall perform the duties assigned to it in this

Charter and such other duties as may be assigned to it in other inter-American treaties and agreements.

32. Guatemala

THE POLITICS OF GUATEMALA *turned liberal in 1944, for the first time in that tiny nation's history. For a decade there was a free press, unrestricted trade unions, and uncontrolled elections in which even illiterates were allowed to vote. Such an opportunity was used by the country's small group of Communist activists. On the other side of the political spectrum, the landowners were alarmed by proposals for land reform. In the resultant muddle it began to appear as if Communism might triumph. Secretary of State Dulles may have had forebodings of the sort of trouble that would appear some years later in Cuba. In any event both he and President Eisenhower decided that Communism would get no foothold in the Western Hemisphere if they could do anything to prevent it. They encouraged a rebellion against President Jacobo Arbenz Guzmán, which succeeded. Actually, as Eisenhower's memoirs show, the Central Intelligence Agency's director, Allen W. Dulles, was not the éminence grise of the Guatemalan counterrevolution in 1954. The secretary of state's brother took a pessimistic view of the chances of besting the Arbenz regime. At one crucial point Eisenhower went against Director Dulles's pessimism and against the legal advice of the assistant secretary of state for Latin American affairs, Dr. Henry F. Holland, and replaced the two old American bombing planes the rebels had lost. Whereupon the rebel leader, Colonel Carlos Enrique Castillo Armas, triumphed, and Arbenz received sanctuary in Czechoslovakia. It was a successful counter-revolution, but Secretary Dulles took the prior situation very seriously and set out his concerns in a radio and television address on June 30, 1954.*

For several years international communism has been probing here and there for nesting places in the Americas. It finally chose Guatemala as a spot which it could turn into an official base from which to breed subversion which would extend to other American Republics.

This intrusion of Soviet despotism was, of course, a direct challenge to our Monroe Doctrine, the first and most fundamental of our foreign policies.

SOURCE: *American Foreign Policy: 1950–1955*, 2 vols. (Washington, D.C., 1957), I, pp. 1311–15.

It is interesting to recall that the menace which brought that doctrine into being was itself a menace born in Russia. It was the Russian Czar Alexander and his despotic allies in Europe who, early in the last century, sought control of South America and the western part of North America. In 1823 President Monroe confronted this challenge with his declaration that the European despots could not "extend their political system to any portion of either continent without endangering our peace and happiness. We would not," he said, "behold such interposition in any form with indifference."

These sentiments were shared by the other American Republics, and they were molded into a foreign policy of us all. For 131 years that policy has well served the peace and security of this hemisphere. It serves us well today.

In Guatemala, international communism had an initial success. It began 10 years ago, when a revolution occurred in Guatemala. The revolution was not without justification. But the Communists seized on it, not as an opportunity for real reforms, but as a chance to gain political power.

Communist agitators devoted themselves to infiltrating the public and private organizations of Guatemala. They sent recruits to Russia and other Communist countries for revolutionary training and indoctrination in such institutions as the Lenin School at Moscow. Operating in the guise of "reformers" they organized the workers and peasants under Communist leadership. Having gained control of what they call "mass organizations," they moved on to take over the official press and radio of the Guatemalan Government. They dominated the social security organization and ran the agrarian reform program. Through the technique of the "popular front" they dictated to the Congress and the President.

The judiciary made one valiant attempt to protect its integrity and independence. But the Communists, using their control of the legislative body, caused the Supreme Court to be dissolved when it refused to give approval to a Communist-contrived law. Arbenz, who until this week was President of Guatemala, was openly manipulated by the leaders of communism.

Guatemala is a small country. But its power, standing alone, is not a measure of the threat. The master plan of international communism is to gain a solid political base in this hemisphere, a base that can be used to extend Communist penetration to the other peoples of the other American Governments. It was not the power of the Arbenz government that concerned us but the power behind it.

If world communism captures any American State, however small, a new and perilous front is established which will increase the danger to the entire free world and require even greater sacrifices from the American people.

This situation in Guatemala had become so dangerous that the American States could not ignore it. At Caracas last March the American States held their Tenth Inter-American Conference. They then adopted a momentous statement. They declared that "the domination or control of the political institutions of any American State by the international Communist movement . . . would constitute a threat to the sovereignty and political independence of the American States, endangering the peace of America."

There was only one American State that voted against this declaration. That State was Guatemala.

This Caracas declaration precipitated a dramatic chain of events. From their European base the Communist leaders moved rapidly to build up the military power of their agents in Guatemala. In May a large shipment of arms moved from behind the Iron Curtain into Guatemala. The shipment was sought to be secreted by false manifests and false clearances. Its ostensible destination was changed three times while en route.

At the same time, the agents of international communism in Guatemala intensified efforts to penetrate and subvert the neighboring Central American States. They attempted political assassinations and political strikes. They used consular agents for political warfare.

Many Guatemalan people protested against their being used by Communist dictatorship to serve the Communists' lust for power. The response was mass arrests, the suppression of constitutional guaranties, the killing of opposition leaders, and other brutal tactics normally employed by communism to secure the consolidation of its power.

In the face of these events and in accordance with the spirit of the Caracas declaration, the nations of this hemisphere laid further plans to grapple with the danger. The Arbenz government responded with an effort to disrupt the inter-American system. Because it enjoyed the full support of Soviet Russia, which is on the

Security Council, it tried to bring the matter before the Security Council. It did so without first referring the matter to the American regional organization as is called for both by the United Nations Charter itself and by the treaty creating the American organization.

The Foreign Minister of Guatemala openly connived in this matter with the Foreign Minister of the Soviet Union. The two were in open correspondence and ill-concealed privity. The Security Council at first voted overwhelmingly to refer the Guatemala matter to the Organization of American States. The vote was 10 to 1. But that one negative vote was a Soviet veto.

Then the Guatemalan Government, with Soviet backing, redoubled its efforts to supplant the American States system by Security Council jurisdiction.

However, last Friday, the United Nations Security Council decided not to take up the Guatemalan matter but to leave it in the first instance to the American States themselves. That was a triumph for the system of balance between regional organization and world organization, which the American States had fought for when the charter was drawn up at San Francisco.

The American States then moved promptly to deal with the situation. Their peace commission left yesterday for Guatemala. Earlier the Organization of American States had voted overwhelmingly to call a meeting of their Foreign Ministers to consider the penetration of international communism in Guatemala and the measures required to eliminate it. Never before has there been so clear a call uttered with such a sense of urgency and strong resolve.

Throughout the period I have outlined, the Guatemalan Government and Communist agents throughout the world have persistently attempted to obscure the real issue—that of Communist imperialism—by claiming that the United States is only interested in protecting American business. We regret that there have been disputes between the Guatemalan Government and the United Fruit Company. We have urged repeatedly that these disputes be submitted for settlement to an international tribunal or to international arbitration. That is the way to dispose of problems of this sort. But this issue is relatively unimportant. All who know the temper of the U.S. people and Government must realize that our overriding concern is that which, with others, we recorded at

Caracas, namely, the endangering by international communism of the peace and security of this hemisphere.

The people of Guatemala have now been heard from. Despite the armaments piled up by the Arbenz government, it was unable to enlist the spiritual cooperation of the people.

Led by Colonel Castillo Armas, patriots arose in Guatemala to challenge the Communist leadership—and to change it. Thus, the situation is being cured by the Guatemalans themselves.

33. The Alliance for Progress

IN THE LAST DAYS of the Eisenhower administration, attitudes toward Latin America began to change. Relations with the Soviet Union were not going well and Latin American affairs seemed to be more easily controllable; it was felt that the late Secretary Dulles had neglected Latin America; for several years President Eisenhower's brother Milton, a university president, had been making trips to Latin America and found dissatisfaction over the unconcern of the Colossus of the North; and there surfaced complaints of Latin Americans that the Marshall Plan and other acts of largesse by the United States government had gone to Europe or to Asia but not to what should be the area of United States concern, its own backyard. All these feelings came together to create what in the new Kennedy administration became known as the Alliance for Progress. At a White House reception for Latin American diplomats and members of Congress on March 13, 1961, President Kennedy gave a speech setting out the new idea in ten points, the first of which was, "I propose that the American Republics begin on a vast new 10-year plan for the Americas, a plan to transform the 1960s into an historic decade of democratic progress." Representatives of the American republics met at Punta del Este in Uruguay August 5–17, 1961, and on the last day of their sessions announced a declaration and a charter.

This declaration expresses the conviction of the nations of Latin America that these profound economic, social, and cultural changes can come about only through the self-help efforts of each country. Nonetheless, in order to achieve the goals which have been established with the necessary speed, domestic efforts must be reinforced by essential contributions of external assistance.

SOURCE: American Foreign Policy: Current Documents, 1961 (Washington, D.C., 1965), pp. 343–47.

The United States, for its part, pledges its efforts to supply financial and technical cooperation in order to achieve the aims of the Alliance for Progress. To this end, the United States will provide a major part of the minimum of twenty billion dollars, principally in public funds, which Latin America will require over the next ten years from all external sources in order to supplement its own efforts.

The United States will provide from public funds, as an immediate contribution to the economic and social progress of Latin America, more than one billion dollars during the twelve months which began on March 13, 1961, when the Alliance for Progress was announced.

The United States intends to furnish development loans on a long-term basis, where appropriate running up to fifty years and in general at very low or zero rates of interest.

For their part, the countries of Latin America agree to devote a steadily increasing share of their own resources to economic and social development, and to make the reforms necessary to assure that all share fully in the fruits of the Alliance for Progress.

Further, as a contribution to the Alliance for Progress, each of the countries of Latin America will formulate a comprehensive and well-conceived national program for the development of its own economy.

Independent and highly qualified experts will be made available to Latin American countries in order to assist in formulating and examining national development plans.

Conscious of the overriding importance of this declaration, the signatory countries declare that the inter-American community is now beginning a new era when it will supplement its institutional, legal, cultural and social accomplishments with immediate and concrete actions to secure a better life, under freedom and democracy, for the present and future generations.

On the same day, August 17, 1961, the delegates signed the charter establishing the Alliance for Progress. But in subsequent years the enthusiasm of the United States government waned as it increased its commitments to the Vietnam War. It also became apparent that the instability of governments in Latin America made private capital hesitant to enter the area. By the end of the decade two American journalists, Jerome Levinson and Juan de Onís, could publish a book entitled The Alliance That Lost Its Way (Chicago: Quadrangle, 1970). By the early

1970s the alliance was dead, and Chile under a new Socialist government was busily expropriating American companies. The violent overthrow of that government in 1973 and the friendliness of its successor, a conservative military junta, toward American businesses meant that in Chile nothing had been solved. Generally in Latin America there were no discernible economic initiatives by the United States government.

34. Cuba

A. Invasion

FROM 1934 TO 1944, and from 1952 to January 1, 1959, the ruler of Cuba was Fulgencio Batista, who had come to power through a revolt by noncommissioned officers of the Cuban army. He ruled first behind a series of nominal presidents and then as president himself. Opposition was suppressed, and although Batista from time to time seemed sympathetic to labor, an attempted revolutionary general strike was ruthlessly crushed in 1935. In 1940 a constitutional convention met that drew up one of the most advanced constitutions in Latin America. Soon afterward Batista was legally elected president and ruled democratically during his four-year term. He honored the constitutional prohibition against succeeding himself, though it is probable that he intended to exercise power through his candidate, and abided by the results of the 1944 election that made his worst enemy the new president. In 1952 he entered the presidential race, but when he saw that he had no chance of winning he seized power by force. In 1954 he was chosen president in an election in which his only opponent withdrew, charging that government terror and bribery had already decided the outcome. With the outbreak of armed resistance led by Fidel Castro in November, 1956, Batista's regime began a campaign of terror against its opponents. It has been estimated that, without legal process, at least 20,000 people were killed—many of them after being tortured—by Batista's forces between November, 1956, and January 1, 1959. In the summer of 1958, Batista's forces failed badly in a major effort to destroy the rebels. Some months later, with the fall of Santa Clara, the provincial capital of Las Villas, Batista concluded that he had lost, and on January 1, 1959, at 3 A.M., fled by plane to the Dominican Republic. The new government under Castro was greeted with enthusiasm both by Cubans and by American citizens resident in Cuba. Many American businesses hastened to pay their taxes in advance, to support the new regime. When public trials of Batista policemen occurred, with some 500 executions by firing squad, opinion in the United States began to turn against the Castro government, even

SOURCE: Current Documents, 1961, p. 295.

*though many of the individuals executed were guilty of hideous crimes.
A series of contentions developed between Washington and Havana
relating to abolition of the special arrangement under which Cuban
sugar was admitted duty-free to the United States; to Cuban expropria-
tion of U.S. property; and to an anti-American propaganda campaign,
both at home and abroad, mounted by the Cuban government. By the
end of 1960 the Eisenhower administration was allowing the Central
Intelligence Agency to train about 1,500 Cuban and other exiles in
Guatemala. President Kennedy inherited this operation and allowed the
exiles to invade Cuba on April 17, 1961, albeit without American air
support. Almost from the beginning of the landing at the Bay of Pigs
the invasion went wrong, and in a few days Castro mopped up the
survivors. Premier Khrushchev meanwhile sent a message to Kennedy
on April 18.*

MR. PRESIDENT: I address this message to you at an alarming
hour which is fraught with danger against universal peace. An
armed aggression has been started against Cuba. It is an open
secret that the armed bands which have invaded that country have
been prepared, equipped, and armed in the United States. The
planes which bomb Cuban towns belong to the United States of
America, the bombs which they drop have been put at their disposal by the American Government.

All this arouses in the Soviet Union, the Soviet Government,
and the Soviet people an understandable feeling of indignation.
Only recently, exchanging views through our representatives, we
talked with you about the mutual wish of the parties to exert joint
efforts directed toward the improvement of relations between our
countries and the prevention of a danger of war. Your statement a
few days ago to the effect that the United States of America would
not participate in military actions against Cuba created an impression that the leading authorities of the United States are aware of
the consequences which aggression against Cuba could have for the
whole world and the United States of America itself.

How are we to understand what is really being done by the
United States now that the attack on Cuba has become a fact?

It is yet not too late to prevent the irreparable. The Government
of the U.S. can still prevent the flames of war kindled by the
interventionists on Cuba from spreading into a conflagration which
it will be impossible to cope with. I earnestly appeal to you, Mr.
President, to call a halt to the aggression against the Republic of

Cuba. The military techniques and the world political situation now are such that any so-called "small war" can produce a chain reaction in all parts of the world.

As for the U.S.S.R., there must be no mistake about our position. We will extend to the Cuban people and its Government all the necessary aid for the repulse of the armed attack on Cuba. We are sincerely interested in the relaxation of international tension, but if others go in for its aggravation, then we will answer them in full measure. In general it is impossible to carry on affairs in such a way that in one area the situation is settled and the fire is put out, and in another area a new fire is lit.

I hope that the U.S. Government will take into consideration these reasons, dictated only by concern that steps should not be permitted which might lead the world to a catastrophe of war.

KENNEDY *responded the same day.*

MR. CHAIRMAN: You are under a serious misapprehension in regard to events in Cuba. For months there has been evident and growing resistance to the Castro dictatorship. More than 100,000 refugees have recently fled from Cuba into neighboring countries. Their urgent hope is naturally to assist their fellow Cubans in their struggle for freedom. Many of these refugees fought alongside Dr. Castro against the Batista dictatorship; among them are prominent leaders of his own original movement and government.

These are unmistakable signs that Cubans find intolerable the denial of democratic liberties and the subversion of the 26th of July Movement by an alien-dominated regime. It cannot be surprising that, as resistance within Cuba grows, refugees have been using whatever means are available to return and support their countrymen in the continuing struggle for freedom. Where people are denied the right of choice, recourse to such struggle is the only means of achieving their liberties.

I have previously stated, and I repeat now, that the United States intends no military intervention in Cuba. In the event of any military intervention by outside force we will immediately honor our obligations under the inter-American system to protect

SOURCE: *Current Documents, 1961,* pp. 296–97.

this hemisphere against external aggression. While refraining from military intervention in Cuba, the people of the United States do not conceal their admiration for Cuban patriots who wish to see a democratic system in an independent Cuba. The United States government can take no action to stifle the spirit of liberty.

I have taken careful note of your statement that the events in Cuba might affect peace in all parts of the world. I trust that this does not mean that the Soviet government, using the situation in Cuba as a pretext, is planning to inflame other areas of the world. I would like to think that your government has too great a sense of responsibility to embark upon any enterprise so dangerous to general peace.

I agree with you as to the desirability of steps to improve the international atmosphere. I continue to hope that you will cooperate in opportunities now available to this end. A prompt cease-fire and peaceful settlement of the dangerous situation in Laos, cooperation with the United Nations in the Congo and a speedy conclusion of an acceptable treaty for the banning of nuclear tests would be constructive steps in this direction. The regime in Cuba could make a similar contribution by permitting the Cuban people freely to determine their own future by democratic processes and freely to cooperate with their Latin American neighbors.

I believe, Mr. Chairman, that you should recognize that free peoples in all parts of the world do not accept the claim of historical inevitability for Communist revolution. What your government believes is its own business; what it does in the world is the world's business. The great revolution in the history of man, past, present and future, is the revolution of those determined to be free.

The correspondence continued with a message from Khrushchev on April 22 in which the premier remarked, "We cannot recognize any U.S. rights to decide the fate of other countries, including the Latin American countries." A statement by the State Department broke off the argument with the comment, "The President will not be drawn into an extended public debate . . . on the basis of this latest . . . Communist distortion of the basic concepts of the rights of man." It was, however, an uneasy exchange. The president had found himself in a weak position. Matters seem not to have been helped by his trip to Vienna in June to meet Khrushchev, who appears to have sized up Kennedy as a young man easy to push around.

B. The Missile Crisis

In the fall of 1962 the situation in Cuba began to appear ominous, for the Russians obviously were up to something there: their technicians were much in evidence. Castro was saying that another American-sponsored invasion would fail. In this climate of opinion the Senate by vote of 86 to 1 and the House by 384 to 7 passed a joint resolution approved by the president on October 3.

Whereas President James Monroe, announcing the Monroe Doctrine in 1823, declared that the United States would consider any attempt on the part of European powers "to extend their system to any portion of this hemisphere as dangerous to our peace and safety"; and

Whereas in the Rio Treaty of 1947 the parties agreed that "an armed attack by any State against an American State shall be considered as an attack against all the American States, and, consequently, each one of the said contracting parties undertakes to assist in meeting the attack in the exercise of the inherent right of individual or collective self-defense recognized by article 51 of the Charter of the United Nations"; and

Whereas the Foreign Ministers of the Organization of American States at Punta del Este in January 1962 declared: "The present Government of Cuba has identified itself with the principles of Marxist-Leninist ideology, has established a political, economic, and social system based on that doctrine, and accepts military assistance from extracontinental Communist powers, including even the threat of military intervention in America on the part of the Soviet Union"; and

Whereas the international Communist movement has increasingly extended into Cuba its political, economic, and military sphere of influence; Now, therefore, be it

Resolved by the Senate and House of Representatives of the United States of America in Congress assembled, That the United States is determined—

a. to prevent by whatever means may be necessary, including the use of arms, the Marxist-Leninist regime in Cuba from extending, by

Source: American Foreign Policy: Current Documents, 1962 (Washington, D.C., 1966), pp. 389–90.

force or the threat of force, its aggressive or subversive activities to any part of this hemisphere;

b. to prevent in Cuba the creation or use of an externally supported military capability endangering the security of the United States; and

c. to work with the Organization of American States and with freedom-loving Cubans to support the aspirations of the Cuban people for self-determination.

WHEN U–2 PHOTOGRAPHS *showed Soviet technicians hastily constructing emplacements for missiles, presumably atomic-armed, Kennedy consulted his closest advisers. Then he appeared before the nation for a showdown with the Soviet Union in a televised speech of October 22.*

GOOD EVENING, MY FELLOW CITIZENS. This Government, as promised, has maintained the closest surveillance of the Soviet military buildup on the island of Cuba. Within the past week unmistakable evidence has established the fact that a series of offensive missile sites is now in preparation on that imprisoned island. The purpose of these bases can be none other than to provide a nuclear strike capability against the Western Hemisphere.

Upon receiving the first preliminary hard information of this nature last Tuesday morning [October 16] at 9:00 A.M., I directed that our surveillance be stepped up. And having now confirmed and completed our evaluation of the evidence and our decision on a course of action, this Government feels obliged to report this new crisis to you in fullest detail.

The characteristics of these new missile sites indicate two distinct types of installations. Several of them include medium-range ballistic missiles capable of carrying a nuclear warhead for a distance of more than 1,000 nautical miles. Each of these missiles, in short, is capable of striking Washington, D.C., the Panama Canal, Cape Canaveral, Mexico City, or any other city in the southeastern part of the United States, in Central America, or in the Caribbean area.

Additional sites not yet completed appear to be designed for intermediate-range ballistic missiles capable of traveling more than twice as far—and thus capable of striking most of the major cities in the Western Hemisphere, ranging as far north as Hudson Bay, Canada, and as far south as Lima, Peru. In addition, jet bombers,

SOURCE: *Current Documents, 1962,* pp. 399–404.

capable of carrying nuclear weapons, are now being uncrated and assembled in Cuba, while the necessary air bases are being prepared.

This urgent transformation of Cuba into an important strategic base—by the presence of these large, long-range, and clearly offensive weapons of sudden mass destruction—constitutes an explicit threat to the peace and security of all the Americas, in flagrant and deliberate defiance of the Rio Pact of 1947, the traditions of this nation and hemisphere, the Joint Resolution of the 87th Congress, the Charter of the United Nations, and my own public warnings to the Soviets on September 4 and 13.

This action also contradicts the repeated assurances of Soviet spokesmen, both publicly and privately delivered, that the arms buildup in Cuba would retain its original defensive character and that the Soviet Union had no need or desire to station strategic missiles on the territory of any other nation.

The size of this undertaking makes clear that it has been planned for some months. Yet only last month, after I had made clear the distinction between any introduction of ground-to-ground missiles and the existence of defensive antiaircraft missiles, the Soviet Government publicly stated on September 11 that, and I quote, "The armaments and military equipment sent to Cuba are designed exclusively for defensive purposes," and, and I quote the Soviet Government, "There is no need for the Soviet Government to shift its weapons for a retaliatory blow to any other country, for instance Cuba," and that, and I quote the Government, "The Soviet Union has so powerful rockets to carry these nuclear warheads that there is no need to search for sites for them beyond the boundaries of the Soviet Union." That statement was false.

Only last Thursday, as evidence of this rapid offensive buildup was already in my hand, Soviet Foreign Minister Gromyko told me in my office that he was instructed to make it clear once again, as he said his Government had already done, that Soviet assistance to Cuba, and I quote, "pursued solely the purpose of contributing to the defense capabilities of Cuba," that, and I quote him, "training by Soviet specialists of Cuban nationals in handling defensive armaments was by no means offensive," and that "if it were otherwise," Mr. Gromyko went on, "the Soviet Government would never become involved in rendering such assistance." That statement also was false.

Neither the United States of America nor the world community of nations can tolerate deliberate deception and offensive threats on the part of any nation, large or small. We no longer live in a world where only the actual firing of weapons represents a sufficient challenge to a nation's security to constitute maximum peril. Nuclear weapons are so destructive and ballistic missiles are so swift that any substantially increased possibility of their use or any sudden change in their deployment may well be regarded as a definite threat to peace.

For many years both the Soviet Union and the United States, recognizing this fact, have deployed strategic nuclear weapons with great care, never upsetting the precarious *status quo* which insured that these weapons would not be used in the absence of some vital challenge. Our own strategic missiles have never been transferred to the territory of any other nation under a cloak of secrecy and deception; and our history, unlike that of the Soviets since the end of World War II, demonstrates that we have no desire to dominate or conquer any other nation or impose our system upon its people. Nevertheless, American citizens have become adjusted to living daily on the bull's eye of Soviet missiles located inside the U.S.S.R. or in submarines.

In that sense missiles in Cuba add to an already clear and present danger—although it should be noted the nations of Latin America have never previously been subjected to a potential nuclear threat.

But this secret, swift, and extraordinary buildup of Communist missiles—in an area well known to have a special and historical relationship to the United States and the nations of the Western Hemisphere, in violation of Soviet assurances, and in defiance of American and hemispheric policy—this sudden, clandestine decision to station strategic weapons for the first time outside of Soviet soil—is a deliberately provocative and unjustified change in the *status quo* which cannot be accepted by this country if our courage and our commitments are ever to be trusted again by either friend or foe.

The 1930's taught us a clear lesson: Aggressive conduct, if allowed to grow unchecked and unchallenged, ultimately leads to war. This nation is opposed to war. We are also true to our word. Our unswerving objective, therefore, must be to prevent the use of these missiles against this or any other country and to secure their withdrawal or elimination from the Western Hemisphere.

Our policy has been one of patience and restraint, as befits a peaceful and powerful nation, which leads a worldwide alliance. We have been determined not to be diverted from our central concerns by mere irritants and fanatics. But now further action is required—and it is underway; and these actions may only be the beginning. We will not prematurely or unnecessarily risk the costs of worldwide nuclear war in which even the fruits of victory would be ashes in our mouth—but neither will we shrink from that risk at any time it must be faced.

Acting, therefore, in the defense of our own security and of the entire Western Hemisphere, and under the authority entrusted to me by the Constitution as endorsed by the resolution of the Congress, I have directed that the following *initial* steps be taken immediately:

First: To halt this offensive buildup, a strict quarantine on all offensive military equipment under shipment to Cuba is being initiated. All ships of any kind bound for Cuba from whatever nation or port will, if found to contain cargoes of offensive weapons, be turned back. This quarantine will be extended, if needed, to other types of cargo and carriers. We are not at this time, however, denying the necessities of life as the Soviets attempted to do in their Berlin blockade of 1948.

Second: I have directed the continued and increased close surveillance of Cuba and its military buildup. The Foreign Ministers of the OAS in their communique of October 3 rejected secrecy on such matters in this hemisphere. Should these offensive military preparations continue, thus increasing the threat to the hemisphere, further action will be justified. I have directed the Armed Forces to prepare for any eventualities; and I trust that, in the interest of both the Cuban people and the Soviet technicians at the sites, the hazards to all concerned of continuing this threat will be recognized.

Third: It shall be the policy of this nation to regard any nuclear missile launched from Cuba against any nation in the Western Hemisphere as an attack by the Soviet Union on the United States, requiring a full retaliatory response upon the Soviet Union.

Fourth: As a necessary military precaution I have reinforced our base at Guantanamo, evacuated today the dependents of our personnel there, and ordered additional military units to be on a standby alert basis.

Fifth: We are calling tonight for an immediate meeting of the

Organ of Consultation, under the Organization of American States, to consider this threat to hemispheric security and to invoke articles 6 and 8 of the Rio Treaty in support of all necessary action. The United Nations Charter allows for regional security arrangements— and the nations of this hemisphere decided long ago against the military presence of outside powers. Our other allies around the world have also been alerted.

Sixth: Under the Charter of the United Nations, we are asking tonight that an emergency meeting of the Security Council be convoked without delay to take action against this latest Soviet threat to world peace. Our resolution will call for the prompt dismantling and withdrawal of all offensive weapons in Cuba, under the supervision of U.N. observers, before the quarantine can be lifted.

Seventh and finally: I call upon Chairman Khrushchev to halt and eliminate this clandestine, reckless, and provocative threat to world peace and to stable relations between our two nations. I call upon him further to abandon this course of world domination and to join in an historic effort to end the perilous arms race and transform the history of man. He has an opportunity now to move the world back from the abyss of destruction—by returning to his Government's own words that it had no need to station missiles outside its own territory, and withdrawing these weapons from Cuba—by refraining from any action which will widen or deepen the present crisis—and then by participating in a search for peaceful and permanent solutions.

This nation is prepared to present its case against the Soviet threat to peace, and our own proposals for a peaceful world, at any time and in any forum—in the OAS, in the United Nations, or in any other meeting that could be useful—without limiting our freedom of action.

We have in the past made strenuous efforts to limit the spread of nuclear weapons. We have proposed the elimination of all arms and military bases in a fair and effective disarmament treaty. We are prepared to discuss new proposals for the removal of tensions on both sides—including the possibilities of a genuinely independent Cuba, free to determine its own destiny. We have no wish to war with the Soviet Union, for we are a peaceful people who desire to live in peace with all other peoples.

But it is difficult to settle or even discuss these problems in an atmosphere of intimidation. That is why this latest Soviet threat— or any other threat which is made either independently or in response to our actions this week—must and will be met with determination. Any hostile move anywhere in the world against the safety and freedom of peoples to whom we are committed—including in particular the brave people of West Berlin—will be met by whatever action is needed.

Finally, I want to say a few words to the captive people of Cuba, to whom this speech is being directly carried by special radio facilities. I speak to you as a friend, as one who knows of your deep attachment to your fatherland, as one who shares your aspirations for liberty and justice for all. And I have watched and the American people have watched with deep sorrow how your nationalist revolution was betrayed and how your fatherland fell under foreign domination. Now your leaders are no longer Cuban leaders inspired by Cuban ideals. They are puppets and agents of an international conspiracy which has turned Cuba against your friends and neighbors in the Americas—and turned it into the first Latin American country to become a target for nuclear war, the first Latin American country to have these weapons on its soil.

These new weapons are not in your interest. They contribute nothing to your peace and well-being. They can only undermine it. But this country has no wish to cause you to suffer or to impose any system upon you. We know that your lives and land are being used as pawns by those who deny you freedom.

Many times in the past the Cuban people have risen to throw out tyrants who destroyed their liberty. And I have no doubt that most Cubans today look forward to the time when they will be truly free—free from foreign domination, free to choose their own leaders, free to select their own system, free to own their own land, free to speak and write and worship without fear or degradation. And then shall Cuba be welcomed back to the society of free nations and to the associations of this hemisphere.

My fellow citizens, let no one doubt that this is a difficult and dangerous effort on which we have set out. No one can foresee precisely what course it will take or what costs or casualties will be incurred. Many months of sacrifice and self-discipline lie ahead— months in which both our patience and our will will be tested, months in which many threats and denunciations will keep us aware of our dangers. But the greatest danger of all would be to do nothing.

The path we have chosen for the present is full of hazards, as all paths are; but it is the one most consistent with our character and courage as a nation and our commitments around the world. The cost of freedom is always high—but Americans have always paid it. And one path we shall never choose, and that is the path of surrender or submission.

Our goal is not the victory of might but the vindication of right—not peace at the expense of freedom, but both peace and freedom, here in this hemisphere and, we hope, around the world. God willing, that goal will be achieved.

After the President's speech the U.S. Navy put the blockade into effect and on Wednesday morning, October 24, word came to the president and his advisers that some Soviet ships approaching the quarantine line had stopped dead in the water, a sign that Moscow was not going to present an immediate confrontation. The crisis wore on for several days as messages went back and forth between Kennedy and Khrushchev. The Soviet premier on Friday, October 26, sent an emotional message to the president indicating he might have overreached himself. (For this message see Department of State Bulletin, November 19, 1973, pp. 640–45.) Meanwhile an important official of the Soviet embassy in Washington had approached a reporter for the American Broadcasting Company, John Scali, and proposed that the Soviet Union would remove the missiles in Cuba, under U.N. supervision and inspection, if the United States would lift the blockade and give a pledge not to invade Cuba. Robert Kennedy and Theodore Sorensen put this technically unofficial proposal into an American note of Saturday, October 27, in which President Kennedy assumed that Khrushchev was willing to agree to the proposal. Khrushchev accepted the arrangement the next day, Sunday, the seventh day—the Sabbath—of the crisis.

35. The Dominican Republic

AFTER SEIZING POWER in the Dominican Republic in 1930, General Rafael Trujillo held it until 1961, when his enemies gunned him down. His had been the worst of all the Latin American dictatorships; his excesses rivaled those of Hitler in Europe, in cruelty, if not in numbers. It was a terrible heritage for the republic after Trujillo, and perhaps for that reason some of the subsequent regimes were military, established by coups. The government of President Juan Bosch was truly democratic, but in 1963 it was ousted by a military man named Elias Wessin y

SOURCE: *American Foreign Policy: Current Documents, 1965* (Washington, D.C., 1968), pp. 1961–65.

Wessin, a deeply religious, fanatical anti-Communist, born of middle-class Lebanese parents, a man completely honest, politically naïve, seeing no difference between the non-Communist revolutionary left and Communism, seeing only black and white. Then on April 24, 1965, a revolution broke out in favor of Bosch, attempting to return to the constitution and to restore the democratically elected president to power. Four days later President Lyndon B. Johnson sent in the marines, to a total of 22,000 troops, with 8,000 sailors manning some 40 ships cruising offshore. Johnson at first said he was intervening to protect American citizens. Later he explained that there was acute danger that the Dominican Republic would fall to Communism. Press reports from the Dominican capital overwhelmingly disputed the American government's positions. President Johnson offered his own explanation in a televised address of May 2, 1965.

GOOD EVENING, LADIES AND GENTLEMEN: I have just come from a meeting with the leaders of both parties in the Congress, which was held in the Cabinet Room of the White House. I briefed them on the facts of the situation in the Dominican Republic. I want to make those same facts known to all the American people and to all the world.

There are times in the affairs of nations when great principles are tested in an ordeal of conflict and danger. This is such a time for the American nations.

At stake are the lives of thousands, the liberty of a nation, and the principles and the values of all the American Republics.

That is why the hopes and the concern of this entire hemisphere are on this Sabbath Sunday focused on the Dominican Republic.

In the dark mist of conflict and violence, revolution and confusion, it is not easy to find clear and unclouded truths.

But certain things are clear. And they require equally clear action. To understand, I think it is necessary to begin with the events of 8 or 9 days ago.

Last week our observers warned of an approaching political storm in the Dominican Republic. I immediately asked our Ambassador [W. Tapley Bennett, Jr.] to return to Washington at once so that we might discuss the situation and might plan a course of conduct. But events soon outran our hopes for peace.

Saturday, April 24—8 days ago—while Ambassador Bennett was conferring with the highest officials of your Government, revolution erupted in the Dominican Republic. Elements of the military forces of that country overthrew their government. However, the rebels themselves were divided. Some wanted to restore former President Juan Bosch. Others opposed his restoration. President Bosch, elected after the fall of Trujillo and his assassination, had been driven from office by an earlier revolution in the Dominican Republic.

Those who opposed Mr. Bosch's return formed a military committee in an effort to control that country. The others took to the street, and they began to lead a revolt on behalf of President Bosch. Control and effective government dissolved in conflict and confusion. . . .

The evidence that we have on the revolutionary movement indicates that it took a very tragic turn. Many of them trained in Cuba, seeing a chance to increase disorder and to gain a foothold, joined the revolution. They took increasing control. What began as a popular democratic revolution that was committed to democracy and social justice moved into the hands of a band of Communist conspirators. . . .

For more than three decades the people of that tragic little island suffered under the weight of one of the most brutal and despotic dictatorships of the Americas. We enthusiastically supported condemnation of that government by the Organization of American States. We joined in applying sanctions, and, when Trujillo was assassinated by his fellow citizens, we immediately acted to protect freedom and to prevent a new tyranny, and since that time we have taken the resources from all of our people at some sacrifice to many, and we have helped them with food and with other resources, with the Peace Corps volunteers, with the AID technicians; we have helped them in the effort to build a new order of progress.

How sad it is tonight that a people so long oppressed should once again be the targets of the forces of tyranny. Their long misery must weigh heavily on the heart of every citizen of this hemisphere. So I think it is our mutual responsibility to help the people of the Dominican Republic toward the day when they can freely choose the path of liberty and justice and progress. This is required of us by the agreements that we are party to and that we have signed. This is required of us by the values which bind us together. . . .

And before I leave you, my fellow Americans, I want to say this personal word: I know that no American serviceman wants to kill anyone. I know that no American President wants to give an order which brings shooting and casualties and death. I want you to know, and I want the world to know, that as long as I am President of this country, we are going to defend ourselves. We will defend our soldiers against attackers. We will honor our treaties. We will keep our commitments. We will defend our nation against all those who seek to destroy not only the United States but every free country of this hemisphere. We do not want to bury anyone, as I have said so many times before. But we do not intend to be buried.

Thank you. God bless you. Good night.

There was very strong adverse reaction to the Dominican intervention, both in Latin America and the United States, and in response the American government proposed an Inter-American Armed Force, which was organized and sent to the Dominican Republic.

Viet Nam, Laos, and Cambodia

XI

Vietnam

Vietnam may not have been the most important problem in American foreign relations after the Second World War, but on no other subject did Americans find themselves so much aroused. If during the first term of President Richard M. Nixon the issue received less attention than in the era of President Johnson, in the early 1970s it still was the most talked about subject in foreign policy. It constituted the one major policy that went wrong with a vengeance: its error represented well over $100 billion in military hardware, troop maintenance, and support of the Saigon government; and close to 50,000 American lives, not to mention the cost to the people of Vietnam.

36. The Roots of Trouble

A. The Beginnings

No SPECIFIC POINT marked the beginning of United States involvement in Vietnam, but by the time of the Korean War the American government was involved. In July, 1941, the Japanese had occupied what then was called Indochina, an act that threatened the Philippines. President Roosevelt in retaliation froze all Japanese credits in the United States, cutting off oil exports to Japan. But this initial involvement was not a quarrel over Indochinese affairs; it was essentially an event in the developing American-Japanese antagonism, an event that happened to occur in Indochina. During the war the president sometimes considered France's position in Indochina, which he believed to be exploitative, and Roosevelt was considering some sort of trusteeship when he died suddenly in April, 1945. His successor, Truman, could not be concerned with Indochina because too many other problems were at hand. The French at the end of the war gave some evidence of being willing to

SOURCE: American Foreign Policy: 1950–1955, 2 vols. (Washington, D.C., 1957), II, p. 2365.

come to terms with Vietnamese nationalism, seeming to be friendly to the Vietminh leader Ho Chi Minh. But then they reneged on an agreement with Ho and in 1946 began a war against him and his supporters that went on until France's defeat in 1954. This war gradually involved the American government. When France joined NATO in 1949, the Americans could no longer overlook the troubles in Indochina that were drawing off French troops from Europe, and the initial steps in involvement occurred shortly afterward, even before the beginning of the Korean War. On February 7, 1950, the State Department announced diplomatic recognition of the three governments in Indochina—Vietnam, Laos, and Cambodia—governments that the French had declared to be independent within the French Union. On May 8, 1950, Secretary of State Acheson, while at a foreign ministers' meeting in Paris, announced extension of military and economic aid. Acheson later defended this action. He knew, of course, that the aid was really going to the French government, to support its military effort to keep Indochina. He knew that the proclaimed independence of Vietnam, Laos, and Cambodia within the French Union was largely a fraud and that the French intended to maintain a tight control. He felt that he was being blackmailed by the French government, that he had to give the Paris regime what it wanted in Indochina in order to get support for NATO in Europe.

The [French] Foreign Minister and I have just had an exchange of views on the situation in Indochina and are in general agreement both as to the urgency of the situation in that area and as to the necessity for remedial action. We have noted the fact that the problem of meeting the threat to the security of Viet Nam, Cambodia, and Laos which now enjoy independence within the French Union is primarily the responsibility of France and the Governments and peoples of Indochina. The United States recognizes that the solution of the Indochina problem depends both upon the restoration of security and upon the development of genuine nationalism and that United States assistance can and should contribute to these major objectives.

The United States Government, convinced that neither national independence nor democratic evolution exist in any area dominated by Soviet imperialism, considers the situation to be such as to warrant its according economic aid and military equipment to the Associated States of Indochina and to France in order to assist them in restoring stability and permitting these states to pursue their peaceful and democratic development.

B. The Geneva Conference

THE FRENCH got ever deeper into the Vietnam quagmire and by the spring of 1954 were in serious trouble when the Vietminh Communists surrounded a large garrison at a place named Dien Bien Phu. At a conference in Geneva called nominally to consider Korean problems, the issue of Vietnam was scheduled to come up early in May. Dien Bien Phu fell to the Communists on May 7, the day before the Vietnam discussion began. The face of the French representative at Geneva, Foreign Minister Georges Bidault, turned pale and then green, when an usher brought in a note containing the message, "DBP fini." The United States found itself an annoyed participant at this meeting. With mainland China in attendance it was embarrassing, because of nonrecognition, to take part. With Britain and France represented and France deeply affected by the conversations and outcome, it was impossible not to be involved. But the French position was militarily impossible. Without much advice from the United States the conference came to its final declaration on July 21, 1954.

FINAL DECLARATION, dated the 21st July, 1954, of the Geneva Conference on the problem of restoring peace in Indo-China, in which the representatives of Cambodia, the Democratic Republic of Viet-Nam, France, Laos, the People's Republic of China, the State of Viet-Nam, the Union of Soviet Socialist Republics, the United Kingdom, and the United States of America took part.

1. The Conference takes note of the agreements ending hostilities in Cambodia, Laos and Viet-Nam and organizing international control and the supervision of the execution of the provisions of these agreements.

2. The Conference expresses satisfaction at the ending of hostilities in Cambodia, Laos and Viet-Nam; the Conference expresses its conviction that the execution of the provisions set out in the present declaration and in the agreements on the cessation of hostilities will permit Cambodia, Laos and Viet-Nam henceforth to play their part, in full independence and sovereignty, in the peaceful community of nations.

3. The Conference takes note of the declarations made by the Governments of Cambodia and of Laos of their intention to adopt measures permitting all citizens to take their place in the national

SOURCE: American Foreign Policy: 1950–1955, I, pp. 785–87.

community, in particular by participating in the next general elections, which, in conformity with the constitution of each of these countries, shall take place in the course of the year 1955, by secret ballot and in conditions of respect for fundamental freedoms.

4. The Conference takes note of the clauses in the agreement on the cessation of hostilities in Viet-Nam prohibiting the introduction into Viet-Nam of foreign troops and military personnel as well as of all kinds of arms and munitions. The Conference also takes note of the declarations made by the Governments of Cambodia and Laos of their resolution not to request foreign aid, whether in war material, in personnel or in instructors except for the purpose of the effective defence of their territory and, in the case of Laos, to the extent defined by the agreements on the cessation of hostilities in Laos.

5. The Conference takes note of the clauses in the agreement on the cessation of hostilities in Viet-Nam to the effect that no military base under the control of a foreign State may be established in the regrouping zones of the two parties, the latter having the obligation to see that the zones allotted to them shall not constitute part of any military alliance and shall not be utilized for the resumption of hostilities or in the service of an aggressive policy. The Conference also takes note of the declarations of the Governments of Cambodia and Laos to the effect that they will not join in any agreement with other States if this agreement includes the obligation to participate in a military alliance not in conformity with the principles of the Charter of the United Nations or, in the case of Laos, with the principles of the agreement on the cessation of hostilities in Laos or, so long as their security is not threatened, the obligation to establish bases on Cambodian or Laotian territory for the military forces of foreign Powers.

6. The Conference recognizes that the essential purpose of the agreement relating to Viet-Nam is to settle military questions with a view to ending hostilities and that the military demarcation line is provisional and should not in any way be interpreted as constituting a political or territorial boundary. The Conference expresses its conviction that the execution of the provisions set out in the present declaration and in the agreement on the cessation of hostilities creates the necessary basis for the achievement in the near future of a political settlement in Viet-Nam.

7. The Conference declares that, so far as Viet-Nam is con-

cerned, the settlement of political problems, effected on the basis of respect for the principles of independence, unity and territorial integrity, shall permit the Viet-Namese people to enjoy the fundamental freedoms, guaranteed by democratic institutions established as a result of free general elections by secret ballot. In order to ensure that sufficient progress in the restoration of peace has been made, and that all the necessary conditions obtain for free expression of the national will, general elections shall be held in July 1956, under the supervision of an international commission composed of representatives of the Member States of the International Supervisory Commission, referred to in the agreement on the cessation of hostilities. Consultations will be held on this subject between the competent representative authorities of the two zones from 20 July 1955 onwards.

8. The provisions of the agreements on the cessation of hostilities intended to ensure the protection of individuals and of property must be most strictly applied and must, in particular, allow everyone in Viet-Nam to decide freely in which zone he wishes to live.

9. The competent representative authorities of the Northern and Southern zones of Viet-Nam, as well as the authorities of Laos and Cambodia, must not permit any individual or collective reprisals against persons who have collaborated in any way with one of the parties during the war, or against members of such persons' families.

10. The Conference takes note of the declaration of the Government of the French Republic to the effect that it is ready to withdraw its troops from the territory of Cambodia, Laos and Viet-Nam, at the request of the governments concerned and within periods which shall be fixed by agreement between the parties except in the cases where, by agreement between the two parties, a certain number of French troops shall remain at specified points and for a specified time.

11. The Conference takes note of the declaration of the French Government to the effect that for the settlement of all the problems connected with the re-establishment and consolidation of peace in Cambodia, Laos and Viet-Nam, the French Government will proceed from the principle of respect for the independence and sovereignty, unity and territorial integrity of Cambodia, Laos and Viet-Nam.

12. In their relations with Cambodia, Laos and Viet-Nam, each member of the Geneva Conference undertakes to respect the sovereignty, the independence, the unity and the territorial integrity of the abovementioned states, and to refrain from any interference in their internal affairs.

13. The members of the Conference agree to consult one another on any question which may be referred to them by the International Supervisory Commission, in order to study such measures as many prove necessary to ensure that the agreements on the cessation of hostilities in Cambodia, Laos and Viet-Nam are respected.

UNDER SECRETARY OF STATE WALTER BEDELL SMITH *was present during part of the Geneva discussions and made a statement at the concluding plenary session on July 21.*

As I stated on July 18, my Government is not prepared to join in a declaration by the Conference such as is submitted. However, the United States makes this unilateral declaration of its position in these matters:

Declaration

The Government of the United States being resolved to devote its efforts to the strengthening of peace in accordance with the principles and purposes of the United Nations takes note of the agreements concluded at Geneva on July 20 and 21, 1954 between (a) the Franco-Laotian Command and the Command of the Peoples Army of Viet-Nam; (b) the Royal Khmer Army Command and the Command of the Peoples Army of Viet-Nam; (c) Franco-Vietnamese Command and the Command of the Peoples Army of Viet-Nam and of paragraphs 1 to 12 inclusive of the declaration presented to the Geneva Conference on July 21, 1954 declares with regard to the aforesaid agreements and paragraphs that (i) it will refrain from the threat or the use of force to disturb them, in accordance with Article 2 (4) of the Charter of the United Nations dealing with the obligation of members to refrain in their international relations from the threat or use of force; and (ii) it would view any renewal of the aggression in violation of the

SOURCE: *American Foreign Policy: 1950–1955,* I, pp. 787–88.

aforesaid agreements with grave concern and as seriously threatening international peace and security.

In connection with the statement in the declaration concerning free elections in Viet-Nam my Government wishes to make clear its position which it has expressed in a declaration made in Washington on June 29, 1954, as follows:

> In the case of nations now divided against their will, we shall continue to seek to achieve unity through free elections supervised by the United Nations to insure that they are conducted fairly.

With respect to the statement made by the representative of the State of Viet-Nam, the United States reiterates its traditional position that peoples are entitled to determine their own future and that it will not join in an arrangement which would hinder this. Nothing in its declaration just made is intended to or does indicate any departure from this traditional position.

We share the hope that the agreements will permit Cambodia, Laos and Viet-Nam to play their part, in full independence and sovereignty, in the peaceful community of nations, and will enable the peoples of that area to determine their own future.

The Geneva decisions did not bind the United States. Nor did the subsequent South Vietnamese regimes consider themselves bound, for the Geneva armistice accords were all between the French on the side and the Vietminh on the other. The South Vietnamese government hence could refuse to cooperate in all-Vietnam elections in 1956.

C. EISENHOWER'S LETTER TO DIEM

PRESIDENT EISENHOWER ON OCTOBER 23, 1954, sent a letter to the then South Vietnamese premier, Ngo Dinh Diem, offering aid with some strings attached.

DEAR MR. PRESIDENT: I have been following with great interest the course of developments in Viet-Nam, particularly since the conclusion of the conference at Geneva. The implications of the agreement concerning Viet-Nam have caused grave concern regarding the future of a country temporarily divided by an artificial military grouping, weakened by a long and exhausting war and faced with enemies without and by their subversive collaborators within.

SOURCE: *American Foreign Policy: 1950–1955*, II, pp. 2401–02.

Your recent requests for aid to assist in the formidable project of the movement of several hundred thousand loyal Vietnamese citizens away from areas which are passing under a de facto rule and political ideology which they abhor, are being fulfilled. I am glad that the United States is able to assist in this humanitarian effort.

We have been exploring ways and means to permit our aid to Viet-Nam to be more effective and to make a greater contribution to the welfare and stability of the Government of Viet-Nam. I am, accordingly, instructing the American Ambassador to Viet-Nam to examine with you in your capacity as Chief of Government, how an intelligent program of American aid given directly to your Government can serve to assist Viet-Nam in its present hour of trial, provided that your Government is prepared to give assurances as to the standards of performance it would be able to maintain in the event such aid were supplied.

The purpose of this offer is to assist the Government of Viet-Nam in developing and maintaining a strong, viable state, capable of resisting attempted subversion or aggression through military means. The Government of the United States expects that this aid will be met by performance on the part of the Government of Viet-Nam in undertaking needed reforms. It hopes that such aid, combined with your own continuing efforts, will contribute effectively toward an independent Viet-Nam endowed with a strong government. Such a government would, I hope, be so responsive to the nationalist aspirations of its people, so enlightened in purpose and effective in performance, that it will be respected both at home and abroad and discourage any who might wish to impose a foreign ideology on your free people.

37. Laotian Neutrality

BY THE END of the Eisenhower administration the experiment, if such it was, in South Vietnam seemed to be working well, although in fact it was not. Diem displaced the Vietnamese emperor, Bao Dai, in 1955 and became president of the Republic of Vietnam; he seemed to be

SOURCE: American Foreign Policy: Current Documents, 1962 (Washington, D.C., 1966), pp. 1075–84.

thoroughly in control. He received American visitors with an indomitable optimism. In Eisenhower's last year or so in office the troubled area in what once had been Indochina appeared to be not Vietnam, but the little kingdom of Laos. Early in the Kennedy administration the United States government, believing that the Soviet Union was backing a Laotian Communist movement, rained down American dollars on the tiny kingdom in proportions almost unheard of in aid programs up to that time. The dollars only exacerbated the factionalism of Laotian politics. In 1961 the Great Powers that had attended the Geneva Conference of 1954 (U.S., U.S.S.R., Great Britain, France, mainland China, together with the successor states of French Indochina (South Vietnam, North Vietnam, Laos, Cambodia), the guarantor nations of the Geneva agreement (Canada, India, Poland), and two neighboring countries of Southeast Asia (Burma, Thailand), assembled an International Conference on the Settlement of the Laotian Question that discussed Laos for months. They signed a declaration at Geneva on July 23, 1962.

The Governments . . .
Welcoming the presentation of the statement of neutrality by the Royal Government of Laos of July 9, 1962, . . .

1. Solemnly declare, in accordance with the will of the Government and people of the Kingdom of Laos, . . . that they recognise and will respect and observe in every way the sovereignty, independence, neutrality, unity and territorial integrity of the Kingdom of Laos.

The same day that American representatives signed this declaration and its accompanying protocol, President Kennedy announced that the Kingdom of Laos stood on the threshold of a new era.

38. The Widening Commitment

A. THE ASSASSINATION OF DIEM

BY THE END of the Kennedy administration in 1963 the war in Vietnam had drawn an American commitment of 15,500 troops in support positions to the South Vietnamese army. Shortly before the assassination of

SOURCE: U.S. Department of Defense, United States–Vietnam Relations: 1945–1967, 12 vols. (Washington, D.C., 1971), XII, p. 574. These volumes are the so-called Pentagon Papers, declassified by the Defense Department and published by the Government Printing Office.

the American president in Dallas, a cabal of South Vietnamese generals overthrew the Diem government and assassinated its head. The American government knew that a plot was afoot and had arranged its policy with care. The following message was sent on October 5, 1963, to Ambassador Henry Cabot Lodge, Jr., in Saigon.

. . . President today approved recommendation that no initiative should now be taken to give any active covert encouragement to a coup. There should, however, be urgent covert effort with closest security under broad guidance of Ambassador to identify and build contacts with possible alternative leadership as and when it appears. Essential that this effort be totally secure and fully deniable and separated entirely from normal political analysis and reporting and other activities of country team. We repeat that this effort is not repeat not to be aimed at active promotion of coup but only at surveillance and readiness. In order to provide plausibility to denial suggest you and no one else in Embassy issue these instructions orally to Acting Station Chief and hold him responsible to you alone for making appropriate contacts and reporting to you alone.

Lodge on October 25 cabled President Johnson's adviser on national security affairs, McGeorge Bundy.

We should not thwart a coup for two reasons. First, it seems at least an even bet that the next government would not bungle and stumble as much as the present one has. Secondly, it is extremely unwise in the long range for us to pour cold water on attempts at a coup, particularly when they are just in their beginning stages. We should remember that this is the only way in which the people in Vietnam can possibly get a change of government. Whenever we thwart attempts at a coup, as we have done in the past, we are incurring very long lasting resentments, we are assuming an undue responsibility for keeping the incumbents in office, and in general are setting ourselves in judgment over the affairs of Vietnam. Merely to keep in touch with this situation and a policy merely limited to "not thwarting" are courses both of which entail some risks but these are lesser risks than either thwarting all coups while they are stillborn or our not being informed of what is happening.

Source: Department of Defense, *U.S.–Vietnam Relations*, p. 591.

All the above is totally distinct from not wanting U.S. military advisors to be distracted by matters which are not in their domain, with which I heartily agree. But obviously this does not conflict with a policy of not thwarting. In judging proposed coups, we must consider the effect on the war effort. Certainly a succession of fights for control of the Government of Vietnam would interfere with the war effort. It must also be said that the war effort has been interfered with already by the incompetence of the present government and the uproar which this has caused.

BUNDY *replied immediately.*

We are particularly concerned about hazard that an unsuccessful coup, however carefully we avoid direct engagement, will be laid at our door by public opinion almost everywhere. Therefore, while sharing your view that we should not be in position of thwarting coup, we would like to have option of judging and warning on any plan with poor prospects of success. We recognize that this is a large order, but President wants you to know of our concern.

SOURCE: Department of Defense, *U.S.–Vietnam Relations*, p. 592.

ON OCTOBER 30 BUNDY sent Lodge what he described as "our present standing instructions for U.S. posture in the event of a coup."

a. U.S. authorities will reject appeals for direct intervention from either side, and U.S.-controlled aircraft and other resources will not be committed between the battle lines or in support of either side, without authorization from Washington.

b. In event of indecisive contest, U.S. authorities may in their discretion agree to perform any acts agreeable to both sides, such as removal of key personalities or relay of information. In such actions, however, U.S. authorities will strenuously avoid appearance of pressure on either side. It is not in the interest of USG to be or appear to be either instrument of existing government or instrument of coup.

c. In the event of imminent or actual failure of coup, U.S. authorities may afford asylum in their discretion to those to whom there is any express or implied obligation of this sort. We believe however that in such a case it would be in our interest and probably in interest of those seeking asylum that they seek protection of other Embassies in addition to our own. This point should be made strongly if need arises.

SOURCE: Department of Defense, *U.S.–Vietnam Relations*, p. 605.

d. But once a coup under responsible leadership has begun, and within these restrictions, it is in the interest of the U.S. Government that it should succeed.

B. The Gulf of Tonkin Resolution

DURING THE SUBSEQUENT PRESIDENTIAL ELECTION YEAR in the United States, 1964, President Johnson anxiously observed cabinets in Saigon shuttling in and out of power, with a steadily worsening military situation. Apparently he began to look for an excuse to intervene, and seems to have instructed or permitted his staff to draft a congressional resolution authorizing intervention, for submission at the proper moment. After incidents involving American destroyers in the Gulf of Tonkin on August 2 and 4, 1964, the president authorized a retaliatory strike by American planes against North Vietnamese shore installations. He also sought congressional authority to take further measures against North Vietnam and received it in a joint resolution that passed the House of Representatives by vote of 416 to 0 on August 7 and the Senate that same day by 88 to 2 (the dissenters were Wayne Morse of Oregon and Ernest Gruening of Alaska). Johnson signed it into law on August 10. He did not tell Congress that the destroyer operations had involved electronic intelligence-gathering of a provocative sort, and that the presumed attacks by North Vietnamese vessels might possibly not have occurred or, if they did, might have involved mistaken identification, for South Vietnamese naval vessels were in the vicinity.

> Whereas naval units of the Communist regime in Vietnam, in violation of the principles of the Charter of the United Nations and of international law, have deliberately and repeatedly attacked United States naval vessels lawfully present in international waters, and have thereby created a serious threat to international peace; and
>
> Whereas these attacks are part of a deliberate and systematic campaign of aggression that the Communist regime in North Vietnam has been waging against its neighbors and the nations joined with them in the collective defense of their freedom; and
>
> Whereas the United States is assisting the peoples of southeast Asia to protect their freedom and has no territorial, military or political ambitions in that area, but desires only that these peoples should be left in peace to work out their own destinies in their own way: Now, therefore, be it

Resolved by the Senate and House of Representatives of the United States of America in Congress assembled, That the Congress approves and supports the determination of the President, as

SOURCE: American Foreign Policy: Current Documents, 1964 (Washington, D.C., 1967), pp. 991–92.

Commander in Chief, to take all necessary measures to repel any armed attack against the forces of the United States and to prevent further aggression.

Sec. 2. The United States regards as vital to its national interest and to world peace the maintenance of international peace and security in southeast Asia. Consonant with the Constitution of the United States and the Charter of the United Nations and in accordance with its obligations under the Southeast Asia Collective Defense Treaty, the United States is, therefore, prepared, as the President determines, to take all necessary steps, including the use of armed force, to assist any member or protocol state of the Southeast Asia Collective Defense Treaty requesting assistance in defense of its freedom.

Sec. 3. This resolution shall expire when the President shall determine that the peace and security of the area is reasonably assured by international conditions created by action of the United Nations or otherwise, except that it may be terminated earlier by concurrent resolution of the Congress.

UPON SIGNING THE TONKIN RESOLUTION *into law on August 10, the president made the following remarks.*

MY FELLOW AMERICANS: One week ago, half a world away, our Nation was faced by the challenge of deliberate and unprovoked acts of aggression in southeast Asia.

The cause of peace clearly required that we respond with a prompt and unmistakable reply.

As Commander in Chief the responsibility was mine—and mine alone. I gave the orders for that reply, and it has been given.

But, as President, there rested upon me still another responsibility—the responsibility of submitting our course to the representatives of the people, for them to verify it or veto it.

I directed that to be done last Tuesday.

Within 24 hours the resolution before me now had been placed before each House of Congress. In each House the resolution was promptly examined in committee and reported for action.

In each House there followed free and serious debate.

SOURCE: *Public Papers of the Presidents of the United States: Lyndon B. Johnson, 1963–64* (Washington, D.C., 1965), II, pp. 946–47.

In each House the resolution was passed on Friday last—with a total of 502 votes in support and 2 opposed.

Thus, today, our course is clearly known in every land.

There can be no mistake—no miscalculation—of where America stands or what this generation of Americans stand for.

The unanimity of the Congress reflects the unanimity of the country.

The resolution is short. It is straightforward. I hope that it will be read around the world.

The position of the United States is stated plainly. To any armed attack upon our forces, we shall reply.

To any in southeast Asia who ask our help in defending their freedom, we shall give it.

In that region there is nothing we covet, nothing we seek—no territory, no military position, no political ambition.

Our one desire—our one determination—is that the people of southeast Asia be left in peace to work out their own destinies in their own way.

This resolution stands squarely within the four corners of the Constitution of the United States. It is clearly consistent with the principles and purposes of the Charter of the United Nations.

This is another new page in the outstanding record of accomplishments the 88th Congress is writing.

Americans of all parties and philosophies can be justly proud— and justly grateful. Proud that democracy has once again demonstrated its capacity to act swiftly and decisively against aggressors. Grateful that there is in our National Government understanding, accord, and unity between the executive and legislative branches— without regard to partisanship.

This is a great strength that we must always preserve.

This resolution confirms and reinforces powers of the Presidency. I pledge to all Americans to use those powers with all the wisdom and judgment God grants to me.

It is everlastingly right that we should be resolute in reply to aggression and steadfast in support of our friends.

But it is everlastingly necessary that our actions should be careful and should be measured.

We are the most powerful of all nations—we must strive also to be the most responsible of nations.

So, in this spirit, and with this pledge, I now sign this resolution.

During the remainder of his years in the White House, President Johnson was accustomed to carry around with him a crumpled piece of paper on which appeared the text of the Tonkin Resolution, and when appropriate he would read its passages to doubters of his Vietnam policy. The House repealed the resolution on December 31, 1970, the Senate on January 2, 1971, and President Nixon signed the bill into law on January 12, 1971. Johnson's successor did not regard repeal as restricting his ability to wage war in Vietnam, for Nixon took the position that the preceding administration had put American troops in and he was following a policy of protecting the positions of those troops.

39. Withdrawal

A. Johnson Announces He Won't Run for Reelection

The year after the Tonkin Resolution, President Johnson acted swiftly when the Saigon government gave every evidence of imminent collapse. He poured American troops into South Vietnam until there were more than a half million; the figure reached 540,000 in the spring of 1968, and this did not include troops in the "pipeline" (support forces), nor troops in such neighboring countries as Thailand, nor sailors and airmen aboard U.S. Navy ships offshore. The enormous effort to protect South Vietnam succeeded in that the Saigon regime did not lapse into chaos, but its hold upon outlying towns and country districts remained shaky. The so-called Tet—or lunar new year—offensive in February, 1968, brought North Vietnamese troops and Vietcong irregulars into Saigon, and a suicide group attacked the American embassy compound. In many towns and country districts the power of the Saigon government collapsed. The American military command requested over 200,000 more troops for Vietnam. President Johnson mulled over this request, together with the dissension within the Democratic party that had become visible in recent months as his Vietnam policy encountered ever more trouble. When Senator Eugene McCarthy did well in the New Hampshire presidential primary, and Senator Robert Kennedy entered the race, President Johnson appeared on national television on March 31, 1968, not merely to announce a change in his Vietnam policy, but to remove himself from the presidential race.

Good evening, my fellow Americans: Tonight I want to speak to you of peace in Vietnam and Southeast Asia.

Source: *Public Papers of the Presidents of the United States: Lyndon B. Johnson, 1968–69*, I (Washington, D.C., 1970), pp. 469–76.

No other question so preoccupies our people. No other dream so absorbs the 250 million human beings who live in that part of the world. No other goal motivates American policy in Southeast Asia.

For years, representatives of our Government and others have traveled the world—seeking to find a basis for peace talks.

Since last September, they have carried the offer that I made public at San Antonio.

That offer was this:

That the United States would stop its bombardment of North Vietnam when that would lead promptly to productive discussions—and that we would assume that North Vietnam would not take military advantage of our restraint.

Hanoi denounced this offer, both privately and publicly. Even while the search for peace was going on, North Vietnam rushed their preparations for a savage assault on the people, the government, and the allies of South Vietnam.

Their attack—during the Tet holidays—failed to achieve its principal objectives.

It did not collapse the elected government of South Vietnam or shatter its army—as the Communists had hoped.

It did not produce a "general uprising" among the people of the cities as they had predicted.

The Communists were unable to maintain control of any of the more than 30 cities that they attacked. And they took very heavy casualties.

But they did compel the South Vietnamese and their allies to move certain forces from the countryside into the cities.

They caused widespread disruption and suffering. Their attacks, and the battles that followed, made refugees of half a million human beings.

The Communists may renew their attack any day.

They are, it appears, trying to make 1968 the year of decision in South Vietnam—the year that brings, if not final victory or defeat, at least a turning point in the struggle.

This much is clear:

If they do mount another round of heavy attacks, they will not succeed in destroying the fighting power of South Vietnam and its allies.

But tragically, this is also clear: Many men—on both sides of the struggle—will be lost. A nation that has already suffered 20 years of warfare will suffer once again. Armies on both sides will take new casualties. And the war will go on.

There is no need for this to be so.

There is no need to delay the talks that could bring an end to this long and this bloody war.

Tonight, I renew the offer I made last August—to stop the bombardment of North Vietnam. We ask that talks begin promptly, that they be serious talks on the substance of peace. We assume that during those talks Hanoi will not take advantage of our restraint.

We are prepared to move immediately toward peace through negotiations.

So, tonight, in the hope that this action will lead to early talks, I am taking the first step to deescalate the conflict. We are reducing—substantially reducing—the present level of hostilities.

And we are doing so unilaterally, and at once.

Tonight, I have ordered our aircraft and our naval vessels to make no attacks on North Vietnam, except in the area north of the demilitarized zone where the continuing enemy buildup directly threatens allied forward positions and where the movements of their troops and supplies are clearly related to that threat.

The area in which we are stopping our attacks includes almost 90 percent of North Vietnam's population, and most of its territory. Thus there will be no attacks around the principal populated areas, or in the food-producing areas of North Vietnam.

Even this very limited bombing of the North could come to an early end—if our restraint is matched by restraint in Hanoi. But I cannot in good conscience stop all bombing so long as to do so would immediately and directly endanger the lives of our men and our allies. Whether a complete bombing halt becomes possible in the future will be determined by events.

Our purpose in this action is to bring about a reduction in the level of violence that now exists.

It is to save the lives of brave men—and to save the lives of innocent women and children. It is to permit the contending forces to move closer to a political settlement.

And tonight, I call upon the United Kingdom and I call upon the Soviet Union—as cochairmen of the Geneva Conferences, and as permanent members of the United Nations Security Council—to do all they can to move from the unilateral act of deescalation that I have just announced toward genuine peace in Southeast Asia.

Now, as in the past, the United States is ready to send its representatives to any forum, at any time, to discuss the means of bringing this ugly war to an end.

I am designating one of our most distinguished Americans, Ambassador Averell Harriman, as my personal representative for such talks. In addition, I have asked Ambassador Llewellyn Thompson, who returned from Moscow for consultation, to be available to join Ambassador Harriman at Geneva or any other suitable place—just as soon as Hanoi agrees to a conference.

I call upon President Ho Chi Minh to respond positively, and favorably, to this new step toward peace.

But if peace does not come now through negotiations, it will come when Hanoi understands that our common resolve is unshakable, and our common strength is invincible.

Tonight, we and the other allied nations are contributing 600,000 fighting men to assist 700,000 South Vietnamese troops in defending their little country.

Our presence there has always rested on this basic belief: The main burden of preserving their freedom must be carried out by them—by the South Vietnamese themselves.

We and our allies can only help to provide a shield behind which the people of South Vietnam can survive and can grow and develop. On their efforts—on their determination and resourcefulness—the outcome will ultimately depend. . . .

Throughout my entire public career I have followed the personal philosophy that I am a free man, an American, a public servant, and a member of my party, in that order always and only.

For 37 years in the service of our Nation, first as a Congressman, as a Senator, and as Vice President, and now as your President, I have put the unity of the people first. I have put it ahead of any divisive partisanship.

And in these times as in times before, it is true that a house divided against itself by the spirit of faction, of party, of region, of religion, of race, is a house that cannot stand.

There is division in the American house now. There is divisiveness among us all tonight. And holding the trust that is mine, as President of all the people, I cannot disregard the peril to the progress of the American people and the hope and the prospect of peace for all peoples.

So, I would ask all Americans, whatever their personal interests or concern, to guard against divisiveness and all its ugly consequences.

Fifty-two months and 10 days ago, in a moment of tragedy and trauma, the duties of this office fell upon me. I asked then for your help and God's, that we might continue America on its course, binding up our wounds, healing our history, moving forward in new unity, to clear the American agenda and to keep the American commitment for all of our people.

United we have kept that commitment. United we have enlarged that commitment.

Through all time to come, I think America will be a stronger nation, a more just society, and a land of greater opportunity and fulfillment because of what we have all done together in these years of unparalleled achievement.

Our reward will come in the life of freedom, peace, and hope that our children will enjoy through ages ahead.

What we won when all of our people united just must not now be lost in suspicion, distrust, selfishness, and politics among any of our people.

Believing this as I do, I have concluded that I should not permit the Presidency to become involved in the partisan divisions that are developing in this political year.

With America's sons in the fields far away, with America's future under challenge right here at home, with our hopes and the world's hopes for peace in the balance every day, I do not believe that I should devote an hour or a day of my time to any personal partisan causes or to any duties other than the awesome duties of this office—the Presidency of your country.

Accordingly, I shall not seek, and I will not accept, the nomination of my party for another term as your President.

But let men everywhere know, however, that a strong, a confident, and a vigilant America stands ready tonight to seek an honorable peace—and stands ready tonight to defend an honored cause—whatever the price, whatever the burden, whatever the sacrifice that duty may require.

Thank you for listening.

Good night and God bless all of you.

B. THE CEASE-FIRE OF 1973

As PRESIDENT JOHNSON RELATED in his address of March, 1968, the United States government long had hoped that South Vietnam could carry its burdens without assistance, and this perhaps obvious goal, which had begun to appear on the bumpers of American automobiles as "Vietnam for the Vietnamese," became the avowed objective of the new Republican administration in 1969. President Nixon promised to reduce the level of American troops in South Vietnam, and by the year 1972 the last American combat troops had departed, so that only 30,000–40,000 support troops remained. In the spring of that year an offensive by the North Vietnamese raised grave questions about the policy of Vietnamization, for the South Vietnamese did not fight at all well against their northern opponents. With American troops rapidly withdrawing and the presidential election in the United States approaching, President Nixon in May announced suddenly that he had allowed the U.S. Navy to mine North Vietnamese harbors, thereby interdicting all shipping. He was careful not to describe this act as a blockade, which would have meant a formal state of war between North Vietnam and the United States. Surprisingly, in view of the dubious constitutionality of this presidential act, accomplished without advice from Congress, there was little protest by the president's countrymen. The military effectiveness of mining the harbors necessarily remained uncertain for some months, as it was an effort to cut off supplies and the North Vietnamese meanwhile could continue to use what they had. In the autumn of 1972 rumor gave way to certainty that negotiations between Hanoi and the president's special assistant for national security affairs, Henry Kissinger, were approaching agreement for a cease-fire and prisoner exchange. Shortly before the presidential election Kissinger announced that peace was "at hand." The negotiations slowed, President Nixon accused the North Vietnamese of bad faith, and in December the bombing resumed, resulting in a carpet bombing of Hanoi. The latter produced a domestic and international outcry when the North Vietnamese revealed that bombs had struck a hospital. The bombing halted, negotiations resumed, and on January 23, 1973, Kissinger and the North Vietnamese envoy, Le Duc Tho, meeting in Paris, initialed an agreement for ending the war. On January 27 in Paris the representatives of the four parties to the agreement—North Vietnam, South Vietnam, the Vietcong, and the United States—duly signed, with Secretary of State William P. Rogers signing for the United States. There was an "agreement on ending the war and restoring peace in Vietnam" together with four technical protocols (on prisoners and detainees, an International Commission of Control and Supervision, Joint Military Commissions, and mine-clearing in North Vietnam). The agreement on ending

SOURCE: Department of State Bulletin, February 12, 1973.

the war was signed by Secretary Rogers in two versions that differed only in their preambles. The first version, signed by all four parties, did not mention the respective governments by name, out of deference to the government of South Vietnam which did not wish to recognize the Vietcong (known as the Provisional Revolutionary Government of the Republic of South Vietnam). The preamble to the second version, signed by the United States and North Vietnam, stated delicately that signature was "with the concurrence of" the Government of the Republic of Vietnam (that is, Saigon) and the Provisional Revolutionary Government of the Republic of South Vietnam.

Article 1

The United States and all other countries respect the independence, sovereignty, unity, and territorial integrity of Vietnam as recognized by the 1954 Geneva Agreements on Vietnam.

Article 2

A cease-fire shall be observed throughout South Vietnam as of 2400 hours G.M.T., on January 27, 1973.

At the same hour, the United States will stop all its military activities against the territory of the Democratic Republic of Vietnam by ground, air and naval forces, wherever they may be based, and end the mining of the territorial waters, ports, harbors, and waterways of the Democratic Republic of Vietnam. The United States will remove, permanently deactivate or destroy all the mines in the territorial waters, ports, harbors, and waterways of North Vietnam as soon as this Agreement goes into effect.

The complete cessation of hostilities mentioned in this Article shall be durable and without limit of time.

Article 3

The parties undertake to maintain the cease-fire and to ensure a lasting and stable peace.

As soon as the cease-fire goes into effect:

(a) The United States forces and those of the other foreign countries allied with the United States and the Republic of Vietnam shall remain in-place pending the implementation of the plan of troop withdrawal. The Four-Party Joint Military Commission described in Article 16 shall determine the modalities.

(b) The armed forces of the two South Vietnamese parties shall remain in-place. The Two-Party Joint Military Commission described in Article 17 shall determine the areas controlled by each party and the modalities of stationing.

(c) The regular forces of all services and arms and the irregular forces of the parties in South Vietnam shall stop all offensive activities against each other and shall strictly abide by the following stipulations:

—All acts of force on the ground, in the air, and on the sea shall be prohibited;
—All hostile acts, terrorism and reprisals by both sides will be banned.

Article 4

The United States will not continue its military involvement or intervene in the internal affairs of South Vietnam.

Article 5

Within sixty days of the signing of this Agreement, there will be a total withdrawal from South Vietnam of troops, military advisers, and military personnel, including technical military personnel and military personnel associated with the pacification program, armaments, munitions, and war material of the United States and those of the other foreign countries mentioned in Article 3 (a). Advisers from the above-mentioned countries to all paramilitary organizations and the police force will also be withdrawn within the same period of time.

Article 6

The dismantlement of all military bases in South Vietnam of the United States and of the other foreign countries mentioned in Article 3 (a) shall be completed within sixty days of the signing of this Agreement.

Article 7

From the enforcement of the cease-fire to the formation of the government provided for in Articles 9 (b) and 14 of this Agreement, the two South Vietnamese parties shall not accept the introduction of troops, military advisers, and military personnel including technical military personnel, armaments, munitions, and war material into South Vietnam.

The two South Vietnamese parties shall be permitted to make periodic replacement of armaments, munitions and war material which have been destroyed, damaged, worn out or used up after the cease-fire, on the basis of piece-for-piece, of the same characteristics and properties, under the supervision of the Joint Military Commission of the two South Vietnamese parties and of the International Commission of Control and Supervision.

Article 8

(a) The return of captured military personnel and foreign civilians of the parties shall be carried out simultaneously with and completed not later than the same day as the troop withdrawal mentioned in Article 5. The parties shall exchange complete lists of the above-mentioned captured military personnel and foreign civilians on the day of the signing of this Agreement.

(b) The parties shall help each other to get information about those military personnel and foreign civilians of the parties missing in action, to determine the location and take care of the graves of the dead so as to facilitate the exhumation and repatriation of the remains, and to take any such other measures as may be required to get information about those still considered missing in action.

(c) The question of the return of Vietnamese civilian personnel captured and detained in South Vietnam will be resolved by the two South Vietnamese parties on the basis of the principles of Article 21 (b) of the Agreement on the Cessation of Hostilities in Vietnam of July 20, 1954. The two South Vietnamese parties will do so in a spirit of national reconciliation and concord, with a view to ending hatred and enmity, in order to ease suffering and to reunite families. The two South Vietnamese parties will do their utmost to resolve this question within ninety days after the cease-fire comes into effect.

Article 9

The Government of the United States of America and the Government of the Democratic Republic of Vietnam undertake to respect the following principles for the exercise of the South Vietnamese people's right to self-determination:

(a) The South Vietnamese people's right to self-determination is sacred, inalienable, and shall be respected by all countries.

(b) The South Vietnamese people shall decide themselves the political future of South Vietnam through genuinely free and democratic general elections under international supervision.

(c) Foreign countries shall not impose any political tendency or personality on the South Vietnamese people.

Article 14

South Vietnam will pursue a foreign policy of peace and independence. It will be prepared to establish relations with all countries irrespective of their political and social systems on the basis of mutual respect for independence and sovereignty and accept economic and technical aid from any country with no political conditions attached. The acceptance of military aid by South Vietnam in the future shall come under the authority of the government set up after the general elections in South Vietnam provided for in Article 9 (b).

Article 18

(a) After the signing of this Agreement, an International Commission of Control and Supervision shall be established immediately. . . .

(d) The International Commission of Control and Supervision shall be composed of representatives of four countries: Canada, Hungary, Indonesia and Poland. The chairmanship of this Commission will rotate among the members for specific periods to be determined by the Commission. . . .

Article 19

The parties agree on the convening of an International Conference within thirty days of the signing of this Agreement to acknowledge the signed agreements; to guarantee the ending of the war, the maintenance of peace in Vietnam, the respect of the Vietnamese people's fundamental national rights, and the South Vietnamese people's right to self-determination; and to contribute to and guarantee peace in Indochina.

The United States and the Democratic Republic of Vietnam, on behalf of the parties participating in the Paris Conference on Vietnam, will propose to the following parties that they participate in this International Conference: the People's Republic of China, the

Republic of France, the Union of Soviet Socialist Republics, the United Kingdom, the four countries of the International Commission of Control and Supervision, and the Secretary General of the United Nations, together with the parties participating in the Paris Conference on Vietnam. . . .

Article 21

The United States anticipates that this Agreement will usher in an era of reconciliation with the Democratic Republic of Vietnam as with all the peoples of Indochina. In pursuance of its traditional policy, the United States will contribute to healing the wounds of war and to postwar reconstruction of the Democratic Republic of Vietnam and throughout Indochina.

In accordance with Article 19 of the cease-fire agreement a conference assembled at Paris on February 26, composed of representatives of the twelve governments mentioned in the article. The secretary general of the United Nations was duly present, but did not sign the declaration of March 2. All the other representatives did. The declaration provided the guarantees required in Article 19 and stipulated that the conference would reassemble upon joint request of the United States and North Vietnam, or upon request by six or more of the signatory governments.

XII

The Diplomatic Revolution: Part One

The invention of atomic weapons in 1945 changed the basis of diplomacy and thereby wrought a diplomatic revolution. Prior to 1945 statesmen everywhere, even American statesmen, had been accustomed to lace their serious diplomatic disagreements with at least some thoughts about the possibility of war and on occasion would hint about war by employing such phrases as "grave consequences" or "incalculable results." Sometimes such a threat was sufficient to change intransigence to sweet reasonableness. Beginning in 1945 this kind of tactic changed; no longer was it possible to base diplomacy upon the possibility of war, for atomic war was humanely impossible. It was not unthinkable, because in the last days of the Second World War the United States had used atomic weapons. The bombings of Hiroshima and Nagasaki, however horrible in their particulars, did not cause as many casualties as did some of the fire bombings toward the end of the war, in Europe (Dresden) as well as in the Far East (Tokyo). But after 1945 the costs of an atomic war became much more ghastly to calculate. The Soviets obtained their own weapons in 1949, and Britain, France, and mainland China followed. The explosive force and heavy fallout of post-1945 weapons made the two atomic bombings of 1945 appear almost as if they belonged to an antediluvian age. After the Second World War no rational statesman was willing to move his country into a conflict involving atomic weapons.

40. The First Years

A. The Atomic Energy Act of 1946

DURING THE THREE WEEKS between the first American atomic explosion (July 16, 1945) and the use of atomic bombs in warfare (August 6, 9) almost no time was available to consider problems relating to civil control of atomic energy. The Far Eastern war was coming to its fiery end, and the highest officials of the government were at the Potsdam Conference and then en route back to the United States. The close of the war made the issue urgent, but the time was not right, for the Truman administration was too busy with reconversion of the economy to peacetime production. Meanwhile the United Nations organization was getting started; the administration prepared to discuss the limitation of atomic weapons there and did so in the spring of 1946, when it advanced the Baruch Plan at a meeting in New York (see pp. 294–99). Slowly a plan evolved for taking control of the atomic weapons program away from the military, which had been running it under the name of the Manhattan Engineer District. Legislation for such a plan passed both houses of Congress, and the president signed the Atomic Energy Act on August 1, 1946.

Be it enacted by the Senate and House of Representatives of the United States of America in Congress assembled,

Section 1.   Declaration of Policy

(a) FINDINGS AND DECLARATION.—Research and experimentation in the field of nuclear chain reaction have attained the stage at which the release of atomic energy on a large scale is practical. The significance of the atomic bomb for military purposes is evident. The effect of the use of atomic energy for civilian purposes upon the social, economic, and political structures of today cannot now be determined. It is a field in which unknown factors are involved. Therefore, any legislation will necessarily be subject to revision from time to time. It is reasonable to anticipate, however, that tapping this new source of energy will cause profound changes in

SOURCE: United States, *Statutes at Large*, vol. 60, pt. 1 (Washington, D.C., 1947), pp. 755–75.

our present way of life. Accordingly, it is hereby declared to be the policy of the people of the United States that, subject at all times to the paramount objective of assuring the common defense and security, the development and utilization of atomic energy shall, so far as practicable, be directed toward improving the public welfare, increasing the standard of living, strengthening free competition in private enterprise, and promoting world peace.

(b) PURPOSE OF ACT.—It is the purpose of this Act to effectuate the policies set out in section 1 (a) by providing, among others, for the following major programs relating to atomic energy:

1. A program of assisting and fostering private research and development to encourage maximum scientific progress;

2. A program for the control of scientific and technical information which will permit the dissemination of such information to encourage scientific progress, and for the sharing on a reciprocal basis of information concerning the practical industrial application of atomic energy as soon as effective and enforceable safeguards against its use for destructive purposes can be devised;

3. A program of federally conducted research and development to assure the Government of adequate scientific and technical accomplishment;

4. A program for Government control of the production, ownership, and use of fissionable material to assure the common defense and security and to insure the broadest possible exploitation of the fields; and

5. A program of administration which will be consistent with the foregoing policies and with international arrangements made by the United States, and which will enable the Congress to be currently informed so as to take further legislative action as may hereafter be appropriate.

Section 2. Organization

(a) ATOMIC ENERGY COMMISSION

1. There is hereby established an Atomic Energy Commission (herein called the Commission), which shall be composed of five members. Three members shall constitute a quorum of the Commission. The President shall designate one member as Chairman of the Commission.

2. Members of the Commission shall be appointed by the President, by and with the advice and consent of the Senate. . . .

4. There are hereby established within the Commission—

A. a General Manager, who shall discharge such of the administrative and executive functions of the Commission as the Commission may direct. . . .

B. a Division of Research, a Division of Production, a Division of Engineering, and a Division of Military Application. . . .

(b) GENERAL ADVISORY COMMITTEE.—There shall be a General Advisory Committee to advise the Commission on scientific and technical matters relating to materials, production, and research and development, to be composed of nine members, who shall be appointed from civilian life by the President. . . .

(c) MILITARY LIAISON COMMITTEE.—There shall be a Military Liaison Committee consisting of representatives of the Departments of War and Navy, detailed or assigned thereto, without additional compensation, by the Secretaries of War and Navy in such number as they may determine. The Commission shall advise and consult with the Committee on all atomic energy matters which the Committees deems to relate to military applications, including the development, manufacture, use, and storage of bombs, the allocation of fissionable material for military research, and the control of information relating to the manufacture or utilization of atomic weapons. The Commission shall keep the Committee fully informed of all such matters before it and the Committee shall keep the Commission fully informed of all atomic energy activities of the War and Navy Departments. The Committee shall have authority to make written recommendations to the Commission on matters relating to military applications from time to time as it may deem appropriate. If the Committee at any time concludes that any action, proposed action, or failure to act of the Commission on such matters is adverse to the responsibilities of the Departments of War or Navy, derived from the Constitution, laws, and treaties, the Committee may refer such action, proposed action, or failure to act to the Secretaries of War and Navy. If either Secretary concurs, he may refer the matter to the President, whose decision shall be final. . . .

Section 3.   Research

(a) RESEARCH ASSISTANCE.—The Commission is directed to exercise its powers in such manner as to insure the continued conduct of research and development activities in the fields specified below by private or public institutions or persons and to assist in the acquisition of an ever-expanding fund of theoretical and practical knowledge in such fields. To this end the Commission is authorized and directed to make arrangements (including contracts, agreements, and loans) for the conduct of research and development activities relating to—

1. nuclear processes;
2. the theory and production of atomic energy, including processes, materials, and devices related to such production;
3. utilization of fissionable and radioactive materials for medical, biological, health, or military purposes;
4. utilization of fissionable and radioactive materials and processes entailed in the production of such materials for all other purposes, including industrial uses; and
5. the protection of health during research and production activities. . . .

Section 4. Production of Fissionable Material

(a) DEFINITION.—As used in this Act, the term "produce," when used in relation to fissionable material, means to manufacture, produce, or refine fissionable material, . . . or to separate fissionable material from other substances in which such material may be contained or to produce new fissionable material.

(b) PROHIBITION.—It shall be unlawful for any person to own any facilities for the production of fissionable material or for any person to produce fissionable material, except to the extent authorized by subsection (c).

(c) OWNERSHIP AND OPERATION OF PRODUCTION FACILITIES.—

1. OWNERSHIP OF PRODUCTION FACILITIES.—The Commission, as agent of and on behalf of the United States, shall be the exclusive owner of all facilities for the production of fissionable material other than facilities which (A) are useful in the conduct of research and development activities in the fields specified in section 3, and (B) do not, in the opinion of the Commission, have a potential production rate adequate to enable the operator of such facilities to produce within a reasonable period of time a sufficient quantity of fissionable material to produce an atomic bomb or any other atomic weapon. . . .

(e) MANUFACTURE OF PRODUCTION FACILITIES.—Unless authorized by a license issued by the Commission, no person may manufacture, produce, transfer, or acquire any facilities for the production of fissionable material. Licenses shall be issued in accordance with such procedures as the Commission may by regulation establish and shall be issued in accordance with such standards and upon such conditions as will restrict the production and distribution of such facilities to effectuate the policies and purposes of this Act. Nothing in this section shall be deemed to require a license for such manufacture, production, transfer, or acquisition incident to or for the conduct of research or development activities in the United States of the types specified in section 3, or to prohibit the Commission from manufacturing or producing such facilities for its own use.

Section 5.   Control of Materials

(a) FISSIONABLE MATERIALS.—

1. DEFINITION.—As used in this Act, the term "fissionable material" means plutonium, uranium enriched in the isotope 235, any other material which the Commission determines to be capable of releasing substantial quantities of energy through nuclear chain reaction of the material, or any material artificially enriched by any of the foregoing. . . .

Section 6.   Military Applications of Atomic Energy

(a) AUTHORITY.—The Commission is authorized to—

1. conduct experiments and do research and development work in the military application of atomic energy; and
2. engage in the production of atomic bombs, atomic bomb parts, or other military weapons utilizing fissionable materials; except that such activities shall be carried on only to the extent that the express consent and direction of the President of the United States has been obtained, which consent and direction shall be obtained at least once each year.

The President from time to time may direct the Commission (1) to deliver such quantities of fissionable materials or weapons to the armed forces for such use as he deems necessary in the interest of national defense or (2) to authorize the armed forces to manufacture, produce, or acquire any equipment or device utilizing fissionable material or atomic energy as a military weapon. . . .

Section 8.   International Arrangements

(a) DEFINITION.—As used in this Act, the term "international arrangement" shall mean any treaty approved by the Senate or international agreement hereafter approved by the Congress, during the time such treaty or agreement is in full force and effect.

(b) EFFECT OF INTERNATIONAL ARRANGEMENTS.—Any provision of this Act or any action of the Commission to the extent that it conflicts with the provisions of any international arrangement made after the date of enactment of this Act shall be deemed to be of no further force or effect.

(c) POLICIES CONTAINED IN INTERNATIONAL ARRANGEMENTS.— In the performance of its functions under this Act, the commission shall give maximum effect to the policies contained in any such international arrangement.

Section 10.   Control of Information

(a) POLICY.—It shall be the policy of the Commission to control the dissemination of restricted data in such a manner as to assure the common defense and security. Consistent with such policy, the Commission shall be guided by the following principles:

1. That until Congress declares by joint resolution that effective and enforceable international safeguards against the use of atomic energy for destructive purposes have been established, there shall be no exchange of information with other nations with respect to the use of atomic energy for industrial purposes; and

2. That the dissemination of scientific and technical information relating to atomic energy should be permitted and encouraged so as to provide that free interchange of ideas and criticisms which is essential to scientific progress.

(b) RESTRICTIONS.—

1. The term "restricted data" as used in this section means all data concerning the manufacture or utilization of atomic weapons, the production of fissionable material, or the use of fissionable material in the production of power, but shall not include any data which the Commission from time to time determines may be published without adversely affecting the common defense and security. . . .

Section 15.   Joint Committee on Atomic Energy

(a) There is hereby established a Joint Committee on Atomic Energy to be composed of nine Members of the Senate to be appointed by the President of the Senate, and nine Members of the House of Representatives to be appointed by the Speaker of the House of Representatives. In each instance not more than five members shall be members of the same political party.

(b) The joint committee shall make continuing studies of the activities of the Atomic Energy Commission and of problems relating to the development, use, and control of atomic energy. The Commission shall keep the joint committee fully and currently informed with respect to the   Commission's activities. All bills, resolutions, and other matters in the Senate or the House of Representatives relating primarily to the Commission or to the development, use, or control of atomic energy shall be referred to the joint committee. The members of the joint committee who are Members of the Senate shall from time to time report to the Senate, and the members of the joint committee who are Members of the House of Representatives shall from time to time report to the House, by bill or otherwise, their recommendations with respect to matters within the jurisdiction of their respective Houses. . . .

On October 11, 1974, President Gerald Ford signed a bill abolishing the Atomic Energy Commission and creating a new Energy Research and Development Administration that could be the forerunner of a new cabinet department replacing the Department of the Interior.

B. The H-Bomb

The AEC commenced operations in January, 1947, under the chairmanship of David E. Lilienthal, who had been chairman of the Tennessee Valley Authority. Already, in the autumn of 1946, the Manhattan Engineer District had conducted bomb tests at Bikini—two explosions (above water and underwater) against a collection of superfluous naval vessels, captured and American. These tests were open to foreign observers. Two years later, in 1948, the AEC conducted closed tests at Eniwetok. Late in August, 1949, the Russians exploded an atomic

SOURCE: Public Papers of the Presidents of the United States: Harry S. Truman, 1950 (Washington, D.C., 1965), p. 138.

test device, which event President Truman announced in September. Almost at once a debate began over whether the United States government should develop a hydrogen bomb, and despite dissent among advisory scientists—a dissent that several years later was to have something to do with the AEC's denial of further clearance to the physicist J. Robert Oppenheimer, who had been in charge of the Los Alamos atomic laboratory during the war—the administration decided to go ahead. President Truman announced the decision in a public statement of January 31, 1950.

It is part of my responsibility as Commander in Chief of the Armed Forces to see to it that our country is able to defend itself against any possible aggressor. Accordingly, I have directed the Atomic Energy Commission to continue its work on all forms of atomic weapons, including the so-called hydrogen or superbomb. Like all other work in the field of atomic weapons, it is being and will be carried forward on a basis consistent with the overall objectives of our program for peace and security.

This we shall continue to do until a satisfactory plan for international control of atomic energy is achieved. We shall also continue to examine all those factors that affect our program for peace and this country's security.

41. Massive Retaliation

IN THE INITIAL YEARS OF THE 1950s the United States found itself confronting Russian atomic power. The Soviets possessed enough weapons to devastate large sections of the continental United States. For a nation that always had considered its homeland virtually impregnable, this was an unprecedented situation. As we can now see, the Soviets, like the Americans, had no intention of beginning an atomic war. Yet neither side was willing to let the other forget about its power. The Soviet Union under Khrushchev showed no hesitation in displaying its atomic strength, at least verbally and sometimes in test demonstrations. The Eisenhower administration did the same thing. Secretary of State Dulles was especially inclined to remind the Soviets of the existence of American weapons and sometimes seemed to enjoy it. In a speech to the Council on Foreign Relations in New York on January 12, 1954, he remarked that in the unknown future the American government would "depend primarily upon a great capacity to retaliate, instantly, by means and at places of our choosing," by which he meant massive retaliation.

SOURCE: Department of State *Bulletin*, January 25, 1954, pp. 107–10.

It is now nearly a year since the Eisenhower administration took office. During that year I have often spoken of various parts of our foreign policies. Tonight I should like to present an overall view of those policies which relate to our security.

First of all, let us recognize that many of the preceding foreign policies were good. Aid to Greece and Turkey had checked the Communist drive to the Mediterranean. The European Recovery Program had helped the peoples of Western Europe to pull out of the postwar morass. The Western powers were steadfast in Berlin and overcame the blockade with their airlift. As a loyal member of the United Nations, we had reacted with force to repel the Communist attack in Korea. When that effort exposed our military weakness, we rebuilt rapidly our military establishment. We also sought a quick buildup of armed strength in Western Europe.

These were the acts of a nation which saw the danger of Soviet communism; which realized that its own safety was tied up with that of others; which was capable of responding boldly and promptly to emergencies. These are precious values to be acclaimed. Also, we can pay tribute to congressional bipartisanship which puts the nation above politics.

But we need to recall that what we did was in the main emergency action, imposed on us by our enemies.

Let me illustrate.

1. We did not send our army into Korea because we judged in advance that it was sound military strategy to commit our Army to fight land battles in Asia. Our decision had been to pull out of Korea. It was Soviet-inspired action that pulled us back.

2. We did not decide in advance that it was wise to grant billions annually as foreign economic aid. We adopted that policy in response to the Communist efforts to sabotage the free economies of Western Europe.

3. We did not build up our military establishment at a rate which involved huge budget deficits, a depreciating currency, and a feverish economy because this seemed, in advance, a good policy. Indeed, we decided otherwise until the Soviet military threat was clearly revealed.

We live in a world where emergencies are always possible, and our survival may depend upon our capacity to meet emergencies. Let us pray that we shall always have that capacity. But, having said that, it is necessary also to say that emergency measures—

however good for the emergency—do not necessarily make good permanent policies. Emergency measures are costly; they are superficial; and they imply that the enemy has the initiative. They cannot be depended on to serve our long-time interests.

This "long time" factor is of critical importance.

The Soviet Communists are planning for what they call "an entire historical era," and we should do the same. They seek, through many types of maneuvers, gradually to divide and weaken the free nations by overextending them in efforts which, as Lenin put it, are "beyond their strength, so that they come to practical bankruptcy." Then, said Lenin, "our victory is assured." Then, said Stalin, will be "the moment for the decisive blow."

In the face of this strategy, measures cannot be judged adequate merely because they ward off an immediate danger. It is essential to do this, but it is also essential to do so without exhausting ourselves.

When the Eisenhower administration applied this test, we felt that some transformations were needed.

It is not sound military strategy permanently to commit U.S. land forces to Asia to a degree that leaves us no strategic reserves.

It is not sound economics, or good foreign policy, to support permanently other countries; for in the long run, that creates as much ill will as good will.

Also, it is not sound to become permanently committed to military expenditures so vast that they lead to "practical bankruptcy."

Change was imperative to assure the stamina needed for permanent security. But it was equally imperative that change should be accompanied by understanding of our true purposes. Sudden and spectacular change had to be avoided. Otherwise, there might have been a panic among our friends and miscalculated aggression by our enemies. We can, I believe, make a good report in these respects.

We need allies and collective security. Our purpose is to make these relations more effective, less costly. This can be done by placing more reliance on deterrent power and less dependence on local defensive power.

This is accepted practice so far as local communities are concerned. We keep locks on our doors, but we do not have an armed guard in every home. We rely principally on a community security system so well equipped to punish any who break in and steal that, in fact, would-be aggressors are generally deterred. That is the modern way of getting maximum protection at a bearable cost.

What the Eisenhower administration seeks is a similar international security system. We want, for ourselves and the other free nations, a maximum deterrent at a bearable cost.

Local defense will always be important. But there is no local defense which alone will contain the mighty landpower of the Communist world. Local defenses must be reinforced by the further deterrent of massive retaliatory power. A potential aggressor must know that he cannot always prescribe battle conditions that suit him. Otherwise, for example, a potential aggressor, who is glutted with manpower, might be tempted to attack in confidence that resistance would be confined to manpower. He might be tempted to attack in places where his superiority was decisive.

The way to deter aggression is for the free community to be willing and able to respond vigorously at places and with means of its own choosing.

So long as our basic policy concepts were unclear, our military leaders could not be selective in building our military power. If an enemy could pick his time and place and method of warfare—and if our policy was to remain the traditional one of meeting aggression by direct and local opposition—then we needed to be ready to fight in the Arctic and in the Tropics; in Asia, the Near East, and in Europe; by sea, by land, and by air; with old weapons and with new weapons.

The total cost of our security efforts, at home and abroad, was over $50 billion per annum, and involved, for 1953, a projected budgetary deficit of $9 billion; and $11 billion for 1954. This was on top of taxes comparable to wartime taxes; and the dollar was depreciating in effective value. Our allies were similarly weighed down. This could not be continued for long without grave budgetary, economic, and social consequences.

But before military planning could be changed, the President and his advisers, as represented by the National Security Council, had to take some basic policy decisions. This has been done. The basic decision was to depend primarily upon a great capacity to retaliate, instantly, by means and at places of our choosing. Now the Department of Defense and the Joint Chiefs of Staff can shape our military establishment to fit what is our policy, instead of having to try to be ready to meet the enemy's many choices. That permits of a selection of military means instead of a multiplication of means. As a result, it is now possible to get, and share, more basic security at less cost.

Let us now see how this concept has been applied to foreign policy, taking first the Far East.

In Korea this administration effected a major transformation. The fighting has been stopped on honorable terms. That was possible because the aggressor, already thrown back to and behind his place of beginning, was faced with the possibility that the fighting might, to his own great peril, soon spread beyond the limits and methods which he had selected.

The cruel toll of American youth and the nonproductive expenditure of many billions have been stopped. Also our armed forces are no longer largely committed to the Asian mainland. We can begin to create a strategic reserve which greatly improves our defensive posture.

This change gives added authority to the warning of the members of the United Nations which fought in Korea that, if the Communists renewed the aggression, the United Nations response would not necessarily be confined to Korea.

I have said in relation to Indochina that, if there were open Red Chinese army aggression there, that would have "grave consequences which might not be confined to Indochina."

I expressed last month the intention of the United States to maintain its position in Okinawa. This is needed to insure adequate striking power to implement the collective security concept which I describe.

All of this is summed up in President Eisenhower's important statement of December 26. He announced the progressive reduction of the U.S. ground forces in Korea. He pointed out that U.S. military forces in the Far East will now feature "highly mobile naval, air and amphibious units"; and he said in this way, despite some withdrawal of land forces, the United States will have a capacity to oppose aggression "with even greater effect than heretofore."

The bringing home of some of our land forces also provides a most eloquent rebuttal to the Communist charge of "imperialism."

If we turn to Europe, we see readjustments in the NATO collective security effort. Senator Vandenberg called the North Atlantic Treaty pledges "the most practical deterrent and discouragement to war which the wit of man has yet devised." But he said also that "if the concept and objective are to build sufficient forces in being to hold the Russian line . . . it presents ruinous corollaries both at home and abroad."

In the first years of the North Atlantic Treaty Organization, after the aggression in Korea, its members made an emergency buildup of military strength. I do not question the judgment of that time. The strength thus built has served well the cause of peace. But the pace originally set could not be maintained indefinitely.

At the April meeting of the NATO Council, the United States put forward a new concept, now known as that of the "long haul." That meant a steady development of defensive strength at a rate which will preserve and not exhaust the economic strength of our allies and ourselves. This would be reinforced by the striking power of a strategic air force based on internationally agreed positions.

We found, at the Council of last December, that there was general acceptance of the "long haul" concept and recognition that it better served the probable needs than an effort to create full defensive land strength at a ruinous price.

One of the emergency aspects of NATO is that it was begun before there was a solid foundation.

For example, Western Europe cannot be successfully defended without a defense of West Germany. West Germany cannot be defended without help from the Germans. German participation is excluded by the armistice arrangements still in force.

The West German Republic needs to be freed from the armistice; and new political arrangements should be made to assure that rearmed Germans will serve the common cause and never serve German militarism.

The French produced a plan to take care of this matter. It was to create a European Defense Community, composed of France, Italy, Belgium, the Netherlands, Luxembourg, and West Germany. They would have a European army, including Germans, but there would be no national armies in West Europe.

A treaty to create this defense community was signed in May 1952. But when the Eisenhower administration took office last

January, no government had sought parliamentary ratification, and the project was nigh unto death.

President Eisenhower is deeply convinced that there can be no long-term assurance of security and vitality for Europe, and therefore for the Western World including the United States, unless there is a unity which will include France and Germany and end the disunity which has led to recurrent wars, and in our generation to two world wars. As NATO's Chief Commander, and now as President, he continues to make clear the importance which the United States attaches to the consummation of the European Defense Community and, we would hope thereafter, a political community.

Until the goals of EDC are achieved, NATO, and indeed future peace, are in jeopardy. Distrust between France and Germany is inflammable, and already Communist agents are looking to it as a means for international arson.

There are of course immense difficulties in the way of the final consummation of Franco-German unity. But we have confidence that peace will soon have the indispensable foundation of the EDC.

New collective security concepts reduce nonproductive military expenses of our allies to a point where it is desirable and practicable also to reduce economic aid. There was need of a more self-respecting relationship, and that, indeed, is what our allies wanted. Trade, broader markets, and a flow of investments are far more healthy than intergovernmental grants-in-aid.

There are still some strategic spots where the local governments cannot maintain adequate armed forces without some financial support from us. In these cases, we take the judgment of our military advisers as to how to proceed in the common interest. For example, we have contributed largely, ungrudgingly, and I hope constructively, to end aggression and advance freedom in Indochina.

The technical assistance program is being continued, and we stand ready to meet nonrecurrent needs due to crop failures or like disasters.

But, broadly speaking, foreign budgetary aid is being limited to situations where it clearly contributes to military strength.

In the ways I outlined we gather strength for the long-term defense of freedom.

We do not, of course, claim to have found some magic formula that insures against all forms of Communist successes. It is normal that at some times and at some places there may be setbacks to the cause of freedom. What we do expect to insure is that any setbacks will have only temporary and local significance, because they will leave unimpaired those free world assets which in the long run will prevail.

If we can deter such aggression as would mean general war, and that is our confident resolve, then we can let time and fundamentals work for us. We do not need self-imposed policies which sap our strength.

The fundamental, on our side, is the richness—spiritual, intellectual, and material—that freedom can produce and the irresistible attraction it then steps up. That is why we do not plan ourselves to shackle freedom to preserve freedom. We intend that our conduct and example shall continue, as in the past, to show all men how good can be the fruits of freedom.

If we rely on freedom, then it follows that we must abstain from diplomatic moves which would seem to endorse captivity. That would, in effect, be a conspiracy against freedom. I can assure you that we shall never seek illusory security for ourselves by such a "deal."

We do negotiate about specific matters but only to advance the cause of human welfare.

President Eisenhower electrified the world with his proposal to lift a great weight of fear by turning atomic energy from a means of death into a source of life. Yesterday, I started procedural talks with the Soviet Government on that topic.

We have persisted, with our allies, in seeking the unification of Germany and the liberation of Austria. Now the Soviet rulers have agreed to discuss these questions. We expect to meet them soon in Berlin. I hope they will come with a sincerity which will equal our own.

We have sought a conference to unify Korea and relieve it of foreign troops. So far, our persistence is unrewarded; but we have not given up.

These efforts at negotiation are normal initiatives that breathe the spirit of freedom. They involve no plan for a partnership division of world power with those who suppress freedom.

If we persist in the courses I outline we shall confront dictatorship with a task that is, in the long run, beyond its strength. For unless it changes, it must suppress the human desires that freedom satisfies—as we shall be demonstrating.

If the dictators persist in their present course, then it is they who will be limited to superficial successes, while their foundation crumbles under the tread of their iron boots.

Human beings, for the most part, want simple things.

They want to worship God in accordance with the dictates of their conscience. But that is not easily granted by those who promote an atheistic creed.

They want to think in accordance with the dictates of their reason. But that is not easily granted by those who represent an authoritarian system.

They want to exchange views with others and to persuade and to be persuaded by what appeals to their reason and their conscience. But that is not easily granted by those who believe in a society of conformity.

They want to live in their homes without fear. But that is not easily granted by those who believe in a police state system.

They want to be able to work productively and creatively and to enjoy the fruits of their labor. But that is not easily granted by those who look upon human beings as a means to create a power-house to dominate the world.

We can be sure that there is going on, even within Russia, a silent test of strength between the powerful rulers and the multitudes of human beings. Each individual no doubt seems by himself to be helpless in this struggle. But their aspirations in the aggregate make up a mighty force.

There are signs that the rulers are bending to some of the human desires of their people. There are promises of more food, more household goods, more economic freedom.

That does not prove that the Soviet rulers have themselves been converted. It is rather that they may be dimly perceiving a basic fact, that is that there are limits to the power of any rulers indefinitely to suppress the human spirit.

In that God-given fact lies our greatest hope. It is a hope that can sustain us. For even if the path ahead be long and hard, it need not be a warlike path; and we can know that at the end may be found the blessedness of peace.

42. Antiballistic Missiles

A. McNamara's Reversal

RUSSIAN MISSILE STRENGTH first appeared as a factor in American diplomacy during the Suez crisis of 1956, when the Soviets indelicately threatened Paris and London, the capitals of the attacking Western powers, with a rain of intermediate-range missiles that the U.S.S.R. had emplaced and presumably stood ready to use. To Washington at this time the Soviets more carefully remarked that both superpowers possessed atomic weapons and the means to deliver them. The next year the Russian Sputnik brought consternation to the American public, a feeling that the Russians might be ahead of the United States in the arms race. This feeling led John F. Kennedy, the Democratic candidate for the presidency in 1960, to accuse the Eisenhower administration of having permitted a missile gap so that the Russians possessed or were about to possess more intercontinental ballistic missiles than the United States. After Kennedy came into office, Under Secretary of Defense Roswell Gilpatric announced publicly that the gap was a myth; the United States, he said, was far ahead of the Soviets in developing and emplacing ICBM's. As the 1960s wore on, the Russians slowly began to close the real missile gap. American electronics manufacturers and some segments of the military began to agitate for protection against Soviet missiles by means of an antiballistic missile system. Secretary of Defense Robert S. McNamara considered an ABM net an absurdity—that the technical problems were huge, and that it was foolish to react to Russian missile strength by boosting the arms race into a new category of expense. Meanwhile, the Vietnam War began to go badly, and the secretary of defense may have felt that he could not resist both the ABM pressure and the anti-Vietnam pressure. He reversed his stance on ABM in a speech in San Francisco on September 18, 1967.

There is evidence that the Chinese are devoting very substantial resources to the development of both nuclear warheads and missile delivery systems. As I stated last January, indications are that they will have medium-range ballistic missiles within a year or so, an initial intercontinental ballistic missile capability in the early 1970's, and a modest force in the midseventies.

SOURCE: *American Foreign Policy: Current Documents, 1967* (Washington, D.C., 1969), pp. 16–25.

Up to now, the leadtime factor has allowed us to postpone a decision on whether or not a light ABM deployment might be advantageous as a countermeasure to Communist China's nuclear development. But the time will shortly be right for us to initiate production if we desire such a system.

China at the moment is caught up in internal strife, but it seems likely that her basic motivation in developing a strategic nuclear capability is an attempt to provide a basis for threatening her neighbors and to clothe herself with the dubious prestige that the world pays to nuclear weaponry. We deplore her development of these weapons, just as we deplore it in other countries. We oppose nuclear proliferation because we believe that in the end it only increases the risk of a common and cataclysmic holocaust.

President Johnson has made it clear that the United States will oppose any efforts of China to employ nuclear blackmail against her neighbors.

We possess now, and will continue to possess for as far ahead as we can foresee, an overwhelming first-strike capability with respect to China. And despite the shrill and raucous propaganda directed at her own people that "the atomic bomb is a paper tiger," there is ample evidence that China well appreciates the destructive power of nuclear weapons.

China has been cautious to avoid any action that might end in a nuclear clash with the United States—however wild her words—and understandably so. We have the power not only to destroy completely her entire nuclear offensive forces but to devastate her society as well.

Is there any possibility, then, that by the mid-1970's China might become so incautious as to attempt a nuclear attack on the United States or our allies? It would be insane and suicidal for her to do so, but one can conceive conditions under which China might miscalculate. We wish to reduce such possibilities to a minimum.

And since, as I have noted, our strategic planning must always be conservative and take into consideration even the possible irrational behavior of potential adversaries, there are marginal grounds for concluding that a light deployment of U.S. ABM's against this possibility is prudent.

The system would be relatively inexpensive—preliminary estimates place the cost at about $5 billion—and would have a much higher degree of reliability against a Chinese attack than the much more massive and complicated system that some have recommended against a possible Soviet attack.

Moreover, such an ABM deployment designed against a possible Chinese attack would have a number of other advantages. It would provide an additional indication to Asians that we intend to deter China from nuclear blackmail and thus would contribute toward our goal of discouraging nuclear weapon proliferation among the present nonnuclear countries.

Further, the Chinese-oriented ABM deployment would enable us to add—as a concurrent benefit—a further defense of our Minuteman sites against Soviet attack, which means that at modest cost we would in fact be adding even greater effectiveness to our offensive missile force and avoiding a much more costly expansion of that force.

Finally, such a reasonably reliable ABM system would add protection of our population against the improbable but possible accidental launch of an intercontinental missile by any one of the nuclear powers.

After a detailed review of all these considerations, we have decided to go forward with this Chinese-oriented ABM deployment; and we will begin actual production of such a system at the end of this year.

In reaching this decision, I want to emphasize that it contains two possible dangers, and we should guard carefully against each.

The first danger is that we may psychologically lapse into the old oversimplification about the adequacy of nuclear power. The simple truth is that nuclear weapons can serve to deter only a narrow range of threats. This ABM deployment will strengthen our defensive posture and will enhance the effectiveness of our land-based ICBM offensive forces. But the independent nations of Asia must realize that these benefits are no substitute for their maintaining, and where necessary strengthening, their own conventional forces in order to deal with the more likely threats to the security of the region.

The second danger is also psychological. There is a kind of mad momentum intrinsic to the development of all new nuclear weaponry. If a weapon system works—and works well—there is strong pressure from many directions to procure and deploy the weapon out of all proportion to the prudent level required.

The danger in deploying this relatively light and reliable Chinese-oriented ABM system is going to be that pressures will develop to expand it into a heavy Soviet-oriented ABM system.

We must resist that temptation firmly, not because we can for a moment afford to relax our vigilance against a possible Soviet first strike but precisely because our greatest deterrent against such a strike is not a massive, costly, but highly penetrable ABM shield but rather a fully credible offensive assured destruction capability.

The so-called heavy ABM shield—at the present state of technology—would in effect be no adequate shield at all against a Soviet attack but rather a strong inducement for the Soviets to vastly increase their own offensive forces. That, as I have pointed out, would make it necessary for us to respond in turn; and so the arms race would rush hopelessly on to no sensible purpose on either side.

Let me emphasize—and I cannot do so too strongly—that our decision to go ahead with a *limited* ABM deployment in no way indicates that we feel an agreement with the Soviet Union on the limitation of strategic nuclear offensive and defensive forces is any the less urgent or desirable.

The road leading from the stone ax to the ICBM, though it may have been more than a million years in the building, seems to have run in a single direction. If one is inclined to be cynical, one might conclude that man's history seems to be characterized not so much by consistent periods of peace, occasionally punctuated by warfare, but rather by persistent outbreaks of warfare, wearily put aside from time to time by periods of exhaustion and recovery that parade under the name of peace.

I do not view man's history with that degree of cynicism, but I do believe that man's wisdom in avoiding war is often surpassed by his folly in promoting it.

However foolish unlimited war may have been in the past, it is now no longer merely foolish, but suicidal as well.

It is said that nothing can prevent a man from suicide if he is sufficiently determined to commit it. The question is what is our determination in an era when unlimited war will mean the death of hundreds of millions—and the possible genetic impairment of a million generations to follow?

Man is clearly a compound of folly and wisdom, and history is clearly a consequence of the admixture of those two contradictory traits. History has placed our particular lives in an era when the consequences of human folly are waxing more and more catastrophic in the matters of war and peace.

In the end, the root of man's security does not lie in his weaponry. In the end, the root of man's security lies in his mind.

What the world requires in its 22d year of the atomic age is not a new race toward armament. What the world requires in its 22d year of the atomic age is a new race toward reasonableness.

We had better all run that race—not merely we the administrators but we the people.

B. SAFEGUARD

WHEN PRESIDENT NIXON took office in January, 1969, he announced that he would reexamine the nation's strategic programs. In a White House press release of March 14, 1969, the president informed his countrymen that he was modifying, "substantially," he said, the so-called Sentinel ABM system for which the Johnson administration had requested funds to begin site construction. President Nixon in a news conference described his revised system as "a safeguard program." While the purpose of Sentinel had been to protect cities (and a furor had arisen when the army began to scout for land in the vicinity of Chicago), Safeguard was designed to protect the country's force of Minuteman missiles, which were all located in trans-Mississippi states with low population densities.

Immediately after assuming office, I requested the Secretary of Defense to review the program initiated by the last administration to deploy the Sentinel ballistic missile defense system.

The Department of Defense presented a full statement of the alternatives at the last two meetings of the National Security Council. These alternatives were reviewed there in the light of the security requirements of the United States and of their probable impact on East-West relations, with particular reference to the prospects for strategic arms negotiations.

After carefully considering the alternatives, I have reached the following conclusions: (1) the concept on which the Sentinel program of the previous administration was based should be substantially modified; (2) the safety of our country requires that we should proceed now with the development and construction of the

SOURCE: Department of State *Bulletin*, March 31, 1969, pp. 273–75.

new system in a carefully phased program; (3) this program will be reviewed annually from the point of view of (a) technical developments, (b) the threat, (c) the diplomatic context, including any talks on arms limitation.

The modified system has been designed so that its defensive intent is unmistakable. It will be implemented not according to some fixed, theoretical schedule but in a manner clearly related to our periodic analysis of the threat. The first deployment covers two missile sites; the first of these will not be completed before 1973. Any further delay would set this date back by at least 2 additional years. The program for fiscal year 1970 is the minimum necessary to maintain the security of our nation. . . .

Modern technology provides several choices in seeking to insure the survival of our retaliatory forces.

First, we could increase the number of sea- and land-based missiles and bombers. I have ruled out this course because it provides only marginal improvement of our deterrent, while it could be misinterpreted by the Soviets as an attempt to threaten their deterrent. It would therefore stimulate an arms race.

A second option is to harden further our ballistic missile forces by putting them in more strongly reinforced underground silos. But our studies show that hardening by itself is not adequate protection against foreseeable advances in the accuracy of Soviet offensive forces.

The third option was to begin a measured construction on an active defense of our retaliatory forces.

I have chosen the third option.

The system will use components previously developed for the Sentinel system. However, the deployment will be changed to reflect the new concept. We will provide for local defense of selected Minuteman missile sites and an area defense designed to protect our bomber bases and our command and control authorities. In addition, this new system will provide a defense of the continental United States against an accidental attack and will provide substantial protection against the kind of attack which the Chinese Communists may be capable of launching throughout the 1970's. This deployment will not require us to place missile and radar sites close to our major cities.

The present estimate is that the total cost of installing this system will be $6–$7 billion. However, because of the deliberate pace of the deployment, budgetary requests for the coming year can be substantially less—by about one-half—than those asked for by the previous administration for the Sentinel system. . . .

. . . I am deeply sympathetic to the concerns of private citizens and Members of Congress that we do only that which is necessary for national security. This is why I am recommending a minimum program essential for our security. It is my duty as President to make certain that we do no less.

The Nixon administration's ardent espousal of ABMs touched off an enormous public and congressional debate, and Safeguard squeaked through the Senate in 1969 by a margin of one vote. In 1970 the Senate margin for additional appropriations rose to five votes, again after long, bitter, much publicized testimony and debate. The next year, 1971, signs appeared that concern over ABM was dying down, for the Senate approved continued deployment of ABM at two Minuteman sites by a vote of 64 to 21, after two hours of moderate debate. Perhaps the relatively low-key debate of 1971 was caused by knowledge or belief in and out of Congress that the president would arrange a nuclear missile détente with the Soviet Union, which he did in May, 1972. For the ABM treaty and the eventual mothballing of the single-site American system at Grand Forks, N.D., see below, pp. 312–17.

XIII

The Diplomatic Revolution: Part Two

While the United States government was deciding its policy on atomic weapons—partly because of the press of events, including Soviet competition—it simultaneously was seeking a limitation of these weapons. From the outset of the atomic era Washington hoped that in some way, which would become apparent sooner or later, it might limit or even prohibit atomic warfare.

43. The Failure to Internationalize Atomic Weapons

A. THE TRUMAN-ATTLEE-KING DECLARATION

As soon as the Second World War was over, the issue of atomic limitation began to press upon the Truman administration, and the new and inexperienced president did not quite know what to do. In a cabinet meeting of September, 1945, Secretary of War Henry L. Stimson proposed (it was Stimson's last cabinet) that the American and Soviet governments get together on a program for limitation and take it to the United Nations after consultation with Great Britain and Canada, who had been cosponsors of the wartime atomic project. After the cabinet meeting a garbled account of the discussion got into the newspapers, and Truman received a visit from Prime Ministers Clement Attlee of Britain and W. L. Mackenzie King of Canada, who virtually demanded a conference on atomic energy with the embarrassed president. They seem to have thought that the Americans contemplated going to the Russians, even giving weapons information to the Russians, without

Source: Charles I. Bevans, comp., Treaties and Other International Agreements of the United States of America: 1776–1949 (Washington, D.C., 1968–), III, pp. 1304–06.

consulting them. At the conference in Washington in November, the wartime scientific adviser, Vannevar Bush, was delegated to draw up an agreement. Bush did so, and the conferees—Truman, Attlee, and King—signed it on November 15, 1945.

1. We recognize that the application of recent scientific discoveries to the methods and practice of war has placed at the disposal of mankind means of destruction hitherto unknown, against which there can be no adequate military defence, and in the employment of which no single nation can in fact have a monopoly.

2. We desire to emphasize that the responsibility for devising means to ensure that the new discoveries shall be used for the benefit of mankind, instead of as a means of destruction, rests not on our nations alone, but upon the whole civilized world. Nevertheless, the progress that we have made in the development and use of atomic energy demands that we take an initiative in the matter, and we have accordingly met together to consider the possibility of international action:

    a. To prevent the use of atomic energy for destructive purposes

    b. To promote the use of recent and future advances in scientific knowledge, particularly in the utilization of atomic energy, for peaceful and humanitarian ends.

3. We are aware that the only complete protection for the civilized world from the destructive use of scientific knowledge lies in the prevention of war. No system of safeguards that can be devised will of itself provide an effective guarantee against production of atomic weapons by a nation bent on aggression. Nor can we ignore the possibility of the development of other weapons, or of new methods of warfare, which may constitute as great a threat to civilization as the military use of atomic energy.

4. Representing as we do, the three countries which possess the knowledge essential to the use of atomic energy, we declare at the outset our willingness, as a first contribution, to proceed with the exchange of fundamental scientific information and the interchange of scientists and scientific literature for peaceful ends with any nation that will fully reciprocate.

5. We believe that the fruits of scientific research should be made available to all nations, and that freedom of investigation and free interchange of ideas are essential to the progress of knowl-

edge. In pursuance of this policy, the basic scientific information essential to the development of atomic energy for peaceful purposes has already been made available to the world. It is our intention that all further information of this character that may become available from time to time shall be similarly treated. We trust that other nations will adopt the same policy, thereby creating an atmosphere of reciprocal confidence in which political agreement and cooperation will flourish.

6. We have considered the question of the disclosure of detailed information concerning the practical industrial application of atomic energy. The military exploitation of atomic energy depends, in large part, upon the same methods and processes as would be required for industrial uses.

We are not convinced that the spreading of the specialized information regarding the practical application of atomic energy, before it is possible to devise effective, reciprocal, and enforceable safeguards acceptable to all nations, would contribute to a constructive solution of the problem of the atomic bomb. On the contrary we think it might have the opposite effect. We are, however, prepared to share, on a reciprocal basis with others of the United Nations, detailed information concerning the practical industrial application of atomic energy just as soon as effective enforceable safeguards against its use for destructive purposes can be devised.

7. In order to attain the most effective means of entirely eliminating the use of atomic energy for destructive purposes and promoting its widest use for industrial and humanitarian purposes, we are of the opinion that at the earliest practicable date a Commission should be set up under the United Nations Organization to prepare recommendations for submission to the Organization.

The Commission should be instructed to proceed with the utmost dispatch and should be authorized to submit recommendations from time to time dealing with separate phases of its work.

In particular the Commission should make specific proposals:

    a. For extending between all nations the exchange of basic scientific information for peaceful ends,

    b. For control of atomic energy to the extent necessary to ensure its use only for peaceful purposes,

c. For the elimination from national armaments of atomic weapons and of all other major weapons adaptable to mass destruction,

d. For effective safeguards by way of inspection and other means to protect complying states against the hazards of violations and evasions.

8. The work of the Commission should proceed by separate stages, the successful completion of each one of which will develop the necessary confidence of the world before the next stage is undertaken. Specifically it is considered that the Commission might well devote its attention first to the wide exchange of scientists and scientific information, and as a second stage to the development of full knowledge concerning natural resources of raw materials.

9. Faced with the terrible realities of the application of science to destruction, every nation will realize more urgently than before the overwhelming need to maintain the rule of law among nations and to banish the scourge of war from the earth. This can only be brought about by giving wholehearted support to the United Nations Organization, and by consolidating and extending its authority, thus creating conditions of mutual trust in which all peoples will be free to devote themselves to the arts of peace. It is our firm resolve to work without reservation to achieve these ends.

B. The Baruch Plan

AFTER THE DEPARTURE OF THE PRIME MINISTERS, Truman appointed a committee chaired by Undersecretary of State Dean Acheson to draw up an American plan of limitation in accord with the Truman-Attlee-King Declaration. Assisted by a panel of experts including J. Robert Oppenheimer and David E. Lilienthal, the committee produced the Acheson-Lilienthal Report, which provided for limitation under the United Nations according to the stages set out in the declaration of November 15, 1945. To the intense irritation of Acheson and Lilienthal, Secretary of State James F. Byrnes then advised the president to appoint First World War production czar Bernard M. Baruch head of the American delegation that would present the American plan to the United Nations Atomic Energy Commission. Baruch was appointed. This self-styled "adviser to presidents" disliked supporting anything that was not "his," and so he made two slight changes in the Acheson-Lilienthal Report and the American public renamed it the Baruch Plan.

SOURCE: *A Decade of American Foreign Policy: Basic Documents, 1941–1949* (Washington, D.C., 1950), pp. 1079–87.

He determined that in case of a violation of the proposed international atomic agreement none of the five Great Powers in the U.N. Security Council could veto any U.N. action and that the violator at once should face "immediate, swift, and sure punishment"—the military might of the other signatories of the limitation pact. The problem with these changes was that (1) to renounce the veto was only a gesture, for the U.N.'s military might against a violator—presumably the Soviet Union —would be American military might and (2) the talk about punishment could only annoy the Russians. Unpersuaded, Baruch offered his plan to the U.N. Atomic Energy Commission during a session in New York on June 14, 1946.

My Fellow Members of the United Nations Atomic Energy Commission, and My Fellow Citizens of the World: We are here to make a choice between the quick and the dead.

That is our business.

Behind the black portent of the new atomic age lies a hope which, seized upon with faith, can work our salvation. If we fail, then we have damned every man to be the slave of Fear. Let us not deceive ourselves: We must elect World Peace or World Destruction. . . .

The United States proposes the creation of an International Atomic Development Authority, to which should be entrusted all phases of the development and use of atomic energy, starting with the raw material and including—

1. Managerial control or ownership of all atomic-energy activities potentially dangerous to world security.

2. Power to control, inspect, and license all other atomic activities.

3. The duty of fostering the beneficial uses of atomic energy.

4. Research and development responsibilities of an affirmative character intended to put the Authority in the forefront of atomic knowledge and thus to enable it to comprehend, and therefore to detect, misuse of atomic energy. To be effective, the Authority must itself be the world's leader in the field of atomic knowledge and development and thus supplement its legal authority with the great power inherent in possession of leadership in knowledge. . . .

When an adequate system for control of atomic energy, including the renunciation of the bomb as a weapon, has been agreed upon and put into effective operation and condign punishments set up for violations of the rules of control which are to be stigmatized as international crimes, we propose that—

1. Manufacture of atomic bombs shall stop;
2. Existing bombs shall be disposed of pursuant to the terms of the treaty, and
3. The Authority shall be in possession of full information as to the know-how for the production of atomic energy.

Let me repeat, so as to avoid misunderstanding: my country is ready to make its full contribution toward the end we seek, subject, of course, to our constitutional processes, and to an adequate system of control becoming fully effective, as we finally work it out.

Now as to violations: in the agreement, penalties of as serious a nature as the nations may wish and as immediate and certain in their execution as possible, should be fixed for:

1. Illegal possession or use of an atomic bomb;
2. Illegal possession, or separation, of atomic material suitable for use in an atomic bomb;
3. Seizure of any plant or other property belonging to or licensed by the Authority;
4. Wilful interference with the activities of the Authority;
5. Creation or operation of dangerous projects in a manner contrary to, or in the absence of, a license granted by the international control body.

It would be a deception, to which I am unwilling to lend myself, were I not to say to you and to our peoples, that the matter of punishment lies at the very heart of our present security system. It might as well be admitted, here and now, that the subject goes straight to the veto power contained in the Charter of the United Nations so far as it relates to the field of atomic energy. The Charter permits penalization only by concurrence of each of the five great powers—Union of Soviet Socialist Republics, the United Kingdom, China, France and the United States.

I want to make very plain that I am concerned here with the veto power only as it affects this particular problem. There must be no veto to protect those who violate their solemn agreements not to develop or use atomic energy for destructive purposes. . . .

I now submit the following measures as representing the fundamental features of a plan which would give effect to certain of the conclusions which I have epitomized.

1. *General.* The Authority should set up a thorough plan for control of the field of atomic energy, through various forms of ownership, dominion, licenses, operation, inspection, research and management by competent personnel. After this is provided for, there should be as little interference as may be with the economic plans and the present private, corporate and state relationships in the several countries involved.

2. *Raw Materials.* The Authority should have as one of its earliest purposes to obtain and maintain complete and accurate information on world supplies of uranium and thorium and to bring them under its dominion. The precise pattern of control for various types of deposits of such materials will have to depend upon the geological, mining, refining, and economic facts involved in different situations.

The Authority should conduct continuous surveys so that it will have the most complete knowledge of the world geology of uranium and thorium. Only after all current information on world sources of uranium and thorium is known to us all can equitable plans be made for their production, refining, and distribution.

3. *Primary Production Plants.* The Authority should exercise complete managerial control of the production of fissionable materials. This means that it should control and operate all plants producing fissionable materials in dangerous quantities and must own and control the product of these plants.

4. *Atomic Explosives.* The Authority should be given sole and exclusive right to conduct research in the field of atomic explosives. Research activities in the field of atomic explosives are essential in order that the Authority may keep in the forefront of knowledge in the field of atomic energy and fulfil the objective of preventing illicit manufacture of bombs. Only by maintaining its position as the best-informed agency will the Authority be able to determine the line between intrinsically dangerous and non-dangerous activities.

5. *Strategic Distribution of Activities and Materials.* The activities entrusted exclusively to the Authority because they are intrinsically dangerous to security should be distributed throughout the world. Similarly, stockpiles of raw materials and fissionable materials should not be centralized.

6. *Non-Dangerous Activities.* A function of the Authority should be promotion of the peacetime benefits of atomic energy.

Atomic research (except in explosives), the use of research reactors, the production of radioactive tracers by means of non-dangerous reactors, the use of such tracers, and to some extent the production of power should be open to nations and their citizens under reasonable licensing arrangements from the Authority. Denatured materials, whose use we know also requires suitable safeguards, should be furnished for such purposes by the Authority under lease or other arrangement. Denaturing seems to have been overestimated by the public as a safety measure.

7. *Definition of Dangerous and Non-Dangerous Activities.* Although a reasonable dividing line can be drawn between dangerous and non-dangerous activities, it is not hard and fast. Provision should, therefore, be made to assure constant reexamination of the questions and to permit revision of the dividing line as changing conditions and new discoveries may require.

8. *Operations of Dangerous Activities.* Any plant dealing with uranium or thorium after it once reaches the potential of dangerous use must be not only subject to the most rigorous and competent inspection by the Authority, but its actual operation shall be under the management, supervision, and control of the Authority.

9. *Inspection.* By assigning intrinsically dangerous activities exclusively to the Authority, the difficulties of inspection are reduced. If the Authority is the only agency which may lawfully conduct dangerous activities, then visible operation by others than the Authority will constitute an unambiguous danger signal. Inspection will also occur in connection with the licensing functions of the Authority.

10. *Freedom of Access.* Adequate ingress and egress for all qualified representatives of the Authority must be assured. Many of the inspection activities of the Authority should grow out of, and be incidental to, its other functions. Important measures of inspection will be associated with the tight control of raw materials, for this is a keystone of the plan. The continuing activities of prospecting, survey, and research in relation to raw materials will be designed not only to serve the affirmative development functions of the Authority, but also to assure that no surreptitious operations are conducted in the raw materials field by nations or their citizens.

11. *Personnel.* The personnel of the Authority should be recruited on a basis of proven competence but also so far as possible on an international basis.

12. *Progress by Stages.* A primary step in the creation of the system of control is the setting forth, in comprehensive terms, of the functions, responsibilities, powers and limitations of the Authority. Once a Charter for the Authority has been adopted, the Authority and the system of control for which it will be responsible will require time to become fully organized and effective. The plan of control will, therefore, have to come into effect in successive stages. These should be specifically fixed in the Charter or means should be otherwise set forth in the Charter for transitions from one stage to another, as contem-

plated in the resolution of the United Nations Assembly which created this Commission.

13. *Disclosures.* In the deliberations of the United Nations Commission on Atomic Energy, the United States is prepared to make available the information essential to a reasonable understanding of the proposals which it advocates. Further disclosures must be dependent, in the interests of all, upon the effective ratification of the treaty. When the Authority is actually created, the United States will join the other nations in making available the further information essential to that organization for the performance of its functions. As the successive stages of international control are reached, the United States will be prepared to yield, to the extent required by each stage, national control of activities in this field to the Authority.

14. *International Control.* There will be questions about the extent of control to be allowed to national bodies, when the Authority is established. Purely national authorities for control and development of atomic energy should to the extent necessary for the effective operation of the Authority be subordinate to it. This is neither an endorsement nor a disapproval of the creation of national authorities. The Commission should evolve a clear demarcation of the scope of duties and responsibilities of such national authorities.

And now I end. . . .

C. The Gromyko Plan

The Soviet representative to the U.N. Atomic Energy Commission, Andrei Gromyko, replied to Baruch on June 19, 1946.

. . . the Soviet delegation proposes that consideration be given to the question of concluding an international convention prohibiting the production and employment of weapons based on the use of atomic energy for the purpose of mass destruction. The object of such a convention should be the prohibition of the production and employment of atomic weapons, the destruction of existing stocks of atomic weapons and the condemnation of all activities undertaken in violation of this convention. The elaboration and conclusion of a convention of this kind would be, in the opinion of the Soviet delegation, only one of the primary measures to be taken to prevent the use of atomic energy to the detriment of mankind. This act should be followed by other measures aiming at the estab-

SOURCE: *American Foreign Policy: 1941–1949,* pp. 1087–93.

lishment of methods to ensure the strict observance of the terms and obligations contained in the above-mentioned convention, the establishment of a system of control over the observance of the convention and the taking of decisions regarding the sanctions to be applied against the unlawful use of atomic energy. The public opinion of the whole civilized world has already rightly condemned the use in warfare of asphyxiating, poisonous and other similar gases, as well as all similar liquids and substances, and likewise bacteriological means, by concluding corresponding agreements for the prohibition of their use. . . .

In preparing their plan and offering it to the United Nations the Russians not only proposed a simple elimination of atomic weapons—they knew this course would have enormous popular appeal and later embodied it in the Stockholm Peace Appeal—but also stressed their opposition to eliminating the veto in the U.N. Council as called for in the Baruch Plan. Elimination of the veto was a minor issue, since in case of a serious breach of an atomic agreement the United States government, the only possible opponent of the Soviet Union might have paid no attention to a Soviet veto. The Russians may have been concerned about the Baruch Plan's requirement of inspection: Stalin's fetish for secrecy was well known. Moreover, the war had hurt the Soviet economy so badly that perhaps the Russians did not wish any observers to see the extent of the damage. The real sticking point, perhaps, was Stalin's desire to have bombs of his own. Whatever the reasoning, the Soviet plan was far apart from the American, and in subsequent discussions at the U.N. the hope for a grand treaty internationalizing atomic power was lost in recriminations.

44. Two *Démarches* of the 1950s

A. ATOMS FOR PEACE

WITH THE FAILURE OF THE BARUCH PLAN for a large atomic treaty, and after a change of administrations, it seemed that smaller moves in regard to atomic energy could meet with success and that a short step forward might lead to a larger step. President Eisenhower and Secretary Dulles also were acutely aware of the new vulnerability of the continental

SOURCE: American Foreign Policy: 1950–1955, 2 vols. (Washington, D.C., 1957), II, pp. 2798–2805.

United States; by 1953 the Russians possessed enough weapons to inflict unacceptable damage. Regardless of Soviet intransigence over atomic limitation at the U.N., it seemed advisable to make an atomic démarche. President Eisenhower addressed the General Assembly on December 8, 1953.

. . . my country's purpose is to help us move out of the dark chamber of horrors into the light, to find a way by which the minds of men, the hopes of men, the souls of men everywhere, can move forward toward peace and happiness and well being.

In this quest, I know that we must not lack patience.

I know that in a world divided, such as ours today, salvation cannot be attained by one dramatic act.

I know that many steps will have to be taken over many months before the world can look at itself one day and truly realize that a new climate of mutually peaceful confidence is abroad in the world.

But I know, above all else, that we must start to take these steps—NOW. . . .

I therefore make the following proposals:

The Governments principally involved, to the extent permitted by elementary prudence, to begin now and continue to make joint contributions from their stockpiles of normal uranium and fissionable materials to an International Atomic Energy Agency. We would expect that such an agency would be set up under the aegis of the United Nations. . . .

Undoubtedly initial and early contributions to this plan would be small in quantity. However, the proposal has the great virtue that it can be undertaken without the irritations and mutual suspicions incident to any attempt to set up a completely acceptable system of world-wide inspection and control.

The Atomic Energy Agency could be made responsible for the impounding, storage, and protection of the contributed fissionable and other materials. The ingenuity of our scientists will provide special safe conditions under which such a bank of fissionable material can be made essentially immune to surprise seizure.

The more important responsibility of this Atomic Energy Agency would be to devise methods whereby this fissionable material would be allocated to serve the peaceful pursuits of mankind. Experts would be mobilized to apply atomic energy to the needs of agriculture, medicine, and other peaceful activities. A special purpose would be to provide abundant electrical energy in the power-starved areas of the world. . . .

. . . the United States pledges before you—and therefore before the world—its determination to help solve the fearful atomic dilemma—to devote its entire heart and mind to find the way by which the miraculous inventiveness of man shall not be dedicated to his death, but consecrated to his life.

The Soviet Union proved unwilling to join in a U.N. atomic program for peace, and the proposal came to nothing. In subsequent years both superpowers carried on their own peaceful programs.

B. Disengagement

With the failure of Eisenhower's proposal *the initiative passed to the Soviet side, and the Russians advanced the principle of disengagement. An attractive idea, it took its origin from the Soviet effort early in the decade to prevent West Germany from joining NATO, in the course of which Stalin in 1952 proposed the unification of Germany as a neutralized state. There could have been no German alliances within a unity so conceived. The nearness of Soviet troops to German territory—they still would have been stationed in Poland—made this proposal unattractive to the West German government of Chancellor Konrad Adenauer. Gradually the original Soviet suggestion was transmuted into a proposal for a nuclear-free zone in Eastern Europe that might include only Germany, some or all of the Eastern European countries, or all of Europe, including the British Isles, perhaps all the emerging countries in Africa, the Middle East, and Asia. The original difficulty remained: disengagement if pushed very far could have broken up NATO and if pushed even further could have forced the U.S. Army to retire back to the continental United States. The remoteness of American troops from Europe and other areas then would have increased greatly the diplomatic and military leverage of the Soviet Union. The former diplomat George Kennan advocated disengagement in a series of lectures over the facilities of the British Broadcasting Corporation in 1957, published in book form the next year. The Polish government in 1957 proposed it to the United Nations. On February 14, 1958, the Polish foreign minister, Adam Rapacki, put this proposal into a formal note to the American ambassador in Warsaw, Jacob D. Beam, with accompanying notes to representatives of other countries, including the U.S.S.R., France, and Great Britain.*

Source: *American Foreign Policy: Current Documents, 1958* (Washington, D.C., 1962), pp. 1445–46.

On October 2, 1957, the Government of the Polish People's Republic presented to the General Assembly of the United Nations a proposal concerning the establishment of a denuclearized zone in Central Europe. The governments of Czechoslovakia and of the German Democratic Republic declared their readiness to accede to that zone.

The Government of the Polish People's Republic proceeded with the conviction that the establishment of the proposed denuclearized zone could lead to an improvement in the international atmosphere and facilitate broader discussions on disarmament as well as the solution of other controversial internal issues, while the continuation of nuclear armaments and making them universal could only lead to a further solidifying of the division of Europe into opposing blocks and to a further complication of this situation, especially in Central Europe.

In December 1957 the Government of the Polish People's Republic renewed its proposal through diplomatic channels.

Considering the wide repercussions which the Polish initiative has evoked and taking into account the propositions emerging from the discussion which has developed on this proposal, the Government of the Polish People's Republic hereby presents a more detailed elaboration of its proposal, which may facilitate the opening of negotiations and reaching of an agreement on this subject.

I. The proposed zones should include the territory of: Poland, Czechoslovakia, German Democratic Republic and German Federal Republic. In this territory nuclear weapons would neither be manufactured nor stockpiled, the equipment and installations designed for their servicing would not be located there; the use of nuclear weapons against the territory of this zone would be prohibited.

II. The contents of the obligations arising from the establishment of the denuclearized zone would be based upon the following premises:

1. The states included in this zone would undertake the obligation not to manufacture, maintain nor import for their own use and not to permit the location on their territories of nuclear weapons of any type, as well as not to install nor to admit to their territories of installations and equipment designed for servicing nuclear weapons, including missiles' launching equipment.

2. The four powers (France, United States, Great Britain, and U.S.S.R.) would undertake the following obligations:

A. Not to maintain nuclear weapons in the armaments of their forces stationed on the territories of states included in this zone; neither to maintain nor to install on the territories of these states any installations or equipment designed for servicing nuclear weapons, including missiles' launching equipment.

B. Not to transfer in any manner and under any reason whatsoever, nuclear weapons nor installations and equipment designed for servicing nuclear weapons—to governments or other organs in this area.

3. The powers which have at their disposal nuclear weapons should undertake the obligation not to use these weapons against the territory of the zone or against any targets situated in this zone.

Thus the powers would undertake the obligation to respect the status of the zone as an area in which there should be no nuclear weapons and against which nuclear weapons should not be used.

4. Other states, whose forces are stationed on the territory of any state included in the zone, would also undertake the obligation not to maintain nuclear weapons in the armaments of these forces and not to transfer such weapons to governments or to other organs in this area. Neither will they install equipment or installations designed for the servicing of nuclear weapons, including missiles' launching equipment, on the territories of states in the zone nor will they transfer them to governments or other organs in this area.

The manner and procedure for the implementation of these obligations could be the subject of detailed mutual stipulations.

III. In order to ensure the effectiveness and implementation of the obligations contained in Part II, paragraphs 1–2 and 4, the states concerned would undertake to create a system of broad and effective control in the area of the proposed zone and submit themselves to its functioning.

1. This system could comprise ground as well as aerial control. Adequate control posts, with rights and possibilities of action which would ensure the effectiveness of inspection, could also be established.

The details and forms of the implementation of control can be agreed upon on the basis of the experience acquired up to the present time in this field, as well as on the basis of proposals submitted by various states in the course of the disarmament negotiations, in the form and to the extent in which they can be adapted to the area of the zone.

The system of control established for the denuclearized zone could provide useful experience for the realization of broader disarmament agreement.

2. For the purpose of supervising the implementation of the proposed obligations an adequate control machinery should be established. There could participate in it, for example, representatives appointed [not excluding additional personal appointments]* by organs of the North Atlantic Treaty Organization and of the Warsaw Treaty. Nationals or representatives of states, which do not belong to any military grouping in Europe, could also participate in it.

The procedure of the establishment, operation and reporting of the control organs can be the subject of further mutual stipulations.

IV. The most simple form of embodying the obligations of states included in the zone would be the conclusion of an appropriate international convention. To avoid, however, implications, which some states might find in such a solution, it can be arranged that:

1. These obligations be embodied in the form of four unilateral declarations, bearing the character of an international obligation deposited with a mutually agreed upon depository state.

2. The obligations of great powers be embodied in the form of a mutual document or unilateral declaration [as mentioned above in paragraph 1];

3. The obligations of other states, whose armed forces are stationed in the area of the zone, be embodied in the form of unilateral declarations [as mentioned above in paragraph 1].

On the basis of the above proposals the government of the Polish People's Republic suggests to initiate negotiations for the purpose of a further detailed elaboration of the plan for the establishment of the denuclearized zone, of the documents and guarantees related to it as well as of the means of implementation of the undertaken obligations.

The government of the Polish People's Republic has reasons to state that acceptance of the proposal concerning the establishment of a denuclearized zone in Central Europe will facilitate the reaching of an agreement relating to the adequate reduction of conventional armaments and of foreign armed forces stationed on the territory of the states included in the zone.

* Brackets here, and below, in source text. [Footnote in *American Foreign Policy*.]

THE UNITED STATES GOVERNMENT ON MAY 3, 1958, *turned down the Rapacki Plan in a note handed by Ambassador Beam to the Polish deputy foreign minister.*

Recognizing that the initiative of the Polish Government stems from a desire to contribute to the attainment of a stable and durable peace, my Government has given these proposals serious and careful consideration. On the basis of this study it has concluded that they are too limited in scope to reduce the danger of nuclear war or provide a dependable basis for the security of Europe. They neither deal with the essential question of the continued production of nuclear weapons by the present nuclear powers nor take into account the fact that present scientific techniques are not adequate to detect existing nuclear weapons. The proposed plan does not affect the central sources of power capable of launching a nuclear attack, and thus its effectiveness would be dependent on the good intentions of countries outside the area. The proposals overlook the central problems of European security because they provide no method for balanced and equitable limitations of military capabilities and would perpetuate the basic cause of tension in Europe by accepting the continuation of the division of Germany.

An agreement limited to the exclusion of nuclear weapons from the territory indicated by your Government without other types of limitation would, even if it were capable of being inspected, endanger the security of the Western European countries in view of the large and widely deployed military forces of the Soviet Union. Unless equipped with nuclear weapons, Western forces in Germany would find themselves under present circumstances at a great disadvantage to the numerically greater mass of Soviet troops stationed within easy distance of Western Europe which are, as the Soviet leaders made clear, being equipped with the most modern and destructive weapons, including missiles of all kinds. . . .

Your note speaks of the existence of opposing military groupings in Central Europe as being responsible for tensions in the area. It should not be necessary for me to recall that the present division of Europe stems primarily from the decision of the Soviet Union not to permit Eastern European nations to participate in the European

SOURCE: *Current Documents, 1958,* pp. 1447–48.

Recovery Plan. Nor need I repeat the many assurances given as to the defensive character of the North Atlantic Treaty Organization which is reflected in its entire organizational and command structure. The entire history of its creation and development testify to this, though persistent efforts are made in some quarters to portray it otherwise.

45. Three Treaties of the 1960s

A. THE PARTIAL TEST BAN TREATY

IN 1954 THE UNITED STATES GOVERNMENT exploded a huge hydrogen bomb at Bikini with extraordinary fallout that swept downwind for seventy miles, well beyond the calculated danger area of the explosion, and fell upon a Japanese tuna trawler named, ironically, the Lucky Dragon. One of the crewmen eventually died of secondary causes. The issue of radiation thereby entered into public debate. In subsequent years it received thorough discussion throughout the Western world, and because of alarming increases in atmospheric contamination resulting from American and Soviet bomb tests and perhaps also because both countries had accumulated a vast amount of test data and may not have needed much more, it became possible for the United States, Great Britain, and the U.S.S.R. to sign a partial test ban treaty in Moscow on August 5, 1963.

Article I

1. Each of the Parties to this Treaty undertakes to prohibit, to prevent, and not to carry out any nuclear weapon test explosion, or any other nuclear explosion, at any place under its jurisdiction or control:

a. in the atmosphere; beyond its limits, including outer space; or underwater, including territorial waters or high seas; or

b. in any other environment if such explosion causes radioactive debris to be present outside the territorial limits of the State under whose jurisdiction or control such explosion is conducted. It is understood in this connection that the provisions of this subparagraph are

SOURCE: *United States Treaties and Other International Agreements: 1963*, pt. 2 (Washington, D.C., 1964), pp. 1314–19.

without prejudice to the conclusion of a treaty resulting in the permanent banning of all nuclear test explosions, including all such explosions underground, the conclusion of which, as the Parties have stated
in the Preamble to this Treaty, they seek to achieve.

2. Each of the Parties to this Treaty undertakes furthermore to
refrain from causing, encouraging, or in any way participating in,
the carrying out of any nuclear weapon test explosion, or any other
nuclear explosion, anywhere which would take place in any of the
environments described, or have the effect referred to, in paragraph
1 of this Article.

Article II

1. Any Party may propose amendments to this Treaty. The text
of any proposed amendment shall be submitted to the Depositary
Governments which shall circulate it to all Parties to this Treaty.
Thereafter, if requested to do so by one-third or more of the
Parties, the Depositary Governments shall convene a conference,
to which they shall invite all the Parties, to consider such
amendment.
2. Any amendment to this Treaty must be approved by a majority of the votes of all the Parties to this Treaty, including the votes
of all of the Original Parties. The amendment shall enter into force
for all Parties upon the deposit of instruments of ratification by a
majority of all the Parties, including the instruments of ratification
of all of the Original Parties.

Article IV

This Treaty shall be of unlimited duration.
Each Party shall in exercising its national sovereignty have the
right to withdraw from the Treaty if it decides that extraordinary
events, related to the subject matter of this Treaty, have jeopardized the supreme interests of its country. It shall give notice of
such withdrawal to all other Parties to the Treaty three months in
advance.

*Although it was effective among the signatories and obtained many
adherents, the treaty proved less efficacious than its signatories had
hoped, for it did not gain the adherence of France and the People's
Republic of China.*

B. The Treaty on Outer Space

The United States, Britain, and the Soviet Union on January 27, 1967, signed a "treaty on principles governing the activities of states in the exploration and use of outer space, including the moon and other celestial bodies," and opened it for adherence by all the states of the world. The Senate consented to the treaty on April 25, 1967, by vote of 88 to 0.

Article I

The exploration and use of outer space, including the moon and other celestial bodies, shall be carried out for the benefit and in the interests of all countries, irrespective of their degree of economic or scientific development, and shall be the province of all mankind.

Outer space, including the moon and other celestial bodies, shall be free for exploration and use by all States without discrimination of any kind, on a basis of equality and in accordance with international law, and there shall be free access to all areas of celestial bodies.

There shall be freedom of scientific investigation in outer space, including the moon and other celestial bodies, and States shall facilitate and encourage international co-operation in such investigation.

Article II

Outer space, including the moon and other celestial bodies, is not subject to national appropriation by claim of sovereignty, by means of use or occupation, or by any other means.

Article IV

States Parties to the Treaty undertake not to place in orbit around the Earth any objects carrying nuclear weapons or any other kinds of weapons of mass destruction, install such weapons on celestial bodies, or station such weapons in outer space in any other manner.

Source: *United States Treaties and Other International Agreements: 1967*, pt. 3 (Washington, D.C., 1969), pp. 2410–21.

The moon and other celestial bodies shall be used by all States Parties to the Treaty exclusively for peaceful purposes. The establishment of military bases, installations and fortifications, the testing of any type of weapons and the conduct of military maneuvers on celestial bodies shall be forbidden. . . .

By declaring outer space to be different from air space, the treaty on uses of outer space fulfilled the very special purpose of declaring as international law the right of such nations as the Soviet Union and the United States to orbit reconnaissance satellites. Ironically it was the U.S.S.R., traditional exponent of secrecy, that made this new legality possible, for in 1957 the Soviets had put up the first Sputnik without seeking permission for it to traverse the territory of other nations. Without reconnaissance satellites it would have been impossible for the U.S. and the U.S.S.R. to have concluded the ABM treaty and the five-year freeze on strategic weapons signed at Moscow in 1972 (see pp. 312–22).

C. The Nonproliferation Treaty

THE MOST IMPORTANT NUCLEAR TREATY OF THE 1960s dealt with that word of the atomic age, "nonproliferation." The United States, Great Britain, and the Soviet Union signed the treaty on July 1, 1968, and opened it for adherence.

Article I

Each nuclear-weapon State Party to the Treaty undertakes not to transfer to any recipient whatsoever nuclear weapons or other nuclear explosive devices or control over such weapons or explosive devices directly, or indirectly; and not in any way to assist, encourage, or induce any non-nuclear-weapon State to manufacture or otherwise acquire nuclear weapons or other nuclear explosive devices, or control over such weapons or explosive devices.

Article II

Each non-nuclear-weapon State Party to the Treaty undertakes not to receive the transfer from any transferor whatsoever of nuclear weapons or other nuclear explosive devices or of control over such weapons or explosive devices directly, or indirectly; not to manufacture or otherwise acquire nuclear weapons or other nuclear

SOURCE: *United States Treaties and Other International Agreements:1970*, pt. 1 (Washington, D.C., 1971), pp. 483–94.

explosive devices; and not to seek or receive any assistance in the manufacture of nuclear weapons or other nuclear explosive devices.

Article III

1. Each non-nuclear-weapon State Party to the Treaty undertakes to accept safeguards, as set forth in an agreement to be negotiated and concluded with the International Atomic Energy Agency in accordance with the Statute of the International Atomic Energy Agency and the Agency's safeguards system, for the exclusive purpose of verification of the fulfillment of its obligations assumed under this Treaty with a view to preventing diversion of nuclear energy from peaceful uses to nuclear weapons or other nuclear explosive devices. Procedures for the safeguards required by this article shall be followed with respect to source or special fissionable material whether it is being produced, processed or used in any principal nuclear facility or is outside any such facility. The safeguards required by this article shall be applied on all source or special fissionable material in all peaceful nuclear activities within the territory of such State, under its jurisdiction, or carried out under its control anywhere.

2. Each State Party to the Treaty undertakes not to provide: (a) source or special fissionable material, or (b) equipment or material especially designed or prepared for the processing, use or production of special fissionable material, to any non-nuclear-weapon State for peaceful purposes, unless the source or special fissionable material shall be subject to the safeguards required by this article. . . .

Article VI

Each of the Parties to the Treaty undertakes to pursue negotiations in good faith on effective measures relating to cessation of the nuclear arms race at an early date and to nuclear disarmament, and on a treaty on general and complete disarmament under strict and effective international control.

Article VII

Nothing in this Treaty affects the right of any group of States to conclude regional treaties in order to assure the total absence of nuclear weapons in their respective territories.

Article X

1. Each Party shall in exercising its national sovereignty have the right to withdraw from the Treaty if it decides that extraordinary events, related to the subject matter of this Treaty, have jeopardized the supreme interests of its country. It shall give notice of such withdrawal to all other Parties to the Treaty and to the United Nations Security Council three months in advance. Such notice shall include a statement of the extraordinary events it regards as having jeopardized its supreme interests. . . .

Despite a large number of adherents, the treaty disappointed its signatories because two members of the nuclear club of the 1960s, France and the People's Republic of China, did not sign. Nor did Israel, a disquieting fact because Israel possessed a reactor provided by France, had the technical know-how, presumably could go nuclear without difficulty, and by failing to sign was subtly signaling this possibility to its fearful, jealous, hypersensitive Arab neighbors, who might apply to the Soviet Union for help.

46. The Strategic Arms Limitation Agreements of 1972

A. THE ABM TREATY

AFTER CONSIDERABLE PROGRESS in a series of U.S.–U.S.S.R. technical atomic arms limitation discussions that alternated between Vienna and Helsinki, the so-called Strategic Arms Limitation Talks (SALT), President Nixon journeyed to Moscow and on May 26, 1972, signed with Leonid I. Brezhnev, the general secretary of the Soviet Communist party, two interdependent instruments that established a nuclear arms modus vivendi between the supepowers. Both governments hoped that other arrangements might follow. Indeed, the second instrument, an executive agreement (see pp. 318–21), was admittedly temporary. The first dealt with ABMs and was in the form of a treaty.

SOURCE: Department of State *Bulletin*, June 26, 1972, pp. 918–20.

Article I

1. Each Party undertakes to limit anti-ballistic missile (ABM) systems and to adopt other measures in accordance with the provisions of this Treaty.

2. Each Party undertakes not to deploy ABM systems for a defense of the territory of its country and not to provide a base for such a defense, and not to deploy ABM systems for defense of an individual region except as provided for in Article III of this Treaty.

Article II

1. For the purposes of this Treaty an ABM system is a system to counter strategic ballistic missiles or their elements in flight trajectory, currently consisting of:

a. ABM interceptor missiles, which are interceptor missiles constructed and deployed for an ABM role, or of a type tested in an ABM mode;

b. ABM launchers, which are launchers constructed and deployed for launching ABM interceptor missiles; and

c. ABM radars, which are radars constructed and deployed for an ABM role, or of a type tested in an ABM mode.

2. The ABM system components listed in paragraph 1 of this Article include those which are:

a. operational;
b. under construction;
c. undergoing testing;
d. undergoing overhaul, repair or conversion; or
e. mothballed.

Article III

Each Party undertakes not to deploy ABM systems or their components except that:

a. within one ABM system deployment area having a radius of one hundred and fifty kilometers and centered on the Party's national capital, a Party may deploy: (1) no more than one hundred ABM launchers and no more than one hundred ABM interceptor missiles at launch sites, and (2) ABM radars within no more than six ABM radar complexes, the area of each complex being circular and having a diameter of no more than three kilometers; and

b. within one ABM system deployment area having a radius of one hundred and fifty kilometers and containing ICBM silo launchers, a Party may deploy: (1) no more than one hundred ABM launchers and no more than one hundred ABM interceptor missiles at launch sites, (2) two large phased-array ABM radars comparable in potential to corresponding ABM radars operational or under construction on the date of signature of the Treaty in an ABM system deployment area containing ICBM silo launchers, and (3) no more than eighteen ABM radars each having a potential less than the potential of the smaller of the above-mentioned two large phased-array ABM radars.

Article IV

The limitations provided for in Article III shall not apply to ABM systems or their components used for development or testing, and located within current or additionally agreed test ranges. Each Party may have no more than a total of fifteen ABM launchers at test ranges.

Article V

1. Each Party undertakes not to develop, test, or deploy ABM systems or components which are sea-based, air-based, space-based, or mobile land-based.

2. Each Party undertakes not to develop, test, or deploy ABM launchers for launching more than one ABM interceptor missile at a time from each launcher, nor to modify deployed launchers to provide them with such a capability, nor to develop, test, or deploy automatic or semi-automatic or other similar systems for rapid reload of ABM launchers.

Article VI

To enhance assurance of the effectiveness of the limitations on ABM systems and their components provided by this Treaty, each Party undertakes:

a. not to give missiles, launchers, or radars, other than ABM interceptor missiles, ABM launchers, or ABM radars, capabilities to counter strategic ballistic missiles or their elements in flight trajectory, and not to test them in an ABM mode; and

b. not to deploy in the future radars for early warning of strategic ballistic missile attack except at locations along the periphery of its national territory and oriented outward.

Article VII

Subject to the provisions of this Treaty, modernization and replacement of ABM systems or their components may be carried out.

Article VIII

ABM systems or their components in excess of the numbers or outside the areas specified in this Treaty, as well as ABM systems or their components prohibited by this Treaty, shall be destroyed or dismantled under agreed procedures within the shortest possible agreed period of time.

Article IX

To assure the viability and effectiveness of this Treaty, each Party undertakes not to transfer to other States, and not to deploy outside its national territory, ABM systems or their components limited by this Treaty.

Article X

Each Party undertakes not to assume any international obligations which would conflict with this Treaty.

Article XI

The Parties undertake to continue active negotiations for limitations on strategic offensive arms.

Article XII

1. For the purpose of providing assurance of compliance with the provisions of this Treaty, each Party shall use national technical means of verification at its disposal in a manner consistent with generally recognized principles of international law.

2. Each Party undertakes not to interfere with the national technical means of verification of the other Party operating in accordance with paragraph 1 of this Article.

3. Each Party undertakes not to use deliberate concealment measures which impede verification by national technical means of compliance with the provisions of this Treaty. This obligation shall not require changes in current construction, assembly, conversion, or overhaul practices.

Article XIII

1. To promote the objectives and implementation of the provisions of this Treaty, the Parties shall establish promptly a Standing Consultative Commission, within the framework of which they will:

a. consider questions concerning compliance with the obligations assumed and related situations which may be considered ambiguous;

b. provide on a voluntary basis such information as either Party considers necessary to assure confidence in compliance with the obligations assumed;

c. consider questions involving unintended interference with national technical means of verification;

d. consider possible changes in the strategic situation which have a bearing on the provisions of this Treaty;

e. agree upon procedures and dates for destruction or dismantling of ABM systems or their components in cases provided for by the provisions of this Treaty;

f. consider, as appropriate, possible proposals for further increasing the viability of this Treaty, including proposals for amendments in accordance with the provisions of this Treaty;

g. consider, as appropriate, proposals for further measures aimed at limiting strategic arms.

2. The Parties through consultation shall establish, and may amend as appropriate, Regulations for the Standing Consultative Commission governing procedures, composition and other relevant matters.

Article XIV

1. Each Party may propose amendments to this Treaty. Agreed amendments shall enter into force in accordance with the procedures governing the entry into force of this Treaty.

2. Five years after entry into force of this Treaty, and at five year

intervals thereafter, the Parties shall together conduct a review of this Treaty.

Article XV

1. This Treaty shall be of unlimited duration.

2. Each Party shall, in exercising its national sovereignty, have the right to withdraw from this Treaty if it decides that extraordinary events related to the subject matter of this Treaty have jeopardized its supreme interests. It shall give notice of its decision to the other Party six months prior to withdrawal from the Treaty. Such notice shall include a statement of the extraordinary events the notifying Party regards as having jeopardized its supreme interests.

The Senate consented to the ABM treaty on August 3, 1972, by a vote of 88 to 2. The treaty went into effect on October 3. The reader should notice that it amended the initial deployment of Safeguard, which was to be at two Minuteman sites; according to the treaty, protection could cover only one Minuteman site, with Washington, D.C., a second area of protection. This would permit the Russians to retain their ABM protection of Moscow already constructed. Critics of the agreement felt this amendment tended to nullify the logic of Safeguard, for in his announcement of 1969 the president had said that to place ABM around cities was futile. In the present state of the art, he had declared, ABM could give moderate protection to an ICBM site, sufficient to allow survival of enough missiles to ensure a second-strike capability and hence maintain a strategic deterrent, but it could not give the absolute protection almost mandatory for cities; that is, it could not prevent what was known euphemistically as "leakage," the occasional penetration of enemy warheads. In 1974 during a meeting in Moscow an agreement was signed by President Nixon and Chairman Brezhnev reducing ABM sites for each country from two to one. Here was recognition that the Soviets did not desire a site for protection of missiles outside the Moscow area; nor had it proved feasible for American congressmen to vote construction of an ABM site for the protection of Washington while leaving their constituents exposed. With the United States limited to a single site, the administration virtually admitted the vulnerability of that site's radars; two sites would have provided alternate radar assistance in case of attack. Hence the decision to mothball the Grand Forks site within months of its completion. That site alone had cost about $5½ billion, the figure that Secretary McNamara in 1967 had estimated would be the cost for the entire Sentinel system, the predecessor of Safeguard.

B. The Five-Year Strategic Arms Freeze

WHILE IN MOSCOW *the president also signed the temporary agreement on limitation of strategic arms.*

The United States of America and the Union of Soviet Socialist Republics, hereinafter referred to as the Parties,

Convinced that the Treaty on the Limitation of Anti-Ballistic Missile Systems and this Interim Agreement on Certain Measures with Respect to the Limitation of Strategic Offensive Arms will contribute to the creation of more favorable conditions for active negotiations on limiting strategic arms as well as to the relaxation of international tension and the strengthening of trust between States,

Taking into account the relationship between strategic offensive and defensive arms,

Mindful of their obligations under Article VI of the Treaty on the Non-Proliferation of Nuclear Weapons,

Have agreed as follows:

Article I

The Parties undertake not to start construction of additional fixed land-based intercontinental ballistic missile (ICBM) launchers after July 1, 1972.

Article II

The Parties undertake not to convert land-based launchers for light ICBMs, or for ICBMs of older types deployed prior to 1964, into land-based launchers for heavy ICBMs of types deployed after that time.

Article III

The Parties undertake to limit submarine-launched ballistic missile (SLBM) launchers and modern ballistic missile submarines to the numbers operational and under construction on the date of signature of this Interim Agreement, and in addition to launchers

SOURCE: Department of State *Bulletin*, June 26, 1972, pp. 920–21.

and submarines constructed under procedures established by the Parties as replacements for an equal number of ICBM launchers of older types deployed prior to 1964 or for launchers on older submarines.

Article IV

Subject to the provisions of this Interim Agreement, modernization and replacement of strategic offensive ballistic missiles and launchers covered by this Interim Agreement may be undertaken.

Article V

1. For the purpose of providing assurance of compliance with the provisions of this Interim Agreement, each Party shall use national technical means of verification at its disposal in a manner consistent with generally recognized principles of international law.

2. Each Party undertakes not to interfere with the national technical means of verification of the other Party operating in accordance with paragraph 1 of this Article.

3. Each Party undertakes not to use deliberate concealment measures which impede verification by national technical means of compliance with the provisions of this Interim Agreement. This obligation shall not require changes in current construction, assembly, conversion, or overhaul practices.

Article VI

To promote the objectives and implementation of the provisions of this Interim Agreement, the Parties shall use the Standing Consultative Commission established under Article XIII of the Treaty on the Limitation of Anti-Ballistic Missile Systems in accordance with the provisions of that Article.

Article VII

The Parties undertake to continue active negotiations for limitations on strategic offensive arms. The obligations provided for in this Interim Agreement shall not prejudice the scope or terms of the limitations on strategic offensive arms which may be worked out in the course of further negotiations.

Article VIII

1. This Interim Agreement shall enter into force upon exchange of written notices of acceptance by each Party, which exchange shall take place simultaneously with the exchange of instruments of ratification of the Treaty on the Limitation of Anti-Ballistic Missile Systems.

2. This Interim Agreement shall remain in force for a period of five years unless replaced earlier by an agreement on more complete measures limiting strategic offensive arms. It is the objective of the Parties to conduct active follow-on negotiations with the aim of concluding such an agreement as soon as possible.

3. Each Party shall, in exercising its national sovereignty, have the right to withdraw from this Interim Agreement if it decides that extraordinary events related to the subject matter of this Interim Agreement have jeopardized its supreme interests. It shall give notice of its decision to the other Party six months prior to withdrawal from this Interim Agreement. Such notice shall include a statement of the extraordinary events the notifying Party regards as having jeopardized its supreme interests.

ON THE SAME DAY *that President Nixon concluded the two major agreements in Moscow, he signed a protocol to the five-year freeze.*

The Parties understand that, under Article III of the Interim Agreement, for the period during which that Agreement remains in force:

The U.S. may have no more than 710 ballistic missile launchers on submarines (SLBMs) and no more than 44 modern ballistic missile submarines. The Soviet Union may have no more than 950 ballistic missile launchers on submarines and no more than 62 modern ballistic missile submarines.

Additional ballistic missile launchers on submarines up to the above-mentioned levels, in the U.S.—over 656 ballistic missile launchers on nuclear-powered submarines, and in the U.S.S.R.—over 740 ballistic missile launchers on nuclear-powered submarines, operational and under construction, may become operational as replacements for equal numbers of ballistic missile launchers of

SOURCE: Department of State *Bulletin*, June 26, 1972, p. 921.

older types deployed prior to 1964 or of ballistic missile launchers on older submarines.

The deployment of modern SLBMs on any submarine, regardless of type, will be counted against the total level of SLBMs permitted for the U.S. and the U.S.S.R.

This Protocol shall be considered an integral part of the Interim Agreement.

The five-year freeze was a complex proposition that answered some questions and raised others. Although President Nixon could have concluded a simple executive agreement without consulting Congress, he made it understood that this important arms arrangement would require majority approval by both houses of Congress. After approval by a vote of 88 to 2 in the Senate on September 14, and 306 to 4 in the House on September 25, the president signed the joint resolution on September 30, 1972. It allowed the United States to maintain its 1,054 intercontinental ballistic missiles and the Soviet Union to keep its 1,618 missiles. According to the protocol to the freeze, the United States would be limited to no more than 710 ballistic missile launchers on submarines and to a maximum of 44 modern ballistic missile submarines; the Soviet Union would have 950 launchers and 62 ballistic missile submarines. The numerical edge granted the Soviet Union in both land-based missiles and submarines resulted from United States possession of multiple warheads (several warheads in the same nose cone, with independent missions—known as MIRV, for Multiple Independently targeted Reentry Vehicle). At the time the Moscow accords were signed in May, 1972, the United States possessed 5,700 warheads, and the Rusians 2,500. The Soviets did not test MIRVs until 1973, which placed them five years behind the Americans; the presumption was that the United States would be safe with a five-year freeze. But at least three problems stood in the way of future negotiation, the discussions known collectively as SALT II that began in November 1972. The first was the qualified nature of the Senate resolution approving the freeze, for the resolution provided, in an amendment offered by Senator Henry M. Jackson of Washington, that under any future Soviet-American treaty on offensive strategic arms there must be equality in the numbers and total payload of weapons. Even though this proviso did not bind the House of Representatives, it passed the Senate by vote of 56 to 35, and the Senate will have to consent to any future arms treaty by a two-thirds majority. The Jaskson amendment tied the president's hands in SALT II. A second problem was the Nixon administration's ardent pursuit of MIRVs, its apparent willingness to convert most of the atomic missiles in its arsenal into MIRVs. By definition, the freeze looked to a continuation of the status quo, and continued American development of MIRV threatened to break it. And in addition to the MIRV problem presented by the United States and the relative rigidity of the future

American arms position because of the Jackson amendment, SALT II faced a threat from the Soviet side, a threat that not only concerned the five-year freeze and its replacement by a treaty, but also applied to the ABM treaty. The very foundation of the Moscow agreements lay in Article V of the five-year freeze and Article XIII of the ABM treaty, which mutatis mutandis were identical and acknowledged the right of each country to employ reconnaissance satellites to test the good will of the other. Both countries have been using such satellites regularly, the first American reconnaissance satellite apparently having orbited on January 30, 1961, and the Russians sending up their own spy satellites somewhat later. But for reasons of delicacy—that is, in 1961 the recent U–2 affair—the United States at the outset did not announce what it was up to. The Soviet Union silently accepted this charade and likewise has never admitted to having a reconnaissance satellite program. All this despite an agreement in accord with which each country reports every satellite it lofts; the reported information makes it easily possible for an expert to calculate the purpose of a launching. In the 1972 agreements signed in Moscow, it was nonetheless necessary to employ a euphemism about satellites: "national technical means of verification." How long could this unavowed system of inspection last? In 1968 the Soviet Union had conducted a curious series of experiments with three satellites in which, when Cosmo 249 and later Cosmos 252 passed near Cosmos 248 in orbit, they were destroyed in explosions. The experiments raised the possibility that the U.S.S.R. might either be working on a satellite destroyer or had perfected one. When the issue arose during the SALT discussions, Soviet negotiators claimed to know nothing about the tests, which may well have been true; Soviet and American negotiators at the SALT talks had managed a considerable personal rapport, and it was entirely possible that the Soviet side had not been informed of its own government's activities. The 1968 explosions did cast a shadow over the future of the 1972 agreements.

XIV

Constitutional Crisis

In the early 1970s, with the Vietnam War concluded (so far as involved American troops), with a détente toward the Soviet Union symbolized by arms and trade agreements, and with a similar détente toward the People's Republic of China illustrated by a dramatic presidential visit, a very serious constitutional conflict was arising between the president and Congress over which branch of government possessed preeminent authority in foreign affairs. There were two main questions, and they were crucial to the issue of who was in control. Did the president in his constitutional role as commander-in-chief have the right to send American forces—naval, air, ground—abroad and keep them there without consent of Congress through a formal declaration of war? And did all important international agreements require treaties rather than executive agreements? The presumption of Congress, especially the Senate, where the issues were under lively and continuous debate, was that according to the Constitution the declaration of war was a congressional prerogative. On that score it was difficult for a president to advance a counterargument, except to cite practices that related either to extremely recent situations or to fairly minor episodes in the nation's past. As for the question of treaties versus executive agreements, the intent of the Founding Fathers in 1787 was clearly in favor of Congress, but in practice presidents in the twentieth century had defied the Constitution's intent and gotten away with it. The grand question in the 1970s was whether President Nixon and his successors would be able to continue widening the precedents of executive power into what was becoming, in American foreign relations, virtually presidential dictatorship.

47. The Right to Declare War

A. The Case for the Executive

At the outset of the Korean War the president's prerogatives as commander-in-chief concerned the Department of State, and department officers drew up a memorandum dated July 3, 1950, published in the Department of State Bulletin for July 31.

The President, as Commander in Chief of the Armed Forces of the United States, has full control over the use thereof. He also has authority to conduct the foreign relations of the United States. Since the beginning of United States history, he has, upon numerous occasions, utilized these powers in sending armed forces abroad. The preservation of the United Nations for the maintenance of peace is a cardinal interest of the United States. Both traditional international law and article 39 of the United Nations Charter and the resolution pursuant thereto [the Security Council resolution of June 27, 1950] authorize the United States to repel the armed aggression against the Republic of Korea.

The President's control over the Armed Forces of the United States is based on article 2, section 2 of the Constitution which provides that he "shall be Commander in Chief of the Army and Navy of the United States."

In *United States v. Sweeny*, the Supreme Court said that the object of this provision was "evidently to vest in the President the supreme command over all the military forces—such supreme and undivided command as would be necessary to the prosecution of a successful war."[1]

That the President's power to send the Armed Forces outside

Source: *American Foreign Policy: 1950–1955*, 2 vols. (Washington, D.C., 1957), II, pp. 2542–49.

1. 157 U.S. (1895) 281, 284. [All citations, except in footnote 19, appeared in the original memorandum (in the main text, however, rather than as footnotes). Footnotes 5, 8, and 19 are part of the memorandum as it appears in *American Foreign Policy: 1950–1955*.]

the country is not dependent on Congressional authority has been repeatedly emphasized by numerous writers.

For example, ex-President William Howard Taft wrote:

> The President is made Commander in Chief of the Army and Navy by the Constitution evidently for the purpose of enabling him to defend the country against invasion, to suppress insurrection and to take care that the laws be faithfully executed. If Congress were to attempt to prevent his use of the Army for any of these purposes, the action would be void. . . . Again, in the carrying on of war as Commander in Chief, it is he who is to determine the movements of the Army and of the Navy. Congress could not take away from him that discretion and place it beyond his control in any of his subordinates, nor could they themselves, as the people of Athens attempted to carry on campaigns by votes in the market-place.[2]

Professor Willoughby writes:

> As to his constitutional power to send United States forces outside the country in time of peace when this is deemed by him necessary or expedient as a means of preserving or advancing the foreign interests or relations of the United States, there would seem to be equally little doubt, although it has been contended by some that the exercise of this discretion can be limited by congressional statute. That Congress has this right to limit or to forbid the sending of United States forces outside of the country in time of peace has been asserted by so eminent an authority as ex-Secretary Root. It would seem to [the] author, however, that the President, under his powers as Commander in Chief of the Army and Navy, and his general control of the foreign relations of the United States, has this discretionary right constitutionally vested in him, and, therefore, not subject to congressional control. Especially, since the argument of the court in *Myers* v. *United States* with reference to the general character of the executive power vested in the President, and, apparently, the authority impliedly vested in him by reason of his obligation to take care that the laws be faithfully executed, it is reasonable to predict that, should the question be presented to it, the Supreme Court will so hold. Of course, if this sending is in pursuance of express provisions of a treaty, or for the execution of treaty provisions, the sending could not reasonably be subject to constitutional objection.[3]

In an address delivered before the American Bar Association in 1917 on the war powers under the Constitution, Mr. Hughes stated that "There is no limitation upon the authority of Congress

2. *Our Chief Magistrate and His Powers*, 1916, pp. 128–129.
3. *The Constitutional Law of the United States*, 1929, vol. III, p. 1567.

to create an army and it is for the President as Commander-in-Chief to direct the campaigns of that Army wherever he may think they should be carried on." He referred to a statement by Chief Justice Taney in *Fleming* v. *Page* in which the Chief Justice said that as Commander in Chief the President "is authorized to direct the movements of the naval and military forces placed by law at his command."[4]

At the time the approval of the Treaty of Versailles was under consideration in the Senate, there was under discussion a reservation to article 10, presented by Senator Lodge, to the effect that "Congress . . . under the Constitution, has the sole power to declare war or authorize the employment of the military or naval forces of the United States." Senator Walsh of Montana stated in debate on November 10, 1919 that the statement was a recital of "What is asserted to be a principle of constitutional law." He said that if—

> . . . any declaration of that character should ever be made by the Senate of the United States, it would be singularly unfortunate. It is not true. It is not sound. It is fraught with the most momentous consequences, and may involve disasters the extent of which it is hardly possible to conceive.
>
> The whole course of our history has been a refutation of such a declaration, namely, that the President of the United States, the Chief Executive of the United States, the Commander in Chief of the Army of the United States, has no power to employ the land or naval forces without any express authorization upon the part of Congress. Since the beginning of our Government, our Navy has been sent over the seven seas and to every port in the world. Was there ever any congressional act authorizing the President to do anything of that kind?

He stated that our Navy travels the sea "in order to safeguard and protect the rights of American citizens in foreign lands. Who can doubt that the President has no [sic] authority thus to utilize the naval and land forces of the United States?"

Mr. Borah stated:

> I agree fully with the legal or constitutional proposition which the Senator states, and I hope this [reservation][5] will be stricken out. It is an act of supererogation to put it in. It does not amount to anything. It is a recital which is not true.

4. S. Doc. 105, 65th Cong., 1st sess. p. 7.
5. Bracketed insertion in the original memorandum.

It can not change the Constitution, and it ought not to be there. . . . It would simply be vain and futile and, if I may say so, with due respect to those who drew it, the doing of an inconsequential thing.[6]

Not only is the President Commander in Chief of the Army and Navy, but he is also charged with the duty of conducting the foreign relations of the United States and in this field he "alone has the power to speak or listen as a representative of the Nation."[7]

Obviously, there are situations in which the powers of the President as Commander in Chief and his power to conduct the foreign relations of this country complement each other.

The basic interest of the United States is international peace and security. The United States has, throughout its history, upon orders of the Commander in Chief to the Armed Forces and without congressional authorization, acted to prevent violent and unlawful acts in other states from depriving the United States and its nationals of the benefits of such peace and security. It has taken such action both unilaterally and in concert with others. A tabulation of 85 instances of the use of American Armed Forces without a declaration of war was incorporated in the *Congressional Record* for July 10, 1941.[8]

It is important to analyze the purposes for which the President as Commander in Chief has authorized the despatch of American troops abroad. In many instances, of course, the Armed Forces have been used to protect specific American lives and property. In other cases, however, United States forces have been used in the broad interests of American foreign policy, and their use could be characterized as participation in international police action.

The traditional power of the President to use the Armed Forces of the United States without consulting Congress was referred to in debates in the Senate in 1945. Senator Connally remarked:

6. 58 Cong. Rec., pt. 8, p. 8195, Nov. 10, 1919, 66th Cong., 1st sess.
7. *United States v. Curtiss-Wright Export Corp. et al.* (299 U.S. [1936] 304, 319).
8. A copy of the tabulation was annexed to the memorandum. It is printed in the Department of State *Bulletin*, July 31, 1950, pp. 177–178, and in the above-cited H. Rept. No. 2495, pp. 67–68. At this point in the memorandum appeared a sentence (omitted in the *Bulletin* but printed in H. Rept. No. 2495, p. 64) which cited a pamphlet by James Grafton Rogers entitled *World Policing and the Constitution.*

"The historical instances in which the President has directed armed forces to go to other countries have not been confined to domestic or internal instances at all." Senator Millikin pointed out that "in many cases the President has sent troops into a foreign country to protect our foreign policy . . . notably in Central and South America." "That was done," he continued, "in order to keep foreign countries out of there—was not aimed at protecting any particular American citizen. It was aimed at protecting our foreign policy." To his remark that he presumed that by the Charter of the United Nations we had laid down a foreign policy which we could protect, Senator Connally replied that that was "absolutely correct." He added:

> I was trying to indicate that fact by reading the list of instances of intervention on our part in order to keep another government out of territory in this hemisphere. That was a question of carrying out our international policy, and not a question involving the protection of some American citizen or American property at the moment.[9]

During the Boxer Rebellion in China in 1900–1901, the President sent about 5,000 troops to join with British, Russian, German, French, and Japanese troops to relieve the siege of the foreign quarters in Peking and reestablish the treaty status. This was done without express congressional authority. In defining United States policy at the time Secretary of State Hay said:

> . . . The purpose of the President is, as it has been heretofore, to act concurrently with the other powers; first, in opening up communication with Peking and rescuing the American officials, missionaries, and other Americans who are in danger; secondly, in affording all possible protection everywhere in China to American life and property; thirdly, in guarding and protecting all legitimate American interests; and, fourthly, in aiding to prevent a spread of the disorders to the other provinces of the Empire and a recurrence of such disasters. It is, of course, too early to forecast the means of attaining this last result; but the policy of the Government of the United States is to seek a solution which may bring about permanent safety and peace to China, preserve Chinese territorial and administrative entity, protect all rights guaranteed to friendly powers by treaty and international law, and safeguard for the world the principle of equal and impartial trade with all parts of the Chinese Empire.[10]

9. Cong. Rec., 79th Cong., 1st sess., vol. 91, pt. 8, Nov. 26, 1945, p. 10967.
10. John Bassett Moore, A Digest of International Law, vol. V, p. 482. See also Taft, op. cit. pp. 114–115; Rogers, op. cit. pp. 58–62.

After the opening up of Japan to foreigners in the 1850's through the conclusion of commercial treaties between Japan and certain Western powers, antiforeign disturbances occurred. In 1863, the American Legation was burned following previous attacks on the British Legation. The commander of the U. S. S. *Wyoming* was instructed to use all necessary force for the safety of the legation or of Americans residing in Japan. Secretary of State Seward said that the prime objects of the United States were:

> First, to deserve and win the confidence of the Japanese Government and people, if possible, with a view to the common interest of all the treaty powers; secondly, to sustain and cooperate with the legations of these powers, in good faith, so as to render their efforts to the same end effective.[11]

In 1864, the Mikado, not recognizing the treaties with the Western powers, closed the straits of Shimonoseki. At the request of the Tycoon's government (opposed to the Mikado), American, British, French, and Netherlands forces, in a joint operation, opened the straits by force. The object of the Western powers was the enforcement of treaty rights, with the approval of the government that granted them.[12]

Again, in 1868, a detachment of Japanese troops assaulted foreign residents in the streets of Hiogo. One of the crew of the *Oneida* was seriously wounded. The safety of the foreign population being threatened, naval forces of the treaty powers made a joint landing and adopted measures to protect the foreign settlement.[13]

Former Assistant Secretary of State James Grafton Rogers has characterized these uses of force as "international police action," saying:

> They amounted to executive use of the Armed Forces to establish our own and the world's scheme of international order. Two American Presidents used men, ships and guns on a large and expensive scale.[14]

11. John Bassett Moore, A *Digest of International Law*, vol. V, pp. 747–748.
12. *Ibid.*, p. 750; S. Ex. Doc. 58, 41 Cong. 2d sess.
13. *Report of the Secretary of the Navy*, 1868, p. xi.
14. *World Policing and the Constitution*, published by the World Peace Foundation, 1945, pp. 66, 67.

In 1888 and 1889, civil war took place in Samoa where the United States, Great Britain, and Germany had certain respective treaty rights for the maintenance of naval depots. German forces were landed, and the German Government invited the United States to join in an effort to restore calm and quiet in the islands in the interest of all the treaty powers. The commander of the United States naval forces in the Pacific was instructed by the Secretary of the Navy that the United States was willing to cooperate in restoring order "on the basis of the full preservation of American treaty rights and Samoan authority, as recognized and agreed to by Germany, Great Britain, and the United States." He was to extend full protection and defense to American citizens and property, to protest the displacement of the native government by Germany as violating the positive agreement and understanding between the treaty powers, but to inform the British and German Governments of his readiness to cooperate in causing all treaty rights to be respected and in restoring peace and order on the basis of the recognition of the Samoan right to independence.[15]

On July 7, 1941, the President sent to the Congress a message announcing that as Commander in Chief he had ordered the Navy to take all necessary steps to insure the safety of communications between Iceland and the United States as well as on the seas between the United States and all other strategic outposts and that American troops had been sent to Iceland in defense of that country. The United States, he said, could not permit "the occupation by Germany of strategic outposts in the Atlantic to be used as air or naval bases for eventual attack against the Western Hemisphere." For the same reason, he said, substantial forces of the United States had been sent to the bases acquired from Great Britain in Trinidad and British Guiana in the South to forestall any pincers movement undertaken by Germany against the Western Hemisphere.[16]

Thus, even before the ratification of the United Nations Charter, the President had used the Armed Forces of the United States without consulting the Congress for the purpose of protecting the foreign policy of the United States. The ratification of the United Nations Charter was, of course, a landmark in the develop-

15. John Bassett Moore, A Digest of International Law, vol. I, pp. 545–546.
16. Cong. Rec., 77th Cong., 1st sess., vol. 87, pt. 6, July 7, 1941, p. 5868.

ment of American foreign policy. As noted above, Senator Connally and Senator Millikin agreed that the President was entitled to use armed forces in protection of the foreign policy represented by the Charter. This view was also expressed in the Senate debates in connection with the ratification of the Charter. For example, Senator Wiley made the following pertinent statement:

It is my understanding, according to the testimony given before the Foreign Relations Committee of the Senate, that the terms "agreement or agreements" as used in article 43 are synonymous with the word "treaty." On the other hand, I recognize that Congress might well interpret them as agreements brought about by the action of the Executive and ratified by a joint resolution of both Houses. These agreements would provide for a police force and the specific responsibility of each nation. But outside of these agreements, there is the power in our Executive to preserve the peace, to see that the "supreme laws" are faithfully executed. When we become a party to this charter, and define our responsibilities by the agreement or agreements, there can be no question of the power of the Executive to carry out our commitments in relation to international policing. His constitutional power, however, is in no manner impaired.[17]

An even fuller exposition of the point was made by Senator Austin, who stated:

Mr. President, I am one of those lawyers in the United States who believe that the general powers of the President—not merely the war powers of the President but the general authority of the President—are commensurate with the obligation which is imposed upon him as President, that he take care that the laws are faithfully executed. That means that he shall take all the care that is required to see that the laws are faithfully executed.

Of course, there are other specific references in the Constitution which show that he has authority to employ armed forces when necessary to carry out specific things named in the Constitution; but the great over-all and general authority arises from his obligation that he take care that the laws are faithfully executed. That has been true throughout our history, and the Chief Executive has taken care, and has sent the armed forces of the United States, without any act of Congress preceding their sending, on a great many occasions. I have three different compilations of those occasions. One of them runs as high as 150 times; another of them 72 times, and so forth. It makes a difference whether we consider the maneuvers which were merely shows of force as combined [comprised?] in the exercise of this authority—as I do—or whether we limit the count to those

17. *Cong. Rec.*, 79th Cong., 1st sess., vol. 91, July 27, 1945, pp. 8127–8128.

cases in which the armed forces have actually entered upon the territory of a peaceful neighbor. But there is no doubt in my mind of his obligation and authority to employ all the force that is necessary to enforce the laws.

It may be asked, How does a threat to international security and peace violate the laws of the United States? Perhaps, Mr. President, it would not have violated the laws of the United States previous to the obligations set forth in this treaty. Perhaps we have never before recognized as being true the fundamental doctrine with which I opened my remarks. But we are doing so now. We recognize that a breach of the peace anywhere on earth which threatens the security and peace of the world is an attack upon us; and after this treaty is accepted by 29 nations, that will be the express law of the world. It will be the law of nations, because according to its express terms it will bind those who are nonmembers, as well as members, and it will be the law of the United States, because we shall have adopted it in a treaty. Indeed, it will be above the ordinary statutes of the United States, because it will be on a par with the Constitution, which provides that treaties made pursuant thereto shall be the supreme law of the land.

So I have no doubt of the authority of the President in the past, and his authority in the future, to enforce peace. I am bound to say that I feel that the President is the officer under our Constitution in whom there is exclusively vested the responsibility for maintenance of peace.[18]

Action contrary to the Charter of the United Nations is action against the interests of the United States. Preservation of peace under the Charter is a cornerstone of American foreign policy. President Truman said in his inaugural address in 1949:

In the coming years, our program for peace and freedom will emphasize four major courses of action.

First, we will continue to give unfaltering support to the United Nations and related agencies, and we will continue to search for ways to strengthen their authority and increase their effectiveness.[19]

In the Korean situation, the resolution of the Security Council of June 25 determined, under article 39 of the Charter, that the action of the North Koreans constituted a breach of the peace and called upon "the authorities in North Korea (a) to cease hostilities forthwith; and (b) to withdraw their armed forces to the thirty-eighth parallel." It also called upon "all Members to render every

18. *Ibid.*, July 26, 1945, pp. 8064–8065.
19. Address of Jan. 20, 1949; Department of State *Bulletin*, Jan. 30, 1949, p. 124.

assistance to the United Nations in the execution of this resolution." This is an application of the principles set forth in article 2, paragraph 5 of the Charter, which states: "All Members shall give the United Nations every assistance in any action it takes in accordance with the present Charter . . ." The Security Council resolution of June 27, passed after the North Korean authorities had disregarded the June 25 resolution, recommended "that Members of the United Nations furnish such assistance to the Republic of Korea as may be necessary to repel the armed attack and to restore international peace and security in the area." This recommendation was also made under the authority of article 39 of the Charter.

The President's action seeks to accomplish the objectives of both resolutions.

The continued defiance of the United Nations by the North Korean authorities would have meant that the United Nations would have ceased to exist as a serious instrumentality for the maintenance of international peace. The continued existence of the United Nations as an effective international organization is a paramount United States interest. The defiance of the United Nations is in clear violation of the Charter of the United Nations and of the resolutions adopted by the Security Council of the United Nations to bring about a settlement of the problem. It is a threat to international peace and security, a threat to the peace and security of the United States and to the security of United States forces in the Pacific.

These interests of the United States are interests which the President as Commander in Chief can protect by the employment of the Armed Forces of the United States without a declaration of war. It was they which the President's order of June 27 did protect. This order was within his authority as Commander in Chief.

B. The Case for Congress: The Javits Act

When the debacle of the Vietnam War brought into sharpest relief the dangers of presidential war-making, Senator Jacob K. Javits on June 15, 1970, introduced a bill to forbid use of American armed forces in

Source: U.S. Congress, Senate, Committee on Foreign Relations, *Hearings on War Powers Legislation*, 92d Cong., 1st sess., 1972, pp. 75–77, 80–83.

combat for longer than thirty days without consent of Congress. A distinguished group of historians testified in favor of the bill during hearings of the Foreign Relations Committee on March 8 and 9, 1971. One of them was Richard B. Morris, Gouverneur Morris Professor at Columbia University, the nation's outstanding historian of colonial and revolutionary America, author of many books, and editor of many others. His remarks follow.

I shall . . . concentrate . . . on the early years of the Republic when the great precedents were shaped.

Repeatedly have the historical and constitutional origins of the warmaking power been subjected to close scrutiny without having any noticeably deterrent effect upon this Nation's proclivity for embarking upon undeclared war. Contrariwise, the last quarter century has witnessed undeclared wars assuming a shape and dimension of fearsome proportions, and with fearsome results. The undeclared war that is now being waged in Indochina tragically divides the American people, diverts resources from the most urgent tasks of domestic reconstruction, fans the fires of inflation, seriously diminishes our prestige and credibility abroad, and even threatens the constitutional fabric of the Nation, aside from the toll it is exacting in blood and treasure.

I am impelled to support this prudent and well-conceived bill, S. 731 [the Javits bill], to regulate undeclared wars, not only by the urgency of Congress's acting promptly to define and delineate the warmaking powers under the Constitution, but as an historian of the founding years of the Republic I am especially concerned that so awesome a power should not be exercised in derogation of the letter of the Constitution and in contravention of its spirit.

Our Nation's independence was achieved in the first anticolonial war of modern times, but it was at its inception dedicated to peace not war. Only a peaceful climate, it was believed, would guarantee the American people life, liberty, and the pursuit of happiness. The Founding Fathers, along with friends abroad, considered that the American Revolution would, as Tom Paine felicitously phrased it, "form a new era and give a new turn to human affairs." Turn to the reverse side of any dollar bill and you will find engraved thereon the Great Seal of the United States, an everlasting pyramid carrying the date 1776, and underneath, the Latin motto: *Novus Ordo Seclorum*—A new order of the ages is born. Every dollar that we spend abroad, carrying this adaptation of an inspired phrase of Virgil, conveys this message of hope. Silas Deane, Franklin's fellow commissioner in France, made the point that for economic reasons, if for no other, it would ever be the interest of Americans "to pursue an inviolable peace with the states of Europe." . . .

Added to this pervasive antimilitary cast of mind was an abiding fear of executive usurpation, expressed both on the State and the national levels. The State constitutions narrowly defined the powers granted to their Governors, and four States used the term "president" instead of Governor, indicating in fact that the executive authority was shared with a council of state. Even more significant for the exercise of war power, the Continental Congress, both the first and second, designated its chairman as "The President," but that official's duties were largely confined to presiding over the Congress, and he possessed scarcely a shred of executive or administrative functions.

In practice these fundamental principles profoundly shaped the conduct of the Revolutionary War and the administration of military affairs during the years of the Confederacy. Certain policies and certain decisions taken as early as 1775 were not only to determine the locus of the warmaking power, the control of the army, and the making of the peace, but were to cast a long shadow ahead. . . .

The Constitution as finally adopted, in article I, section 8, vests in Congress the right to declare war and to raise and support armies, but limits appropriations of money for their use to a maximum of 2 years. It further empowers Congress to provide and maintain a navy, to make rules for the government and regulation of the land and naval forces, and to call forth the militia to execute the laws of the Union, suppress insurrections and repel invasion. Article II, section 2, describes the President as Commander in Chief. Thus the Constitution clearly distinguishes between declaring war and supporting it on the one hand and conducting its operations on the other. So far the country was prepared to go in 1787 in entrusting to the Executive a portion of the war powers, but no further. . . .

To allay fears that the warmaking powers under the Constitution would subvert republican institutions, the authors of The Federalist papers took pains to construe the President's role rather narrowly. So ardent an advocate of executive energy as Alexander Hamilton felt it expedient to remind his readers in *Federalist* No. 69 that the President as Commander in Chief had far less powers than the King of Great Britain. The latter could not only declare war but could raise and regulate fleets and armies, "all which, by the Constitution under consideration, would appertain to the legislature." . . .

So much for the warmaking powers spelled out in the Constitution. Let us now consider briefly how these powers were executed in practice by the earliest presidents. Fortunate indeed was the country in its early Chief Executives who executed their powers as Commander in Chief with prudence and restraint. As Commander in Chief during the American Revolution, Washington, at the time of the Newburgh address, had demonstrated his abhorrence of the use of military power to coerce the Congress. His disinterested stand has long been cited as a classic example of military restraint and stands as a noble tribute to the republican principle that the civilian arm is supreme over the military. . . .

Not only did President Adams seek to construe his war powers strictly and in accordance with the congressional mandate, but he went so far as in effect to divest himself of his role as Commander in Chief and, with Senate approval, confer it upon George Washington. Had the more extreme members of the President's own party possessed the votes, they would have issued a declaration of war over the President's head, a possibility that also confronted President McKinley in the Spanish-American War. Both occasions posed serious threats that Congress, or a portion thereof, would declare war without a recommendation by the President. Instead, President Adams showed admirable restraint, and has provided us with a model for our own day of how to wind down an undeclared war. . . .

If John Adams were here today I am confident that he would give his wholehearted support to the proposed bill, S. 731, to "make rules respecting military hostilities in the absence of a declaration of war." . . . it is calculated to provide those safeguards for the exercise of warmaking intended by the drafters and ratifiers of the Constitution without hampering the President in his capacity as Commander in Chief to act in defense of national security.

ALFRED H. KELLY, *professor of history at Wayne State University and coauthor of the most widely used college textbook on American constitutional history, also testified in favor of the bill.*

The underlying reasons for the major disturbance in the constitutional balance in warmaking power between Congress and the Executive which characterize the last 30 years are rather evident to everyone in this room and need no extensive elucidation here. They include the destruction, between 1914 and 1950, of the self-maintaining European balance of power system, together with the concomitant destruction of the ocean barrier, which to paraphrase Walter Lippmann has ceased to be a barrier and has become instead a three- or four-dimensioned highway. Equally evident is the role of atomic weaponry in impinging upon the area of discretionary rational calculation with respect to decisions to pass from peace to war, so that the rationalistic enlightenment assumption of reasonable calculation, embedded as it is in our constitutional system, has been upset and in part thrust into the background. It is in this sense, in part, that the initiation of war, as distinct from the waging of war, has to some extent tended to become an irrational act.

Third, and this is perhaps the most devastating development of all, the emergence of the United States as the principal guardian of a gigantic power sphere in which a constant posture of war-willingness against a series of potential aggressor imperiums has tended to undermine if not destroy entirely the "peace is normal; war is abnormal" conception both of constitutional life and of the international order as they developed in the 19th century. . . .

There were two decisive "breaks" in the continuity of the peace-war relationship between the Executive and the Congress, which tended, when taken together, to damage very badly the traditional balance of power with respect to peace-war decisions between Congress and the Executive.

The first occurred between May of 1940 and December 7, 1941, when President Roosevelt was able to mobilize mass popular support to sanction a series of Executive acts of war—properly de-

SOURCE: U.S. Senate, *Hearings on War Powers Legislation*, pp. 88–91.

scribed as that when seen in the context of international law—beginning with the destroyer base deal and ending with the convoy system instituted against the "rattlesnakes of the Atlantic" which took from congressional hands the discretionary peace-war decision with respect to the struggle in Europe. This is intended as no criticism of Franklin Roosevelt. On the contrary, the constitutional tragedy lies precisely in the fact, seen in the light of our present knowledge of the historical events involved, that exercise of Presidential prerogative which stretched the limits of the Constitution well beyond the breaking point, as Professor Corwin pointed out at the time, appears to have been necessary to national survival. The Presidential measures were not acts of irresponsible Executive despotism; rather the contrary, although I have always regarded it as doubly tragic that they did on occasion involve some considerable manipulation both of factual and legal realities, a state of affairs which has been known to recur since that time.

The second major "break" in congressional-Executive relations with respect to the war power came in two developments in 1950, both of them in connection with the defense of the newly emergent American power sphere in Asia and Europe, which the United States now was charged with maintaining and defending. The first was President Truman's decision in June 1950 to intervene militarily against the Communist aggression in South Korea, and thus to take the United States, by an act of Executive discretion alone, into a large-scale war on the continent of Asia. I am aware that the President acted nominally in defense of obligations of the United States to the United Nations, in spite of the fact that the United States had never assigned police forces to the United Nations, nor had it implemented the earlier United Nations Participation Act of 1945.

The second, and closely related circumstance in point of time and national policy, was the decision of the Truman administration that year to place seven divisions in Germany as a kind of trip wire against potential Soviet aggression.

Now in spite of the argument to the contrary which relies heavily upon the 140 precedents cited earlier, I would contend that from a constitutional point of view this move was entirely unprecedented. Seen from our vantage point now, it constituted a dangerous break in constitutional continuity. For never before had a President moved armed forces of such force, number, and character as to imply total national military commitment outside the confines of the United States or its territorial environs and possessions, let alone overseas into the ancient cockpit of European wars. To compare this situation with President Wilson's landing the Marines at Vera Cruz in 1914, or the first Roosevelt's intervention in Santo Domingo in 1904 is to ignore power relations, war potential, commitment, and geography. Again, the Executive's decision cannot be condemned merely as an act of irresponsible Presidential despotism. The decision, with all its tragic potential, was in a sense necessary. It was in support of the North Atlantic Alliance, for one thing. Furthermore, there was not technically a state of peace in Germany as yet. But it exposed a certain tragic inconsistency between the ancient peace-war balance between Congress and the Executive in the American constitutional system and the exigencies of the decisionmaking process in the marginal area between diplomacy and war inherent in the defense of the new American power system. . . .

It would be too much to label the various senatorial and congressional resolutions since 1950 which represent attempts to recoup the congressional discretion in the war declaratory power as exercises in futility, but they certainly have not succeeded to any important degree in restoring the constitutional balance which existed in the matter before that time. The outcome of the "great debate," staged in the Senate early in 1951 over Presidential versus congressional war power—a debate precipitated by Senator Robert Taft's stern speech denouncing executive "usurpation of power" in "violation of the Constitution and laws of the United States"— was a serious defeat for the champions of congressional constitutional war-declaring prerogative. Not only did the President refuse to yield up any acknowledgment of wrong-doing either in Europe or America; what was more significant, the Senate itself finally in effect quietly resigned itself to the adoption of a very weak resolution declaring it to be "the sense of the Senate" that "in the interests of sound constitutional process congressional approval should be obtained on any policy requiring the movement of American troops abroad."

The precedents here were decisive. President Eisenhower did gain congressional concurrence in his decision to defend the offshore Chinese islands in 1958. But the Executive-determined military intervention in Lebanon in 1958, the Kennedy moves in 1962 into Thailand and Vietnam, the "Cuban naval quarantine" of that same year—polite terminology for a blockade, a state of affairs described in all textbooks in international law as recognizing the technical existence of a state of war—all were taken without so much as a prior bow toward the congressional war-declaring discretion. In the same class was the 1965 intervention in Santo Domingo. And while the Tonkin Gulf Resolution of August 1964 represented a certain recognition of congressional constitutional right, its ultimate effect was to weaken rather than to strengthen congressional prerogative, since the President used what amounted in force to nothing like a full declaration of war to mount a full-scale war in Southeast Asia. . . .

Let me now say a few words in support of the Senate 731, the Javits bill. The measure obviously poses few constitutional problems in the immediate sense, since however unprecedented, it is in direct pursuance of the congressional war power. As an attempt to repair, implement and revitalize congressional discretion with respect to the war power, I believe that it expresses the will of the American people in their long-standing conviction that "peace is normal; war is abnormal"; that for that reason a declaration of war requires some formal national affirmation, usually a democratic affirmation in support of the idea of a *bellum justum*. It is as a reaffirmation of this spirit that the measure, I believe, has its chief value.

HENRY STEELE COMMAGER, *whose remarks follow, is professor of history at Amherst College, coauthor of a well-known textbook on general American history, author of many volumes, and editor of the most widely read documentary account of the nation's history.*

Now the original assumption of our Constitution framers, that the President could not engage in war on his own, was greatly strengthened by the elementary fact that he could not if he wanted to because there were no armies or navies with which to make war. At the time of the ratification of the U.S. Constitution the U.S. Army consisted of 719 officers and men, not a formidable force for military adventures. The situation did not change perceptibly over the years. Our Armed Forces increased to some 20,000 by 1840, to

SOURCE: U.S. Senate, *Hearings on War Powers Legislation*, pp. 10–11, 16–19.

28,000 on the eve of the Civil War, and to 38,000 by 1890. Even in 1915, with the world locked in mortal combat, the Armed Forces of the United States were less than 175,000. With the worst will in the world, therefore, there was little Presidents could do with these forces—little that would involve us in the kind of embroilments in which we now find ourselves.

Now we are in a wholly new situation. Not only do we keep some 3 million men under arms at all times—since 1951 the number has rarely fallen below that—but we have the greatest and most formidable armaments that any nation ever commanded. What this means is quite simply that while in the past Presidents could not involve the Nation, or the world, very deeply in war without congressional approval, now they can, and do.

The symbol of our new power is the nuclear weapon. Doubtless the threat of nuclear war goes far to justify giving the Executive whatever discretion is necessary to secure survival in the face of attack. Correspondingly our possession of the most formidable nuclear armaments places upon us a graver responsibility, graver than we have had to observe in the past. We should, therefore, make it our first objective to minimize the risk of a nuclear showdown. This we are not doing. Our invasion of Vietnam, Cambodia, Laos, is a temptation, indeed almost a challenge, to China to come into the war, as she came into the war in Korea; such a confrontation conjures up the spectre of a nuclear war. As for chemical and biological warfare, it is notorious that we have used and are still using chemical defoliants and that only a public outcry and congressional protest brought some modification of the use of chemicals and the adoption of new policies for the disposition of nerve gases. . . .

These are new ingredients within the matrix of the presidential power, and they change the constitutional mix, for the Constitution, after all, is not static but dynamic. The problem is complicated by a new terminology: the obsolescence of older terms which once had clear legal meaning, and the emergence of new terms, some of them (like "combat" meaning only ground troops, or "protective reaction") designed to deceive. Thus it is conceded that the President has authority to "repel" attacks, but the term has been drained of meaning—certainly of the meaning that a Madison or a Jefferson read into it. . . .

"Reason may mislead us. Experience must be our guide," said

James Madison at the Constitutional Convention. By "reason" he meant theory or doctrine. Experience must indeed be our guide, and on the basis of a century and three-quarters of experience, confirmed by a quarter century of intensive modern experience, we can say with, I think, some confidence that:

1. With the exception of the Civil War—a very special case—and perhaps of the Korean War where the President responded to the decision of the Security Council—there are no instances in our history where the use of warmaking powers by the Executive without authority of Congress was clearly and incontrovertibly required by the nature of the emergency which the Nation faced, but that on the contrary in almost every instance the long run interests of the Nation would have been better promoted by consultation and delay.

2. That great principles of government are not to be decided on the basis of the argumentum ad horrendum—by conjuring up hypothetical dangers and insisting that the structure and operations of government must be based on the chance of these rather than on experience. It was to this kind of argument that Thomas Jefferson said, "Shake not your raw head and bloody bones at me."

3. But that if such an emergency were to arise, it is amply provided for by the provisions of Senator Javits' bill. . . .

The problems that confront us cannot be solved by debates over precedents, by appeals to constitutional probity, or by confronting presidential power with congressional. These may mitigate but will not resolve our crisis. For all of these gestures address themselves to symptoms rather than to the fundamental disease. That disease is the psychology of the cold war; that disease is our obsession with power; that disease is our assumption that the great problems that glare upon us so hideously from every corner of the horizon can be solved by force.

Abuse of power by Presidents is a reflection, and perhaps a consequence, of abuse of power by the American people and Nation. For two decades now we have misused our prodigious power. We misused our economic power, not least in associating economic with military assistance, and in imposing economic sanctions against nations who did not see eye to eye with us about trade with our "enemies." We misused our political power by trying to force neutrals onto our side in the cold war, and by bringing pressure on the nations of Latin America to support our short-sighted policy of excluding China from the United Nations—surely the most egregious blunder in the history of modern diplomacy.

We misused our political power by planting the CIA in some 60 countries to carry on what we chose to regard as National Defense but what was in the eyes of its victims the work of subversion. We misused our military power in forcing our weapons on scores of nations throughout the globe, maintaining military alliances like NATO and SEATO and imposing our will upon these where we were able. We misused our international power by flouting the sovereign rights of neighboring nations like Cuba and Guatemala and the Dominican Republic and violating our obligations under the OAS Treaty and the United Nations. And we are even now engaged in a monstrous misuse of power in waging war on a distant people that does not accept our ideology, or our determination of its future. Is it any wonder that against this almost lurid background, Presidents misuse their power?

As we have greater power than any other nation, so we should display greater moderation in using it, greater humility in justifying it, and greater magnanimity in withholding it. We display neither moderation nor humility nor magnanimity, but that arrogance of power which your chairman has so somberly deplored.

In the long run, the abuse of the executive power cannot be divorced from the abuse of national power. If we subvert world order and threaten world peace, we must inevitably subvert and threaten our own political institutions first. This we are in process of doing.

In 1972 THE SENATE passed the Javits bill by a vote of 68 to 16. The House approved a much weaker version that required only that the president tell Congress when he was using troops in hostilities, and the bill died in conference. Reintroduced in 1973, it found more support because the Watergate scandals had dramatically lowered the prestige of the Nixon administration, and especially because of revelations that the administration had sponsored secret bombings in Cambodia. It passed both houses and received a presidential veto on October 24; the president said that such a measure would "seriously undermine this nation's ability to act decisively and convincingly in times of international crisis." The veto was overriden on November 7, by a vote of 287 to 135 in the House, 75 to 18 in the Senate. In the House, 198 Demo-

SOURCE: New York Times, Nov. 8, 1973.

crats and 86 Republicans voted to override the veto, while 32 Democrats and 103 Republicans voted against overriding. In the Senate, 50 Democrats and 25 Republicans voted to override while 3 Democrats and 15 Republicans voted against. The Javits Act of 1973 differed from the proposal of three years earlier, notably in extension of the time limit during which a president might act without congressional approval. The act was a fairly long document, reflecting the need to fence in contingencies. The most important sections follow.

Section 1

This joint resolution may be cited as the "war-powers resolution."

Section 2

(A) It is the purpose of this joint resolution to fulfill the intent of the framers of the Constitution of the United States and insure that the collective judgment of both the Congress and the President will apply to the introduction of United States armed forces into hostilities, or into situations where imminent involvement in hostilities is clearly indicated by the circumstances, and to the continued use of such forces in hostilities or in such situations. . . .

Section 4

(A) In the absence of a declaration of war, in any case in which United States armed forces are introduced

(1) into hostilities or into situations where imminent involvement in hostilities is clearly indicated by the circumstances;

(2) into the territory, airspace or waters of a foreign nation, while equipped for combat, except for deployments which relate solely to supply, replacement, repair, or training of such forces; or

(3) in numbers which substantially enlarge United States armed forces equipped for combat already located in a foreign nation; the President shall submit within 48 hours to the Speaker of the House of Representatives and to the President pro Tempore of the Senate a report, in writing, setting forth

(a) the circumstances necessitating the introduction of the United States armed forces;

(b) the Constitutional and legislative authority under which such introduction took place; and

(c) the estimated scope and duration of the hostilities or involvement.

(B) The President shall provide such other information as the Congress may request in the fulfillment of its Constitutional responsibilities with respect to committing the nation to war and to the use of United States armed forces abroad.

(C) Whenever United States armed forces are introduced into hostilities or into any situation described in subsection (A) of this section, the President shall, so long as such armed forces continue to be engaged in such hostilities or situation, report to the Congress periodically on the status of such hostilities or situation, but in no event shall he report to the Congress less often than once every six months.

Section 5

. . . (B) Within 60 calendar days after a report is submitted or is required to be submitted pursuant to Section 4 (A) (1), whichever is earlier, the President shall terminate any use of United States armed forces with respect to which such report was submitted (or required to be submitted), unless the Congress (1) has declared war or has enacted a specific authorization for such use of United States armed forces, (2) has extended by law such 60-day period, or (3) is physically unable to meet as a result of an armed attack upon the United States. Such 60-day period shall be extended for not more than an additional 30 days if the President determines and certifies to the Congress in writing that unavoidable military necessity respecting the safety of United States armed forces requires the continued use of such armed forces in the course of bringing about a prompt removal of such forces.

(C) Notwithstanding subsection (B), at any time that United States armed forces are engaged in hostilities outside the territory of the United States, its possessions and territories without a declaration of war or specific statutory authorization, such forces shall be removed by the President if the Congress so directs by concurrent resolution.

48. Treaties versus Executive Agreements

SINCE THE END OF THE SECOND WORLD WAR the number of treaties and executive agreements concluded by the United States has increased in spectacular fashion. Of all the treaties and executive agreements, bilateral and multilateral, signed by the government's agents since the Declaration of Independence, about two thirds of them have been entered into since 1945. There has been an especially large rise in executive agreements. In the 150 years prior to 1939, the United States entered into 799 treaties and one-and-one-half times as many executive agreements, 1,182. In the twenty-six years after 1945, according to State Department compilations, 368 treaties were concluded, and fifteen times that many executive agreements were signed—a total of 5,590. In addition there were more than 400 secret agreements, the nature of which the department refused to reveal. Actually, other government departments had concluded thousands upon thousands of executive agreements, and the State Department was listing only its own. Secretary John Foster Dulles in 1953 told a Senate subcommittee that 10,000 agreements had been made to carry out the NATO treaty. No one, of course, wanted to bring all these technical executive agreements to a Senate vote. The senators' concern was with the important agreements that they felt should be in the form of treaties and thereby subject to committee hearings and formal debate upon the floor.

A. THE CASE ACT

CONGRESSIONAL CONCERN for the rise in the number of important executive agreements, in particular the discovery of secret executive agreements signed in the 1960s with Ethiopia, Laos, Thailand, South Korea, and Spain, produced several proposals for a different manner of handling the country's foreign relations. On February 16, 1972, the Senate voted 81 to 0 in favor of the Case bill, sponsored by Senator Clifford P. Case. This was just before President Nixon's trip to China, and the Senate's vote at such a time might have been viewed as an implicit warning to the president not to sign some executive agreement with the Chinese; although perhaps the timing was coincidental. The bill passed the House on August 14, by voice vote, and the president signed it into law on August 22.

SOURCE: United States, Statutes at Large, vol. 86 (Washington, D.C., 1973), p. 619.

The Secretary of State shall transmit to the Congress the text of any international agreement, other than a treaty, to which the United States is a party as soon as practicable after such agreement has entered into force with respect to the United States but in no event later than sixty days thereafter. However, any such agreement the immediate public disclosure of which would, in the opinion of the President, be prejudicial to the national security of the United States shall not be so transmitted to the Congress but shall be transmitted to the Committee on Foreign Relations of the Senate and the Committee on Foreign Affairs of the House of Representatives under an appropriate injunction of secrecy to be removed only upon due notice from the President.

B. THE ERVIN BILL

SENATOR SAM J. ERVIN, JR., *proposed an even stronger measure.*

SECTION 1. (a) In furtherance of the provisions of the United States Constitution regarding the sharing of powers in the making of international agreements, any executive agreement made on or after the date of enactment of this Act shall be transmitted to the Secretary of State, who shall then transmit such agreement (bearing an identification number) to the Congress. However, any such agreement the immediate disclosure of which would, in the opinion of the President, be prejudicial to the security of the United States shall instead be transmitted by the Secretary to the Committee on Foreign Relations of the Senate and the Committee on Foreign Affairs of the House of Representatives under an appropriate written injunction of secrecy to be removed only upon due notice from the President. Each committee shall personally notify the Members of its House that the Secretary has transmitted such an agreement with an injunction of secrecy, and such agreement shall thereafter be available for inspection only by such members.

(b) . . . any such executive agreement shall come into force with respect to the United States at the end of the first period of sixty calendar days of continuous session of Congress after the date

SOURCE: U.S. Congress, Senate, committee print of S. 3475, 92d Cong., 2d sess., April 11, 1972.

on which the executive agreement is transmitted to Congress or such committees, as the case may be, unless, between the date of transmittal and the end of the sixty-day period, both Houses pass a concurrent resolution stating in substance that both Houses do not approve the executive agreement. . . .

Note on Sources

The most important international arrangements of the United States, treaties and executive agreements, have long been published in haphazard form, but it is gratifying to remark that soon the inquiring student will be able to find authentic texts in one of two places. For instruments through the year 1949, recourse should be to Charles I. Bevans, comp., *Treaties and Other International Agreements of the United States of America: 1776–1949* (Washington, D.C., 1968–). This new series by the State Department's assistant legal adviser is in two parts, multilateral and bilateral. The first part has now been published in four volumes; the second, in progress alphabetically by countries, has now (1974) passed "United Arab Republic," and when finished will run to a dozen or more volumes. The series will save considerable time for anyone seeking a text, and ensure that the text will be printed correctly. The second resort, for texts dating from 1950 onward, is *United States Treaties and Other International Agreements* (Washington, D.C., 1950–). Several volumes are published for each year. Treaties appear in a somewhat confused order, according to their publication in the State Department's pamphlet series for treaties and executive agreements.

For diplomatic correspondence the best printed source is *Foreign Relations of the United States*, the grand documentary compilation that dates back to the beginning of the Civil War and has appeared in one or more annual volumes, with the exception of the year 1869, until, at the present writing, 1949. As the years have passed, *Foreign Relations* has increased in size, from the initial volume for 1861, to two volumes for the 1920s, until twelve volumes were necessary for 1945 and eleven for 1946; the hope is to hold the annual volumes for years thereafter to seven or eight. Standards of editing for the volumes have gone up markedly since the series became a professional publication in the 1920s when Tyler Dennett took up the editorship. At the present time the leadership of the State Department's Historical Office is dedicated to the highest standards of scholarship. The director of the office is William M. Franklin; the deputy director is Richardson Dougall; the chief of the *Foreign Relations* branch is Fredrick Aandahl. The office covers the documentation of American foreign affairs not only from the department's own records, but also from records of such other government agencies as might have affected the negotiations. The department's historians have obtained material from many private collections of personal papers, such as the Henry L. Stimson papers in the Yale University Library.

For the years after 1945 the editors of *Foreign Relations* are probably going to encounter increasing trouble in keeping up the standards of the series, for several reasons. For one, the documentation has spread from the department to other agencies, notably the National Security Council beginning in 1947. This proliferation of authority produces difficulties of both compilation and clearance. Another problem is that American foreign relations have simply become so important, not only to the United States but to all nations of the world, that their historical documentation possesses dangers hitherto unknown. In the old days, even during the era prior to the Second World War, no one cared what the American government thought about many issues. Now that feelings may be hurt, feathers ruffled, caution will seem more in order, and the clearing of *Foreign Relations* becomes complicated for that special reason. A third problem is the sheer bulk of documentation: the task of getting through it is difficult. And some of it is in disorder; many files now stored in various repositories have been dumped into boxes without numerical indexing, in so-called "lots," in their original order or confusion, and in an arrangement that must be divined by an official researcher (and later, the nongovernment researcher).

A positive note for the appearance of *Foreign Relations* occurred on March 8, 1972, when after sensational leakage of official documents by former government employees, notably revelation of the Pentagon Papers and their publication by newspapers, commercial presses, and the government itself, the sensitivity to clearance problems and the danger of more unofficial declassification led President Nixon to announce in a memorandum to Secretary of State Rogers that within the next three years *Foreign Relations* should be brought up to a twenty-year line—to coverage of events twenty years removed from the present. If carried out, this order by the president meant that by 1976 volumes of *Foreign Relations* would be appearing for events of 1956, such as the Suez crisis, a documentation historians at the present time would find fascinating. The only problem with the presidential order was that somewhat similar presidential jogging had occurred before, without much result because of bureaucratic inertia or reluctance: President Kennedy had sought to open more government records to historians and not much had happened.

For documentation of events closer to the present than volumes of *Foreign Relations*, the student must turn for the most part to a series of weighty green books published by the Department of State over a period of a dozen years, from 1957 to 1969. These books contain documents culled from various sources, frequently the department *Bulletin*, brought together by editors in the Historical Office. The initial volume in the series (not bound in green, because it is Senate Doc. 123, 81st Cong., 1st sess.) was entitled *A Decade of American Foreign Policy: Basic Documents, 1941–1949* (Washington, D.C., 1950). It was followed by two thick volumes, *American Foreign Policy: Current Documents, 1950–1955* (Washington, D.C., 1957). Beginning with events for the year 1956, an annual volume appeared two or three years after the date of its material; the series covered events through the year 1967, after which the Historical Office found itself squeezed by budget economies and by editorial problems incident to the bulging of *Foreign Relations* for the last years of the Second World War and the immediate postwar era, and *Current Documents* expired. Apparently there is no hope of its resurrection, at least within the State Department. The Council on Foreign Relations publishes an annual documentary volume entitled *Documents on American Foreign Relations* a year or two after events, but it is a much less ambitious undertaking, with far fewer pages (some *Current Documents* volumes ran more than 1,500 pages, compared to the perhaps 500 pages of the Council volumes; and *CD* contained far more words per page). The weekly Department of State *Bulletin* must now be consulted for foreign policy documentation since 1967.

In recent years the Government Printing Office has been bringing out handsomely produced volumes of presidential papers: *Public Papers of the Presidents of the United States.* They contain speeches, press statements, press conferences, and so forth, and are complete for Presidents Truman, Eisenhower, Kennedy, and Johnson. These books relate to the edition of President Franklin D. Roosevelt's papers published commercially under the editorship of Judge Samuel I. Rosenman. It is a pity that a gap now exists in compilation of presidential material between the end of the old series assembled by James D. Richardson, published under congressional authority in 1896–99 and covering the years 1789–1897, and the beginning of the Roosevelt material in 1933.

Students of foreign affairs of the years since 1945 thus have a more full documentation, within fewer sources, than for any previous period of American foreign relations. Still, the foreign policy of the United States is so varied, its ramifications so far-flung, its sensitivities so numerous, that even the several series mentioned above will not provide enough information. It is necessary to go elsewhere, to employ the customary ingenuity of students wishing to know. As the present volume shows, the text of at least one of the recent alliances of the United States has had substantial alteration by executive interpretation communicated privately by the secretary of state; this fact emerged in 1969 in Senate subcommittee hearings, the proceedings of which were published that same year. The Pentagon Papers, for all of their incompleteness, offer documentation on the involvement of the United States in Vietnam far ahead of the *Foreign Relations* series. The *New York Times,* in addition to being a publisher of the Pentagon Papers and the Anderson Papers, often contains extraordinary insights obtained from the questioning of officials, on and off the record, by its reporters. And authors of books sometimes manage to ferret out novel information. Henry Brandon's *The Retreat of American Power* (Garden City, N.Y.: Doubleday, 1973) related in detail the effort of the Soviet Union to establish a nuclear submarine base at Cienfuegos, Cuba, in 1970. John Newhouse's *Cold Dawn: The Story of Salt* (New York: Holt, Rinehart and Winston, 1973) first reported the existence during the past few years of Soviet diplomatic feelers—virtual proposals—for an alliance with the United States to contain mainland China. All these revelations, documented or reported, modify and sometimes drastically change official government documentation. There always has been this uncontrolled side to public affairs in a democratic country such as America, and probably always will be. Its existence, the need to watch for it, if possible to discover it, makes the study of American foreign relations a continually fascinating enterprise.

Composite Index

This book completes a three-volume documentary history of American diplomacy. The index below is a composite work for all three volumes in the series:

Volume I: *Foundations of American Diplomacy, 1775–1872*
Volume II: *America as a World Power, 1872–1945*
Volume III: *America in a Divided World, 1945–1972*

Within each entry, an italic roman numeral is used to indicate the volume reference; page references are given in arabic numerals.

Composite Index